EXCEL® VBA 24-HOUR TRAINER

INTRODUCTION xxvii

▶ **SECTION I** **UNDERSTANDING THE BASICS**

LESSON 1 Introducing VBA 3

LESSON 2 Getting Started with Macros 9

LESSON 3 Introducing the Visual Basic Editor 19

LESSON 4 Working in the VBE 27

▶ **SECTION II** **DIVING DEEPER INTO VBA**

LESSON 5 Object-oriented Programming — An Overview 43

LESSON 6 Variables, Data Types, and Constants 49

LESSON 7 Understanding Objects and Collections 61

LESSON 8 Making Decisions with VBA 69

▶ **SECTION III** **BEYOND THE MACRO RECORDER: WRITING YOUR OWN CODE**

LESSON 9 Repeating Actions with Loops 85

LESSON 10 Working with Arrays 99

LESSON 11 Automating Procedures with Worksheet Events 111

LESSON 12 Automating Procedures with Workbook Events 123

LESSON 13 Using Embedded Controls 135

LESSON 14 Programming Charts 151

LESSON 15 Programming PivotTables and PivotCharts 163

LESSON 16 User Defined Functions 183

LESSON 17 Debugging Your Code 195

Continues

▶ SECTION IV   ADVANCED PROGRAMMING TECHNIQUES

LESSON 18   Creating UserForms...215

LESSON 19   UserForm Controls and Their Functions 231

LESSON 20   Advanced UserForms 249

LESSON 21   Class Modules...263

LESSON 22   Add-Ins...279

LESSON 23   Managing External Data 295

LESSON 24   Data Access with ActiveX Data Objects.....................307

LESSON 25   Not Gone, Not Forgotten..................................315

▶ SECTION V   INTERACTING WITH OTHER OFFICE APPLICATIONS

LESSON 26   Overview of Office Automation from Excel 327

LESSON 27   Working with Word from Excel..............................333

LESSON 28   Working with Outlook from Excel 343

LESSON 29   Working with Access from Excel 353

LESSON 30   Working with PowerPoint from Excel 363

APPENDIX   What's on the DVD?.......................................371

INDEX...375

Excel® VBA

24-HOUR TRAINER

Excel® VBA

24-HOUR TRAINER

Tom Urtis

WILEY

Wiley Publishing, Inc.

Excel® VBA 24-Hour Trainer

Published by
Wiley Publishing, Inc.
10475 Crosspoint Boulevard
Indianapolis, IN 46256
www.wiley.com

Copyright © 2011 by Wiley Publishing, Inc., Indianapolis, Indiana

Published by Wiley Publishing, Inc., Indianapolis, Indiana

Published simultaneously in Canada

ISBN: 978-0-470-89069-1

Manufactured in the United States of America

10 9 8 7 6 5 4 3 2 1

For general information on our other products and services please contact our Customer Care Department within the United States at (877) 762-2974, outside the United States at (317) 572-3993 or fax (317) 572-4002.

Wiley also publishes its books in a variety of electronic formats. Some content that appears in print may not be available in electronic books.

Library of Congress Control Number: 2011922792

To Bill and Mary Urtis

ABOUT THE AUTHOR

 **TOM URTIS** is a Microsoft Office developer and programming expert with over 20 years of experience in developing customized Office programs with Visual Basic for Applications (VBA) and Application Programming Interface (API). In 2000 Tom founded Atlas Programming Management (www.atlaspm.com), an Office solutions company in Silicon Valley that specializes in Excel to provide consulting, project development, training, and support for a diverse international clientele. As an Excel trainer, Tom created the Excel Aptitude Test (XAT, www.xatcorp.com), which measures knowledge of Excel for a customized training curriculum based on the test score.

Tom is co-author of *Holy Macro! It's 2,500 Excel VBA Examples*, and he has served as a technical editor and consultant for other Excel books and training materials. Tom received the Most Valuable Professional award for Excel from Microsoft in 2008, and it has been renewed each year thereafter in recognition of his Excel skills and contributions to the Excel community. Tom is one of some 100 Excel experts worldwide who hold the Excel MVP award.

A native of New York state, Tom is a graduate of Michigan State University, and has lived and worked in the San Francisco Bay Area for 30 years. Tom is an avid sports fan and collector of rare sports memorabilia, and he enjoys the outdoor life that California offers. He can be reached by email, at tom@atlaspm.com.

ABOUT THE TECHNICAL EDITOR

MIKE ALEXANDER is a Microsoft MVP and the author of several books on advanced business analysis with Microsoft Access and Excel. He has more than 15 years of experience consulting and developing Office solutions. In his spare time he runs a free tutorial site, www.datapigtechnologies.com, where he shares basic Access and Excel tips with the Office community.

CREDITS

EXECUTIVE EDITOR
Carol Long

PROJECT EDITOR
Christopher J. Rivera

DEVELOPMENT EDITOR
Kezia Endsley

TECHNICAL EDITOR
Michael Alexander

PRODUCTION EDITOR
Kathleen Wisor

COPY EDITOR
Kim Cofer

EDITORIAL DIRECTOR
Robyn B. Siesky

EDITORIAL MANAGER
Mary Beth Wakefield

FREELANCER EDITORIAL MANAGER
Rosemarie Graham

ASSOCIATE DIRECTOR OF MARKETING
David Mayhew

PRODUCTION MANAGER
Tim Tate

VICE PRESIDENT AND EXECUTIVE GROUP PUBLISHER
Richard Swadley

VICE PRESIDENT AND EXECUTIVE PUBLISHER
Barry Pruett

ASSOCIATE PUBLISHER
Jim Minatel

PROJECT COORDINATOR, COVER
Katie Crocker

COMPOSITOR
JoAnn Kolonick,
Happenstance Type-O-Rama

PROOFREADER
Louise Watson, Word One

INDEXER
Robert Swanson

COVER DESIGNER
Michael Trent

COVER IMAGE
© Richard Cano

ACKNOWLEDGMENTS

THE PRODUCTION OF THIS BOOK was made possible by the combined efforts of highly talented people, starting with the entire Wiley Publishing team. Thanks to Carol Long, the Executive Editor, who got the project approved and kept the process moving from start to finish. Thanks to Mike Alexander, who introduced me to Wiley Publishing and was the Technical Editor. Thanks to Ed Connor and Christopher Rivera, the Project Editors, and to Kim Cofer, who edited copy. Thanks to Kezia Endsley, the Design Editor. Thanks to Rosemarie Graham, Carol Kessel, Mary Beth Wakefield, and Ashley Zurcher of Wiley Publishing for all their assistance. Many thanks to the Excel development team at Microsoft Corporation for improving Excel with each new release of Office, while considering suggestions from Excel users. Finally, a special thanks to the global Excel community. You've shown me creative ways to use Excel over the years, and taught me how to explain technical concepts to beginning Excel users.

CONTENTS

INTRODUCTION   *xxvii*

SECTION I: UNDERSTANDING THE BASICS

LESSON 1: INTRODUCING VBA   3

What Is VBA?   3
A Brief History of VBA   4
What VBA Can Do for You   5
    Automating a Recurring Task   5
    Automating a Repetitive Task   5
    Running a Macro Automatically if Another Action Takes Place   5
    Creating Your Own Worksheet Functions   5
    Simplifying the Workbook's Look and Feel for Other Users   5
    Controlling Other Office Applications from Excel   6
Liabilities of VBA   7
Try It   8

LESSON 2: GETTING STARTED WITH MACROS   9

Composing Your First Macro   9
    Accessing the VBA Environment   9
    Using the Macro Recorder   12
Running a Macro   16
    The Macro Dialog Box   16
    Shortcut Key   17
Try It   17
    Lesson Requirements   18
    Step-by-Step   18

LESSON 3: INTRODUCING THE VISUAL BASIC EDITOR   19

What Is the VBE?   19
How To Get Into the VBE   20

Understanding the VBE	**20**
The Project Explorer Window	21
The Code Window	21
The Properties Window	22
The Immediate Window	22
Understanding Modules	**22**
Using the Object Browser	**23**
Exiting the VBE	**24**
Try It	**25**

LESSON 4: WORKING IN THE VBE	**27**
Toolbars in the VBE	**27**
Macros and Modules	**28**
Locating Your Macros	28
Understanding the Code	29
Editing a Macro with Comments and Improvements to the Code	30
Deleting a Macro	33
Inserting a Module	33
Renaming a Module	34
Deleting a Module	36
Locking and Protecting the VBE	**36**
Try It	**37**
Lesson Requirements	37
Step-by-Step	37

SECTION II: DIVING DEEPER INTO VBA	

LESSON 5: OBJECT-ORIENTED PROGRAMMING — AN OVERVIEW	**43**
What "Object-Oriented Programming" Means	**43**
The Object Model	**44**
Properties	45
Methods	46
Collections	46
Try It	**47**

LESSON 6: VARIABLES, DATA TYPES, AND CONSTANTS	**49**
What Is a Variable?	**49**
Assigning Values to Variables	**50**
Why You Need Variables	**50**

Data Types	51
Understanding the Different Data Types	51
Declaring a Variable for Dates and Times	53
Declaring a Variable with the Proper Data Type	53
Forcing Variable Declaration	**54**
Understanding a Variable's Scope	**56**
Local Macro Level Only	56
Module Level	56
Application Level	57
Constants	**57**
Choosing the Scope and Lifetime of Your Constants	58
Try It	**58**
Lesson Requirements	58
Step-by-Step	58

LESSON 7: UNDERSTANDING OBJECTS AND COLLECTIONS — 61

Workbooks	**61**
Worksheets	**62**
Cells and Ranges	**63**
SpecialCells	**64**
Try It	**65**
Lesson Requirements	65
Step-by-Step	65

LESSON 8: MAKING DECISIONS WITH VBA — 69

Understanding Logical Operators	**69**
AND	70
OR	70
NOT	71
Choosing Between This or That	**72**
If...Then	72
If...Then...Else	73
If...Then...ElseIf	74
Select Case	74
Getting Users to Make Decisions	**76**
Message Boxes	76
Input Boxes	77
Try It	**78**
Lesson Requirements	78
Step-by-Step	78

SECTION III: BEYOND THE MACRO RECORDER: WRITING YOUR OWN CODE

LESSON 9: REPEATING ACTIONS WITH LOOPS — 85

What Is a Loop? — 85
Types of Loops — 86
    For...Next — 87
    For...Each...Next — 88
    Exiting a For... Loop — 89
    Looping In Reverse with Step — 90
    Do...While — 91
    Do...Until — 91
    Do...Loop...While — 93
    Do...Loop...Until — 94
    While...Wend — 94
Nesting Loops — 94
Try It — 95
    Lesson Requirements — 96
    Step-by-Step — 96

LESSON 10: WORKING WITH ARRAYS — 99

What Is an Array? — 99
    What Arrays Can Do for You — 101
    Declaring Arrays — 102
The Option Base Statement — 103
Boundaries in Arrays — 104
Declaring Arrays with Fixed Elements — 104
Declaring Dynamic Arrays with ReDim and Preserve — 105
Try It — 107
    Lesson Requirements — 107
    Step-by-Step — 107

LESSON 11: AUTOMATING PROCEDURES WITH WORKSHEET EVENTS — 111

What Is an "Event"? — 111
Worksheet Events — an Overview — 112
    Where Does the Worksheet Event Code Go? — 112
    Enabling and Disabling Events — 114

Examples of Common Worksheet Events   **115**

Worksheet_Change Event   115
Worksheet_SelectionChange Event   116
Worksheet_BeforeDoubleClick Event   116
Worksheet_BeforeRightClick Event   117
Worksheet_FollowHyperlink Event   117
Worksheet_Activate Event   117
Worksheet_Deactivate Event   118
Worksheet_Calculate Event   118
Worksheet_PivotTableUpdate Event   119

Try It   **119**

Lesson Requirements   119
Step-by-Step   119

LESSON 12: AUTOMATING PROCEDURES WITH WORKBOOK EVENTS   **123**

Workbook Events — An Overview   **123**

Where Does the Workbook Event Code Go?   123
Entering Workbook Event Code   125

Examples of Common Workbook Events   **126**

Workbook_Open Event   126
Workbook_BeforeClose Event   127
Workbook_Activate Event   127
Workbook_Deactivate Event   128
Workbook_SheetChange Event   128
Workbook_SheetSelectionChange Event   128
Workbook_SheetBeforeDoubleClick Event   129
Workbook_SheetBeforeRightClick Event   129
Workbook_SheetPivotTableUpdate Event   130
Workbook_NewSheet Event   130
Workbook_BeforePrint Event   130
Workbook_SheetActivate Event   131
Workbook_SheetDeactivate Event   131
Workbook_BeforeSave Event   131

Try It   **132**

Lesson Requirements   132
Step-by-Step   132

LESSON 13: USING EMBEDDED CONTROLS   135

Working with Forms Controls and ActiveX Controls   **135**
The Forms Toolbar   136
The Control Toolbox   140
Try It   **144**
Lesson Requirements   144
Step-by-Step   144

LESSON 14: PROGRAMMING CHARTS   151

Adding a Chart to a Chart Sheet   **152**
Adding an Embedded Chart to a Worksheet   **154**
Moving a Chart   **155**
Looping Through All Embedded Charts   **157**
Deleting Charts   **158**
Renaming a Chart   **159**
Try It   **160**
Lesson Requirements   160
Step-by-Step   160

LESSON 15: PROGRAMMING PIVOTTABLES AND PIVOTCHARTS   163

Creating a PivotTable Report   **163**
Hiding the PivotTable Field List   167
Using the Report Filter Area   167
Formatting Numbers in the Values Area   168
Why It's Called a PivotTable   **170**
Creating a PivotChart   **171**
Understanding PivotCaches   **173**
Manipulating PivotFields in VBA   **176**
Manipulating PivotItems with VBA   **177**
Creating a PivotTables Collection   **177**
Try It   **178**
Lesson Requirements   178
Step-by-Step   179

LESSON 16: USER DEFINED FUNCTIONS   183

What Is a User Defined Function?   **183**
Characteristics of User Defined Functions   184
Anatomy of a UDF   184
UDF Examples That Solve Common Tasks   185

Volatile Functions	**188**
The Name of the Active Worksheet and Workbook	189
UDFs with Conditional Formatting	190
Calling Your Function from a Macro	190
Adding a Description to the Insert Function Dialog	191
Try It	**193**
Lesson Requirements	193
Step-by-Step	193

LESSON 17: DEBUGGING YOUR CODE — **195**

What Is Debugging?	**195**
What Causes Errors?	**196**
Weapons of Mass Debugging	**198**
The Debugging Toolbar	198
Trapping Errors	**207**
Error Handler	207
Bypassing Errors	208
Try It	**210**
Lesson Requirements	210
Step-by-Step	210

SECTION IV: ADVANCED PROGRAMMING TECHNIQUES

LESSON 18: CREATING USERFORMS — **215**

What Is a UserForm?	**215**
Creating a UserForm	**216**
Designing a UserForm	**218**
Showing a UserForm	**225**
Where Does the UserForm's Code Go?	**225**
Closing a UserForm	**226**
Unloading a UserForm	226
Hiding a UserForm	227
Try It	**228**
Lesson Requirements	228
Step-by-Step	228

LESSON 19: USERFORM CONTROLS AND THEIR FUNCTIONS 231

Understanding the Frequently Used UserForm Controls 231
   CommandButtons 232
   Labels 232
   TextBoxes 234
   ListBoxes 236
   ComboBoxes 238
   CheckBoxes 240
   OptionButtons 241
   Frames 243
   MultiPages 245
Try It 246
   Lesson Requirements 246
   Step-by-Step 246

LESSON 20: ADVANCED USERFORMS 249

The UserForm Toolbar 249
Modal versus Modeless 250
Disabling the UserForm's Close Button 250
Maximizing Your UserForm's Size 252
Selecting and Displaying Photographs on a UserForm 252
Unloading a UserForm Automatically 253
Pre-Sorting the ListBox and ComboBox Items 253
Populating ListBoxes and ComboBoxes with Unique Items 255
Display a Real-Time Chart in a UserForm 258
Try It 259
   Lesson Requirements 259
   Step-by-Step 259

LESSON 21: CLASS MODULES 263

What Is a Class? 263
What Is a Class Module? 264
Creating Your Own Objects 265
An Important Benefit of Class Modules 266
Creating Collections 268
Class Modules for Embedded Objects 269
Try It 272
   Lesson Requirements 272
   Step-by-Step 272

LESSON 22: ADD-INS — 279

What Is an Excel Add-In?	279
Creating an Add-In	280
Converting a File to an Add-In	284
Installing an Add-In	286
Creating a User Interface for Your Add-In	288
Changing the Add-In's Code	290
Closing Add-Ins	290
Removing an Add-In from the Add-Ins List	291
Try It	291
Lesson Requirements	291
Step-by-Step	291

LESSON 23: MANAGING EXTERNAL DATA — 295

Creating QueryTables from Web Queries	295
Creating a QueryTable for Access	299
Using Text Files to Store External Data	301
Try It	304
Lesson Requirements	304
Step-by-Step	304

LESSON 24: DATA ACCESS WITH ACTIVEX DATA OBJECTS — 307

Introducing ADO	307
The Connection Object	309
The Recordset Object	309
The Command Object	310
An Introduction to Structured Query Language (SQL)	310
The SELECT Statement	311
The INSERT Statement	311
The UPDATE Statement	312
The DELETE Statement	312
Try It	313

LESSON 25: NOT GONE, NOT FORGOTTEN — 315

Using Dialog Sheets	315
What Does a Dialog Sheet Look Like?	316
Option to Show Message Only Once	318

Using XLM Get.Cell Functions   321
Using the SendKeys Method   322
Try It   323
   Lesson Requirements   323
   Step-by-Step   323

SECTION V: INTERACTING WITH OTHER OFFICE APPLICATIONS

LESSON 26: OVERVIEW OF OFFICE AUTOMATION FROM EXCEL   327

Why Automate Another Application?   327
Understanding Office Automation   328
   Early Binding   328
   Late Binding   329
   Which One Is Better?   330
Try It   330
   Lesson Requirements   330
   Step-by-Step   330

LESSON 27: WORKING WITH WORD FROM EXCEL   333

Activating a Word Document   333
   Activating the Word Application   334
   Opening and Activating a Word Document   334
Creating a New Word Document   336
Copying an Excel Range to a Word Document   337
Printing a Word Document from Excel   337
Importing a Word Document to Excel   338
Try It   339
   Lesson Requirements   339
   Step-by-Step   339

LESSON 28: WORKING WITH OUTLOOK FROM EXCEL   343

Opening Outlook   343
Composing an E-mail in Outlook from Excel   344
   Creating a MailItem Object   344
   Transferring an Excel Range to the Body of Your E-mail   345
   Putting It All Together   346
E-mailing a Single Worksheet   348
Try It   348
   Lesson Requirements   348
   Step-by-Step   348

LESSON 29: WORKING WITH ACCESS FROM EXCEL   353

Adding a Record to an Access Table   353
Exporting an Access Table to an Excel Spreadsheet   356
Creating a New Table in Access   358
Try It   359
    Lesson Requirements   359
    Step-by-Step   360

LESSON 30: WORKING WITH POWERPOINT FROM EXCEL   363

Creating a New PowerPoint Presentation   363
Copying a Worksheet Range to a PowerPoint Slide   364
Copying Chart Sheets to PowerPoint Slides   365
Running a PowerPoint Presentation from Excel   367
Try It   368
    Lesson Requirements   368
    Step-by-Step   368

APPENDIX: WHAT'S ON THE DVD?   371

INDEX   *375*

INTRODUCTION

CONGRATULATIONS ON MAKING TWO EXCELLENT CHOICES! You want to learn programming for Microsoft Excel with Visual Basic for Applications (VBA), and you've purchased this book to teach you. Excel is the most powerful and widely used spreadsheet application in the world. VBA enables you to become much more productive and efficient, while getting your everyday Excel tasks done more quickly and with fewer errors. You'll gain a programming skill that is in high demand, which will improve your value in the workplace and your marketability when searching for employment.

This book covers VBA from the ground up, and assumes you have never programmed Excel before. If you've never recorded or written an Excel macro, this book will show you how. If you've worked with VBA before, this book has examples of programming techniques you might not have seen. The instruction and examples in this book teach VBA concepts that range in levels from fundamental to advanced. The techniques in this book will apply just as well to the Excel business power user as to the keeper of the family budget.

VBA is the programming language for Microsoft's popular Office suite of applications, including Excel, Word, Access, PowerPoint, and Outlook. A full section of this book explains how to control each of those applications from Excel with VBA. By the time you complete this book, you will have learned how to record, write, and run your own macros. You'll learn how to make VBA run itself by programming Excel to monitor and respond to users' actions, and how to create friendly, customized interfaces that the users of your workbooks will enjoy.

The future of VBA is solid. Microsoft has confirmed time and again that VBA will be supported in versions of Excel into the foreseeable future. The programming skills you learn in this book will serve you throughout your career. You'll be able to apply the principles you learn in this book to other tasks that can be automated in Excel and Microsoft's other Office applications. VBA is an enormous programming language, and combined with Excel, it's an ongoing, rewarding process of learning something new every day. With this book as your entry into the world of VBA programming, you are well on your way.

WHO THIS BOOK IS FOR

This book is for Excel users who have never programmed Excel before. You are an Excel user who has been doing a frequent task manually, and you are ready to automate the task with VBA. You might also be a job seeker, and you want to improve your chances of being hired in this difficult job market by learning a valuable skill. Whether your Excel tasks are large or small, this book is for you. You'll learn how to use VBA to automate your work, from recording a simple one-line macro to writing a complex program with a customized, user-friendly interface that will look nothing like Excel. There is something in this book for everyone, but especially for the person who wants to dive right into VBA from square one and learn to use its powerful programming tools.

WHAT THIS BOOK COVERS

This book contains 30 lessons, which are broken into five sections.

➤ **Section I: Understanding the BASICs** — Section I includes Lessons 1 to 4, introducing you to VBA by providing a historical background and a discussion of what VBA is and what it can do for you. Section I familiarizes you with the Macro Recorder and the Visual Basic Editor, where VBA code is maintained.

➤ **Section II: Diving Deeper into VBA** — Section II includes Lessons 5 to 8, which discuss VBA topics including an overview of object-oriented programming, variable declaration, objects and collections, and arrays.

➤ **Section III: Beyond the Macro Recorder: Writing Your Own Code** — Section III includes Lessons 9 to 17. You learn how to write your own macros without help from the Macro Recorder. You become familiar with loops, event programming at the workbook and worksheet levels, charts, PivotTables, and User Defined Functions, and learn how to debug your VBA code.

➤ **Section IV: Advanced Programming Techniques** — Section IV includes Lessons 18 to 25, and deals with the more advanced topics of UserForms, class modules, add-ins, retrieving external data, and backwards-compatible features that have been all but forgotten but are still fully supported in all Excel versions.

➤ **Section V: Interacting with Other Office Applications** — Section V includes Lessons 26 to 30, dealing with how to control Access, Word, Outlook, and PowerPoint from Excel.

HOW THIS BOOK IS STRUCTURED

My primary goal in this book is to teach you what you need to know in VBA. I tried to write this book as if you and I were sitting down in front of your computer, and I was explaining Excel and VBA's technical concepts in an informal tutorial session. The book is structured such that each lesson teaches you the theory of a topic, followed by one or more coded examples, with plenty of screenshots and notes to help you follow along. To avoid redundancy of instruction, the lessons build on each other, so the later chapters assume you've read, or are already familiar with, the material discussed in earlier lessons. I strongly recommend that you watch the videos. You will get more out of them than you might imagine, because they include bonus information about Excel, such as tips and tricks, that will help you manage your workbooks with greater ease and efficiency.

WHAT YOU NEED TO USE THIS BOOK

What you need is this book and a fully installed version of Microsoft Office. If you only have Excel installed, that will suffice for lessons up to and including Lesson 25. Lessons 26 to 30 deal with controlling other Office applications from Excel. VBA ships with Excel so you already have all the programming tools you need, but make sure your installation has provided you with access to the VBE and Help files. It's possible to exclude those items in the installation process. The version of Windows is not important. In many examples, different versions of Excel are represented, with Excel's latest version at this writing, version 2010, shown most frequently. Almost everything discussed in this book has VBA example code to go along with it, with notes in the code (lines of text in VBA code that start with an apostrophe) that explain what the code is doing, and why. There are plenty of screenshots to help you see beforehand what to expect, and help you after you've tested your code to confirm you followed the steps correctly.

There's one other item you need, which only you are in control of, and that is arranging a quiet period of time for yourself on a regular basis, so you can read this book and view its video Try It lessons uninterrupted. Everyone studies and retains new material differently, and we all live in a busy world. But do what you can to carve out some "you time" as you make your way through the book. You'll find a lot of useful material that will lead you to think of other situations you typically encounter in Excel that can be solved with the concepts you'll be learning.

INSTRUCTIONAL VIDEOS ON DVD

Twenty-six of the 30 lessons in this book are brought to life through hours of instructional video that are included on the DVD. Those lessons with video conclude with a tutorial. Both the content of the lesson and the accompanying tutorial are covered in the video. You may want to watch the video before you read each lesson or vice versa. The choice is up to you.

CONVENTIONS

To help you get the most from the text and keep track of what's happening, we've used a number of conventions throughout the book.

> *Boxes with a warning icon like this one hold important, not-to-be-forgotten information that is directly relevant to the surrounding text.*

> *The pencil icon indicates notes, tips, hints, tricks, or asides to the current discussion.*

> *References like this one point you to the DVD to watch the instructional video that accompanies a given lesson.*

As for styles in the text:

➤ We *highlight* new terms and important words when we introduce them.

➤ We show keyboard strokes like this: Ctrl+A.

➤ We show file names, URLs, and code within the text like so: `persistence.properties`.

We present code in two different ways:

```
We use a monofont type with no highlighting for most code examples.
We use bold to emphasize code that is particularly important in the present context
or to show changes from a previous code snippet.
```

SUPPORTING WEBSITES AND CODE

As you work through each lesson I recommend that you type in all of the code. However, depending on how you learn, you may prefer to download the code. The code is available on the DVD and at `www.wrox.com`. You can use the search box on the website to locate this title. After you have located this book, click the **Download Code** link to access the files that can be downloaded. You can download the files via HTTP or FTP. All of the files are stored as ZIP files.

> The ISBN for this book is 978-0-470-89069-1. You may find it easier to search by the ISBN than by the title of the book.

You can also download the code from the main Wrox download page, `www.wrox.com/dynamic/books/download.aspx`. Click the link to the Excel VBA 24-Hour Trainer to access the files that can be downloaded.

ERRATA

We make every effort to ensure that there are no errors in the text or in the code. However, no one is perfect, and mistakes do occur. If you find an error in one of our books, like a spelling mistake or faulty piece of code, we would be very grateful for your feedback. By sending in errata, you may save another reader hours of frustration, and at the same time, you will be helping us provide even higher quality information.

To find the errata page for this book, go to `www.wrox.com` and locate the title using the Search box or one of the title lists. Then, on the book details page, click the Book Errata link. On this page, you can view all errata that have been submitted for this book and posted by Wrox editors. A complete book list, including links to each book's errata, is also available at `www.wrox.com/misc-pages/booklist.shtml`.

If you don't spot "your" error on the Book Errata page, go to www.wrox.com/contact/techsupport .shtml and complete the form there to send us the error you have found. We'll check the information and, if appropriate, post a message to the book's errata page and fix the problem in subsequent editions of the book.

P2P.WROX.COM

For author and peer discussion, join the P2P forums at p2p.wrox.com. The forums are a web-based system for you to post messages relating to Wrox books and related technologies and interact with other readers and technology users. The forums offer a subscription feature to e-mail you topics of interest of your choosing when new posts are made to the forums. Wrox authors, editors, other industry experts, and your fellow readers are present on these forums.

At p2p.wrox.com, you will find a number of different forums that will help you, not only as you read this book, but also as you develop your own applications. To join the forums, just follow these steps:

1. Go to p2p.wrox.com and click the Register link.

2. Read the terms of use and click Agree.

3. Complete the required information to join, as well as any optional information you wish to provide, and click Submit.

4. You will receive an e-mail with information describing how to verify your account and complete the joining process.

> *You can read messages in the forums without joining P2P, but in order to post your own messages, you must join.*

Once you join, you can post new messages and respond to messages other users post. You can read messages at any time on the Web. If you would like to have new messages from a particular forum e-mailed to you, click the Subscribe to this Forum icon by the forum name in the forum listing.

For more information about how to use the Wrox P2P, be sure to read the P2P FAQs for answers to questions about how the forum software works, as well as many common questions specific to P2P and Wrox books. To read the FAQs, click the FAQ link on any P2P page.

Excel® VBA 24-Hour Trainer

SECTION I
Understanding the BASICs

▶ **LESSON 1:** Introducing VBA

▶ **LESSON 2:** Getting Started with Macros

▶ **LESSON 3:** Introducing the Visual Basic Editor

▶ **LESSON 4:** Working in the VBE

1

Introducing VBA

Welcome to your first lesson in Visual Basic for Applications! A good place to start is at the beginning, where you'll find it useful to get an understanding of where VBA came from and what VBA is today. Once you get a feel for how VBA fits into the overall Excel universe, you'll learn how to use VBA to manipulate Excel in ways you might never have thought possible.

WHAT IS VBA?

Visual Basic for Applications (VBA) is a programming language created by Microsoft to automate operations in applications that support it, such as Excel. VBA is an enormously powerful tool that enables you to control Excel in countless ways that you cannot do manually.

In fact, VBA is also the language that manipulates Microsoft Office applications in Access, Word, PowerPoint, and Outlook. For the purposes here, VBA is the tool you'll use to develop macros and manipulate the kinds of objects you will learn about in this book to control Excel, and to control other Office applications from Excel.

You do not need to purchase anything more than the Office suite (or the individual application) to also own VBA. If you have Excel on your computer, you have VBA on your computer.

> ### WHAT IS A "MACRO," ANYWAY?
>
> Back in the day, a programming language was often called a "macro language" if its capabilities included the automation of a sequence of commands in spreadsheet or word processor applications. With Microsoft's release of Office 5, VBA set a new bar for how robust a programming language can be, with capabilities extending far beyond those of earlier programming languages, such as the ability to create and control objects within Excel, or to have access to disk drives and networks.
>
> *continues*

(continued)

So, VBA is a programming language and it is also a macro language. Confusion of terminology arises when referring to VBA code that is a series of commands written and executed in Excel. Is it a macro, a procedure, or a program? Since Microsoft commonly refers to its VBA procedures as macros, that's good enough for me to call them macros as well. Outside of a few exceptions that'll be discussed when the time comes, I'll be referring to VBA procedures as macros.

A BRIEF HISTORY OF VBA

VBA is a present-day dialect of the BASIC (Beginner's All-purpose Symbolic Instruction Code) programming language that was developed in the 1960s. BASIC became widely used in many software applications throughout the next two decades, because it was easy to learn and understand.

Over the years, BASIC has evolved and improved in response to advancing technology and increased demands by its users for greater programming flexibility. In 1985, Microsoft released a much richer version of BASIC, named QuickBASIC, which boasted the most up-to-date features found in programming languages of the day. In 1992, Microsoft released Visual Basic for Windows, designed to work within the burgeoning Windows environment.

Meanwhile, various software publishers were making their own enhancements to BASIC for their products' programming languages, resulting in a wide and confusing range of functionality and commands among software applications that were using BASIC. Microsoft recognized the need for developing a standardized programming language for its software products, and created Visual Basic for Applications.

VBA was first released by Microsoft with Excel 5 in the Office 1995 suite. Since then, VBA has become the programming language for Microsoft's other popular Office applications, as well as for external software customers of Microsoft to whom VBA has been licensed for use.

DON'T CONFUSE VB WITH VBA!

With all the acronyms bandied about in the world of computing, it's easy to get some terms confused. "VB" stands for Visual Basic and it is not the same as VBA. Though both VB and VBA are programming languages derived from BASIC and created by Microsoft, they are otherwise very different.

VB is a language that allows you to create standalone executable applications that do not even require its users to have Office or Excel loaded onto their computers. On the other hand, VBA cannot create standalone applications, and it exists within a host application such as Excel and the workbook containing the VBA code. For a VBA macro to run, its host application workbook must be open. This book is about VBA, and how it controls Excel.

WHAT VBA CAN DO FOR YOU

Everyone reading this book uses Excel for their own needs, such as financial budgeting, forecasting, analyzing scientific data, creating invoices, or charting the progress of their favorite basketball team. One thing all readers have in common is the need to automate some kind of frequently encountered task that is either too time-consuming or too cumbersome to continue doing manually. That's where VBA comes in.

The good news is, utilizing VBA does not mandate that you first become a world-class professional programmer. Many VBA commands are at your disposal and, as this book will show you, are relatively easy to implement and customize for your everyday purposes.

Anything you can do manually you can do with VBA, but faster and with a minimized risk of human error. Many things that Excel does not allow you to do manually, you can do with VBA. The following sections describe a handful of examples of what VBA can do for you.

Automating a Recurring Task

If you find yourself needing to produce weekly or monthly sales and expense reports, a macro can create them in no time flat, in a style and format you (and more importantly, your boss) will be thrilled with. And if the source data changes later that day and you need to produce the updated report again, no problem — just run the macro again!

Automating a Repetitive Task

When faced with needing to perform the same task on every worksheet in your workbook, or in every workbook in a particular file folder, you can create a macro to "loop" through each object and do the deed. You learn how to repeat actions with various looping methods in Lesson 9.

Running a Macro Automatically if Another Action Takes Place

In some situations you'll want a macro to run automatically, so you don't have to worry about remembering to run it yourself. For example, to automatically refresh a pivot table the moment its source data changes, you can monitor those changes with VBA, assuring that your pivot table always displays real-time results. This is called "event" programming, which is cool stuff, and is discussed in Lessons 11 and 12.

Creating Your Own Worksheet Functions

You can create your own worksheet functions, known as "User Defined Functions," to handle custom calculations that Excel's built-in functions do not provide for, or would be too complicated to use even if such functions were available. For example, you'll see how to add up numbers in cells that are formatted a certain color. UDFs, as these custom functions are called, are covered in Lesson 16.

Simplifying the Workbook's Look and Feel for Other Users

When you create a workbook for others to use, there will inevitably be users who know little to nothing about Excel, but who will still need to work in that file. You can build a customized interface with user-friendly menus and informational pop-up boxes to guide your novice users throughout their activities in the workbook. You might be surprised at how un-Excel-looking an Excel workbook can be, with VBA providing a visually comfortable and interactive experience for users unfamiliar with Excel, enabling them to get their work done. Figure 1-1 shows an example of accomplishing this with UserForms, which are discussed in Lessons 18, 19, and 20.

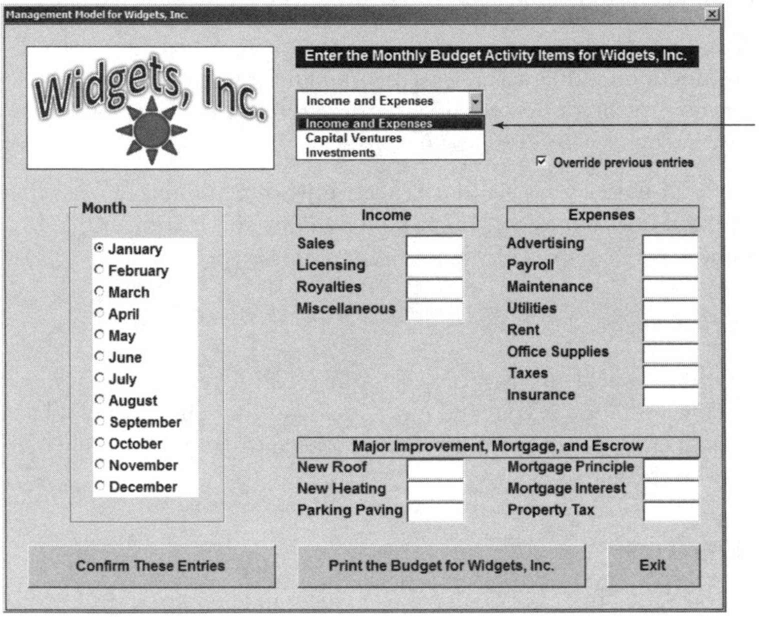

FIGURE 1-1

Controlling Other Office Applications from Excel

If you create narrative reports in Word that require an embedded list of data from Excel, or if you need to import a table from Access into an Excel worksheet, VBA can automate the process. VBA is the programming language for Microsoft's other Office applications, enabling you to write macros in Excel to perform tasks in those other applications, with the users being none the wiser that they ever left Excel while the macro was running.

As you can imagine, the list of advantages to using VBA could fill a city telephone book. The point is, there are sure to be tasks in your everyday dealings with Excel that can be accomplished more quickly and efficiently with VBA, and this book will show you how.

LIABILITIES OF VBA

Although VBA is a tremendously useful and versatile tool, alas, it is not an elevator to Excel nirvana. The pros far outweigh the cons, but learning and using VBA comes with a few caveats that you need to be aware of:

➤ With each version release of Excel, Microsoft may add new VBA commands or stop supporting existing VBA commands, sometimes without advance warning. Surprises do happen, as was especially the case when Office 2007 was released with all its added features. Such is life in the world of Excel VBA; you will probably learn of coding errors from people who have upgraded to a newer version and are using the workbook you created in an earlier version.

➤ VBA does not run uniformly in all computer operating environments. Sometimes, no matter how extensively you test your code and how flawlessly the macros run on your computer, there will be users of your workbook who will report an error in your code. It won't be your fault or VBA's fault, it's just the idiosyncrasies of how programming languages such as VBA mix with various operating systems, Office versions, and network configurations. Debugging your code is the subject of Lesson 17.

➤ Programming languages, including VBA, are not warmly received by all workplace IT departments. Many companies have set internal policies that forbid employees from downloading malicious software onto workplace computers. This is an understandable concern, but the corporate safety nets are sometimes cast far and wide to include Excel workbooks with VBA code. The tug of war in companies between the security interests of IT, and the work efficiency needs of management, can determine whether the VBA code you install will actually be allowed for use in some company venues.

➤ Finally, VBA is a large program. It has thousands of keywords and the language library is only getting larger. Actually, I see this as a good thing, because the more VBA you learn, the more productivity and control you will have with Excel. Just as with any language, be it spoken or programming, there is a level of rolling-up-your-shirtsleeves commitment that'll be needed to learn VBA. Even the longest journey starts with a first step, and this book will get you on your way.

> *VBA has a bright, stable future. An occasional rumor will make the rounds on the Internet, claiming the imminent demise of VBA. Do not believe it. VBA is here to stay, and Microsoft has publicly said so, time and again. The facts are, in 2007, Microsoft closed its VBA licensing program to new customers, and VBA is not supported in the 2008 version of Office for the Mac. However, Microsoft has consistently made very clear its plan for supporting VBA in future versions of Excel for Windows.*

TRY IT

There's nothing specific to try based on the material in this lesson. What you could do is make a list of some of your most frequent everyday Excel tasks. Chances are, those frequently recurring tasks will be good candidates for the first VBA macros you'll be composing when you practice macro-writing on your own.

2

Getting Started with Macros

In Lesson 1, you read that VBA is the programming language of Microsoft Excel and that a macro is a sequence of VBA commands to run a task automatically instead of manually. In this lesson, you learn how to create a simple macro, what its code looks like, and a few options for how you can run the macro.

COMPOSING YOUR FIRST MACRO

This lesson leads you through the process of composing a macro to sort and format a range of data. But even before the first line of programming code is written, you'll want to set up shop by giving yourself easy access to the VBA-related tools you'll be using. The following house-keeping tips usually need to be done only once, and are worth taking the time to do now, if you haven't already done so.

Accessing the VBA Environment

At the time of this writing, Excel is at a unique stage in its ongoing evolution, because three of its versions are being used with substantial popularity. Version 2003 (also known as version 11) was the final Excel version having the traditional menu bar interface of File, Edit, View, and so on. Then came version 2007 (also known as version 12) with Office's new Ribbon interface, and most recently, version 2010 (also known as version 14) has taken its place among the community of Excel users.

As with other tasks you typically do in Excel, the actions you take to create, view, edit, or run VBA code usually start by clicking the on-screen icon relating to that task. Exactly what those VBA-related icons look like, and what you need to do to make them easily accessible to you, will depend on the particular version of Excel you are working with.

Start by making sure that the VBA-related icons you'll be using most frequently are already displayed whenever you open Excel.

For versions of Excel up to and including 2003, from your worksheet menu, click View ⇨ Toolbars ⇨ Visual Basic as shown in Figure 2-1. This displays the Visual Basic toolbar, as shown in Figure 2-2, which you can dock just as you do with your other toolbars.

For versions of Excel after 2003 (that is, starting with Excel 2007), the Ribbon user interface has replaced the menu interface, resulting in a different look to the VBA-related icons and a different set of steps required to see them.

In versions 2007 and 2010, these VBA icons are located on the Developer tab. By default, the Developer tab is not automatically displayed along with the other Ribbon tabs. You need to do a set of one-time mouse clicks to show the Developer tab, and to keep it visible whenever you open Excel. Although the steps to do this are easy, they are different between versions 2007 and 2010.

FIGURE 2-1

In Excel 2007, click the round Office button near the top-left corner of your screen. Then, click the Excel Options button located at the bottom of that menu, as shown in Figure 2-3.

FIGURE 2-2

In the Excel Options dialog box, click the Popular item at the upper left, and select the Show Developer tab in the Ribbon option, as shown in Figure 2-4.

For Excel version 2010, showing the Developer tab is a bit different. A new Ribbon tab named File has supplanted the Office button. Click the File tab and then click the Options button as shown in Figure 2-5.

In the Excel Options dialog box for version 2010, click the Customize Ribbon item at the left, which displays two vertical lists as shown in Figure 2-6. Notice that the list on the right has
a drop-down menu above it called Customize the Ribbon. Select the Main Tabs item from that drop-down. In the list of Main Tabs, select Developer and click OK.

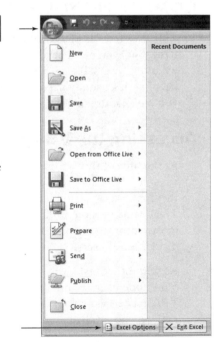

FIGURE 2-3

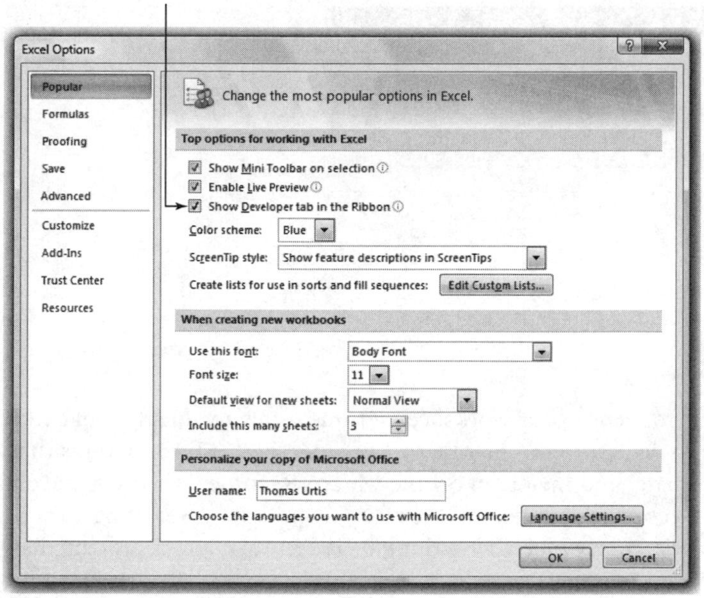

FIGURE 2-4

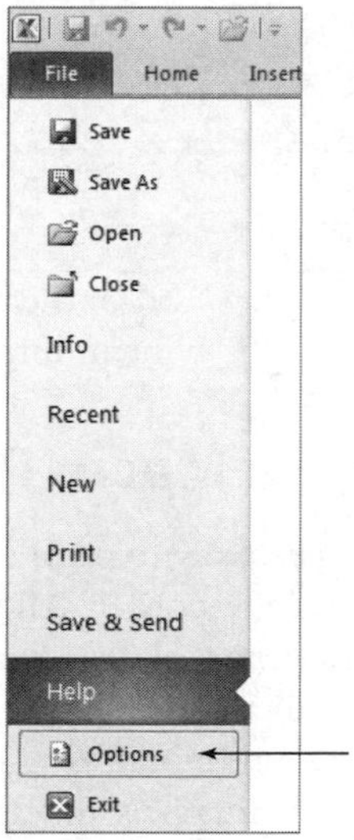

FIGURE 2-5

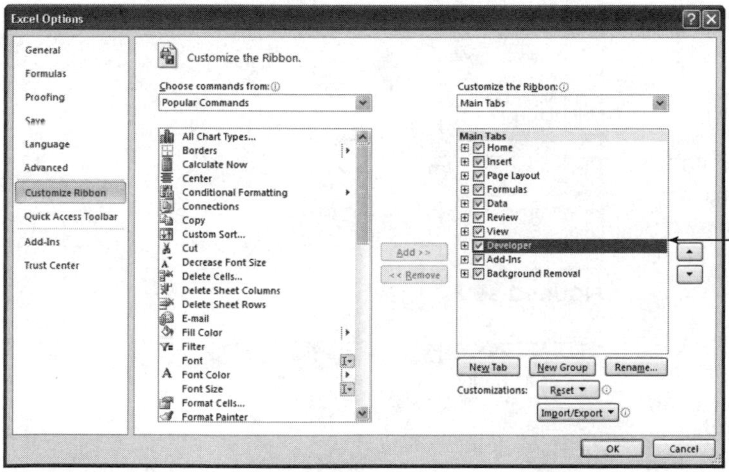

FIGURE 2-6

Figure 2-7 shows the Developer tab on the Ribbon with its related icons.

FIGURE 2-7

Using the Macro Recorder

The easiest way to create a macro is to record your worksheet actions using a valuable tool called the Macro Recorder. All you need to do is turn on the Macro Recorder, perform the actions that comprise the task you want to automate, and then turn off the Macro Recorder when you have finished your task. While the Macro Recorder is turned on, every action you do — selecting a cell, entering a number, formatting a range, pretty much everything — is recorded and represented as VBA code in a new macro. As you'll see, when you run the macro created by the Macro Recorder, your task will be completed automatically, just as you did it manually.

The Macro Recorder comes in handy for repetitive (and sometimes mundane) common tasks that you'd rather not have to keep manually doing over and over. For example, say you manage a table of data every day, such as shown in Figure 2-8, that shows how many items your company sold in its East, West, North, and South regions.

	A	B	C	D	E	F	G
1	Item	Region	Count				
2	Widgets	North	40931				
3	Wombats	West	48521				
4	Wombats	East	37883				
5	Wallabees	South	82943				
6	Widgets	West	8010				
7	Warlocks	South	65065				
8	Wallabees	West	76781				
9	Wallabees	East	29023				
10	Widgets	North	72685				
11	Widgets	South	2371				
12	Warlocks	East	40681				
13	Wallabees	West	91831				
14							
15							

FIGURE 2-8

The everyday task at hand is to sort the table primarily by Region, then by Item, then by Count. Your boss wants the Item and Region columns to switch places, so that Region occupies column A and Item occupies column B. To improve readability, the numbers in the Count column must be formatted with the thousands comma separator, and the headers for Item, Region, and Count must be bolded. Figure 2-9 shows the finished table, the way your boss wants it.

	A	B	C	D	E	F	G
1	**Region**	**Item**	**Count**				
2	East	Wallabees	29,023				
3	East	Warlocks	40,681				
4	East	Wombats	37,883				
5	North	Widgets	40,931				
6	North	Widgets	72,685				
7	South	Wallabees	82,943				
8	South	Warlocks	65,065				
9	South	Widgets	2,371				
10	West	Wallabees	76,781				
11	West	Wallabees	91,831				
12	West	Widgets	8,010				
13	West	Wombats	48,521				
14							
15							

FIGURE 2-9

This is normally a six-step process, which is quite boring, but it's part of your job responsibilities. To complete the task you might:

1. Insert a new column at column A.

2. Select the Region column, cut it, and paste it to empty column A, to the left of the Item column.

3. Delete the now-empty column from where the Region column was cut.

4. Select range A1:C13 and sort in ascending order by Region, Item, and Count.

5. Select range C2:C13 and format the numbers with the thousands comma separator.

6. Select range A1:C1 and format those cells as Bold.

Not only are these steps monotonous, but also an invitation to honest mistakes due to eventual human error. The good news is, if you perform the necessary steps perfectly for the Macro Recorder, the task can be reduced to a simple mouse click or keyboard shortcut, with VBA doing the grunt work for you.

> *Any time you create a macro, it's wise to plan ahead about why you are creating the macro, and what you want the macro to do. This is especially important with complex macros, because you will want your macros to operate efficiently and accurately, with just the code that's necessary to get the job done properly. By avoiding excessive code, your macros will run faster and be easier to edit or troubleshoot. For example, get your workbook ready beforehand to avoid unnecessary coded actions. Have the worksheet that you'll be working on active, with the range of interest already visible. Mistakes are recorded too! Practice the steps first, so your macro is not longer than it needs to be.*

Because you know what manual steps are required for this daily task, you are ready to create your macro. The first thing to do is turn on the Macro Recorder. In Excel versions 2003 or before, click

the Record Macro button on the Visual Basic toolbar as shown in Figure 2-10. For later Excel versions, click the Record Macro button in the Code section of the Developer tab on the Ribbon, as shown in Figure 2-11.

FIGURE 2-10   **FIGURE 2-11**

What you see next will look much like Figure 2-12. A small dialog box titled Record Macro will appear, with default information that only needs your approval by clicking OK to start recording your macro. Resist the temptation to accept the defaults because now's the time to get into a few good habits.

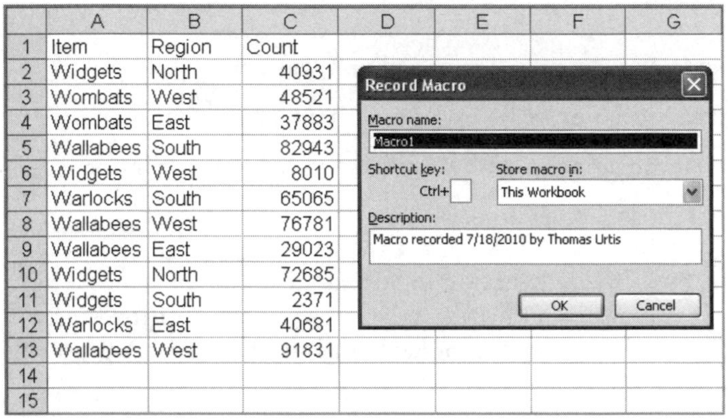

	A	B	C	D	E	F	G
1	Item	Region	Count				
2	Widgets	North	40931				
3	Wombats	West	48521				
4	Wombats	East	37883				
5	Wallabees	South	82943				
6	Widgets	West	8010				
7	Warlocks	South	65065				
8	Wallabees	West	76781				
9	Wallabees	East	29023				
10	Widgets	North	72685				
11	Widgets	South	2371				
12	Warlocks	East	40681				
13	Wallabees	West	91831				
14							
15							

Record Macro

Macro name:
Macro1

Shortcut key: Store macro in:
Ctrl+ [ ] This Workbook

Description:
Macro recorded 7/18/2010 by Thomas Urtis

[OK] [Cancel]

FIGURE 2-12

The Macro Recorder is an excellent teaching tool, and hardly a day goes by when I do not use it in some way. VBA is just too voluminous a programming language to memorize its every keyword and nuance. Often as not, I'll record a macro just to look at the code it produces to learn the proper syntax of a task dealing with some larger macro I am working on. You will find yourself using the Macro Recorder in the same way; it's a terrific source for learning VBA code, as Excel developers of any skill level will attest.

For this example, the macro you are creating is one you will want to keep and use often. A little customization is strongly recommended to help you down the road, when you'll want to remember what the macro does, why you created it, and what optional keyboard shortcut you assigned to run it.

In the Record Macro dialog box, give the macro a meaningful name. Macro names cannot contain spaces and they cannot begin with a numeral. Because you are the person doing the sorting, and you don't want to make the macro name too long, naming it `mySort` gives the macro more meaning than the default name of `Macro1`.

In Figure 2-12, notice the small box to the right of Ctrl+ in the Shortcut Key section. You can place any letter of the alphabet in that field, which, when pressed with the Ctrl key, will be one method (and a convenient one at that) by which you can run the macro.

> *A shortcut key is not mandatory; in fact, most of your macros will not have one or need one. But if you do want to assign a shortcut key, get into the good habit of assigning it with the Ctrl+Shift combination rather than with just the Ctrl key. Excel has assigned almost all 26 letters of the alphabet to serve as shortcuts with the Ctrl key for various tasks, and you will do well to avoid overriding that built-in functionality. For example, Ctrl+C is typically the key combination you use to copy text. However, if you assign the shortcut key Ctrl+C to your macro, you will override the default for that key combination and will not be able to use Ctrl+C to copy text.*

To take advantage of the Shortcut Key option, click in the Shortcut Key field, press the Shift key, and also press a key such as the letter S. You will have created the keyboard shortcut Ctrl+Shift+S, which will not interfere with any of Excel's significant built-in keyboard shortcuts.

Most macros you record will be stored in the workbook you are working with. For now, you can keep the default selection of This Workbook in the Store Macro In field.

Finally, in the Description field, enter a brief but meaningful explanation of what the macro does. When you are finished making these minor changes to the Record Macro dialog box, it will look similar to Figure 2-13. Go ahead and click OK, which will turn on the Macro Recorder, and you can proceed to manually perform the steps you want to automate.

	A	B	C	D	E	F	G
1	Item	Region	Count				
2	Widgets	North	10931				
3	Wombats	West	48521				
4	Wombats	East	37883				
5	Wallabees	South	82943				
6	Widgets	West	8010				
7	Warlocks	South	65065				
8	Wallabees	West	76781				
9	Wallabees	East	29023				
10	Widgets	North	72685				
11	Widgets	South	2371				
12	Warlocks	East	40681				
13	Wallabees	West	91831				
14							
15							

Record Macro

Macro name:
mySort

Shortcut key: Ctrl+Shift+ S   Store macro in: This Workbook

Description:
Arrange the columns and sort ascending by Region, Item, and Count. Bold headers and format Count.

OK   Cancel

FIGURE 2-13

In versions 2003 and before, you will see a tiny floating toolbar while the Macro Recorder is on. That is the Stop Recording toolbar, with a Stop Recording button you will click when you are finished recording your actions. When you have completed the steps to your task, turn off the Macro Recorder in version 2003 by clicking the Stop Recording button, as shown in Figure 2-14.

FIGURE 2-14

If you are working in a later version of Excel, click the Stop Recording button from the Developer tab in the Ribbon, as shown in Figure 2-15. Clicking the Stop Recording button ends the recording session, and you will have created your macro.

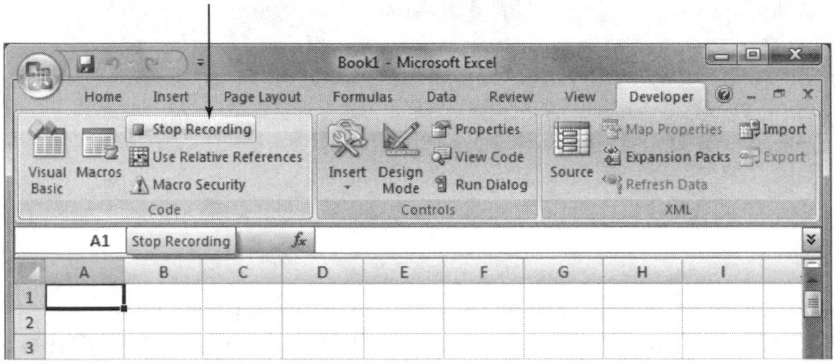

FIGURE 2-15

HEY, MY STOP RECORDING BUTTON DISAPPEARED!

If you are using Excel version 2003 or before, the Stop Recording toolbar might seem to suddenly disappear on you from time to time. This is almost always due to unwittingly closing that toolbar by clicking the "X" close button on its title bar instead of the Stop Recording button. It happens to the best of us. To show the Stop Recording toolbar again, start to record a new macro, then from the worksheet menu click View ⇨ Toolbars ⇨ Stop Recording. Click the Stop Recording button to end the macro, and the next time you record a macro, the Stop Recording toolbar will be its normal visible self.

RUNNING A MACRO

You have many ways to run a macro, most of which are demonstrated in later lessons. As you will see, the method(s) you choose for running your macros may depend on complex reasons such as the workbook design, or may be based on a simpler factor such as what feels most intuitive and convenient for you. To wrap up this lesson, following are a couple of commonly used options for running your macros.

The Macro Dialog Box

When you create recorded macros, their names will appear listed in a dialog box called, appropriately enough, the Macro dialog box. To show the Macro dialog box in version 2003 or before, click the Run Macro button on the Visual Basic toolbar as shown in Figure 2-16. The title of that button, Run Macro, is a bit of a misnomer, because just by clicking

FIGURE 2-16

it, you are not actually running a macro yet. All you'll be doing is displaying the Macro dialog box, from which you can run a macro but also edit and examine macros.

In versions later than 2003, the button to click is more logically labeled Macros, as shown in Figure 2-17.

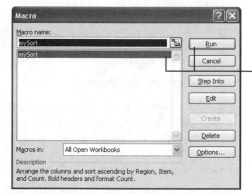

FIGURE 2-17

Regardless of the Excel version, pressing Alt+F8 displays the Macro dialog box — no mouse clicks needed.

Figure 2-18 shows the Macro dialog box with the one and only `mySort` macro listed. As you create more macros in this workbook, their names will be listed in the Macro dialog box in alphabetical order. To run your macro, select its name in the list and click the Run button as indicated by the black arrows. You could also run the macro by double-clicking its name in the list.

Shortcut Key

Recall that you assigned the shortcut key Ctrl+Shift+S to this macro at the start of the macro recording process. Because you did that, you do not need to bother with the Macro dialog box if you don't want to; you can run the `mySort` macro simply by pressing Ctrl+Shift+S.

FIGURE 2-18

TRY IT

In this lesson, you practice creating a recorded macro.

Lesson Requirements

For this lesson, you create a macro by turning on the Macro Recorder, copying a range of formula-containing cells, and using Paste Special to convert the formulas in that range to values.

Step-by-Step

Start by establishing a situation where you have dynamic formulas in cells where you prefer to show static values. In a fresh worksheet, select cell A1:D10, and type the formula `=INT(RAND()*1000)`. Press Ctrl+Enter, which will insert formulas in A1:D10 that return a random number between 0 and 199. Select any single cell to deselect range A1:D10.

Create a macro that copies the range of dynamic RAND numbers, and paste the numbers over the range as values to obtain static numbers:

1. Turn on the Macro Recorder by clicking the Record Macro button.

2. In the Record Macro dialog box, name the macro **ValuesOnly** and assign it the shortcut Ctrl+Shift+C.

3. Click OK to start recording your ValuesOnly macro.

4. Select range A1:D10.

5. Press Ctrl+C to copy the selected range.

6. Right-click within the selected range.

7. Left-click Paste Special, select Values, and click OK.

8. Press the Esc key to exit copy mode.

9. Click cell A1 to deselect all cells except A1.

10. Turn off the Macro Recorder by clicking the Stop Recording button.

11. Re-enter formulas in range A1:D10 and test your macro with the shortcut Ctrl+Shift+C, or by displaying the Macro dialog box, selecting the ValuesOnly macro name in the list, and clicking the Run button.

Once you run your macro, the formulas you entered will now be hard numbers.

To get the sample database files, you can download Lesson 2 from the book's website at www.wrox.com.

 Please select Lesson 2 on the DVD to view the video that accompanies this lesson.

3

Introducing the Visual Basic Editor

In Lesson 2, you learned how to create a macro, and you saw a couple of easy ways to run the macro you created. Now it's time to view your macro and have a look at the environment called the Visual Basic Editor (VBE), within which all macros and VBA procedures are stored. Seeing where macros live and breathe will improve your understanding of the VBA programming process, especially when you start to edit existing macros or create new macros without the Macro Recorder.

WHAT IS THE VBE?

It's fair to say that for many users of Excel, the worksheets, pivot tables, charts, and hundreds of functions are all the tools they need to satisfactorily handle their spreadsheet activities. For them, the familiar workbook environment is the only side of Excel they see, and understandably the only side of Excel they are probably aware of.

But Excel has a separate, less visible environment working behind the scenes — the Visual Basic Editor — which is interconnected with the workbook environment even if no programming code exists in the workbook. Both environments are constantly but quietly working together, sharing information back and forth about the entire workbook. The Visual Basic Editor is a user-friendly development environment where programmed instructions are maintained in order to make your spreadsheet applications work.

HOW TO GET INTO THE VBE

With Excel open, a fast and easy way to get into the Visual Basic Editor
is to press Alt+F11 on your keyboard. You can do this from any worksheet. It's just as quick with your mouse too, by clicking the Visual Basic
Editor icon on the Visual Basic toolbar in versions up to 2003, as shown
in Figure 3-1, or the Visual Basic button from the Developer tab on the
Ribbon in later versions, as shown in Figure 3-2.

FIGURE 3-1

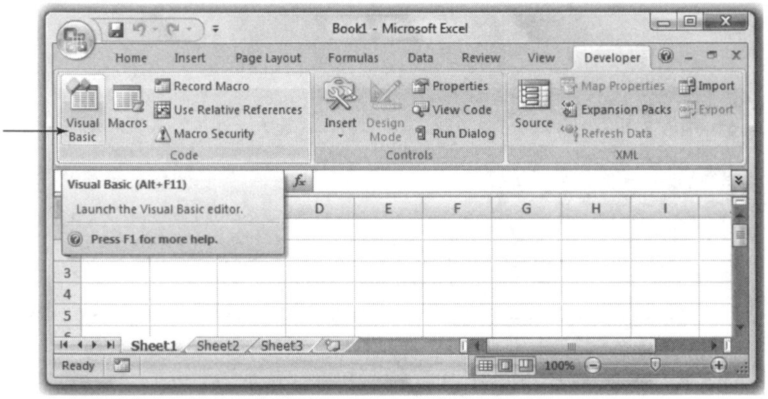

FIGURE 3-2

CAREFUL, THAT WAS *ALT*+F11!

The Ctrl key is commonly used in conjunction with other keys for keyboard shortcuts. By force of habit, you might mistakenly press Ctrl+F11 instead of Alt+F11
when attempting to go to the VBE. However, pressing Ctrl+F11 has a curious result:
you won't be taken to the VBE, but instead you will have created and find yourself
on an outdated type of sheet called a macro sheet, with the strange tab name of
Macro1. Prior to Excel version 97, macros were stored on macro sheets, which can
still be created, though they have no practical use with today's Excel, and they no
longer hold any programming code. It's OK to just delete the macro sheet if you create one, and take another stab at the Alt key with F11 to get into the VBE.

UNDERSTANDING THE VBE

The Visual Basic Editor can show a number of different windows depending on what you want to
see or do. For the majority of work you'll be doing with the help of this book, you'll want to eventually become familiar with four windows: the Project Explorer window, the Code window, the
Properties window, and the Immediate window. Figure 3-3 shows what the VBE looks like with
these four windows.

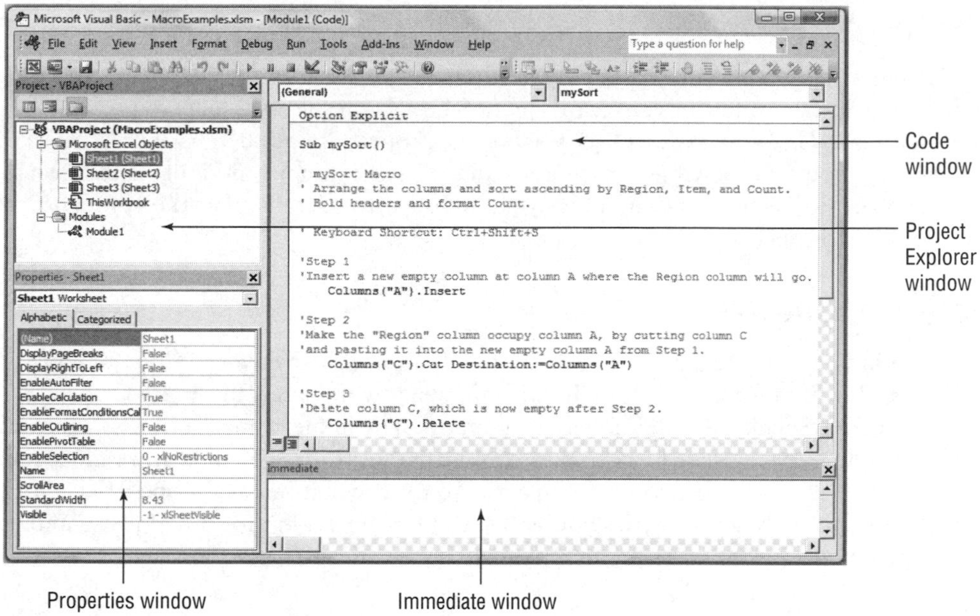

FIGURE 3-3

The Project Explorer Window

The Project Explorer is a vertical pane on the left side of the VBE. It behaves similarly to Windows Explorer, with folder icons that expand and collapse when clicked. If you do not see the Project Explorer window in your VBE, press Ctrl+R, or from the VBE menu bar, click View ➪ Project Explorer. As the first item showing at the top of the Project Explorer window in Figure 3-3, the name of the workbook I am using (in Excel terms, the VBAProject) is MacroExamples.xlsm.

VBA code is kept in objects known as *modules*, which are discussed later in further detail. Figure 3-3 shows one module called Module1. Double-clicking a module name in the Project Explorer displays that module's VBA code contents in the Code window, as you see in Figure 3-3.

The Code Window

The Code window is where the code for macros and VBA procedures is located. The VBE provides separate code windows for each module. A good way to think of this is, for every object (worksheet, module, and so on) you see listed in the Project Explorer, the VBE has provided a code window. You will note that the drop-down in the upper right-hand corner of Figure 3-3 displays the name of the macro that is currently showing in the Code window (mySort). As you create multiple macros, you can use this drop-down to quickly move from one macro to another.

The Properties Window

The Properties window is located in the left vertical pane near the bottom of the VBE. If you do not see the Properties window in your VBE, press F4, or from the VBE menu bar click View ⇨ Properties Window. This window displays a list of the properties and their assigned values of whatever object is selected in the Project Explorer window. For example, in Figure 3-3, Sheet1 has been selected and the Properties window shows you, among other details, that the Name property for the selected object is Sheet1.

The Immediate Window

The Immediate window is located at the bottom of the VBE, usually below the Code window as depicted in Figure 3-3. If you do not see the Immediate window in your VBE, press Ctrl+G, or from the VBE menu bar, click View ⇨ Immediate Window. The name "Immediate" has nothing to do with urgency, but rather with the notion that you can query a line of code and immediately obtain its returned result, without having to run a macro to see what that code line does. This comes in handy for code debugging tactics you will see in Lesson 17, but for now I just wanted to point out the Immediate window to familiarize you with its name and location.

UNDERSTANDING MODULES

I touched on modules earlier but they are worth another mention. A module is a container for your code. A single module may hold one or many macros, depending on the workbook and your preference for how you manage your code. For smaller projects with maybe two or three macros, just one module is sufficient. If you develop larger projects with dozens of macros, you will want to organize them among several modules by theme or purpose.

Several types of modules exist:

➤ **Standard Modules** — These are the kind you have seen already, which hold macros you create from scratch on your own or from the Macro Recorder.

➤ **UserForm Modules** — These belong to a custom user interface object called a userform, which is covered in Lessons 18, 19, and 20.

➤ **Class Modules** — These contain the kind of VBA code that allows you to create your own objects programmatically. Creating your own classes is very cool, and you learn about that in Lesson 21.

➤ **Worksheet Modules** — These hold VBA code that looks and acts like macros, but to make things interesting Microsoft refers to that code as a procedure instead of as a macro. Worksheet-level procedures are tied to various actions called "events," such as selecting a range or entering a value in a cell.

➤ **Workbook Module** — Not to be outdone, the workbook itself has its own module, named by default as ThisWorkbook, where code is maintained for handling workbook-level events.

The point is, several types of modules exist but the concept is the same — modules hold code for the object(s) they serve.

USING THE OBJECT BROWSER

The VBE offers a useful tool you should know about, called the Object Browser. This section gives some background on the Object Browser and how you can use it to familiarize yourself with locating objects and their associated properties and methods.

The ability to program Excel is based on tapping into any of several libraries of objects in the Microsoft Office objects model. For example, there is an Office library, a VBA library, and of course, an Excel library. Some libraries have hundreds of objects, and each object has many properties, methods, and in some cases, associated events. The interwoven collection of object libraries and their keyword kin is enormous. Fortunately, there is the Object Browser to guide your search for information about objects and their properties for whatever library you are interested in.

To see the Object Browser in the VBE, press the F2 key or click View ⇨ Object Browser. It will look similar to Figure 3-4 — it covers the area normally occupied by the Code window.

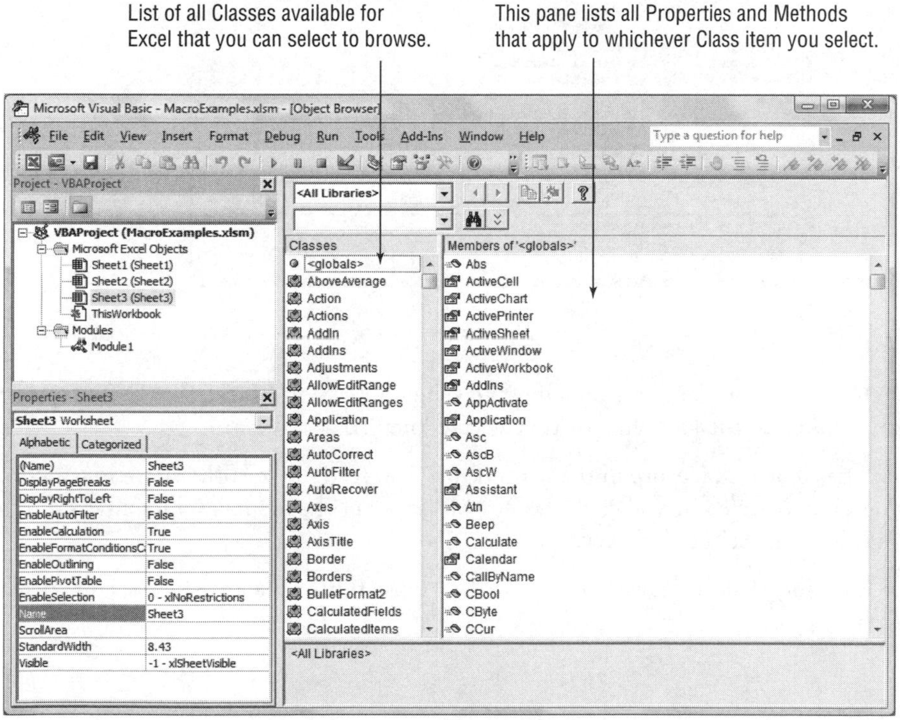

List of all Classes available for Excel that you can select to browse.

This pane lists all Properties and Methods that apply to whichever Class item you select.

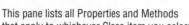

FIGURE 3-4

To get a feel for the Object Browser, click the drop-down arrow next to <All Libraries> and select Excel. When you do that, in the Classes pane, you will see the classes belonging to Excel. Click the Application class and you will see the larger Members pane display the properties and methods relating to the Application object. Click the ActiveWorkbook member and look at the bottom of the Object Browser. You see that ActiveWorkbook is a property that itself is a Workbook object.

Following those steps, the Object Browser will look like Figure 3-5, with the black arrows pointing to what you clicked. If you click the green Workbook link at the bottom, the Object Browser will take you to the `Workbook` class, and display the properties and methods for `Workbook`.

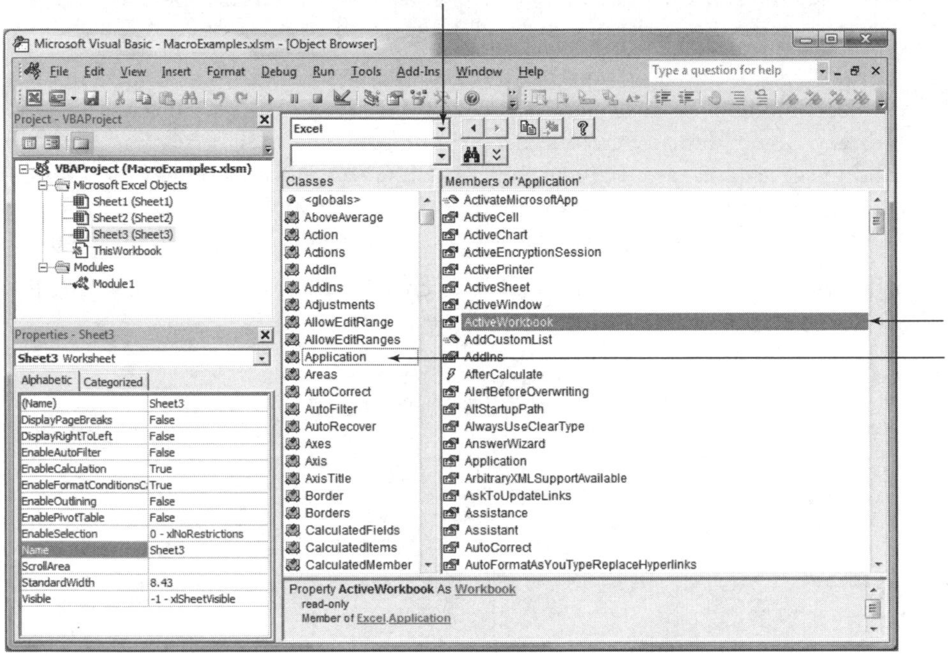

FIGURE 3-5

With a class or member item selected, you can click the yellow Question Mark icon at the top of the Object Browser to be taken to the Help file for that selected item.

The Object Browser has a Search feature in the drop-down field to the left of the Binoculars icon. If you type a term you are interested in and click the Binoculars icon, the associated members of that term will be displayed for the selected library.

To exit the Object Browser, click the lower of the two "X" close buttons near the top-right corner of the VBE.

EXITING THE VBE

To exit the VBE and return to the worksheets, you can either press Alt+Q, or click the topmost "X" close button at the top-right corner of the VBE.

TRY IT

Because this lesson is an introduction to the Visual Basic Editor environment, there are no programming techniques to try, but you can get a jump on your familiarity with the VBE by considering these items:

1. There are several ways to get into the VBE, but which way works best for you? As you've seen, Alt+F11 works on all Excel versions, but if you are more of a mouse user than a keyboard user, there are several options depending on what's easiest for you:

   ➤ In version 2003 you can click Tools ⇨ Macro ⇨ Visual Basic Editor, or you can keep the Visual Basic toolbar visible, and click the Visual Basic Editor icon. You can also right-click the workbook icon near the upper left corner of the Excel window (just to the left of the File menu item), and select View Code, which will take you to that workbook's module in the VBE.

   ➤ In versions 2007 and 2010, you can click the Visual Basic Editor icon on the Developer tab.

   ➤ In any version of Excel, you can right-click a worksheet tab and select "View Code," which will take you to that worksheet's module in the VBE.

2. Take another look at the Object Browser and click around its classes and members. The VBA object model is a vast library of information that no one would attempt to memorize, but the idea here is to get a feel for the interwoven relationships among objects' classes, properties, and methods.

3. In the Project Explorer window, if you double-click an object such as a worksheet, workbook, or module name, you will be taken directly to that object's Code window. But also, notice the pop-up menu when you right-click an object's name in the Project Explorer. Go ahead and click onto any of those menu items to get the gist of where they lead you and what purpose they serve.

4. Get a bit of practice in with the Immediate window. If you were to enter some value into cell A1, and then format cell A1 in bold font, you can enter these expressions in the Immediate window and press Enter for each one:

   ? `Range("A1").Value` (will return whatever value you entered into A1).

   ? `Range("A1").Font.Bold` (will return True if you bolded A1, or False if you did not).

   ? `Range("A1").ClearContents` (will return True and clear the contents of cell A1).

There is no video to accompany this lesson.

4

Working in the VBE

In Lesson 3, you took a bird's eye view of the Visual Basic Editor, and you became familiar with the names and locations of its most frequently used windows. In this lesson, you navigate through those VBE windows for the purpose of demonstrating how to handle the kinds of maintenance tasks you will often encounter in the VBE.

TOOLBARS IN THE VBE

The first thing you may have noticed about the VBE interface is that there is no Ribbon. The traditional VBE menu bar is pretty much the same interface for all versions of Excel after 1997.

Because you will be spending more time in the VBE, you'll want convenient access to the toolbar icons relating to the work you'll be doing. If you have not already done so, press Alt+F11 to get into the VBE, and show the Edit and Standard toolbars whose icons will soon come in handy. From the menu at the top of the VBE, click View ⇨ Toolbars ⇨ Edit and again View ⇨ Toolbars ⇨ Standard, as depicted in Figure 4-1.

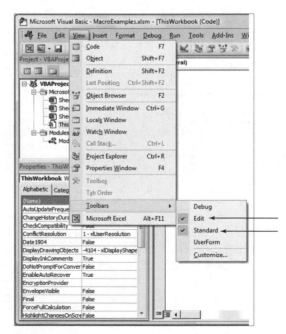

FIGURE 4-1

MACROS AND MODULES

In Lesson 2, you used the Macro Recorder to create a macro named mySort. You learned how to assign a shortcut key to the macro, and how to enter a brief description of what the macro does. You also learned about a couple of ways to run the macro by using either the shortcut key or the Macro dialog box. One thing you have not been shown yet is the macro itself, or even how to find it.

Locating Your Macros

When the Macro Recorder created the mySort macro in Lesson 2, it also created a module in which to store the macro. If this module happens to be the first module of the workbook, as was the case for mySort, the Macro Recorder will name the new module Module1 by default. If the Macro Recorder creates another module after that, it assigns the default name of Module2, and so on.

In the Project Explorer window, expand the bolded VBAProject title (my Project workbook name is MacroExamples.xlsm) and expand the yellow Modules folder to show the module named Module1. To see the VBA code in that module, you can double-click the module name, or you can right-click the module name and choose View Code as shown in Figure 4-2.

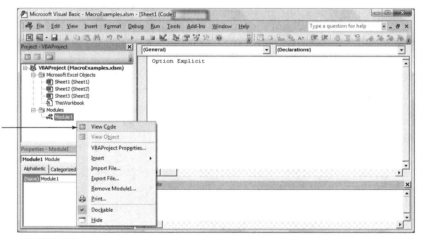

FIGURE 4-2

The mySort macro will appear in the Code window for Module1. Based on the steps you took while recording the mySort macro in Chapter 2, Figure 4-3 shows the exact code that was produced by Macro Recorder in Excel version 2003.

```
Sub mySort()
'
' mySort Macro
' Arrange the columns and sort ascending by Region, Item, and Count.
' Bold headers and format Count.
'
' Keyboard Shortcut: Ctrl+Shift+S
'
    Columns("A:A").Select
    Selection.Insert Shift:=xlToRight
    Columns("C:C").Select
    Selection.Cut Destination:=Columns("A:A")
    Columns("C:C").Select
    Selection.Delete Shift:=xlToLeft
    Range("A1:C13").Select
    Selection.Sort Key1:=Range("A2"), Order1:=xlAscending, Key2:=Range("B2") _
        , Order2:=xlAscending, Key3:=Range("C2"), Order3:=xlAscending, Header:= _
        xlGuess, OrderCustom:=1, MatchCase:=False, Orientation:=xlTopToBottom, _
        DataOption1:=xlSortNormal, DataOption2:=xlSortNormal, DataOption3:= _
        xlSortNormal
    Range("C2:C13").Select
    Selection.NumberFormat = "#,##0"
    Range("A1:C1").Select
    Selection.Font.Bold = True
End Sub
```

FIGURE 4-3

> *If you are using Excel version 2007 or 2010, your recorded code will look a bit different from the 2003 version code. However, this macro produced by the Macro Recorder in version 2003 will work just fine in those later versions.*

Understanding the Code

All macros start with a Sub statement (Sub is short for Subroutine, commonly referred to as a macro) that includes the name of the macro, followed by a pair of parentheses. Here, the Sub statement is simply Sub mySort().

Because this macro was recorded, there is a series of comment lines below the Sub statement that the Macro Recorder wants you to know about. For example, you see the macro name, the description of the macro you entered into the Record Macro dialog box, and the notation that the shortcut Ctrl+Shift+S has been assigned to this macro.

Comment lines start with an apostrophe, are green in color to help you identify them, and are not executed as VBA code, as opposed to the other lines of VBA code that actually do something when the macro is running.

The remaining lines in the macro are VBA statements, and they represent every action that was taken while the Macro Recorder was on:

1. The first thing you did was select column A.

2. Next, you inserted a new column at column A.

3. Next, you selected column C, cut that column, and pasted it to column A.

4. Next, you went back to select column C because it was empty, and you deleted it.

5. Next, you selected range A1:C13 where the table of data was.

6. Next, you sorted the selected range.

7. Next, you selected range C2:C13, which contained numbers you wanted to format.

8. Next, you formatted the selected cells with the thousands comma separator.

9. Next, you selected range A1:C1 where the column labels were.

10. Next, you formatted the selected range in order to Bold the font of those label cells.

11. Finally, you turned off the Macro Recorder, which produced the End Sub line. All macros end with the End Sub statement.

That's quite a few "Nexts" in the explanation for what is going on! Fortunately, you can edit a macro by typing your own descriptive comments, and you can consolidate a lot of the code so it runs faster and looks cleaner.

Editing a Macro with Comments and Improvements to the Code

As good as the Macro Recorder is at teaching VBA code, it is woefully lacking in the efficiency department with the volume of code it produces. To be fair, the Macro Recorder was never meant to be a lean, mean coding machine. Its primary function, which it performs flawlessly, is to produce VBA code that represents your every on-screen action.

It should be said, there is no law in the universe dictating that you must modify your every recorded macro. Sometimes, for simple macros that do the job, leaving them in their original recorded state is fine — if they work the way you want them to, you've won that round.

However, for the majority of VBA code that gets produced by the Macro Recorder, the superfluous and inefficient nature of its excessive code will be impossible to ignore. Besides, when you send your VBA workbook masterpieces to other users, you'll want your code to look and act beyond the beginner stage of recorded code.

> *You will find that editing a macro in the Code window is very similar to editing a Word document. Of course, rules exist for proper syntax of VBA code lines, but the principles of typing text, selecting words and deleting them with the Delete key, pressing Enter to go to the next line down — all these word processor kinds of behaviors with which you are familiar — will help make the macro edit process an intuitive one.*

A rule of thumb in VBA development is, don't select or activate objects unless you need to. The methods of Select and Activate are among the biggest culprits of slow, meandering macro execution. For example, the first two lines of code in the recorded macro are:

```
Columns("A:A").Select
Selection.Insert Shift:=xlToRight
```

Those two lines can and should be consolidated into one line, bypassing the selection activity:

```
Columns("A").Insert Shift:=xlToRight
```

Same with the next two statements...

```
Columns("C:C").Select
Selection.Cut Destination:=Columns("A:A")
```

...which can be expressed more succinctly as

```
Columns("C").Cut Destination:=Columns("A")
```

You can see where I am going with this. In VBA, you can act directly upon most objects, most of the time, without needing to select them. When you deleted column C, you never needed to touch it in order for VBA to do the work for you because this...

```
Columns("C:C").Select
Selection.Delete Shift:=xlToLeft
```

...can become this:

```
Columns("C").Delete Shift:=xlToLeft
```

Figure 4-4 shows how the original 13 lines of code in the mySort macro have been reduced to a much more readable and highly efficient six lines. Also notice how comments can be added for the purpose of enhancing the organized look of the macro. Your comments will help you, and anyone reading the macro, to understand what the code lines are doing, and why they are doing it.

```
Sub mySort()

' mySort Macro
' Arrange the columns and sort ascending by Region, Item, and Count.
' Bold headers and format Count.

' Keyboard Shortcut: Ctrl+Shift+S

'Step 1
'Insert a new empty column at column A where the Region column will go.
    Columns("A").Insert

'Step 2
'Make the "Region" column occupy column A, by cutting column C and pasting it
'into the new empty column A from Step 1.
    Columns("C").Cut Destination:=Columns("A")

'Step 3
'Delete column C, which is now empty after Step 2.
    Columns("C").Delete

'Step 4
'Sort range A1:C13 by column A ("Region"), column B ("Item"), and column C ("Count").
    Range("A1:C13").Sort Key1:=Range("A2"), Order1:=xlAscending, Key2:=Range("B2"), _
        Order2:=xlAscending, Key3:=Range("C2"), Order3:=xlAscending, Header:=xlYes

'Step 5
'Format the numbers in the Count column to show the thousands comma separator.
    Range("C2:C13").NumberFormat = "#,##0"

'Step 6
'Bold the header labels of "Region", "Item", and "Count" in range A1:C1.
    Range("A1:C1").Font.Bold = True
End Sub
```

FIGURE 4-4

You've now seen plenty of comments in the example macros, and how useful comments can be in your VBA code. To enter a comment line of text, simply type in the apostrophe character, and everything you type after that, on that same line, will be regarded as a comment and not executed as VBA code. Usually, comments are written as stand alone lines of text, meaning the very first character on that line is the apostrophe. However, some programmers prefer to place comments on the same line as actual VBA code, for example:

Range("A1").Clear 'Make cell A1 be empty for the next user.

In any case, comments will be green in color by default, and will not be executed as VBA code.

Another way you can speed up your macros is to use the `With` statement when you are performing multiple actions to the same object, such as to a range of cells. Suppose as part of your macro, you need to clear a range of cells and format the range for the next user. If you use the Macro Recorder to do this, here is the code you might get:

```
Range("A1:D8").Select
Selection.Clear
Selection.Locked = False
Selection.FormulaHidden = False
Selection.Font.Bold = True
Selection.Font.Italic = True
```

Notice there are five lines of code that all start with the `Selection` object, which refers to the selected range of A1:D8. If this code was to run as the Macro Recorder produced it, VBA would need to resolve the `Selection` object for each line of code.

You can do two key edits to these lines of code by avoiding the `Select` method altogether and referring to the range object only once at the beginning of a `With` structure. Between the `With` and `End With` statements, every line of code that starts with a dot shall be evaluated by VBA as belonging to the same range object, meaning the range reference need only be resolved once. Here is the condensed code using a `With` structure for greater efficiency:

```
With Range("A1:D8")
.Clear
.Locked = False
.FormulaHidden = False
.Font.Bold = True
.Font.Italic = True
End With
```

Deleting a Macro

There will be many times when you have recorded or composed a macro that you don't need any more. Instead of having a useless macro hanging around doing no good, it's better to delete it. To delete a macro, you can select its entire code in the Code window (be sure you only select from and including the Sub line, to and including the End Sub line) and press the Delete key.

By the way, you can delete a macro from outside the VBE. While on any worksheet, if you press Alt+F8 to call the Macro dialog box, you can select the macro name in the list and click the Delete button.

Inserting a Module

With larger VBA projects, you'll want to distribute your macros among two or more modules. With large projects, you'll be organizing your macros by some kind of theme or purpose. For example, the macros in your company's budget workbook that deal with reports might be placed in their own module. Sometimes you will have no choice in the matter, because modules do have a limit as to how much code they can individually support. To insert a new module, from the VBE menu bar, click Insert ⇨ Module as shown in Figure 4-5.

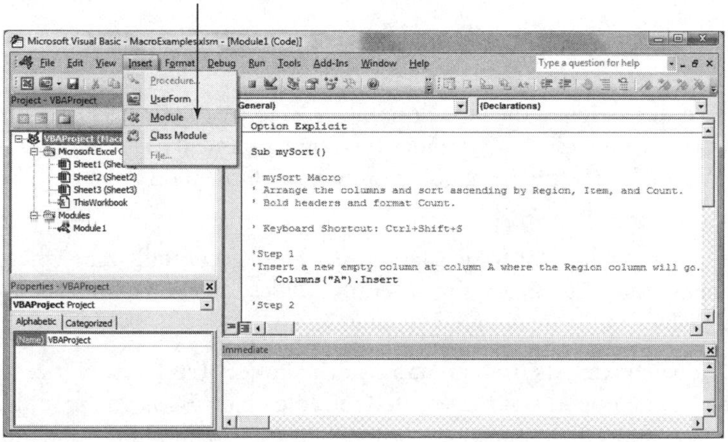

FIGURE 4-5

You'll see that your new module appears in the Project Explorer window. The entry cursor will be blinking in the new Code window, all primed and ready for you to enter VBA code into your new module, as depicted in Figure 4-6.

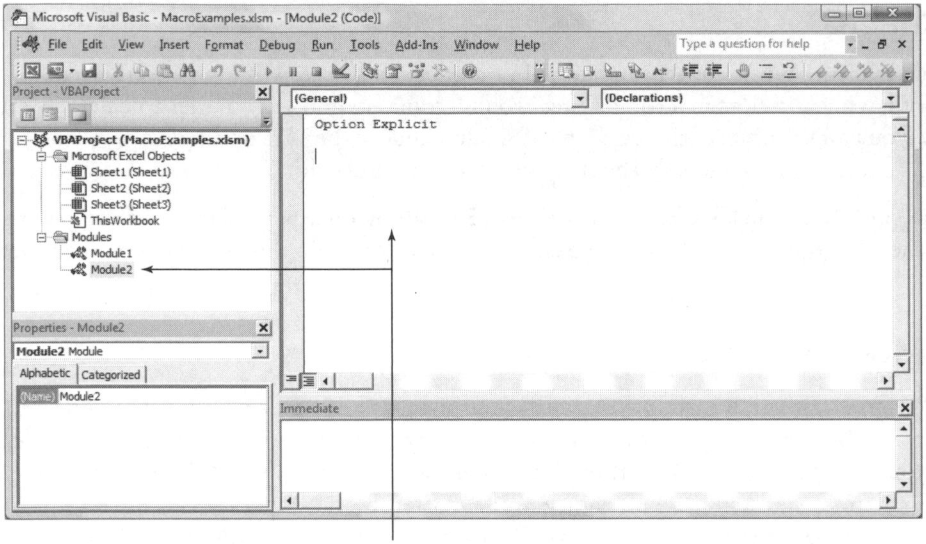

FIGURE 4-6

Renaming a Module

You've noticed that the Macro Recorder assigned the default name of Macro1 to the module it created, and just now with Module2 you see how Excel continues to assign a sequential default name to subsequent modules you insert. Yep, definitely a pattern going on here with the module names, but it doesn't mean those names need to stay that way.

A module name can be changed, and it makes a lot of sense to do so. This is especially true when you have a complex workbook containing many macros in several modules, and you want the module names to describe the overall themes of the macros they contain.

To change a module name, select it by clicking its original name in the Project Explorer. Notice in the Properties window that the Name property of the selected module object is, as you would expect, Module2. In the Properties window, use your mouse to select the entire module name property, such as you see in Figure 4-7.

Now, it's a simple task of typing over the selected Module2 text in the Properties window as you enter whatever new name you want to give to that module. For this demonstration, name the module Test. Just type the word **Test** and press Enter. The successful result is shown in Figure 4-8.

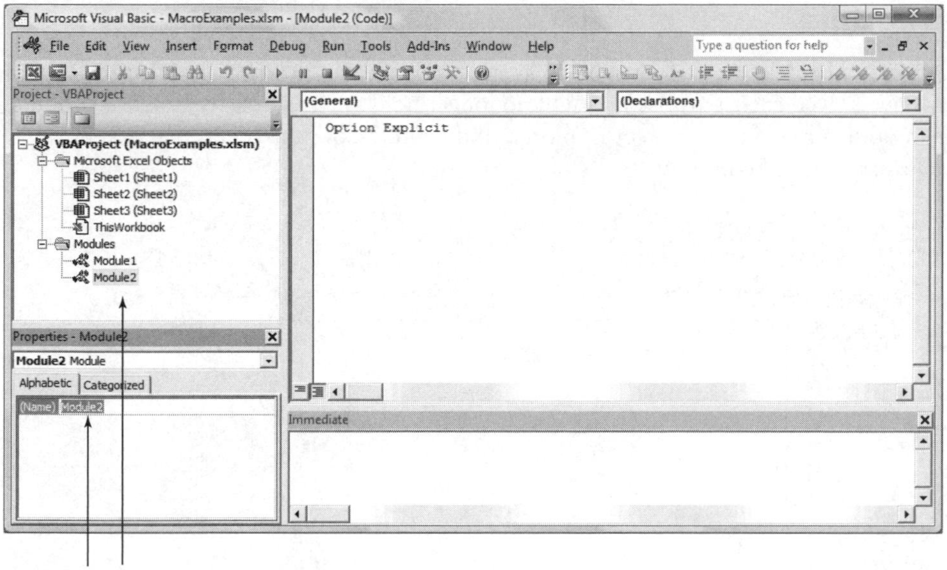

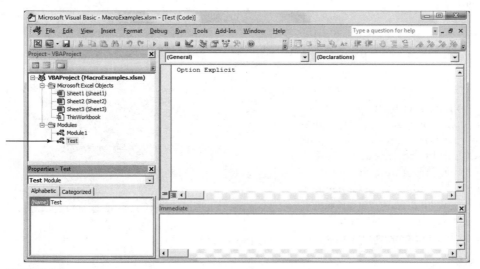

FIGURE 4-7

FIGURE 4-8

Deleting a Module

An entire module can be deleted, and it's wise to keep your projects uncluttered of unused module objects if they have served their purpose and will no longer hold any macros. To delete a module, right-click the module name in the Project Explorer, and from the pop-up menu, click Remove [module name] as shown in Figure 4-9.

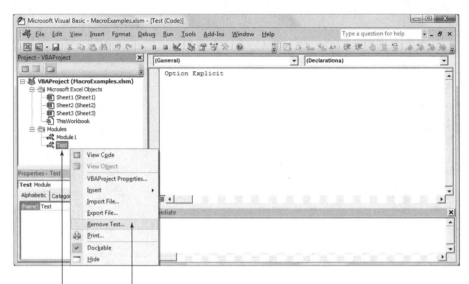

FIGURE 4-9

You will be prompted with a message to confirm your intentions, along with a question as to whether you want to export your module elsewhere. In very remote instances you will need to export a module, but personally, I have never come across a need to do that. Although the default button on the message is Yes, click the No button as shown in Figure 4-10 to confirm the deletion of that module.

FIGURE 4-10

LOCKING AND PROTECTING THE VBE

The beauty of macros is that when they are properly constructed, you can count on them to do their job. The last thing you want is for another user of your workbook to wander into the Visual Basic Editor by mistake, and make any kind of keystroke in a Code window. Especially when other people are using your workbook, you will want to protect your code.

To limit access to the VBE, click Tools ⇨ VBAProject Properties, which calls the VBAProject - Project Properties dialog box. Click to select the Protection tab. Place a checkmark in the box next to Lock Project for Viewing. Enter a password you will remember, and confirm it as shown in Figure 4-11.

Click OK to exit the dialog box. For the locked protection to take effect, you need to save the workbook and close it. Now, each time the workbook is reopened, the Visual Basic Editor will require your password if you or anyone tries to gain access to the VBE.

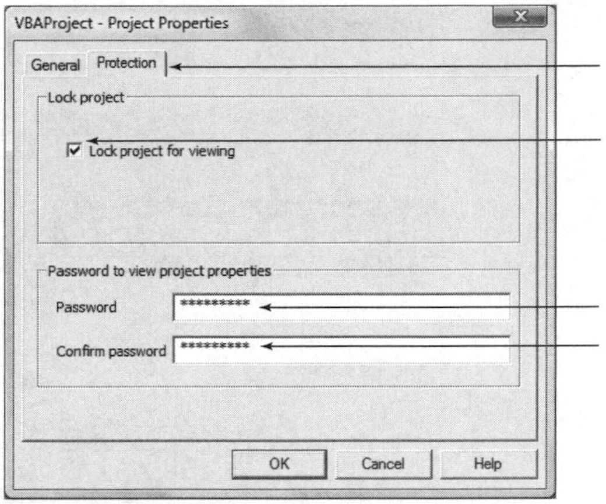

FIGURE 4-11

TRY IT

In this lesson, you practice placing a macro into a new module. You type a short macro into Notepad. The idea is to start getting accustomed to writing VBA code, and also to practice copying a macro from outside of Excel (such as from a newsgroup or website) and pasting it into a new module in Excel.

Lesson Requirements

None.

Step-by-Step

Place a macro from an external application into a new Excel module. In this exercise, Windows Notepad is being used as the external application. To open Notepad, click the Start button at the lower left corner of your screen, and from the Start menu select Programs (in later versions of Windows it may be All Programs) ⇨ Accessories ⇨ Notepad.

1. Open Notepad, and type these four statements just as you see them, which is a VBA macro named `Example`:

```
Sub Example()
Range("A1").Value = "Hello"
MsgBox "You just entered Hello in cell A1."
End Sub
```

2. Open Excel.

3. Return to Notepad, select the `Example` macro you just composed, and press Ctrl+C.

4. Return to Excel and, from your worksheet, press Alt+F11. That will take you to the Visual Basic Editor.

5. The left pane should be visible and titled Project - VBA Project. That is called the Project Explorer. If it is not visible, press Ctrl+R to access it.

6. Find the bold name of your workbook in the syntax "VBAProject (YourWorkbookName.xls)." Click it once to select it.

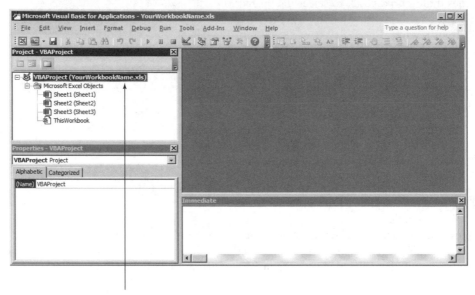

FIGURE 4-12

7. From the menu bar, click Insert ➪ Module.

8. A cursor will be blinking in the large white pane on the right, which is the new module. Press Ctrl+V to paste the copied `Example` macro into your new module. Figure 4-13 shows the macro that's been copied into your new module.

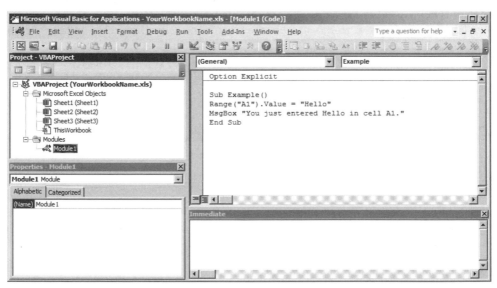

FIGURE 4-13

9. Press Alt+Q to return to the worksheet.

10. Press Alt+F8 to display the Macro dialog box.

11. In the larger white box of that Macro dialog box you will see "Example", as shown in Figure 4-14. Double-click it, or single-click it (that is, select it) and click the Run button. Either one of those two actions will run the `Example` macro.

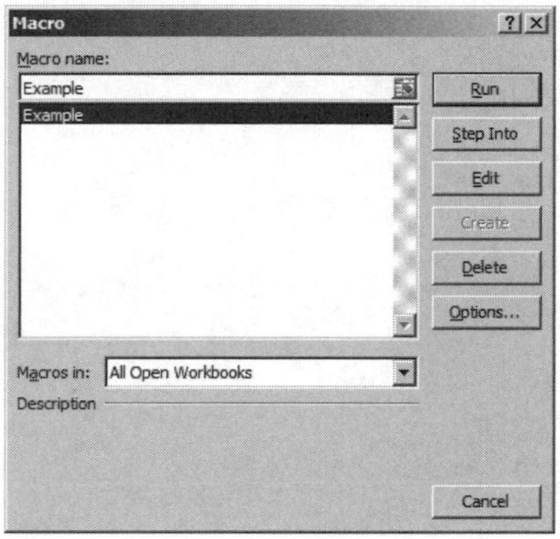

FIGURE 4-14

To get the sample database files, you can download Lesson 4 from the book's website at `www.wrox.com`.

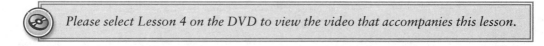

Please select Lesson 4 on the DVD to view the video that accompanies this lesson.

SECTION II
Diving Deeper into VBA

▶ **LESSON 5:** Object-oriented Programming — An Overview

▶ **LESSON 6:** Variables, Data Types, and Constants

▶ **LESSON 7:** Understanding Objects and Collections

▶ **LESSON 8:** Making Decisions with VBA

5

Object-oriented Programming — An Overview

In Lesson 1, you saw a brief historical synopsis of VBA. One particular facet of VBA's evolution that is worth more explanation is object-oriented programming, or OOP.

Object-oriented programming came about in the 1980s as a new concept in computer programming. Its popularity grew over time, and with good reason — OOP's original precepts are at the core of today's VBA programming language for Excel.

WHAT "OBJECT-ORIENTED PROGRAMMING" MEANS

Visual Basic for Applications is an object-oriented programming language. The basic concept of object-oriented programming is that a software application (Excel in this case) consists of various individual objects, each of which has its own set of features and uses. An Excel application contains cells, worksheets, charts, pivot tables, drawing shapes — the list of Excel's objects is seemingly endless. Each object has its own set of features, which are called *properties*, and its own set of uses, called *methods*.

You can think of this concept just as you would the objects you encounter every day, such as your computer, your car, or the refrigerator in your kitchen. Each of those objects has identifying qualities, such as height, weight, and color. They each have their own distinct uses, such as your computer for working with Excel, your car to transport you over long distances, and your refrigerator to keep your perishable foods cold.

VBA objects also have their identifiable properties and methods of use. A worksheet cell is an object, and among its describable features (its properties) are its address, its height, its formatted color, and so on. A workbook is also a VBA object, and among its usable features (its methods) are its abilities to be opened, closed, and have a chart or pivot table added to it.

Therefore, we can say that object-oriented programming, upon which VBA is based, is a style of programming language that cares primarily about objects, and how those objects can be manipulated based on their inherent qualities.

THE OBJECT MODEL

The Excel object model is the heart and soul of how VBA is used in Excel. While VBA is the programming language for Excel, it is also the programming language for Office applications in Word, Access, PowerPoint, and Outlook. Even though all these applications are programmable with VBA, they have their own programming needs because they are different software applications and hence are designed to serve different functions. Excel does not receive e-mails as Outlook does, and Word does not produce reports from its own database tables as Access does.

Every VBA action you take in your Excel workbook sends a command through the Excel object model. The object model is a large list of objects that relate to Excel, such as worksheets, cells, ranges, and charts. The VBA code in your macro that adds a worksheet to the workbook will make sense to Excel, because it is communicating with the objects that are recognized to be present in the Excel object model. For example, that same macro to add a worksheet would not work in Outlook. The Outlook object model does not include worksheets because Outlook is an application that maintains e-mails and appointment calendars, not worksheets.

The object model of any VBA application is hierarchical by design. In the Excel object model, the `Application` object is at the top of the model because it is the entire Excel application. Under the `Application` object is a whole host of other objects, one of them being the `Workbook` object. Under `Workbook` is the `Worksheet` object, among many others, and under the `Worksheet` object are `Range` and `Cell` objects, and so on.

The result of this hierarchy is what drives the proper syntax for your VBA macros. For example, if you want to enter the word "Hello" in cell A1 of Sheet1 of the workbook you are currently working in, the line of code to handle that could be:

```
Application.ActiveWorkbook.Worksheets("Sheet1").Range("A1").Value = "Hello"
```

VBA is a smart language. It knows you are working in Excel if you are specifying a `Workbook` object. It also knows you are doing something in a workbook if you are specifying a `Worksheet` object. Therefore, the preceding line of code can be shortened to:

```
Worksheets("Sheet1").Range("A1").Value = "Hello"
```

And that can be shortened further if you are working on Sheet1 when the code line is executed. If the parent `Worksheet` object is not specified, VBA's default assumption is that you want the active worksheet to receive the word "Hello" in cell A1, and in that scenario the line of code would simply be:

```
Range("A1").Value = "Hello"
```

A bit of theory on the subject of objects. In an object-oriented programming environment, VBA regards as an Excel object pretty much any element of the Excel application you can think of, whether it is a button, or a row, or a window — even the Excel application itself.

When you add an object to your workbook with VBA — for example, if you run a macro that creates a chart — VBA is at work behind the scenes, storing information about that `Chart` object, and assigning default values to its properties that were not specified in the macro. I mention this as a piece of good news, because with VBA filling in the blanks as it does, it's that much less about VBA you need to learn in order to start writing advanced macros. This advantage will become clearer as you progress into more complex programming techniques.

Properties

As noted earlier, VBA objects have inherent qualities, called *properties*, similar to any objects you may deal with in the real world. Properties define what the object looks like and how it acts. If you own a red bicycle, you can change its `Color` property by painting the bicycle a different color. For a `Cell` object on a worksheet, you can change its color property by formatting the cell with a different color.

In VBA code, you refer to the property of an object by first referring to the object, then the property, separated by a dot. Following are examples of a few of the many properties belonging to the `Cell`, `Worksheet`, and `Workbook` objects:

➤ This line of code would format the active cell's `Locked` property:

```
ActiveCell.Locked = True
```

➤ The `Name` property of the `Worksheet` object represents the worksheet's tab name. For example, this expression in the Immediate window would return the name of the active worksheet:

```
? ActiveSheet.Name
```

➤ This expression would change the `Name` property of the active worksheet to "Hello," and when executed would result in "Hello" being the active worksheet's new tab name:

```
ActiveSheet.Name = "Hello"
```

➤ This expression will change the Color property of the active worksheet's tab to yellow:

```
ActiveSheet.Tab.Color = vbYellow
```

➤ Workbooks have a `Saved` property that indicates if the workbook has been saved since its most recent change. For example, if you save your workbook and then enter the following expression in the Immediate window, VBA will return True:

```
? ThisWorkbook.Saved
```

➤ If you were to make some change to the workbook, such as entering a number in a cell, and immediately re-evaluate the expression `? ThisWorkbook.Saved`, False would be returned because VBA knows that the workbook has not been saved since it was last changed.

Methods

Methods are actions that can be performed by objects. VBA objects have inherent behavioral abilities. Following are examples of Excel objects and some of their methods:

➤ The `Range` object of A1:D10 can have its cells' contents cleared with the `ClearContents` method:

```
Range("A1:D10").ClearContents
```

➤ Workbooks and worksheets can be activated with the `Activate` method:

```
Workbooks("Book1.xlsx").Activate
Worksheets("Sheet2").Activate
```

➤ Here's a more complicated example, to call your attention to the fact that objects can contain objects, not just properties. Suppose you have three pivot tables on Sheet1, and you only want to refresh the pivot table named PivotTable2. As far as VBA is concerned, what you really want to refresh is the PivotCache object of the PivotTable2 object of the Sheet1 worksheet object. This line of code would accomplish that, using the `Refresh` method:

```
Worksheets("Sheet1").PivotTables("PivotTable2").PivotCache.Refresh
```

> *This multiple-object syntax might look daunting at first, but you can take some comfort in knowing that you've been writing VBA code in this manner since Day 1. All objects (except the Application object, which is Excel itself) have a Parent property, that is, another object to which they belong. In many cases, you don't need to specify the Parent object because it is inferred by default. For example, if you are referring to cell A1 on your active worksheet, you do not need to (though you could) express it as ActiveSheet.Range("A1") — you only need to express it as Range("A1"). In the preceding example, however, pivot tables are embedded objects for which VBA requires you to specify the Parent worksheet object. If all this talk of properties and methods is not clear yet, don't worry, it will all make perfect sense when you see the theory in action.*

Collections

Some of the VBA programming you learn in later lessons will involve the concept of collections, and it is a topic I'll touch on here. In object-oriented programming, a *Collection* is an object that contains a group of like objects. For example, there is a `Worksheets` collection object that is the entire group of `Worksheet` objects in your workbook. Even if one worksheet contains hundreds of formulas and another worksheet is totally empty, both those worksheets are like objects because they are both worksheets, and therefore they both are a part of the `Worksheets` collection.

As you'll see, invoking the `Collection` object in your code is a terrific way to take some action on all the objects in that collection, without needing to know anything specific about the collected objects. For example, say you want to add some boilerplate text to every comment on your worksheet. Employing a `For…Each` loop (loops are covered in Lesson 9) to edit every comment in the `Comments` collection would make the task simple, because each comment would belong to the `Comments` collection, and you'd be confident knowing you hit all comments without needing to know what cells they are in.

> *A good rule of thumb in recognizing a* Collections *object is to notice that its name ends with the letter "s," as a pluralized form of its singular object item name. Examples of this are the* Names *collection of individual* Name *objects, the* Charts *collection of individual* Chart *objects, the* Workbooks *collection of individual* Workbook *objects, and so on.*

TRY IT

This lesson provided an overview of object-oriented programming. There are no programming techniques to try based on the material in this lesson, but here are some important concepts to keep in mind:

1. Excel is replete with objects, such as workbooks, worksheets, and cells, and each object has its own set of properties that can be altered to suit your application project's design.

2. If you should need to refer to an object's container, such as when you refer to a worksheet in another workbook, just use the object's `Parent` property. All objects (except `Application`) have a `Parent` property that is the object within which they are contained. For example, if your active workbook object is Book2 but you want to refer to Sheet1 in Book1, you'd precede the Sheet1 object with its parent Book1object name, like this: Workbooks("Book1.xlsm").Worksheets("Sheet1").Range("A1").Value = "Hello"

3. The `Application` object indeed holds the highest order of Excel's objects, but as you will see, it also offers many useful methods and properties. The `Application` object provides the ability to insert worksheet functions (SUM, AVERAGE, VLOOKUP, and so on), as well as commands to control Excel's display options for worksheet gridlines, tabs, and window sizes.

 There is no video to accompany this lesson.

6

Variables, Data Types, and Constants

Many of the macros you develop will involve the need for referencing an item you are working on without specifying that item by its name, amount, or location. This concept may sound strange at first, but you will quickly discover with your macros that in many situations it makes sense, and indeed is necessary, to manipulate or analyze data in one part of your macro, and hold the results in virtual memory for later use.

WHAT IS A VARIABLE?

VBA stores data in memory using a *variable*. A variable is a name given by you, to which you assign a piece of data that is stored in an area of the computer's memory, allowing you to refer to that data when you need to later in the macro. VBA handles the task of finding an appropriate place in the computer's memory to store your variable data, and dutifully retrieves the data when you ask for it by its variable name.

Variables hold values of different data types (more on this later) that are specified when the variable is declared. When you declare a variable, you do so by entering a declaration statement that includes four keywords in a particular order:

1. The Dim statement (VBA's abbreviation for "Dimension"), which all variable declarations start with.

2. The name of your variable, which you create, such as myValue.

3. The word As.

4. The type of data being stored.

One common data type is called `Integer`, which, as you will see in Table 6-1, refers to whole numbers within a certain range. Using the preceding four steps as a sequential construction guide, here is a typical-looking variable declaration statement:

```
Dim myValue As Integer
```

You'll soon see the enormous benefit that this kind of innocent-looking statement can have in your macro. Although a few wrinkles exist in the variable declaration process, a variable declaration statement will often look no more complicated than this.

> *You will find that editing a macro in the Code window is very similar to editing a Word document. Of course, rules exist for proper syntax of VBA code lines, but the principles of typing text, selecting words and deleting them with the Delete key, pressing Enter to go to the next line down — all these word-processor kinds of behaviors with which you are familiar — will help make the macro editing process an intuitive one.*

ASSIGNING VALUES TO VARIABLES

After the variable declaration statement, which might be the next code line or 100 code lines later in your macro, depending on what you are doing, you will have a statement that assigns a value to the `myValue` variable. Here's an example of assigning the number in cell A1 to the `myValue` variable:

```
myValue = Range("A1").Value
```

The value you assign might be an actual value that is stored in a cell, as in the preceding example, or it might be a value you create, again, depending on the task at hand. This notion will become clearer with more examples you'll be seeing throughout the book.

WHY YOU NEED VARIABLES

I mentioned earlier that in some situations, employing a variable will be a sensible option. Suppose you have a number in cell A1 that you are referring to for several analytical purposes throughout your macro. You could retrieve that number by referring to its A1 cell address every time, but that would force Excel to look for the same cell address and to recommit the same number to memory every time.

As a simplified example, here is a macro with four commands, all invoking the value in cell A1:

```
Sub WithoutVariable()
Range("C3").Value = Range("A1").Value
Range("D5").Value = Range("A1").Value / 12
Range("E7").Value = Range("A1").Value * 365
MsgBox "The original value is " & Range("A1").Value
End Sub
```

For VBA to execute this macro, it must go through the same behind-the-scenes gyrations four separate times to satisfy each of the four commands that reference range A1. And if your workbook design changes, where you move the number of interest from cell A1 to cell K5, you need to go into the code, find each related code line, and change the cell reference from A1 to K5.

Fortunately, there is a better way to handle this kind of situation — by declaring a variable to refer to the value in cell A1 just once, like this:

```
Sub WithVariable()
Dim myValue As Integer
myValue = Range("A1").Value
Range("C3").Value = myValue
Range("D5").Value = myValue / 12
Range("E7").Value = myValue * 365
MsgBox "The original value is " & myValue
End Sub
```

By assigning the number value in cell A1 to the `myValue` variable, you've increased your code's efficiency and its readability, and VBA will keep the number value in memory without having to reevaluate cell A1. Also, if your cell of interest changes from A1 to some other cell, say cell K5, you only need to edit the cell address in the assignment code line to refer to cell K5, like so:

```
myValue = Range("K5").Value
```

As you've probably noticed in this situational example, a variable declaration is advisable, but it is not an absolute requirement for the `WithoutVariable` macro to function. However, as you will see in the upcoming lessons, variable declaration will be a necessary practice for handling more complex tasks that involve loops, object manipulation, and conditional decision-making. Don't worry — after you see a few examples of variables in action and start practicing with them on your own, you'll quickly get the hang of when and how to declare variables.

DATA TYPES

Simply stated, VBA's role in life is to manipulate data in a way your computer can understand it. A computer sees information only as a series of binary numbers such as 0s and 1s — very differently than how humans see information as numerals, symbols, and letters of the alphabet.

Your macros will inevitably manipulate data of varying types, such as text, or numbers, or range objects. Part of VBA's job is to bridge the communication gap between humans and computers, by providing a method for telling the computer what type of data is being referred to in code. When you specify a data type in VBA, you help the computer to know how it should regard your data so that your macros will produce the results you'd expect, based on the types of data you are manipulating.

Understanding the Different Data Types

Data types are the different kinds of ways you can store data in memory. Table 6-1 shows a list of common data types, with their descriptions and memory usage.

TABLE 6-1: Data Types

DATA TYPE	DESCRIPTION	MEMORY
Boolean	True or False; 1 or 0; On or Off.	2 bytes
Byte	An integer from 0 to 255.	1 byte
Currency	A positive or negative number with up to 15 digits to the left of the decimal point and up to 4 digits to the right of it.	8 bytes
Date	A floating-point number with the date to the left of the decimal point and the time to the right of it.	8 bytes
Decimal	An unsigned integer scaled to the power of 10. The power of 10 scaling factor specifies the number of digits to the right of the decimal point, and ranges from 0 to 28.	12 bytes
Double	A floating point number ranging in value from −1.79769313486231E308 to −4.94065645841247E-324 for negative values and from 4.94065645841247E-324 to 1.79769313486232E308 for positive values.	8 bytes
Integer	An integer ranging from −32,768 to 32,767.	2 bytes
Long	An integer ranging from −2,147,483,648 to 2,147,483,647.	4 bytes
Object	A reference to an object, such as a range of cells, a chart, a pivot table, a workbook, a worksheet, or any one of the many other objects that are a part of the Excel application.	4 bytes
Single	A floating-point number ranging in value from −3.402823E38 to −1.401298E-45 for negative values and from 1.401298E-45 to 3.402823E38 for positive values.	4 bytes
String	There are two kinds of strings: variable-length and fixed-length. A variable-length string can contain up to approximately 2 billion characters. A fixed-length string can contain 1 to approximately 64,000 characters.	For a variable-length string, 10 bytes plus storage for the string. For a fixed-length string, the storage for the string
Variant	Data type for all variables that are not explicitly declared as some other type, which can contain any kind of data except fixed-length String data.	For containing numbers, 16 bytes. For containing characters, 22 bytes plus storage for the characters

Declaring a Variable for Dates and Times

The `Date` data type is worth an extra look, because it is the data type with which variables for both dates and times can be declared. You can assign values to a date variable by enclosing them in the # number sign character, with the value being recognizable to Excel as either a date or time. For example:

```
myDate = #09 October 1958#
```

or

```
myDate = #October 9, 1958#
```

or

```
myTime = #9:10 PM#
```

or

```
myTime = #10/9/1958 9:10:00 PM#
```

> *When entering dates, get into the good habit of entering the year as a full four-digit number. The year 2029 is the dividing line in VBA for two-digit years belonging to either the twentieth or twenty-first centuries. All two-digit years from 00 to and including 29 are regarded as belonging to the 2000s, and 30 to 99 are regarded as belonging to the 1900s. For example, the expression 10/10/29 in Excel is October 10, 2029, but 10/10/30 is regarded by Excel as October 10, 1930.*

Declaring a Variable with the Proper Data Type

As you become more familiar with VBA, you'll notice that different developers have their preferred writing styles when declaring variables. For example, you can declare several variables on one line, each separated by a comma, like this:

```
Dim myValue1 as Integer, myValue2 as Integer, myValue3 as Integer
```

There is nothing wrong with that construction, but be careful not to make this common mistake:

```
Dim myValue1, myValue2, myValue3 as Integer
```

If you do not specify a data type after a variable name, such as in the latter case with `myValue1` and `myValue2`, VBA will assign the `Variant` data type. Only the `Value3` variable has been specified the `Integer` data type. `Variant` is a catch-all data type that is the most memory-intensive, and the least helpful in understanding the purpose of its associated variables if anyone else should read your code.

The Variant data type does have its place, for instance when dealing with arrays or conversions of data types, but you should take care to specify the appropriate data types of all your variables. In so doing, your macros will run faster, they'll be easier to read, and they'll be more reliable.

FORCING VARIABLE DECLARATION

Declaring your variables can only be a good thing. It takes a little extra thought and effort, but not declaring your variables can cause a lot more trouble when reading or debugging your code. Macros run faster and use less memory when all variables are properly declared.

You can tell if variable declaration is being enforced by seeing if the statement Option Explicit is at the top of your module. If you do see the Option Explicit statement, write a quick macro that tries to call an undeclared variable, such as you see depicted in Figure 6-1. When you attempt to run the macro, you'll receive a compile error as shown in Figure 6-1, informing you a variable is not defined. In this scenario, the error occurred because the myName variable was not declared with a statement such as Dim myName as String.

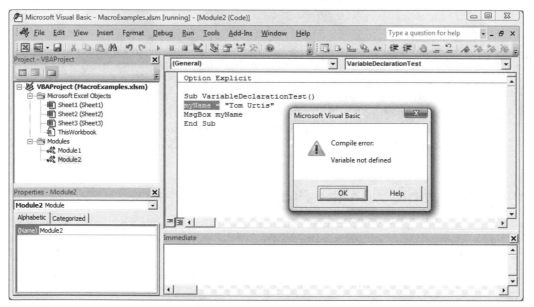

FIGURE 6-1

If you do not see the Option Explicit statement at the top of your modules, go into the VBE and from the menu bar, click Tools ➪ Options as shown in Figure 6-2.

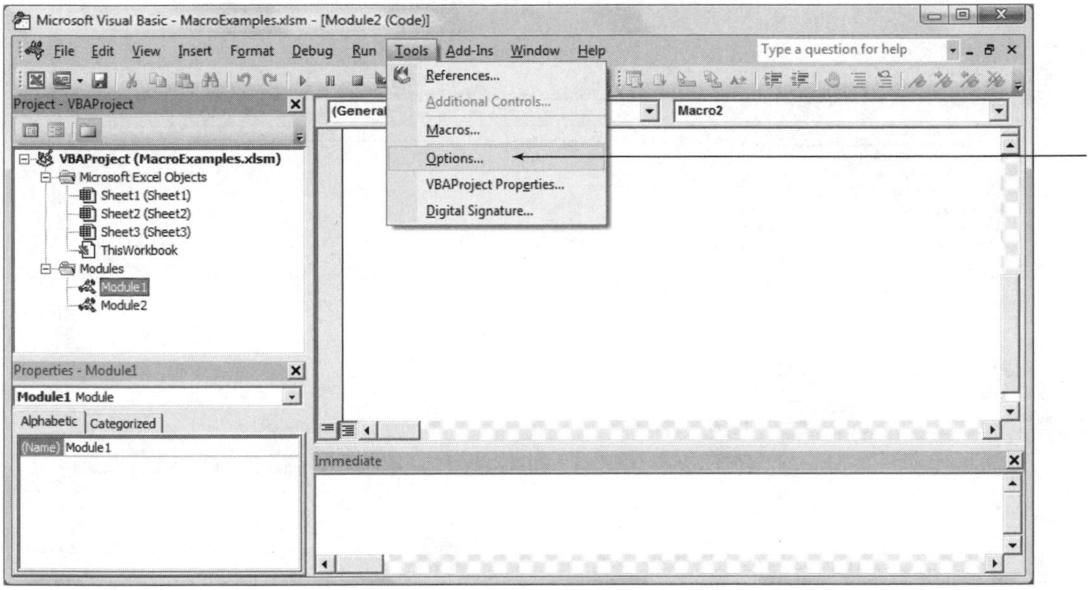

FIGURE 6-2

You will see the Options dialog box. On the Editor tab, select the option Require Variable Declaration as shown in Figure 6-3, and click OK.

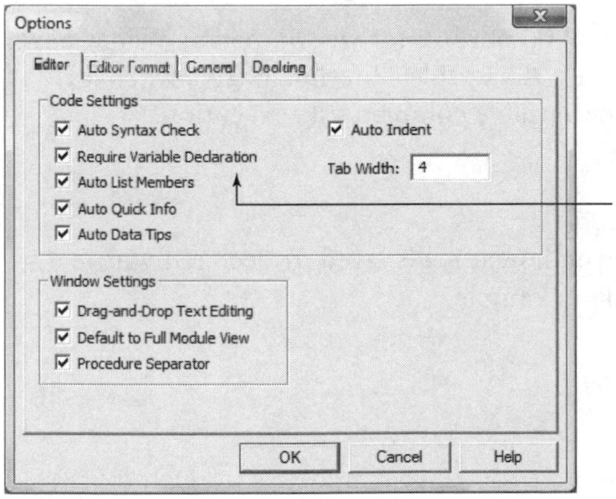

FIGURE 6-3

Figure 6-4 shows the `Option Explicit` statement at the top of the module, which will appear in every new module you insert thereafter.

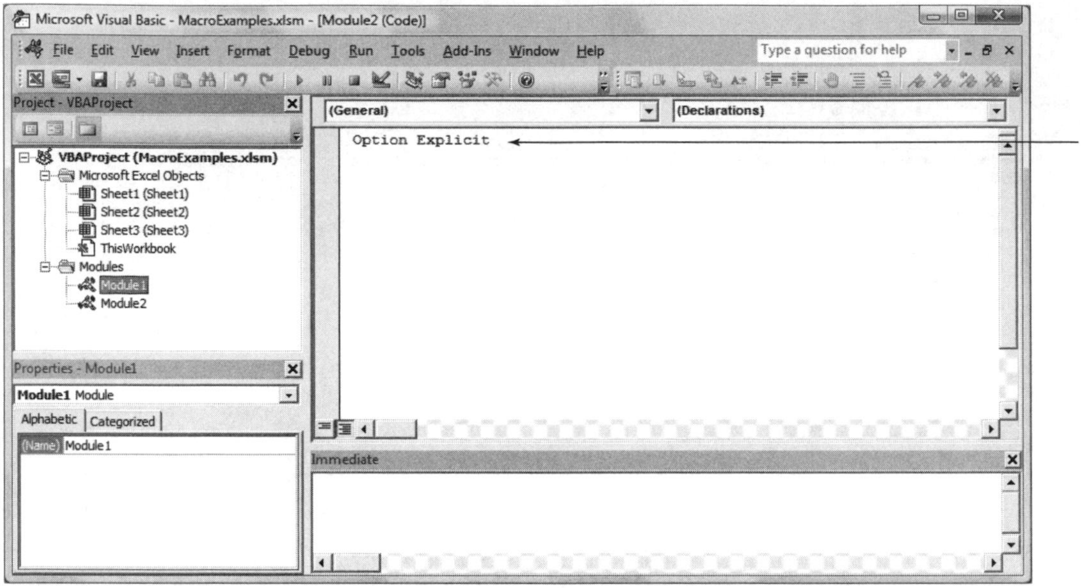

FIGURE 6-4

UNDERSTANDING A VARIABLE'S SCOPE

Variables and constants (explained in the next section) do not live forever in memory. They have a set lifetime and visibility within macros and modules. A variable's lifetime begins when it is declared, and ends when the macro that declared the variable completes its execution.

Local Macro Level Only

The visibility of a variable or constant also depends on how it is declared. If declared within a macro, a variable can only be used by that macro. For example:

```
Sub Macro1()
Dim intAdd As Integer, intSum As Integer
intAdd = 31
intSum = intAdd + 10
MsgBox intSum
End Sub
```

Module Level

It is possible for a variable to be visible and usable in more than one macro by having the declaration statement at the top of the module instead of inside a particular macro. In Figure 6-5, both Macro1 and Macro2 can utilize the int.Sum and intAdd variables.

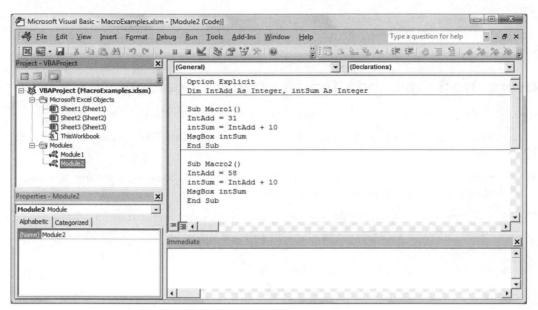

FIGURE 6-5

Application Level

Finally, you can declare the variables as `Public`, which will make them visible to all macros in all modules. You only need to place the statements at the top of one standard module, like so:

```
Public intAdd As Integer
Public intSum As Integer
```

CONSTANTS

A variable's value may often change during a macro's execution, but some macros are better served with a reference to a particular value that will not change. A *constant* is a value in your macro that does not change while the macro is running. Essentially, constants are variables that do not change.

When you declare a constant, you do so by entering a declaration statement that starts with the `Const` statement, followed by the constant's name you specify, then the data type, and finally the value, all on one line. Here is an example:

```
Const myMonths as Integer = 12
```

It's a good practice to use constants for the same reasons you would use a variable. Instead of hard-coding the same value in your macro over and over, you define the constant just once and use the reference as you need to. For example, your macro may be analyzing the company's sales amounts, and needing to factor in the sales tax at various points in the macro. This constant statement at the start of the macro would allow you to reference the 8.25% sales tax:

```
Const SalesTax as Double = .0825
```

Note that once you declare a constant in the macro, you cannot assign a different value to it later in the macro. If you need the value to change during the macro, what you really need is a variable instead of a constant.

Choosing the Scope and Lifetime of Your Constants

The scope and lifetime of constants are much the same as for variables:

➤ For the constant to be available only to a particular macro, declare the constant within that macro.

➤ For the constant to be available only to the macros that are housed in the same module, declare the constant at the top of that module, above and outside all macros.

➤ For the constant to be available to all macros in all modules, prefix the constant declaration with the `Public` statement, and set it at the top of a standard module, above and outside all macros. For example:

```
Public Const SalesTax as Double = .0825
```

TRY IT

In this lesson you practice creating a macro that includes a declared variable. Create a macro, without using the Macro Recorder, in which you declare a variable for the `String` data type, and you manipulate the string text with a few lines of practice code.

Lesson Requirements

None.

Step-by-Step

Create a macro that includes the following actions:

➤ Declare a `String` type variable.

➤ Assign text to the `String` variable.

➤ Populate a range of cells with the `String` variable's text.

1. Open Excel and add a new workbook.

2. In your active worksheet, enter the text **Hello** in cell A1.

3. Press Alt+F11 to get into the Visual Basic Editor.

4. From the VBE menu, click Insert ➪ Module.

5. In the new module, type in the name of your macro as

```
Sub Test6
```

6. Press the Enter key, which will cause Excel to place a set of parentheses after the `Test6` macro name, and also will create the `End Sub` statement. Your macro so far will look like this:

```
Sub Test6()

End Sub
```

7. In the empty line between `Sub Test6()` and `End Sub`, type **Dim myString As String** and press Enter.

8. Now is the time to define the `myString` variable, by telling VBA that it shall be equal to the value in cell A1, which is the word Hello you entered in Step 2. To do that, type the following line of code into your macro and press Enter: **myString = Range("A1").Value**

9. With your `String` variable defined, try entering its defined text into a few cells, starting with cell B3. If you combine the variable with a space and the word "World", you can programmatically enter the text "Hello World" into B3. To do that, type this line of code into your macro and press Enter: **Range("B3").Value = myString & " World!"**

10. Just for fun, repeat the variable's text three times in succession, which would be HelloHelloHello, and tell VBA to enter that into cell B4. For the next line in your macro, type **Range("B4").Value = myString & myString & myString** and press Enter.

11. As a third and final entry, show the text Hello and Goodbye in cell B5 by typing this last line of code into your macro: **Range("B5").Value = myString & " and Goodbye"**. At this point, your macro is completed, and it will look like this:

```
Sub Test6()
Dim myString As String
myString = Range("A1").Value
Range("B3").Value = myString & " World!"
Range("B4").Value = myString & myString & myString
Range("B5").Value = myString & " and Goodbye"
End Sub
```

12. Press Alt+Q to return to your worksheet.

13. Watch your new macro in action. Press Alt+F8 to display the Macro dialog box.

14. Select the `Test6` macro name in the large window as shown in Figure 6-6, and click the Run button.

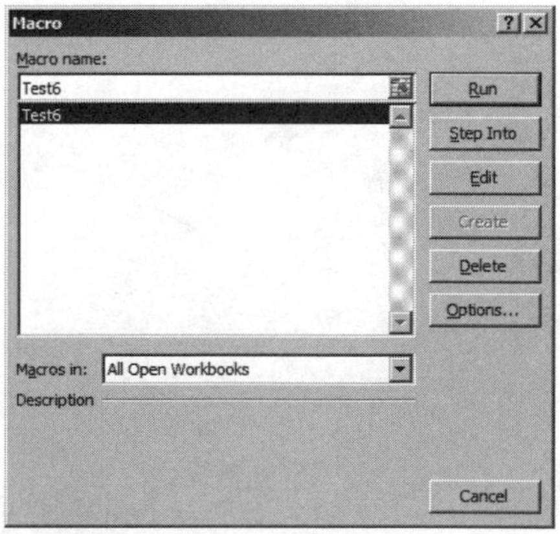

FIGURE 6-6

To get the sample database files, you can download Lesson 6 from the book's website at
`www.wrox.com`.

Please select Lesson 6 on the DVD to view the video that accompanies this lesson.

7

Understanding Objects and Collections

Lesson 5 introduced the topic of *collections*, which are objects that contain a group of like objects. This lesson adds some detail to the topic and goes over some programming techniques to deal with the most common types of object collections you will encounter: workbooks, worksheets, cells, and ranges.

WORKBOOKS

An Excel file is a `Workbook` object. You might wonder how workbooks have a collection, seeing as you can only work in one workbook at a time, and even then you are usually manipulating objects at a lower level, such as worksheets or cells.

> *Do not confuse the* `Application` *object with the* `Workbook` *object. In VBA, the* `Application` *object is at the very top of the food chain; there is nothing higher than* `Application` *in the Excel object model.* `Application` *represents the entire Excel program, whereas* `Workbook` *represents an individual Excel file.*

The `Workbooks` collection contains the references to every `Workbook` object that is open in the same instance of Excel. You will need to call upon the `Workbooks` collection when you want to do some task in every open workbook, or when you want to activate a particular workbook whose name is not known.

Here is an example. In VBA, this will add a new workbook:

```
Workbooks.Add
```

When this code line is executed, the active workbook becomes the new workbook you added, same as the effect of manually adding a new workbook from your existing one, when the workbook you added becomes the active workbook.

What if your project calls for you to add two workbooks to the existing one, and you want to end the macro with the first added workbook being the active one, instead of the last added workbook being the active one? In your `Workbooks` collection, how do you specify which `Workbook` object you want to do something with, when you don't know the names of any open workbooks?

VBA offers several methods to solve this problem, one being an ability to assign a variable to each workbook you add, and then to activate the workbook whose variable you care about. For example, this macro will add two workbooks and end with the first added workbook being the active one:

```
Sub AddWorkbooks()
Dim WorkbookAdd1 As Workbook
Dim WorkbookAdd2 As Workbook
Set WorkbookAdd1 = Workbooks.Add
Set WorkbookAdd2 = Workbooks.Add
WorkbookAdd1.Activate
End Sub
```

`Workbook` objects have a number of methods as you would expect, such as `Open`, `Save`, and `Close`. Lesson 9 delves into the practice of repeating actions with loops, but here's a sneak peek at a loop that saves and closes every workbook that is currently open in your copy of Excel, except for the workbook you are working in. Notice what you don't see, which is a concern about how many workbooks are open, or what their names are; you only need to tell VBA to look for `Workbook` objects in the `Workbooks` collection.

```
Sub CloseAllWorkbooks()
Dim wkb As Workbook
For Each wkb In Workbooks
If wkb.Name <> ThisWorkbook.Name Then
wkb.Close SaveChanges:=True
End If
Next wkb
End Sub
```

WORKSHEETS

The `Worksheets` collection allows you to refer to the `Worksheets` objects' names or index numbers, which is the numerical position of worksheets as you see their tabs in order from left to right. Referring to names tends to be a safer practice, but as you saw with workbooks, and as you will learn with looping techniques, a variable can be assigned to each `Worksheets` object to access all worksheets without caring where they are in the workbook or what their tab names are.

Say you want to add a new worksheet, and give it the name Test1. No problem there, but now you are asked to add the new worksheet such that its placement shall be the last (rightmost) worksheet in the workbook. You have no idea how many sheets exist already. You don't know the name of the last worksheet in order to reference its location but even if you did know that today, there could easily be a differently named worksheet in that index position tomorrow.

This one-line macro will add a new worksheet, name it as you specify, and place it at the far right end of the worksheets, which is the highest worksheet index number based on the count of existing worksheets:

```
Sub WorksheetTest1()
Worksheets.Add(After:=Worksheets(Worksheets.Count)).Name = "Test1"
End Sub
```

You can place a worksheet relative to another worksheet's name, this time adding a worksheet, and placing it before Sheet2:

```
Sub WorksheetTest2()
Worksheets.Add(Before:=Worksheets("Sheet2")).Name = "Test2"
End Sub
```

> *The preceding examples will work without any problem, as long as the workbook does not already contain a worksheet with the name Test1 or Test2. Excel does not allow worksheets to be given duplicate names in the same workbook, and attempting to do so will result in an error. You'll learn about handling VBA errors in Lesson 17.*

You may want to relocate an existing worksheet from its current position to a particular index position for the convenience of your workbook's users. Suppose that during the course of your macro, you want the active worksheet to occupy the number two worksheet index position — that is, to be the worksheet that is located second from the left as you see the worksheet tabs. To accomplish this, you can place the active worksheet after the first index worksheet, as shown in the following example.

> *A word of caution about the* Worksheets *collection: there is a difference between the* Sheets *collection and the* Worksheets *collection. You probably know about Chart sheets, and if your workbook has one, you need to be mindful to cycle through the* Worksheets *collection only if you are interested in manipulating worksheets. If you cycle through the* Sheets *collection, all sheets, including a Chart sheet (or outmoded Dialog Sheets or Macro sheets) will be included in the procedure. If you only want to act on worksheets, specify the* Worksheets *collection.*

CELLS AND RANGES

The Range object is probably the most utilized object in VBA. A range can be a single cell or a range of cells that spans any size area. A Range object, then, is a cell or block of cells that is contained on a Worksheet object. Though a Range object can be a union of several noncontiguous blocks of cells, it is always the case that a VBA Range object is contained on one worksheet. There is no such thing as a Range object that includes cells on different worksheets.

A single cell is a range as far as VBA is concerned, and `ActiveCell` is the object name in VBA of the single active cell on the active worksheet. There is no such object as "ActiveRange," but there are many ways to identify particular ranges, one of the most common being the `Selection` object.

If you were to select any range of cells, and execute this line of code, all cells in that selection would immediately contain the word "Hello":

```
Selection.Value = "Hello"
```

You may be interested to know that named ranges are fair game for VBA to refer to and manipulate, just like any other range. In fact there is a `Names` collection object for named ranges.

As an example, say you have previously named a range `myRange`. This line of code in a VBA macro would place the word "Hello" in all cells in your named range:

```
Range("myRange").Value = "Hello"
```

As you have seen, you do not need to select your range in order to work with it. For most operations on cells or ranges, you can refer to the range and its parent worksheet. The following line of code can be executed from any worksheet in your workbook, as an example of establishing a bold format for a range of cells on Sheet1.

```
Worksheets("Sheet1").Range("A1:D25").Font.Bold = True
```

There are times when you will want to refer to all the cells on a worksheet, instead of limiting your operation to a particular range. For example, suppose as part of your macro you want to clear the contents of every cell on the worksheet. Starting with version 2007, clearing the contents of the entire grid of worksheet cells can be expressed as `Range("A1:XFD1048576").ClearContents`. However, if the workbook is being used in a version of Excel prior to 2007, that same operation could be expressed as `Range("A1:IV65536").ClearContents`. Fortunately, you can avoid errors and confusion by using the `Cells` object as shown in the following example, which refers to all worksheet cells in whichever version of Excel is being used at the moment:

```
Cells.ClearContents
```

You can do some useful operations using the `Cells` object when you want to involve the entire worksheet. Suppose you have set up Sheet1 as a template, with formatted ranges, labels, values, and formulas, and you want Sheet2 to be established the same way. This line of code will copy the Sheet1 cells and paste them to Sheet2.

```
Worksheets("Sheet1").Cells.Copy Worksheets("Sheet2").Cells
```

SPECIALCELLS

An interesting brand of range objects is Excel's group of *SpecialCells*. If you have not yet examined `SpecialCells`, press the F5 key to call the Go To dialog. Click the Special button and you will see more than a dozen classifications of `SpecialCells`.

Cells on your worksheet that contain comments are regarded by Excel as `SpecialCells`. So are cells containing Data Validation, or cells that contain formulas, or cells that contain constants, such as text or data you have manually entered. With the combinations of `SpecialCells`, the possibilities are enormous for identifying various kinds of ranges based on all sorts of criteria.

Say in range A1:A10 you have some cells that contain formulas, some cells that contain numbers you have manually entered, and some cells that contain nothing. If you want to select all individual cells in range A1:A10 that contain formulas, and not include in your selection any of the other cells in that range, this macro would do that:

```
Sub FindFormulas()
Range("A1:A10").SpecialCells(xlCellTypeFormulas).Select
End Sub
```

TRY IT

In this lesson you practice with the useful Intellisense tool to help you become familiar with the properties and methods of VBA objects. VBA's *"IntelliSense"* feature offers you VBA syntax assistance in the VBE. You learn how to use it for the purpose of seeing a list of your objects' properties and methods in your VBE Code window.

Lesson Requirements

None.

Step-by-Step

VBA's IntelliSense feature is an incredibly useful tool that helps you write your macros faster and smarter. I use it all the time to help me write code in the proper VBA syntax. As you learned, VBA has hundreds of objects and each object can have dozens of methods and properties. IntelliSense can display a list of an object's methods and properties while you are typing your code, and it can quickly call the Help feature for a topic you select.

1. Open Excel and press Alt+F11 to go to the Visual Basic Editor.

2. If you have not already done so, from the VBE menu, click Tools ➪ Options as shown in Figure 7-1.

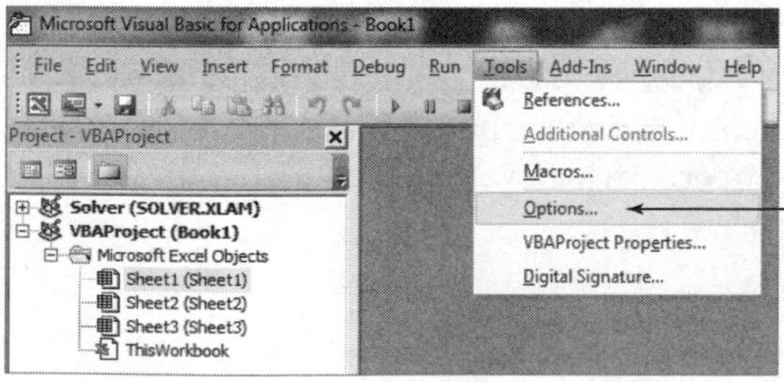

FIGURE 7-1

3. In the Options dialog on the Editor tab, make sure there is a checkmark in the box next to Auto List Members as shown in Figure 7-2, and click OK.

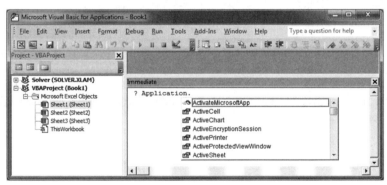

FIGURE 7-2

4. Press Ctrl+G to be taken into the Immediate window.

5. Type in the question mark character, then press the spacebar, type the word **Application**, and press the dot key on your keyboard. A list of the `Application` object's members, properties, and methods will be displayed, as shown in Figure 7-3.

FIGURE 7-3

6. Now, practice using IntelliSense. Press the N key and you will be taken to the first item in the `Application` object's list of members that begins with the letter N. In this case, that member happens to be the `Name` property, which will be highlighted by selection as shown in Figure 7-4.

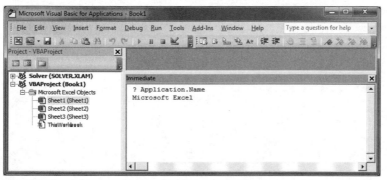

FIGURE 7-4

7. With the `Name` property item selected, either double-click it or press the Alt key to accept and enter the `Name` property for the `Application` object, and then press the Enter key. The Immediate window will return the result "Microsoft Excel" as shown in Figure 7-5.

FIGURE 7-5

8. Continue to explore on your own. Press the Enter key in the Immediate window to start a new line, enter the question mark character and press the spacebar, and scroll through the member list of other objects such as `ActiveWorkbook` or `Range`. Keep in mind that many objects are parents of other objects, so you can go two or more members deep to gather some information. For example, the `ActiveWorkbook` object has a `Worksheets` collection, and the `Worksheets` collection has a `Count` property. Therefore, if you type the line `? activeworkbook.Worksheets.Count` into the Immediate window, VBA will return the number of worksheets the active workbook contains.

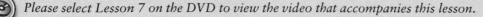

Please select Lesson 7 on the DVD to view the video that accompanies this lesson.

8

Making Decisions with VBA

So far, all the macros you've created share a common trait of being executed line by line, starting with the very first line of code below the Sub name, and ending at the EndSub line. You might think that this is the very purpose of a VBA macro, for all its code lines to be run in sequence from start to finish. After all, isn't that why VBA code is in a macro in the first place?

It turns out that VBA can do a lot more with your macros than just serve the purpose of executing every line of code in them. You will encounter many instances when you'll need to guide the user into making a decision about whether to do one thing or another. There are also times when you will want VBA to just go ahead and make a decision about something, without any input from the user.

Depending on the decisions that get made during the course of a macro, you'll want VBA to execute only the code relating to the selected choice, while bypassing the alternative code relating to which choice was not selected. This lesson shows you how to ask the user for information when the situation calls for it, and also how to simply let VBA do the decision-making on the fly, in circumstances when the user does not even need to be involved in the decision process.

UNDERSTANDING LOGICAL OPERATORS

Logical operators are terms in VBA that you can use for evaluating or comparing a combination of individual expressions in order to make a decision in your macro, and for VBA to carry out the code relating to that decision. The three most commonly used logical operators are AND, OR, and NOT, and all three have the same logical effect in VBA as they do in Excel's worksheet functions.

To understand how and why to use these logical operators in your macro, it's important to take a look at the conditions under which each one will yield a positive (True) result, or a negative (False) result. A truth table is a good way to illustrate each logical operator's True or False outcome, depending on the combinations of all possible results from the VBA expressions being compared. Once you understand the theory of logical operators, you will see how to put them to practical use when your macros call for decisions to be made.

AND

The AND logical operator performs a conjunction by comparing two expressions. The result of the AND operation is True only if both conditions are True. If either or both conditions are False, the And operation will evaluate to False.

For example, say you enter the number 500 in cell A1, and you enter the number 850 in cell B1. The following statement with the AND operator will evaluate to True, because both conditions are true at the same time:

```
Range("A1").Value > 300 AND Range("B1").Value > 700
```

Keeping the same numbers in cells A1:B1, the following statement would evaluate to False, because even though the first condition is True, the second condition is False:

```
Range("A1").Value > 300 AND Range("B1").Value >900
```

This next statement would also evaluate to False, because even though the second condition is True, the first condition is False:

```
Range("A1").Value >620 AND Range("B1").Value > 700
```

The final possibility is if both conditions are False, with this statement for example, which would evaluate to False:

```
Range("A1").Value <200 AND Range("B1").Value < 700
```

Table 8-1 summarizes each possible result of the AND logical operator more succinctly.

TABLE 8-1: Truth Table for the AND Logical Operator

EXPRESSION 1	EXPRESSION 2	LOGICAL RESULT
True	True	True
True	False	False
False	True	False
False	False	False

OR

The OR operator performs a logical disjunction, whereby if either condition is True, or if both conditions are True, the result is True. If both conditions are False, the OR operation will result in False. For example, using the same cell values as the previous AND example, with 500 in cell A1 and 850 in cell B1, you can see how differently the four statements will evaluate, using OR instead of AND as the logical operator.

The first statement will evaluate to True, not necessarily because both conditions arc Truc, but because at least one condition is True:

```
Range("A1").Value > 300 OR Range("B1").Value > 700
```

The following statement would evaluate to True, on the strength of the first condition being True, even though the second condition is False:

```
Range("A1").Value > 300 OR Range("B1").Value >900
```

This next statement would also evaluate to True because, despite the first condition being False, the second condition is True:

```
Range("A1").Value >620 OR Range("B1").Value > 700
```

The final possibility is if both conditions are False, meaning that in this case, because neither condition is True, the statement would evaluate to False:

```
Range("A1").Value <200 OR Range("B1").Value < 700
```

Table 8-2 summarizes each possible result of the OR logical operator.

TABLE 8-2: Truth Table for the OR Logical Operator

EXPRESSION 1	EXPRESSION 2	LOGICAL RESULT
True	True	True
True	False	True
False	True	True
False	False	False

> *Careful! Comparing logical expressions does not mean you can compare the impossible. Consider the following example:*
>
> ```
> Dim intNumber As Integer
> intNumber = 0
> MsgBox intNumber <= 5 Or 10 / intNumber > 5
> ```
>
> *Because it is impossible to divide a number by zero, this code will produce an error even though the first condition evaluated to True.*

NOT

The NOT operator performs logical negation. Similar to the negative sign in front of a worksheet formula, the NOT operator will invert an expression's True or False evaluation. For example, this line of code will toggle as on or off the display of gridlines on the active worksheet:

```
ActiveWindow.DisplayGridlines = Not ActiveWindow.DisplayGridlines
```

The logic behind this use of the NOT operator is to make the status of an object's property be opposite of whatever its current status is. In this case, the DisplayGridlines property of the ActiveWindow object can only be True (show the gridlines) or False (do not show the gridlines). Therefore, using the

NOT operator in this way, you get the effect of toggling between showing and not showing the active worksheet's gridlines at each re-execution of this line of code.

Table 8-3 summarizes each possible result of the NOT logical operator.

TABLE 8-3: Truth Table for the OR Logical Operator

EXPRESSION	LOGICAL RESULT
True	False
False	True

CHOOSING BETWEEN THIS OR THAT

This lesson began by mentioning that some code in your macros will need to be purposely bypassed. Most computer programming languages, VBA included, provide for the flexibility of structuring your code so that every command does not need to be run in every case. Many times, you will write macros wherein you will want the program to run certain commands if the user clicks Yes, and alternative commands if the user clicks No. All of the commands are a part of the macro code, but only one set of them will execute.

If...Then

Among VBA's arsenal of decision-making commands, the If...Then statement is probably the simplest and most commonly utilized approach to structure your conditional scenarios. For example, consider this line of code:

```
If Weekday(VBA.Date) = 6 Then MsgBox "Have a nice weekend!", , "Today is Friday!"
```

You may recall from your experience with Excel's WEEKDAY worksheet function that to Excel, weekday number 1 is Sunday, weekday number 2 is Monday, and so on. VBA would look at this line of code and display the message box only if the line of code is being executed on a Friday because Friday is weekday number 6. If the weekday is any day other than Friday, VBA bypasses this line of code.

In your prior VBA travels, you might have only seen an If statement with an accompanying End If statement below it, and you might be wondering why and how the previous example can be successfully executed without having or needing an End If statement. The previous example could have been written in "block" style like this:

```
If Weekday(VBA.Date) = 6 Then
MsgBox "Have a nice weekend!", , "Today is Friday!"
End If
```

When evaluating for a single condition, and the conditional code is one task as shown in this example, you can write the entire If...Then statement as a single

> *line of code as you saw. Some programmers prefer a single If line for their one-condition evaluations, and other programmers prefer the block style. It comes down to a personal preference and whatever feels more intuitive to you.*

If...Then...Else

More often than not, your evaluations will involve two or more conditions instead of just one. When you have two conditions and each has its own set of tasks to carry out, you need to separate the two conditions with the `Else` statement in a block `If` structure.

Expanding on the previous example, say you want to display a message box if today is Friday, but a different message box if today is not Friday. Here is the format you would use in your macro:

```
If Weekday(VBA.Date) = 6 Then
MsgBox "Have a nice weekend!", , "Today is Friday!"
Else
MsgBox "Alas, today is not Friday.", , "Not Friday yet!"
End If
```

Notice that the `Else` statement stands alone on its own dedicated line, separating the two conditions' respective commands. Only one condition can possibly evaluate to True in this example, because today is either Friday or it is some day other than Friday. This block of code is designed to always be executed such that only one of the message box commands would appear, but never both during the same run.

> *Here's a design tip to speed up your programs. In a block If structure with multiple conditions, VBA will look at each condition in turn, and basically stop at, and execute the conditional code for, the first condition that is found to evaluate to True. With two or three conditions, it might not be a big deal in which order you set your conditions in the If structure. But sometimes you will be programming for multiple conditions, and the point is, you will want VBA to execute its process as efficiently as possible. A good habit to get into is to design your If structures by setting the first condition to be the one that's most likely to be the case. That way, most of the time, the first condition will be the True condition and VBA will not waste time evaluating the alternative unlikelier scenarios. With this in mind, the previous example is a good opportunity to show how to make your code run faster. You can see that the first condition dealt with the current weekday being Friday. If you think about it, there is only one chance in seven that that will be the case. Mostly, the macro will be run on one of the other days of the week. A better way to write the If code is to consider which condition will be True more often than the other condition(s). Six out of seven days will not be a Friday, so that condition should be placed first, as shown in this example:*
>
> ```
> If Weekday(VBA.Date) <> 6 Then
> MsgBox "Alas, today is not Friday.", , "Not Friday yet!"
> Else
> MsgBox "Have a nice weekend!", , "Today is Friday!"
> End If
> ```

If...Then...ElseIf

VBA provides an extended way to utilize the If...Then...Else conditional structure when more than two conditions must be evaluated. Say you want to display a custom message for every day of the traditional five-day work week. You'll need a way to express your conditions in a single If structure with five possible courses of action, depending on which day of the week the macro is run.

One way you can accomplish this is with an If...Then...ElseIf structure as shown in the following example. Recall from the discussion about logical operators at the beginning of this lesson, that you can evaluate two or more conditions in one line of code. Notice that the first five conditions coincide with the five workdays from Monday to Friday. The final condition uses the OR operator to identify a weekend day of either Saturday or Sunday.

```
Sub WeekdayTest()

'Monday
If Weekday(VBA.Date) = 2 Then
MsgBox "Ugghhh - - Back to work.", , "Today is Monday"

'Tuesday
ElseIf Weekday(VBA.Date) = 3 Then
MsgBox "At least it's not Monday anymore!", , "Today is Tuesday"

'Wednesday
ElseIf Weekday(VBA.Date) = 4 Then
MsgBox "Hey, we're halfway through the work week!", , "Today is Wednesday"

'Thursday
ElseIf Weekday(VBA.Date) = 5 Then
MsgBox "Looking forward to the weekend.", , "Today is Thursday"

'Friday
ElseIf Weekday(VBA.Date) = 6 Then
MsgBox "Have a nice weekend!", , "Today is Friday!"

'Saturday or Sunday
ElseIf Weekday(VBA.Date) = 7 Or Weekday(VBA.Date) = 1 Then
MsgBox "Hey, it's currently the weekend!", , "Today is a weekend day!"

End If

End Sub
```

Select Case

As you are fully aware, the world is a complicated place and your macros will sometimes need to take into consideration not just one, two, or five courses of action, but possibly ten, hundreds, or even thousands depending on the situation. There are also times when several possible different conditions will require the same course of action. For these complex evaluations, the Select Case statement is a perfect solution.

You will want to become familiar with Select Case. It is simple to use, and it is easier to follow in your code than an extensive If structure. Similar to If and ElseIf keywords, you use the Case keyword in a Select Case structure to test for the True evaluation of a particular condition or set of conditions. You can have as many Case statements as you want, and only the code associated with the first Case that evaluated to True will be executed.

The best way to understand Select Case is to see it in action with a few examples. The following macro named WeekdayTestSelectCase is actually the previous WeekdayTest macro, which accomplishes the same result, but uses Select Case instead of If...Then...ElseIf:

```
Sub WeekdayTestSelectCase()
Select Case Weekday(VBA.Date)

Case 2 'Monday
MsgBox "Ugghhh - - Back to work.", , "Today is Monday"

Case 3 'Tuesday
MsgBox "At least it's not Monday anymore!", , "Today is Tuesday"

Case 4 'Wednesday
MsgBox "Hey, we're halfway through the work week!", , "Today is Wednesday"

Case 5 'Thursday
MsgBox "Looking forward to the weekend.", , "Today is Thursday"

Case 6 'Friday
MsgBox "Have a nice weekend!", , "Today is Friday!"

Case 1,  7 'Saturday or Sunday
MsgBox "Hey, it's currently the weekend!", , "Today is a weekend day!"

End Select
End Sub
```

You'll notice less redundancy of each condition (each Case), because the primary item of interest, Weekday(VBA.Date), needs to be named only once in the Select Case statement, instead of in every ElseIf statement. Also, each Case is very clear, and the entire macro is just easier to read.

A useful tactic with Select Case is the ability to group several different conditions into a single Case if it satisfies a particular test. For example, if your company operates its budget on a calendar year basis, that means the months of January, February, and March belong to Quarter 1; April, May, and June belong to Quarter 2, and so on.

With Select Case, you can group different conditions into the same Case in order to arrive at a common result. It is not just that January has a one-to-one association with Quarter 1, because the months of February and March also comprise Quarter 1. If you want to produce a message box that displays the current Quarter, this macro shows how to group the months into cases.

```
Sub CurrentQuarter()
Select Case Month(VBA.Date)
Case 1 To 3: MsgBox "Quarter 1"
Case 4 To 6: MsgBox "Quarter 2"
```

```
Case 7 To 9: MsgBox "Quarter 3"
Case 10 To 12: MsgBox "Quarter 4"
End Select
End Sub
```

As you can see, you don't need 12 separate statements to handle each conditional month; you can simply state the range of months using the `To` statement in each `Case`. I put a new wrinkle in that macro to point out a VBA feature, that being the colon character (:), which can be used to separate multiple statements on the same line that would otherwise each require their own line. I don't usually use the colon character this way, but sometimes it comes in handy by helping the readability of small macros like this.

GETTING USERS TO MAKE DECISIONS

Thus far you have seen examples of VBA's decision-making abilities that have not required any input from the user. The time will come when you'll either want or need information from the user in order for decisions to be made that only the user can provide. Message boxes and `InputBoxes` are excellent tools to interact with your users in such situations.

Message Boxes

Up to this point in the book, you have seen many examples of code that include a message box. In all those examples, the message box was a simple pop-up box that displayed an informational text message, with an OK button for you to acknowledge the information.

Message boxes are flexible tools that allow you to customize the buttons while asking questions directly to the users that will force them to select one option or the other. Instead of OK, you can display a Yes button and a No button on your message box, and write the code that will be followed if the user clicks Yes, or the user clicks No. An example of such a message box is shown in Figure 8-1.

FIGURE 8-1

Say you have a macro to perform a task that your users should confirm they really want to do as a final OK. Some macros are quite large and virtually irreversible, or the task at hand will alter the workbook in a significant way. In the following simplified example, the active worksheet will be copied and placed before Sheet1, but only if the user first clicks the Yes button to confirm his intention for this to happen. If the user clicks No, a friendly message box will advise the user that the macro will not run because No was clicked.

```
Sub ConfirmExample()
Select Case MsgBox( _
"Do you really want to copy this worksheet?", _
vbYesNo + vbQuestion, _
"Please confirm...")
```

```
Case vbNo
MsgBox _
"No problem, this worksheet will not be copied.", _
vbInformation, _
"You clicked No."
Exit Sub

Case vbYes
MsgBox _
"Great - - click OK to run the macro.", _
vbInformation, _
"Thanks for confirming."
ActiveSheet.Copy Before:=Sheets("Sheet1")

End Select
End Sub
```

As you look at the `MsgBox` line, note that the message box arguments are contained within parentheses. A message box has two mandatory arguments: the *prompt*, which is the text you place in the body of the message box, and the button configuration. Other combinations of buttons include `OKCancel`, `YesNoCancel`, and `AbortRetryIgnore`. The title of the message box is optional, but I always enter it to offer a more customized experience for the user.

> *In the Try It section at the end of Lesson 7, you learned about VBA's IntelliSense feature. I recommend you activate IntelliSense if you have not already done so, because when composing message boxes, you'll be reminded of the available arguments and their proper syntax while you are writing your code.*

Input Boxes

When you need a piece of specific information from the user, such as a text string or a number, an `InputBox` was made for the job. An `InputBox` looks like a distant cousin of a message box, with the prompted text that tells the user what to do, OK and Cancel buttons (which cannot be reconfigured as a message box's buttons can), and an optional title argument.

An `InputBox` requires a prompt argument, and it provides a field wherein the user would enter the kind of information as needed for the macro to continue. The entry would return a `String` type variable. If no entry is made, that is, the text field is left empty, the `InputBox` would return a null string, which is usually regarded by VBA the same as if the user clicked the Cancel button.

The following example uses an `InputBox` to ask the user to enter a number to represent how many rows will be inserted below the active cell's row. Figure 8-2 shows what the `InputBox` looks like for this macro.

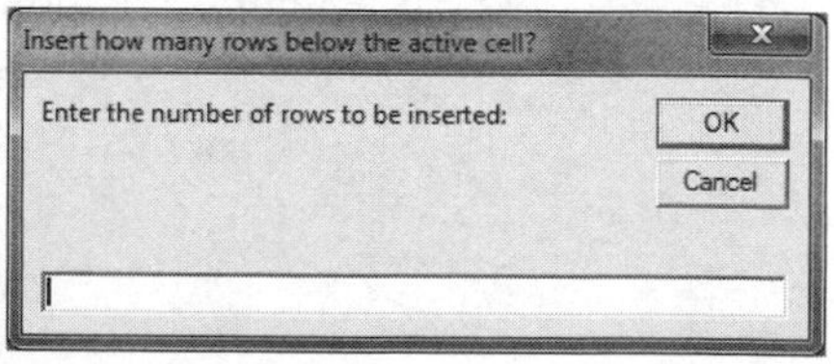

FIGURE 8-2

```
Sub InsertRows()
'Declare the string variable for the InputBox entry.
Dim CountInsertRows As String
'Define the String variable as the InputBox entry.
```

```
CountInsertRows = InputBox( _
"Enter the number of rows to be inserted:", _
"Insert how many rows below the active cell?")
'Verify that a number was entered.
'The Val function returns the numbers contained in a string as a numeric value.
If CountInsertRows = "" Or Val(CountInsertRows) < 1 Then Exit Sub
'Insert as many rows as the number that was entered.
'The Resize property returns a Range object based on the number of rows
'and columns in the new range. The number that was entered in the InputBox
'represents how many rows shall be inserted.  The count of columns, which is
'the other optional argument for Resize, need not be specified because it is
'only rows being inserted.
Rows(ActiveCell.Row + 1).Resize(Val(CountInsertRows)).Insert
End Sub
```

TRY IT

In this lesson, you write a macro that includes a single-line `If` statement, an `If…Then` structure, a `Select Case` structure, a message box to ask the user a Yes or No question, and an `InputBox` to accept a text entry from the user.

Lesson Requirements

For this lesson, the active worksheet is currently protected with a password, and you ask the workbook's users if they want to unprotect the worksheet. If they answer No, the macro will terminate. If they answer Yes, the macro will proceed to ask them for the password. If the attempted password is incorrect, the user will be informed of that, the worksheet will remain protected, and the macro will terminate. If the attempted password is correct, the user will then be allowed to unprotect the worksheet.

Step-by-Step

1. Start by opening a new workbook and password protecting Sheet1 with the password "hello" (without the quotes, all lowercase just as you see it here).

2. With your Sheet1 worksheet protected, press Alt+F11 to go to the Visual Basic Editor.

3. From the menu at the top of the VBE, click Insert ⇨ Module.

4. In the module you just created, type **Sub PasswordTest** and press Enter. VBA will automatically place a pair of empty parentheses at the end of the `Sub` line, followed by an empty line, and the `End Sub` line below that. Your macro will look like this so far:

    ```
    Sub PasswordTest()

    End Sub
    ```

5. Begin a `Select Case` structure with a Yes No Question message box to ask the users to confirm their intention to unprotect the worksheet:

```
Select Case MsgBox( _
"Do you want to unprotect the worksheet?", _
vbYesNo + vbQuestion, _
"Please confirm your intentions.")
```

6. Handle the case for a No answer by informing the user that the macro will not continue, and then exit the macro with the `Exit Sub` statement:

```
Case vbNo
MsgBox "No problem -- this macro will end.", vbInformation, "You clicked No."
Exit Sub
```

7. Handle the case for a Yes answer:

```
Case vbYes
```

8. Provide an `InputBox` for the user to enter the password. Declare a `String` type variable, and define it as the text that will be entered into the `InputBox`.

```
Dim myPassword As String
'myPassword = _
InputBox("Please enter the case-sensitive password:", _
"A password is required to unprotect this worksheet.")
```

9. Here is an opportunity to add a single-line `If` statement to end the macro if the user clicks Cancel, or clicks OK without entering anything into the `InputBox`. The pair of double quotes with nothing between them is interpreted by VBA as a zero-length string.

```
If myPassword = "" Then Exit Sub
```

10. Begin an `If...Then` structure to determine if the `InputBox` entry matches the password "hello" that was used to protect the worksheet:

```
If myPassword <> "hello" Then
```

11. If the `InputBox` entry is anything other than "hello," enter the code you would want executed when an incorrect password is entered, which you can do with a friendly message box:

```
MsgBox _
"Sorry, " & myPassword & " is not the correct Password.", _
vbCritical, _
"Incorrect."
```

12. Enter your `Else` statement and supply the code to be executed only if the correct password is entered:

```
Else
MsgBox _
"Thank you.  Please click OK to unprotect the worksheet.", _
vbInformation, _
"You entered the correct password!!"
ActiveSheet.Unprotect "hello"
```

13. End the `If` structure that determined if the `InputBox` entry matched the password "hello":

```
End If
```

14. End the `Select Case` structure for the users to confirm their intention of unprotecting the worksheet:

```
End Select
```

15. Here is what the complete macro would look like:

```
Sub PasswordTest()

'Ask the user if they want to unprotect the worksheet.
Select Case MsgBox( _
"Do you want to unprotect the worksheet?", _
vbYesNo + vbQuestion, _
"Please confirm your intentions.")

'Handle the case for a No answer by informing the user
'that the macro will not continue,
'and then exit the subroutine with the Exit Sub statement.
Case vbNo
MsgBox "No problem -- this macro will end.", vbInformation, "You clicked No."
Exit Sub

'Handle the case for a Yes answer by providing an InputBox
'for the user to enter the password.
Case vbYes

'Declare a String type variable.
Dim myPassword As String
'Define the String variable as the text that will be entered into the InputBox.
myPassword = _
InputBox("Please enter the case-sensitive password:", _
"A password is required to unprotect this worksheet.")

'A one-line If statement to end the macro if the user clicks Cancel,
'or clicks OK without entering anything into the InputBox.
If myPassword = "" Then Exit Sub

'If structure to determine if the InputBox entry matches the password "hello"
'that was used to protect the worksheet.
If myPassword <> "hello" Then

'The code line to be executed if an incorrect password is entered.
MsgBox _
"Sorry, " & myPassword & " is not the correct Password.", _
vbCritical, _
"Incorrect."

Else
'The code to execute only if the correct password is entered.
MsgBox _
```

```
"Thank you.  Please click OK to unprotect the worksheet.", _
vbInformation, _
"You entered the correct password!!"
ActiveSheet.Unprotect "hello"

'End the If structure that determined if the InputBox entry
'matched the password "hello".
End If

'End the Select Case structure for the users to confirm their intention
'of unprotecting the worksheet.
End Select

End Sub
```

 Please select Lesson 8 on the DVD to view the video that accompanies this lesson.

SECTION III
Beyond the Macro Recorder: Writing Your Own Code

▶ **LESSON 9:** Repeating Actions with Loops

▶ **LESSON 10:** Working with Arrays

▶ **LESSON 11:** Automating Procedures with Worksheet Events

▶ **LESSON 12:** Automating Procedures with Workbook Events

▶ **LESSON 13:** Using Embedded Controls

▶ **LESSON 14:** Programming Charts

▶ **LESSON 15:** Programming PivotTables and PivotCharts

▶ **LESSON 16:** User Defined Functions

▶ **LESSON 17:** Debugging Your Code

9

Repeating Actions with Loops

Suppose you need to perform the same action, or the same sequence of several actions, many times in your macro. For example, you may need to unhide all worksheets that are hidden, or add 12 worksheets to your workbook and name them for each month of the year.

The fact is, you'll encounter many circumstances for which a repetition of similar commands is a necessary part of the job. In most cases it will be impractical, and sometimes downright impossible, to write an individual command for each performance of the action. The need for handling a repetitive set of commands efficiently is exactly what loops are made for.

WHAT IS A LOOP?

A *loop* is a method of performing a task more than once. You may need to copy each worksheet in your workbook and save it as the only worksheet in its own separate workbook. Or, you may have a list of thousands of records and want to insert an empty row where the value of a cell in column A is different than the value of the cell below it. Maybe your worksheet has dozens of cells that contain comments, and you want to add the same preceding text to every comment's existing text without having to edit every comment one at a time.

Instead of doing these kinds of tasks manually, or recording an impractical (and sometimes impossible) macro to handle the repetition, you can use loops to get the job done with less code while keeping more flexible control over the number of necessary repetitions. In VBA, a loop is a structure that executes one or more commands, and then cycles through the process again within the structure, for as many times as you specify. Each cycle of executing the loop structure's command(s) is called an *iteration*.

> *Loops are great, but you're not obligated to use one just because you need to repeat an action two or three times. You'll come across situations that you know will always require the same commands to be repeated the same way, for the same number of times. If you feel like coding each action separately, and you can live with the longer code, go ahead and hard-code the separate commands if that's what works for you. Beyond three potential iterations, however, you really should go the loop route. It'll save you a lot of work, and the code will be easier to maintain.*

The number of a loop's iterations will depend on the nature of the task at hand. All loops fall into one of two categories. A *fixed-iteration loop* executes a specified number of times that you hard-code directly as a numeric expression. An *indefinite loop* executes a flexible number of times that is usually defined by a logical expression.

For example, a fixed iteration loop dealing with a year's worth of data might need to cycle through 12 iterations, one for each month. An indefinite loop might need to cycle through every worksheet in your workbook, taking into consideration that because worksheets can be added or deleted at any time, the exact count of worksheets can never be known in advance.

TYPES OF LOOPS

VBA provides several different looping structures, and at least one of them will be suited for any looping requirement you'll encounter. Table 9-1 shows an overview of the types of loops in VBA.

TABLE 9-1: Types of Loops in VBA

LOOP STRUCTURE	CATEGORY	EXPLANATION
For...Next	Fixed	Repeats an action for a specified number of times.
For...Each...Next	Fixed	Repeats an action upon an object in a Collection. For example, you can perform a task for each worksheet in the workbook.
Do...While	Indefinite	Executes an action if the condition is True, and repeats the action until the condition is False.
Do...Until	Indefinite	Executes an action if the condition is False, and repeats the action until the condition is True.
Do...Loop...While	Indefinite	Executes an action once, and repeats the action while the condition is True, until it is False.
Do...Loop...Until	Indefinite	Executes an action once, and repeats the action while the condition is False, until it is True.
While...Wend	Indefinite	Same as the Do...While loop structure, still supported by VBA but obsolete.

For...Next

The For...Next loop structure is a simple and effective way to repeat an action for a specified number of times. For example, if you want to add five new worksheets to your workbook, you could declare an Integer type variable and repeat the action five times, like this:

```
Sub AddFiveWorksheets()
'Declare your Integer or Long variable.
Dim intCounter As Integer
'Open the For loop structure.
For intCounter = 1 To 5
'Enter the command(s)that will be repeated.
Worksheets.Add
'Loop to the next iteration.
Next intCounter
End Sub
```

> *Although it is technically correct that the* Next *statement can stand alone, do yourself a favor by getting into the good habit of including the variable in the* Next *statement. For example, writing your code as* Next intCounter *instead of just as* Next *will make it easier for you to read.*

When VBA executes a For...Next loop, by default it increments by 1 the value of the declared Integer or Long type variable. Because the objective was to add five worksheets, the easiest way to keep a running count of the process is to iterate five times, just as if you were counting the occurrence of each action from 1 to 5.

You can take advantage of the fixed nature of a For...Next loop by asking for the number of worksheets that are to be added. In the following example, an InputBox engages the user by asking for a number that represents how many worksheets will be added:

```
Sub ForNextExample2()
'Declare your Integer or Long variables.
Dim MoreSheets As Integer, intCounter As Integer
'Define the MoreSheets variable with an InputBox.
MoreSheets = InputBox( _
"How many worksheets do you want to add?", _
"Enter a number")
'Open the For loop structure.
For intCounter = 1 To MoreSheets
'Enter the command(s)that will be repeated.
Worksheets.Add
'Loop to the next iteration.
Next intCounter
End Sub
```

You don't always need to start counting from the number 1 in a For...Next loop; you can pretty much count from any number to any number. Suppose you want to hide rows 6, 7, and 8. A For...Next loop to accomplish that task could look like this:

```
Sub ForNextExample3()
'Declare your Integer or Long variable.
Dim intCounter As Integer
'Open the For loop structure.
For intCounter = 6 To 8
'Enter the command(s)that will be repeated.
Rows(intCounter).Hidden = True
'Loop to the next iteration.
Next intCounter
End Sub
```

For...Each...Next

The For...Each...Next loop executes an action for a fixed number of times just as the For...Next construct does, but unlike For...Next, For...Each...Next does not keep a count along the way of how many iterations it performs. The count of iterations is not important with For...Each...Next because the objective is to execute an action for however many objects exist in a specified VBA collection. Maybe there will be hundreds of iterations to occur; maybe there will be none.

Suppose that as part of your workbook project's design, a particularly lengthy macro will run faster and less confusingly for the user if all other Excel workbooks are closed. Naturally, you can never know in advance if the user will have 10 other workbooks open in addition to yours, or if your workbook is the only open workbook. A For...Each...Next loop would be the perfect way to save and close all other workbooks that might be open, such as with this example:

```
Sub CloseWorkbooks()
'Declare your object variable.
Dim wb As Workbook
'Open the For loop structure.
For Each wb In Workbooks
'Enter the command(s)that will be repeated.
If wb.Name <> ThisWorkbook.Name Then
wb.Save
wb.Close
End If
'Loop to the next iteration.
Next wb
End Sub
```

Notice that an object variable is declared for Workbook, and the Workbooks collection is being evaluated with an If structure for the presence of any and all workbooks that are named differently than your workbook. The code will complete its mission with the same result of your workbook being the only one that's open, regardless of whether it was the only one open from the start, or whether 50 other workbooks had also been open at the time.

One of Excel's oddities is that you can hide any number of worksheets at the same time, but if you have multiple worksheets that are hidden, you can unhide only one worksheet at a time. With this macro as another example of a For...Each...Next loop, you can quickly unhide all worksheets at once:

```
Sub UnhideSheets()
'Declare your object variable.
Dim ws As Worksheet
'Open a For Ech loop.
For Each ws In Worksheets
'Command(s) to be executed.
ws.Visible = xlSheetVisible
'Loop to the next iteration.
Next ws
End Sub
```

Exiting a For... Loop

Suppose your macro requires that you determine whether a particular workbook named Test.xlsx happens to be open, and if so, you must close it. You might compose a macro with a loop that looks like this:

```
Sub CloseOneWorkbook()
'Declare your object variable.
Dim wb As Workbook
'Open a For Each loop.
For Each wb In Workbooks
'Command(s) to be executed.
If wb.Name = "Test.xlsx" Then
wb.Save
wb.Close
End If
'Loop to the next iteration.
Next wb
End Sub
```

Strictly speaking, the macro will work. But think for a moment — what if a few dozen workbooks are open? In this case, you'd want the loop to do its job only up to the point of encountering the Test.xlsx workbook.

In the preceding CloseOneWorkbook example, even if the Test.xlsx workbook is found to be open and then closed, the loop will still continue its appointed rounds after that by unnecessarily evaluating each open workbook. This would be a waste of time and system resources. Instead, you should insert the Exit For statement to stop the looping process in a For...Next or For...Each...Next loop when a condition has been met and dealt with, and cannot be met thereafter.

Here is an example of how that macro should look, with the Exit For statement placed immediately before the End If statement:

```
Sub CloseOneWorkbookFaster()
'Declare your object variable.
Dim wb As Workbook
For Each wb In Workbooks
'Command(s) to be executed.
```

```
If wb.Name = "Test.xlsx" Then
wb.Save
wb.Close
'Exit For statement to avoid needless iterations if the condition is met.
Exit For
End If
'Loop to the next iteration.
Next wb
End Sub
```

Looping In Reverse with Step

A common request that Excel users have is to insert an empty row when the value of a cell in some particular column does not equal the value of the cell below it. In Figure 9-1, the table of data is sorted by Region in column A, and the request is to visually separate the regions with an empty row at each change in Region name.

When inserting a series of rows like this, it's best to start looping from the bottom of the table, and work your way up to the top. That means your numeric row reference in the loop will be decreasing and not increasing, because your starting point is row 18 (the last row of data) and your ending point is row 2 (the first row of data).

Recall that when VBA executes a For… Next loop, by default it increments by 1 the value of your declared Integer or Long type variable. With For…Next loops, you can specify an alternative increment or decrement value by using the optional Step keyword. You can step forward or backward by as large a numeric value as you like.

Before

	A Region	B Item	C Count	D
1	**Region**	**Item**	**Count**	
2	East	Wombats	116	
3	East	Widgets	654	
4	East	Wallabees	822	
5	East	Wallabees	456	
6	East	Wombats	898	
7	West	Wallabees	605	
8	West	Witches	781	
9	West	Wallabees	990	
10	North	Wallabees	349	
11	North	Wombats	493	
12	North	Widgets	507	
13	North	Widgets	644	
14	South	Widgets	570	
15	South	Widgets	323	
16	South	Wallabees	373	
17	South	Wallabees	900	
18	South	Widgets	962	
19				
20				
21				

After

	A	B	C	D
1	**Region**	**Item**	**Count**	
2	East	Wombats	116	
3	East	Widgets	654	
4	East	Wallabees	822	
5	East	Wallabees	456	
6	East	Wombats	898	
7				
8	West	Wallabees	605	
9	West	Witches	781	
10	West	Wallabees	990	
11				
12	North	Wallabees	349	
13	North	Wombats	493	
14	North	Widgets	507	
15	North	Widgets	644	
16				
17	South	Widgets	570	
18	South	Widgets	323	
19	South	Wallabees	373	
20	South	Wallabees	900	
21	South	Widgets	962	

FIGURE 9-1

In this example, each cell in column A is being evaluated one by one, from row 18 to row 2, so the loop will step by a numeric factor of negative 1. Here is a macro that makes the "Before" image look like the "After" image in Figure 9-1:

```
Sub InsertRows()
'Declare your Integer or Long variable.
Dim xRow As Long
'Open a For Each loop.
For xRow = 18 To 3 Step -1
'Command(s) to be executed.
If Range("A" & xRow).Value <> Range("A" & xRow - 1) Then
Rows(xRow).Resize(1).Insert
End If
'Loop to the next iteration.
Next xRow
End Sub
```

Do...While

The Do statement is an extremely powerful tool with which to gain more flexibility in your looping structures. In a Do...While loop, you test for a condition that must be True before the loop will execute. When the condition is True, the command(s) within the loop are executed.

As a simple example, the DoWhileExample macro will produce five message boxes because the Do...While loop tests for the condition that an Integer variable (named iCounter) has not exceeded the number 5. Notice that the iCounter variable starts at 1 outside the loop and is increased by 1 inside the loop.

```
Sub DoWhileExample()
Dim iCounter As Integer
iCounter = 1
Do While iCounter <= 5
MsgBox "Hello world!", , iCounter
iCounter = iCounter + 1
Loop
End Sub
```

Applying this concept to a more practical activity, suppose you want to open all Excel workbooks that are in a particular file path. The macro named OpenAllFiles will do that using a Do...Loop structure. The Dir function returns the first filename that matches the combination of the specified pathname and an Excel workbook extension containing .xls. Calling the Dir function again would open additional filenames until a filename is encountered that does not match the combination.

```
Sub OpenAllFiles()
Dim myFile As String, myPath As String
myPath = "C:\Your File Path\"
myFile = Dir(myPath & "*.xls*")
Do While myFile <> ""
Workbooks.Open myPath & myFile
myFile = Dir()
Loop
End Sub
```

Do...Until

When VBA runs a Do...Until loop, it tests the logical condition you supply and executes the commands within the loop as long as the condition evaluates to False. When VBA reaches the Loop statement, it re-evaluates the condition and executes the looping commands only if the condition is still False.

This example demonstrates Do...Until by selecting the next worksheet based on the index number from whatever current worksheet you are on. The wrinkle that is taken into consideration by the loop is that the next highest index number worksheet might be hidden, and because you cannot select a hidden worksheet, the loop selects the next highest index number of a worksheet that is also visible.

```
Sub SelectSheet()
'Declare an Integer type variable to handle the Index number property
'of whichever worksheet(s) are being evaluated in the current iteration.
Dim intWS As Integer
'Because you want to activate the next visible worksheet,
```

```
'as a starting point you need to know the next highest Index position
'from whatever worksheet is active at the time.
intWS = ActiveSheet.Index + 1
'If you are on the last worksheet, you'll have reached the end of the line,
'so define the intWS as the first Index worksheet.
If intWS>Worksheets.Count Then intWS = 1
'Open a Do Until loop that determines the next Index number,
'only considering visible worksheets.
Do Until Worksheets(intWS).Visible = True
'Add a 1 to the intWS variable as you iterate to the next highest Index number.
intWS = intWS + 1
If it turns out that the intWS Index variable reaches a number
'that is greater than the count of worksheets in the workbook,
'the intWS number is set back to 1, which is the first Index position.If intWS >
Worksheets.Count Then intWS = 1
'Loop to start evaluation again, until the proper Index number is found.
Loop
'Select the worksheet whose Index property matches the index number
'that has met all the criteria.
Worksheets(intWS).Select
End Sub
```

For another example, suppose you want to update your AutoCorrect list easily and quickly. Say you have a two-column table on your worksheet that occupies columns A and B. In column A, you have listed frequently misspelled words, and in column B are the corrected words that you want Excel to automatically display if you misspell any of those words. For example, in cell A1 you have entered "teh" (without the quotes) and in cell B1 you have entered the correction of "the"(without the quotes). This macro, using a Do…Until loop, will handle each entry in column A and continue to do so until the first empty cell is encountered, indicating the end of the list.

```
Sub AddCorrection()
'Declare a Long type variable to help looping through rows
'of the two-column list.Dim i As Long
'Declare two String type variables:
'one for thr original entry, and the other for the text string replacement.
Dim myMistake As String, myCorrection As String
'Establish the number 1 for the Long Variable, representing row 1
'which is the first row in the example list.
i = 1
'Open a Do Until loop, telling VBA to stop looping when an empty cell
'is encountered in column A, indicating the end of the list.
Do Until IsEmpty(Cells(i, 1))
'Define the myMistake variable as the text contents of the cell in column
A.myMistake = Cells(i, 1).Value
'Define the myCorrection variable as the text contents of the cell in column B.
myCorrection = Cells(i, 2).Value
'VBA tells the Excel Application's AutoCorrect property to update itself with
'the two strings from columns A and B.
Application.AutoCorrect.AddReplacement What:=myMistake, Replacement:=myCorrection
'Add a 1 to the i variable in preparation for evaluating the next row in the list.
i = i + 1
'The Loop statement starts the process again for the next row in the list.
Loop
End Sub
```

This example introduces the `Cells` range method to refer to a cell object. You are already familiar with the `Range("A1")` notation, but the `Cells` method offers more flexibility in VBA when referring to individual cells and ranges. The `Cells` method has two arguments: the first argument is row number, and the second argument is column number. The syntax is `ParentObject .Cells(RowIndex, ColumnIndex)`. For example, the notation `Cells(2, 5)` is the same as `Range("E2")` because for cell E2, column E is also regarded by Excel as column 5, and the numeral 2 in "E2" refers to row 2. You'll be seeing an increased use of the `Cells` method in this book because it is such an easier and more efficient method of referring to dynamic ranges in VBA.

Do...Loop...While

To have VBA test the conditional statement after executing the commands within the loop, you simply place the conditional statement after the `Loop` keyword. The `Do...Loop...While` syntax is:

```
Do
Command statements to be executed within the loop.
Loop While condition
```

When VBA executes the command(s) in a `Do...Loop...While` structure, it does so first, and then at the `Loop While` line, it tests the logical condition. If the condition is True at that point, the loop iterates again, and so on, until the condition evaluates to False.

A common request is to locate all cells in a worksheet that contain a particular value, similar to clicking the Find Next button on the Find dialog box, and then do something to that cell or to the cells around it. Suppose you have a worksheet filled with data and you want to find all cells that contain the word "Hello." These cells can be in any row or column.

For each of those cells where "Hello" is found, you want to place the word "Goodbye" in the cell of the column to the immediate right. The following macro does just that, using a `Do...Loop...While` construction that finds every cell containing "Hello" and identifies its address, so the loop can perform only as many iterations as there are cells containing "Hello":

```
Sub FindHello()
Dim HelloCell As Range, BeginningAddress As String
Set HelloCell = ActiveSheet.UsedRange.Find("Hello", LookIn:=xlValues)
If Not HelloCell Is Nothing Then
BeginningAddress = HelloCell.Address
Do
HelloCell.Offset(0, 1).Value = "Goodbye"
Set HelloCell = ActiveSheet.UsedRange.FindNext(HelloCell)
Loop While Not HelloCell Is Nothing And HelloCell.Address<>BeginningAddress
End If
End Sub
```

Do...Loop...Until

Similar in approach to the Do...Loop...While construct, the Do...Loop...Until loop tests its condition after executing the loop's statements. The Until keyword tells VBA that the statements within the loop will be executed again, for as long as the logical condition evaluates to False. Once VBA tests the condition as True, the loop's iterations will stop, and the macro will resume with the line of code following the Loop keyword.

This macro shows an example of a Do...Loop...Until structure, which creates 365 new worksheets, all named with dates starting from the day you run the macro:

```
Sub YearSheets()
Dim i As Integer
i = 0
Do
Sheets.Add(After:=Sheets(Sheets.Count)).Name = Format(VBA.Date + i, "MM-DD-YYYY")
i = i + 1
Loop Until i = 365
End Sub
```

While...Wend

While...Wend loops have become obsolete and are rarely used because they are not as robust as Do and For loops. VBA still supports While...Wend loops for backward compatibility with prior versions of Excel, and I am not aware of any plans by Microsoft to stop supporting While...Wend.

So, though I recommend you not bother learning how to build a While...Wend loop, the fact is, they are rather uncomplicated constructs and you should have some familiarity with how they look if and when you see them in older code written by others. Here is an example of While...Wend that uses an InputBox that asks for a password, and keeps asking until the correct password is entered, or the message box is cancelled:

```
Sub InputPassword()
While InputBox("Please enter password:", "Password required") <> "MyPassword"
If MsgBox( _
"Sorry, that is not correct.", _
vbOKCancel, _
"Wrong password") _
= vbCancel Then End
Wend
MsgBox "Yes!! You entered the correct password!", vbOKOnly, "Thank you!"
End Sub
```

NESTING LOOPS

Your macros will eventually require that you enclose one loop structure inside another loop structure, referred to as *nesting* loops. For example, you may need to loop through a set of rows in a data table, and each completed set of looped-through rows will represent a single iteration for a larger loop construct for the columns in the table.

When you nest loops, you need to be aware of a few important points:

➤ When you nest For...Next loops, each loop must have its own uniquely named counter variable.

➤ When you nest For...Each...Next loops, each loop must have its own uniquely named object (or element) variable.

➤ If you use an Exit For or Exit Do statement, only the loop that is currently executing will terminate. If that loop is nested within a larger loop, the larger loop will still continue to execute its iterations.

➤ I mentioned this earlier in this lesson, but it especially holds true with nested loops: I strongly recommend you include the variable name in your Next statements.

Here is an example of a macro with a Do loop nested inside a For...Each...Next loop. This macro will produce a list of six unique random numbers between 1 and 54, similar to a lottery drawing.

```
Sub PickSixLottery()

'Declare the Range variables for the entire six-cell range,
'and for each individual cell in the six-cell range.
Dim RandomRange As Range, RandomCell As Range

'Identify the six-cell range where the randomly selected numbers will be listed.
Set RandomRange = Range("A1:A6")

'Before populating the six-cell list range, make sure all its cells are empty.
RandomRange.Clear

'Open a For...Each loop to cycle through each cell in range A1:A6.
For Each RandomCell In RandomRange

'Open a Do...Loop that enters a unique random number between 1 and 54
Do
RandomCell.Value = Int(54 * Rnd + 1)
Loop Until WorksheetFunction.CountIf(RandomRange, RandomCell.Value) = 1

'Iterate to the next cell until all six cells have been populated.
Next RandomCell

End Sub
```

TRY IT

In this lesson, you write a macro with a For...Next loop that adds 12 worksheets to a workbook, and names each of them by month.

Lesson Requirements

For this lesson, you write a macro that uses a `For...Next` loop with an `Integer` type variable that adds 12 worksheets to your workbook, names each worksheet by calendar month ("January," "February," and so on), and places the worksheets' tabs in order of calendar month from left to right.

Step-by-Step

1. Open a new workbook and press Alt+F11 to go to the Visual Basic Editor.

2. From the menu at the top of the VBE, click Insert ➪ Module.

3. In the module you just created, type **Sub LoopTwelveMonths** and press Enter. VBA will automatically place a pair of empty parentheses at the end of the `Sub` line, followed by an empty line, and the `End Sub` line below that. Your macro will look like this so far:

   ```
   Sub LoopTwelveMonths ()

   End Sub
   ```

4. Declare an `Integer` type variable that will iterate 12 times, one for each month of the year:

   ```
   Dim intMonth As Integer
   ```

5. Open a `For...Next` loop that starts from 1 and ends at 12:

   ```
   For intMonth = 1 To 12
   ```

6. With a one-line command, you can add each of the 12 worksheets in turn, while placing their tabs one after another from left to right, and naming each tab by calendar month. The `DateSerial` function is a good way to cycle through month names because it requires integer values for the arguments of Year, Month, and Day, just like the DATE worksheet function. You can use any year, and any day that is not a number greater than 28. For the Month argument, the `intMonth` variable is a perfect fit because it was declared as an `Integer` type.

   ```
   Sheets.Add(After:=Sheets(Sheets.Count)).Name = _
   Format(DateSerial(2011, intMonth, 1), "MMMM")
   ```

7. Enter the `Next` statement for the `intMonth` variable that will produce and name the next month's worksheet up to and including December:

   ```
   Next intMonth
   ```

8. When completed, the macro will look like this, with comments that have been added to explain each step:

   ```
   Sub LoopTwelveMonths()

   'Declare an Integer type variable to iterate twelve times,
   'one for each month of the year.
   Dim intMonth As Integer
   ```

```
'Open a For...Next loop that starts from one and ends at twelve.
For intMonth = 1 To 12

'With a one-line command, you can add each of the twelve worksheets in turn,
'while placing their tabs one after another from left to right.
Sheets.Add(After:=Sheets(Sheets.Count)).Name = _
Format(DateSerial(2011, intMonth, 1), "MMMM")

'The Next statement for the intMonth variable
'produces and names the next month worksheet.
Next intMonth

End Sub
```

 Please select Lesson 9 on the DVD to view the video that accompanies this lesson.

10

Working with Arrays

This lesson introduces you to arrays in VBA. As you will see, arrays are a very useful way to programmatically group and store many items of related data. Once you've collected your array of data items, you can access any of the items individually, or access the group as a whole. Arrays can help you accomplish various tasks in a logical and efficient manner, which is important to remember when you find yourself faced with some tasks for which arrays will be the only alternative.

WHAT IS AN ARRAY?

An *array* is like a variable on steroids. In addition to being a variable, an array also serves as a holding container for a group of individual values, called *elements*, that are of the same data type. You can populate the array yourself by specifying the known elements in your macro, or you can let VBA populate the array during the course of the macro if you don't know how many elements the array will end up containing.

The concept of arrays can be challenging to grasp at first, so a real-world analogy might help. Suppose you are a fan of classic movies, and you keep a CD library at home of perhaps 100 movies. Among those 100 movies are five that are your favorite classics. You can declare a variable named myFavoriteMovies, and create a String array with this macro:

```
Sub FavoriteMovies()

Dim myFavoriteMovies(1 to 5) as String

myFavoriteMovies (1) = "Gone With The Wind"
myFavoriteMovies (2) = "Casablanca"
myFavoriteMovies (3) = "Citizen Kane"
myFavoriteMovies (4) = "Sunset Boulevard"
myFavoriteMovies (5) = "Modern Times"

MsgBox myFavoriteMovies(3)

End Sub
```

Elements in an array are variables, and you can refer to a specific element by its index number inside the array. Because the array name is myFavoriteMovies, and the Message Box is referring to the third element in that array, when you run this macro, the Message Box will display Citizen Kane.

You have created an array which is a collection of your favorite classic movies. You can loop through each element in that collection — that is, each movie title — by referring to its index number inside the myFavoriteMovies array. The following macro shows how to display each movie title element in a Message Box.

```
Sub FavoriteMoviesLoop()

Dim myFavoriteMovies(1 To 5) As String
Dim intCounter As Integer

myFavoriteMovies(1) = "Gone With The Wind"
myFavoriteMovies(2) = "Casablanca"
myFavoriteMovies(3) = "Citizen Kane"
myFavoriteMovies(4) = "Sunset Boulevard"
myFavoriteMovies(5) = "Modern Times"

For intCounter = 1 To 5
MsgBox myFavoriteMovies(intCounter), , _
"Favorite #" & intCounter
Next intCounter

End Sub
```

If you would like to populate a range of cells with the elements of your array, this macro demonstrates how to do that, listing the movie titles in range A1:A5.

```
Sub FavoriteMoviesRange()

Dim myFavoriteMovies(1 To 5) As String
Dim intCounter As Integer

myFavoriteMovies(1) = "Gone With The Wind"
myFavoriteMovies(2) = "Casablanca"
myFavoriteMovies(3) = "Citizen Kane"
myFavoriteMovies(4) = "Sunset Boulevard"
myFavoriteMovies(5) = "Modern Times"

For intCounter = 1 To 5
Cells(intCounter, 1).Value = myFavoriteMovies(intCounter)
Next intCounter

End Sub
```

VBA regards the array itself as one variable, but inside the array is a group of two or more elements that you can work with separately. You can, and often will, refer to each element by its index number, which is its position in the array. This way, you can pick a particular element in the array to work with based on its index number, or you can loop through all the index numbers one after the other, in case your project calls for every element to be worked on.

What Arrays Can Do for You

Arrays are often used for representing data in lists or tables, where each item in the list is of the same data type. Some examples might be a list of your friends' names, all of which would be String data types, or a table of your city's average daily temperatures by month, all of which might be Double data types. Arrays offer you the versatility of storing and manipulating data items through one array variable, which is much more efficient than assigning variables to every element in the array.

Say you want to count how many Excel workbook filenames reside in a particular folder. You don't know how many total files are in that folder, or how many of those total files are Excel files. With an array doing the job, you won't need any worksheet cells to store the filenames. Instead, you can programmatically compile into memory the count of Excel files, and the individual filenames too, all of which you can retrieve later in your macro if need be.

The previous arrays of movie titles are an example of one-dimensional arrays. In the macro named `FavoriteMoviesRange`, the five movies were listed in range A1:A5. VBA regards this as a one-dimensional array because the array elements stand by themselves in a table that is five rows deep and one column wide.

Many arrays you deal with will have more than one dimension. Figure 10-1 expands on this list of classic movies by adding a second column that lists the year each movie was released. This table is composed of five rows and two columns. A two-dimensional String array can be created by associating the movie title elements with their respective year of release elements.

	A	B	C
1	Gone With The Wind	1939	
2	Casablanca	1942	
3	Citizen Kane	1941	
4	Sunset Boulevard	1950	
5	Modern Times	1936	
6			

FIGURE 10-1

The first item of business is to declare a String type variable for the array. The size of the array is specified with the variable, to include the span of rows and columns that make up the array. For example, with five rows and two columns, a variable named `Classics` is declared with the statement `Dim Classics(1 To 5, 1 To 2) As String`. The following macro loops through rows 1 to 5 in column A and rows 1 to 5 in column B. Each value in the array is stored in memory with two Integer type variables for collecting row and column data. Based on Figure 10-1, the Message Box will return 1941 because `Classics(3, 2)` returns the string value of the element that occupies the location of the array's third row and second column.

```
Sub TwoDimensionalArray()

Dim Classics(1 To 5, 1 To 2) As String
Dim intRow As Integer, intColumn As Integer

For intRow = 1 To 5
For intColumn = 1 To 2
Classics(intRow, intColumn) = Cells(intRow, intColumn).Value
Next intColumn
Next intRow

MsgBox Classics(3, 2)

End Sub
```

Declaring Arrays

You declare an array the same way you typically declare variables. The variable declaration starts with the `Dim` statement, followed by the array name and the data type. The array name ends with a pair of parentheses to indicate that it's an array, with the count of elements, if known, placed inside the parentheses.

For example, the following statement declares an array named `myDays`, which will be populated with all seven days of the week. Notice the data type is String, because weekday names are text values, such as "Sunday," Monday," and so on.

```
Dim myDays(6) As String
```

You can also declare arrays using the `Public`, `Private`, and `Static` keywords, just as you can with other variables, with the same results in terms of scope and visibility.

To declare an array as `Public`, place a statement like this at the top of your module:

```
Public MyArray(1) As String
```

With the `Public` declaration, you can share an array across procedures. For example, if you run either of the following two macros, the array elements of Hello and Goodbye will be displayed in a Message Box.

```
Sub PublicArrayExample()

'Fill the array MyArray with values.
MyArray(0) = "Hello"
MyArray(1) = "Goodbye"


'Run the TestPublicArrayExample macro to display MyArray.
Run "TestPublicArrayExample"

End Sub
Sub TestPublicArrayExample()
'Display the values contained in the array MyArray.
Dim i As Integer
For i = 0 To UBound(MyArray, 1)
MsgBox MyArray(i)
Next i
End Sub
```

> *You may have noticed the UBound statement in the preceding macro. You will learn more about upper and lower boundaries in the upcoming section named Boundaries in Arrays.*

A `Static` array is an array that is sized in the declaration statement. For example, the following declaration statement declares an Integer array that has 11 rows and 11 columns:

```
Dim MyArray(10, 10) as Integer
```

THE OPTION BASE STATEMENT

When learning arrays, it's common for some head-scratching and confusion to accompany the concept of zero-based numbering. In the declaration statement Dim myDays(6) As String, you might wonder why the array shows the number 6 in parentheses, when there are seven days in a week.

In zero-based numbering, the first element of any array is represented by the default number of 0. The second element is represented by the number 1, and so on. That is why an array of seven weekday elements is represented by the number 6 in the statement Dim myDays(6) As String.

VBA does provide a way for specifying that the first element of the array be number 1, which is more intuitive for most people. You can do this by placing the statement Option Base 1 at the top of the module. Personally, I have never specified Option Base 1 because I've become accustomed to VBA's default settings.

Here's a visual look at zero-based numbering in action. Figure 10-2 shows five text elements that you might manually place into an array macro.

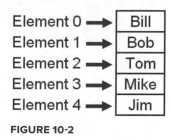

FIGURE 10-2

Note the element index numbers starting with the default of 0. In the following macro, the array named FamilyArray is populated in the order of the pictured elements. Further, a variable named FamilyMember is assigned the element 2 item, which is actually the third item in the list of names because the list starts at number 0. Therefore, when the MsgBox FamilyMember command is executed, Tom will be displayed in the Message Box because Tom occupies the element 2 position in the array named FamilyArray.

```
Sub ArrayTest()
Dim FamilyArray() As Variant
Dim FamilyMember As String
FamilyArray = Array("Bill", "Bob", "Tom", "Mike", "Jim")
FamilyMember = FamilyArray(2)
MsgBox FamilyMember
End Sub
```

To test this concept a bit further, enter the statement Option Base 1 at the very top of the module. When you run the ArrayTest macro again, you'll see that FamilyArray(2) returns Bob, because the array elements were counted starting at base number 1.

> It's a fair question to ask why VBA uses zero-based numbering in the first place. It turns out, most other programming languages use zero-based numbering for their arrays because of the way arrays are stored in memory. The topic is rather complicated, but in simple English, the subscript (the numbers in the parentheses following the array's variable name) refers to an offset position in memory from the array's starting position. Therefore, the first element has a starting position of 1, but the array's subscript is translated into the offset memory address of 0. The second element is offset at 1, and so on.

BOUNDARIES IN ARRAYS

Arrays have two boundaries: a lower boundary, which is the position of the first data element, and an upper boundary representing the count of elements in the array. VBA keeps track of both boundaries' values automatically, with the LBound and UBound functions.

> When you declare an array, you can specify only the upper index boundary. In the example, you have Dim myDays(6) As String *but it could have been* written as Dim myDays(0 to 6) As String. *The "0 to" does not need to be present because the lower index boundary is always assumed to be 0 (or 1 if* Option Base 1 *has been stated at the top of the module). Under the default setting of* Option Base 0, *the number you include in the declaration (which was 6 in this example) is the upper index number of the array, not the actual number of elements.*

Here is an example to demonstrate the LBound and UBound functions in practice. In this example, you fill an array with a number of cell addresses, and the macro enters the word Hello in that array of cell ranges.

```
Sub ArraySheets()

'Declare your variables
Dim sheetName As Variant, i As Integer, TargetCell as Variant

'Populate the array yourself with the known worksheet names.
TargetCell = Array("A1", "B5", "B7", "C1", "C12", "D13", "A12")

'Loop from the lower boundary (the first array element)
'to the upper boundary (last element) of your sheetName array.
For i = LBound(TargetCell) To UBound(TargetCell)

Range(TargetCell(i)).Value = "Hello"

'Continue looping through the array elements to completion.
Next i

'End the macro.

End Sub
```

DECLARING ARRAYS WITH FIXED ELEMENTS

Early in this lesson you saw this array declaration:

```
Dim myDays(6) As String
```

The ultimate objective of that declaration was to build an array containing the seven days of the week, and to transfer that list into range A1:A7, as depicted in Figure 10-3.

The macro to do that could look like the following one named `ArrayWeekdays`. Characteristics of a fixed array include a set of elements that remain constant, such as days of the week, where there will always be seven and their names will never change. The WEEKDAY function returns an integer from 1 to 7 that represents a day of the week. For example, 1 represents Sunday, 2 represents Monday, and so on. If you enter the function =WEEKDAY(5) in a cell, and custom format the cell as DDDD, the cell will display Thursday.

	A	B	C
1	Sunday		
2	Monday		
3	Tuesday		
4	Wednesday		
5	Thursday		
6	Friday		
7	Saturday		
8			
9			
10			

FIGURE 10-3

The comments in the code explain what is happening, and why:

```
Sub ArrayWeekdays()

'Declare the array variable for seven elements (from 0 to 6).
Dim myDays(6) As String

'Declare an Integer type variable to handle the seven indexed elements.
Dim intDay As Integer

'Start to loop through each array element starting at the default 0 lower boundary.
For intDay = 0 To 6

'For each array element, define the myDays String variable
'with its corresponding day of the week.
'There is no such thing as "Weekday 0", because Excel's Weekday function
'is numbered from 1 to 7,so the "+ 1" notation adds 1 to the intDays Integer
'variable which started at the lower bound of 0.
myDays(intDay) = Format(Weekday(intDay + 1), "DDDD")

'Cells in range A1:A7 are populated in turn with the weekday.
Range("A" & intDay + 1).Value = myDays(intDay)

'The loop is continued through to conclusion.
Next intDay

'End of the macro.

End Sub
```

DECLARING DYNAMIC ARRAYS WITH REDIM AND PRESERVE

Unlike an array with a known fixed set of elements, some arrays are built programmatically during the macro. These arrays are called "dynamic." Earlier you read about populating an array with the count of Excel workbook files that exist in a folder. In that case you'd have a "dynamic" array because the file count is subject to change; you would not know ahead of time what the array's size will be. With a dynamic array, you can create an array that is as large or as small as you need to make it.

To attack the problem of an unknown count of elements, you can change the size of an array on the fly with a pair of keywords called ReDim and Preserve. The ReDim statement is short for redimension, a fancy term for resizing the array. When ReDim is used by itself to place an element in the array, it releases whatever data was in the array at the time, and simply adds the element to a new empty array.

The Preserve statement is necessary to keep (preserve) the data that was in the array, and have the incoming element be added to the existing data. In VBA terms, ReDim Preserve raises the array's upper boundary, while keeping the array elements you've accumulated.

The following macro named SelectedWorksheets demonstrates ReDim Preserve in action. The purpose of the array in this example is to collect the names of all worksheets that are concurrently selected, such as when you press the Ctrl key and select a few worksheet tabs.

The comments in the code explain what each line of code is doing, so you can get a feel for how to populate a dynamic array and display its elements (the worksheet names) in a Message Box.

```
Sub SelectedWorksheets()
'Declare the array variable for an unknown count of elements.
Dim WhatSelected() As Variant

'Declare a variable for the Worksheet data type.
Dim wks As Worksheet

'Declare an Integer variable to handle the unknown count of selected worksheets.
Dim intSheet As Integer

'Start to loop through each selected worksheet.
For Each wks In ActiveWindow.SelectedSheets

'An index array element is assigned to each selected worksheet.
intSheet = intSheet + 1

'This macro is building an array as each selected worksheet is encountered.
'The Redim statement adds the newest selected worksheet to the growing array.
'The Preserve statement keeps (preserves) the existing array data,
'allowing the array to be resized with the addition of the next element.
ReDim Preserve WhatSelected(intSheet)

'The corresponding worksheet's tab name is identified with each selected sheet,
'and placed in the "WhatSelected" array for later retrieval.
WhatSelected(intSheet) = wks.Name

'The loop is continued to completion.
Next wks

'Looping through each element in the "WhatSelected" array that was just built,
'a message box displays the name of each corresponding selected worksheet.
For intSheet = 1 To UBound(WhatSelected)
MsgBox WhatSelected(intSheet)
Next intSheet

'End of the macro.

End Sub
```

TRY IT

In this lesson you verify whether a certain string element is part of an array.

You test whether a certain string element is in an array. At the end of the macro, you'll show a Message Box to confirm that the string element either was or was not found to exist in the array.

Like the example earlier in this lesson, say you have this list of names:

> Bill
>
> Bob
>
> Tom
>
> Mike
>
> Jim

Now, say you want to test whether a certain string element is in that array, which in this example you will enter into a worksheet cell. Enter a good-looking name like **Tom** into cell A1 of Sheet1. Put the list of names in an array, and test to see whether "Tom" is among the elements in that list.

Lesson Requirements

To get the sample database files you can download Lesson 10 from the book's website at www.wrox.com.

Step-by-Step

1. Open Excel and add a new workbook.

2. Press Alt+F11 to get into the Visual Basic Editor.

3. From the VBE menu, click Insert ⇨ Module.

4. In the new module, type the name of your macro as

   ```
   Sub TestArray
   ```

5. Press the Enter key, which will cause Excel to place a set of parentheses after the `TestArray` macro name, and also will create the `End Sub` statement. Your macro so far will look like this:

   ```
   Sub TestArray()

   End Sub
   ```

6. For the first line of code, establish that Sheet2 is VeryHidden, as an example to demonstrate the result of an element being found, or not found, in an array. If the element is found, Sheet2 will be unhidden.

   ```
   Worksheets("Sheet2").Visible = xlSheetVeryHidden
   ```

7. For the second line of code, declare a variable for the array of names you'll be creating, and name the variable `myArray`. For the next line of code, assign the variable name to the array. In this case, you know what the list of names contains so you can build the array yourself by simply entering the individual names inside the parentheses. The two lines of code will look like this:

```
Dim myArray As Variant
myArray = Array("Bill", "Bob", "Tom", "Mike", "Jim")
```

8. The next two lines of code would show the String type variable to represent the string element you are attempting to verify, and then code to assign the string to that variable. The String variable, named `strVerify`, refers to a name you would enter into cell A1 of Sheet1 to test the macro. For example:

```
Dim strVerify as String
strVerify = Worksheets("Sheet1").Range("A1").Value
```

9. You will need to declare two more variables. One of these variables will be an Integer type variable, which will help you loop through each of the five elements in the array. The other variable is a Boolean data type, which will help to characterize as True or False that the string in cell A1 of Sheet1 is among the elements in the array.

```
Dim i as Integer, blnVerify as Boolean
```

10. Enter **Tom** in cell A1 of Sheet1.

11. Now, to see whether "Tom"exists in the array, loop through each element and compare it to the string variable. If there is a match, exit the loop and alert the user by unhiding Sheet2. If the String variable is not found, let the user know that as well, and keep Sheet2 hidden.

```
For i = LBound(myArray) To UBound(myArray)
If strVerify = myArray(i) Then
blnVerify = True
MsgBox "Yes! " & myArray(i) & " is in the array!", , "Verified"
Worksheets("Sheet2").Visible = xlSheetVisible
Exit For
End IfNext i

If blnVerify = False Then _
MsgBox strVerify & " is not in the array.", , "No such animal."
```

12. Putting it all together, the macro would look like this:

```
Sub TestArray ()

'Establish that Sheet2 is VeryHidden.
Worksheets("Sheet2").Visible = xlSheetVeryHidden

'Declare and assign a Variant type variable for the array.
Dim myArray As Variant
myArray = Array("Bill", "Bob", "Tom", "Mike", "Jim")
```

```
'Declare and assign a String type variable for the element being evaluated.
Dim strVerify as String
strVerify = Worksheets("Sheet1").Range("A1").Value

'Declare the Integer and Boolean data type variables.
Dim i as Integer, blnVerify as Boolean

'Loop through each element starting with the first one (LBound).
'and continue as necessary through to the last element (UBound).
'If "Tom" is found, exit the loop and alert the user.
'If "Tom" is not found, alert the user of that as well.

For i = LBound(myArray) To UBound(myArray)
If strVerify = myArray(i) Then
blnVerify = True
MsgBox "Yes! " & myArray(i) & " is in the array!", , "Verified"
Worksheets("Sheet2").Visible = xlSheetVisible
Exit For
End If
Next i

If blnVerify = False Then _
MsgBox strVerify & " is not in the array.", , "No such animal."

'End the macro.
End Sub
```

 Please select Lesson 10 on the DVD to view the video that accompanies this lesson.

11

Automating Procedures with Worksheet Events

For the most part, the macros you have seen in this book have been run by pressing a set of shortcut keys, or by going to the Macro dialog box, selecting the macro name, and clicking the Run button. You can take several other actions to run a macro, as you learn in future lessons. The common theme of all these actions is that you have to manually *do something*, whatever it may be, to run a macro.

The question becomes, can a VBA procedure simply know on its own when to run itself, and then just go ahead and do so automatically, without you needing to "do something" to make it run? The answer is yes, and it leads to the subject of event programming, which can greatly enhance the customization and control of your workbooks.

> *So far, this book has used the term "macro" to refer to VBA subroutines. When referring to event code, the term "procedure" is used to differentiate it from macro code.*

WHAT IS AN "EVENT"?

In the Excel object model, an *event* is something that happens to an object, and is recognized by the computer so an appropriate action can be taken. Recall that the Excel application is made up of objects, such as workbooks, worksheets, cells, charts, pivot tables, and so on. Even the entire Excel application is an object.

Virtually everything you do in Excel is in some way invoking an event upon an object. A few examples of events are as follows:

➤ Double-clicking a cell

➤ Adding a worksheet

> ➤ Activating a worksheet

> ➤ Changing a cell value

> ➤ Clicking a hyperlink

> ➤ Right-clicking a cell

> ➤ Calculating a formula

With VBA's event programming capabilities, you can tap into Excel's recognition of when an event occurs and what kind of event it is. This allows you to write VBA code that will execute based on whichever event(s) occur that you want to monitor. This book primarily concentrates on events at two levels:

> ➤ *Worksheet-level events*, which are introduced in this lesson.

> ➤ *Workbook-level events*, which are introduced in the next lesson.

WORKSHEET EVENTS — AN OVERVIEW

Worksheet-level events occur for a particular worksheet. As you might imagine, events occur when something happens to a worksheet, such as entry of new data into a cell, or a formula being calculated, or the worksheet being activated or deactivated. Event code that is associated with any particular worksheet has no direct effect on events that take place on other worksheets in that or any other workbook.

Where Does the Worksheet Event Code Go?

You've become familiar with the concept of modules as being containers for the macros that you or the Macro Recorder creates. You'll be pleased to know that each worksheet already comes with its own built-in module, so you never need to create a module for any worksheet- or workbook-level procedure code.

Worksheet event code always goes into the module of the worksheet for which you are monitoring the event(s). Regardless of the Excel version you are using, the quickest and easiest way to go straight to a worksheet's module is to right-click its sheet tab, and select View Code, as shown in Figure 11-1.

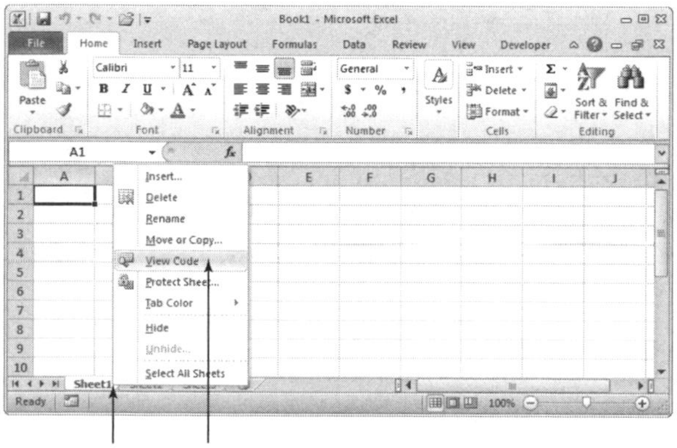

To access the worksheet's module quickly,
right-click the sheet tab and select View Code.

FIGURE 11-1

Immediately after you select View Code, you are taken directly into the Visual Basic Editor, as shown in Figure 11-2. Your mouse cursor will be blinking in the worksheet module's Code window, ready for you to start entering your event procedure code.

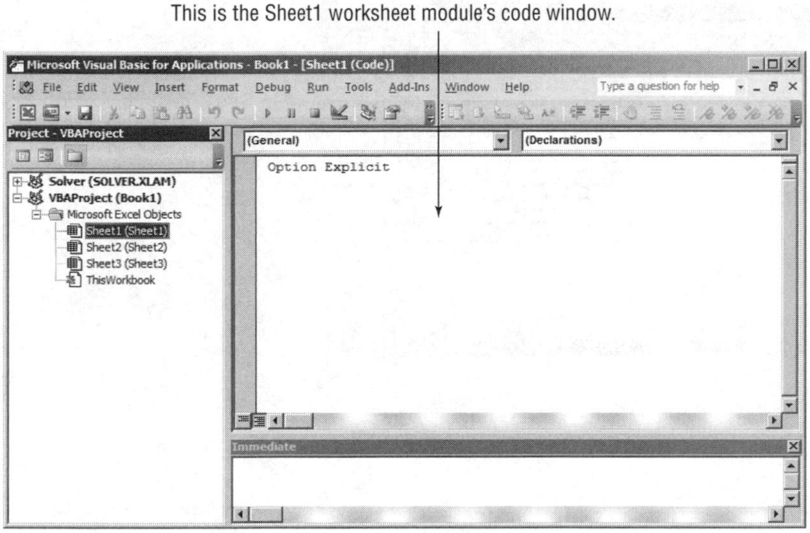

This is the Sheet1 worksheet module's code window.

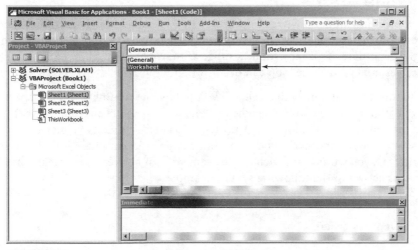

FIGURE 11-2

Immediately above the Code window are two fields with drop-down arrows. The field on the left is the Object field, and when you click its drop-down arrow, you would select the Worksheet object item, as shown in Figure 11-3.

FIGURE 11-3

The field above the worksheet module's Code window, and to the right of the Object field, is the Procedure field. Click the Procedure field's drop-down arrow for a list of the worksheet-level events available to you, as shown in Figure 11-4.

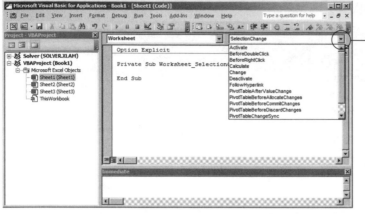

FIGURE 11-4

 When you select an event from the Procedure field's drop-down list, VBA performs the valuable service of entering the procedure statement, with all its argument parameters and an associated End Sub *statement, right there in the worksheet module for you.*

Enabling and Disabling Events

The Excel Application object has an EnableEvents property that is enabled by default. In some cases you will need to temporarily disable events in your event procedure code, and then re-enable them before the end of the procedure. This may sound strange at first, but the reason is that some events can trigger themselves, and an infinite loop can occur if that happens.

For example, if you are monitoring data entry in a cell and you only want a number to be entered, but a non-numeric entry is attempted, you would use the Worksheet_Change event to undo that wrong entry by clearing the cell's contents. However, VBA regards a cell's contents being cleared as a Change event, which would trigger another round of the same Change event procedure that was already running. To avoid this, you would sandwich the relevant code in between statements that disable and enable events, as shown in the following syntax example.

```
Application.EnableEvents = False
'your relevant code
Application.EnableEvents = True
```

 Check out the Try It section at the end of this lesson — you will see two specific examples of disabling and enabling events there!

> *In the preceding syntax example, the* EnableEvents *property of the* Application *object was temporarily set to False with the statement*
>
> ```
> Application.EnableEvents = False
> ```
>
> *and then set back to True at the end of the macro with the statement*
>
> ```
> Application.EnableEvents = True
> ```
>
> *Keep in mind that the* Application *object covers all of Excel. For example, while a macro is running with the* EnableEvents *property of the* Application *object set to False,* EnableEvents *is disabled for all open workbooks in that instance of Excel, not just for the workbook where the VBA code is being executed. Whatever properties of the* Application *object you temporarily change, remember to reset those properties back to their original settings before you exit your macro or procedure.*

EXAMPLES OF COMMON WORKSHEET EVENTS

At the worksheet level, Excel version 2003 has nine events, and five more than that (associated with pivot tables) for a total of 14 in versions 2007 and 2010. The most commonly used worksheet events are the nine that are common to all versions of Excel from 2000 to 2010:

➤ Worksheet_Change

➤ Worksheet_SelectionChange

➤ Worksheet_BeforeDoubleClick

➤ Worksheet_BeforeRightClick

➤ Worksheet_FollowHyperlink

➤ Worksheet_Activate

➤ Worksheet_Deactivate

➤ Worksheet_Calculate

➤ Worksheet_PivotTableUpdate

Worksheet_Change Event

The Worksheet_Change event occurs when cells on the worksheet are changed by the user or by an external link, such as a new value being entered into a cell, or the cell's value being deleted. The following example places the current date in column C next to a changed cell in column B:

```
Private Sub Worksheet_Change(ByVal Target As Range)
If Target.Column <> 2 Then Exit Sub
Target.Offset(0, 1).Value = Format(VBA.Date, "MM/DD/YYYY")
End Sub
```

> *The* Worksheet_Change *event is* not *triggered by a calculation change, such as a formula returning a different value. Use the* Worksheet_Calculate *event to capture the changes to values in cells that contain formulas.*

Worksheet_SelectionChange Event

The Worksheet_SelectionChange event occurs when a cell is selected. The following code highlights the active cell with a yellow color every time a different cell is selected:

```
Private Sub Worksheet_SelectionChange(ByVal Target As Range)
Cells.Interior.ColorIndex = 0
Target.Interior.Color = vbYellow
End Sub
```

> *A word to the wise! This kind of code is fun and has its usefulness, but with each change in cell selection, the Undo stack will be eliminated, essentially negating the Undo feature.*

Worksheet_BeforeDoubleClick Event

The Worksheet_BeforeDoubleClick event is triggered by double-clicking a worksheet cell. The Cancel argument is optional and halts the ability to go into Edit mode for that cell from a double-click.

In this example, if you double-click a cell in range A1:C8, and the cell already contains a number or is empty, the numeric value of that cell increases by 1. All other cells in the worksheet are unaffected.

```
Private Sub Worksheet_BeforeDoubleClick(ByVal Target As Range, _
Cancel As Boolean)
If Intersect(Target, Range("A1:C8")) Is Nothing Then Exit Sub
If IsNumeric(Target.Value) = True Then
Cancel = True
Target.Value = Target.Value + 1
End If
End Sub
```

> *This event does not occur if you double-click the fill handle.*

Worksheet_BeforeRightClick Event

The `Worksheet_BeforeRightClick` event occurs when you right-click a worksheet cell. The optional `Cancel` argument halts the right-click pop-up menu from appearing. In the following example, when you right-click a cell in column E, the current date and time are entered into that cell, and column E's width is autofitted:

```
Private Sub Worksheet_BeforeRightClick(ByVal Target As Range, _
Cancel As Boolean)
If Target.Column <> 5 Then Exit Sub
Cancel = True
Target.Value = Format(VBA.Now, "MMM DD, YYYY, hh:mm AM/PM")
Columns(Target.Column).AutoFit
End Sub
```

Worksheet_FollowHyperlink Event

The `Worksheet_FollowHyperlink` event occurs when you click any hyperlink on the worksheet. You learn more about command buttons in later lessons, but as a sneak preview, Figure 11-5 shows a command button embedded onto a worksheet. The button is captioned with a website address but the caption itself is plain text, not actually a hyperlink. With the following code, when you click the command button, you are taken to that caption's website.

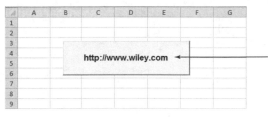

FIGURE 11-5

```
Private Sub CommandButton1_Click()
CommandButton1.Parent.Parent.FollowHyperlink CommandButton1.Caption
End Sub
```

> The `Worksheet_FollowHyperlink` *event is available as a worksheet-level event, but in reality, it is more of a function of the entire workbook. Notice the first three items in the statement:* `CommandButton1.Parent.Parent.` *The parent of the* `CommandButton` *is the worksheet upon which it resides, and the parent of that worksheet is the workbook itself.*

Worksheet_Activate Event

The `Worksheet_Activate` event occurs when you go to a particular worksheet, typically by clicking the worksheet's tab, although any of the other methods of arriving at a worksheet will trigger the `Worksheet_Activate` event. Suppose you have a worksheet with one or more pivot tables on it, and every time you go to that worksheet, you want to know that the pivot tables are all refreshed and up to date. The following event code accomplishes that task:

```
Private Sub Worksheet_Activate()
Dim intCounter As Integer
For intCounter = 1 To ActiveSheet.PivotTables.Count
ActiveSheet.PivotTables(intCounter).PivotCache.Refresh
Next intCounter
End Sub
```

Worksheet_Deactivate Event

The Worksheet_Deactivate event occurs when you activate a different worksheet than the one you were on. Suppose there is a particular cell in a worksheet that you strongly prefer to have some value entered into before the user exits that worksheet. The following Worksheet_Deactivate event code checks to see if cell A1 contains a value. If it does not, a Message Box alerts the users as a reminder of that fact when they deactivate the worksheet.

```
Private Sub Worksheet_Deactivate()
If Len(Me.Range("A1").Value) = 0 Then _
MsgBox "FYI and reminder: you did not enter a value in cell A1" & vbCrLf & _
"in the worksheet named " & Me.Name & ".", _
vbExclamation, _
"Cell A1 should have some value in it!"
End Sub
```

Worksheet_Calculate Event

The Worksheet_Calculate event occurs when the worksheet is recalculated. Suppose you have a budget model and you want to monitor the *bottom-line* number for profit and loss, which is derived by a formula in cell Z135. You could conditionally format the cell when its returned value is outside an acceptable range, but chances are no one will see the formatting due to the location of the cell.

To give the budget model's *bottom-line* number a boost in awareness, utilize the Worksheet_Calculate event to make a Message Box pop up as a warning when the number in cell Z135 becomes lower than $1,000. Also, to make it fun, have a congratulatory message appear if the profit number is greater than or equal to $5,000.

```
Private Sub Worksheet_Calculate()
If Range("Z135").Value < 1000 Then
MsgBox "Profits are too low!!", vbExclamation, "Warning!!"
ElseIf Range("Z135").Value >= 5000 Then
MsgBox "Profits are TERRIFIC!!", vbExclamation, "Wow, good news!!"
End If
End Sub
```

Worksheet_PivotTableUpdate Event

The `Worksheet_PivotTableUpdate` event occurs after a pivot table is updated on a worksheet, such as after a refresh. The following procedure is a simple example of the syntax for this event:

```
Private Sub Worksheet_PivotTableUpdate(ByVal Target As PivotTable)
MsgBox "The pivot table on this worksheet was just updated.", vbInformation, "FYI"
End Sub
```

TRY IT

In this lesson, you write a `Worksheet_Change` event that allows you to sum numbers as they are entered into the same cell. You write a `Worksheet_Change` event for your worksheet, where any cell in column A except for cell A1 will accept a number you enter, add it to whatever number was already in that cell, and display the resulting sum. For example, if cell A9 currently holds the number 2 and you enter the number 3 in that cell, the resulting value of cell A9 will be 5.

Lesson Requirements

To get the sample database files you can download Lesson 11 from the book's website at www.wrox.com.

Step-by-Step

1. Open a new workbook, right-click the Sheet1 tab, and select View Code.

2. Your cursor will be blinking in the Sheet1 worksheet module. Directly above that, click the down arrow belonging to the Object list, and select Worksheet. This will produce the following default lines of code in your worksheet module:

    ```
    Private Sub Worksheet_SelectionChange(ByVal Target As Range)

    End Sub
    ```

3. It is really the `Change` event you are interested in composing, so take one of two actions: either manually edit the `Private Sub Worksheet_SelectionChange(ByVal Target As Range)` statement by deleting the word `Selection`, or click the down arrow above the module for the Procedures list, select the `Change` item, and delete the default `Private Sub Worksheet_SelectionChange(ByVal Target As Range)` statement and its accompanying `End Sub` statement. At this point, the only procedure code you will see in your worksheet module is this:

    ```
    Private Sub Worksheet_Change(ByVal Target As Range)

    End Sub
    ```

4. The event code will monitor column A but you will want the ability to enter some kind of header label into cell A1. Begin the procedure by writing a line of code to exclude cell A1 from the `Change` event:

```
If Target.Address = "$A$1" Then Exit Sub
```

5. Your next consideration is to limit the `Change` event to column A, to avoid imposing the `Change` event onto the entire worksheet. Also, you will want the `Change` event to be in effect for only one cell at a time in column A. One statement can handle both considerations:

```
If Target.Column <> 1 Or Target.Cells.Count > 1 Then Exit Sub
```

Note that column A is the first (leftmost) column in the worksheet grid and is easily referred to in VBA as `Columns(1)`.

6. Pressing the Delete key triggers the `Change` event. You might want to delete a cell's contents and start entering a new set of numbers in an empty cell, so allow yourself the luxury of exiting the `Change` event if the Delete key is pressed:

```
If IsEmpty(Target) Then Exit Sub
```

7. Even though a number is supposed to be entered into column A, never assume that it will always happen that way, because people make mistakes. Provide for the attempt at a non-numeric entry and disallow it:

```
If IsNumeric(Target.Value) = False Then
```

8. Disable events because you are about to undo the non-numeric value; the `Undo` command also triggers the `Change` event:

```
Application.EnableEvents = False
```

9. Execute the `Undo` action so the non-numeric entry is deleted:

```
Application.Undo
```

10. Enable events again:

```
Application.EnableEvents = True
```

11. Remind the user with a Message Box that only numbers are allowed, and exit the `Change` event procedure with the `Exit Sub` statement:

```
MsgBox "You entered a non-numeric value.", _
vbExclamation, _
"Please: numbers only in column A!"
Exit Sub
End If
```

12. Now that all the reasonable safeguards have been met, declare two `Double` type variables: one named `OldVal` for the numeric value that was in the cell before it was changed, and the other variable named `NewVal` for the numeric value that was just entered that triggered this `Change` event:

```
Dim OldVal As Double, NewVal As Double
```

13. Define the `NewVal` variable first, because it is the number that was just entered into the cell:

```
NewVal = Target.Value
```

14. Undo the entry in order to display the old (preceding) value. Again, this requires that you disable events in order not to re-trigger the `Change` event while you are already in a `Change` event:

```
Application.EnableEvents = False
```

15. Execute `Undo` so the previous value is reestablished:

```
Application.Undo
```

16. Define the `OldVal` variable, which is possible to do now that the previous value has been restored:

```
OldVal = Target.Value
```

17. Programmatically enter into the cell the sum of the previous value, plus the new last-entered value, by referring to those two variables in an arithmetic equation just as you would if they were numbers:

```
Target.Value = OldVal + NewVal
```

18. Enable events now that all the changes to the cell have been made:

```
Application.EnableEvents = True
```

19. When completed, the entire procedure will look like this, with comments that have been added to explain each step:

```
Private Sub Worksheet_Change(ByVal Target As Range)

'Allow for a header label to be placed in cell A1.
If Target.Address = "$A$1" Then Exit Sub
'Only apply this effect to column A (column 1 in VBA-Speak).
'At the same time, only allow one cell at a time to be changed.
If Target.Column <> 1 Or Target.Cells.Count > 1 Then Exit Sub
'Pressing the Delete key triggers the Change event.
'You might want to delete the cell's contents and start with
'an empty cell, so exit the Change event if the Delete key is pressed.
If IsEmpty(Target) Then Exit Sub

'Even though a number is *supposed* to be entered into column A,
```

```
'never assume that will always happen because users do make mistakes.
'Provide for the attempt at a non-numeric entry and disallow it.
If IsNumeric(Target.Value) = False Then
'Disable events because you are about to undo the non-numeric value,
'and Undo also triggers the Change event.
Application.EnableEvents = False
'Execute the Undo so the non-numeric entry is deleted.
Application.Undo
'Enable events again.
Application.EnableEvents = True
'Remind the user with a Message Box that only numbers are allowed,
'and exit the Change event procedure with the Exit Sub statement.
MsgBox "You entered a non-numeric value.", _
vbExclamation, _
"Please: numbers only in column A!"
Exit Sub
End If


'Now that all the reasonable safeguards have been met,
'Declare two Double type variables:
'one named OldVal for the numeric value that was in the cell
'before it got changed,
'and the other variable named NewVal for the numeric value
'that was just entered that triggered this Change event.
Dim OldVal As Double, NewVal As Double
'Define the NewVal variable first, as it is the number that
'was just entered into the cell.
NewVal = Target.Value
'Undo the entry in order to display the old (preceding) value.
'Again, this requires that you disable events in order to not
're-trigger the Change event while you are already in a Change event.
Application.EnableEvents = False
'Execute Undo so the previous value is re-established.
Application.Undo
'Define the OldVal variable which is possible to do now that
'the previous value has been restored.
OldVal = Target.Value
'Programmatically enter into the cell the sum of the old previous value,
'plus the new last-entered value, by referring to those two variables
'in an arithmetic equation just as you would if they were numbers.
Target.Value = OldVal + NewVal
'Enable events now that all the changes to the cell have been made.
Application.EnableEvents = True

End Sub
```

20. Press Alt+Q to return to the worksheet. Test the code by entering a series of numbers in any single cell in column A other than cell A1.

Please select Lesson 11 on the DVD to view the video that accompanies this lesson.

12

Automating Procedures with Workbook Events

In Lesson 11, you learned about worksheet-level events and how they are triggered by actions relating to individual worksheets. Workbooks themselves can also recognize and respond to a number of events that take place at the workbook level. This lesson describes how you can further customize your workbooks with VBA procedures for the most commonly used workbook events.

WORKBOOK EVENTS — AN OVERVIEW

Workbook events occur within a particular workbook. Many workbook events occur because something happened to an object in the workbook, such as a worksheet — any worksheet — that was activated, or a cell — any cell — that was changed. Other workbook events occur because the workbook was imposed upon to do something, such as to open or close, or to be saved or printed.

Unless the VBA code itself purposely refers to other workbooks, event procedures at the workbook level affect only the workbook within which the code resides.

Where Does the Workbook Event Code Go?

You saw in Lesson 11 that each individual worksheet has its own module. Workbooks are similar to worksheets in this respect, because a workbook is also an Excel object, and has its own module already present and accounted for when the workbook is created.

> *Workbook-level event code always goes into the workbook module. You never need to create a workbook module or a worksheet module; Excel creates those modules automatically with every new workbook. If a workbook-level event procedure is not in the workbook module (same as if a worksheet-level event procedure is not in a worksheet module), VBA will not be able to execute the event code.*

To arrive at the Code window for your workbook's module, with whatever version of Excel you are using, you can press Alt+F11 to get into the Visual Basic Editor. If you are using a version of Excel prior to 2007, such as version 2003, you can also access the workbook module quickly by right-clicking the Excel workbook icon near the top-left corner of the workbook window, and selecting View Code. This option is shown in Figure 12-1.

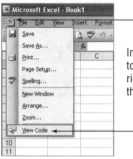

In Excel versions prior to 2007, to access the workbook module quickly, right-click the workbook icon to the left of the File menu item, and select View Code.

FIGURE 12-1

In the VBE, if you do not see the Project Explorer window, go ahead and make it visible by pressing Ctrl+R. In the Project Explorer, find your workbook name; it will be in bold font, with the text *VBAProject (YourWorkbookName.xlsm)*. Directly below that will be a yellow folder named Microsoft Excel Objects. When that folder is expanded, the last item at the bottom of the list is the workbook object, identified by its default name of `ThisWorkbook`.

As shown in Figure 12-2, to get into the Code window of the workbook module, either double-click the `ThisWorkbook` object, or right-click it and select View Code. As soon as you do that, your mouse cursor will be blinking in the workbook module's Code window, ready for you to start entering your workbook-level event procedure code.

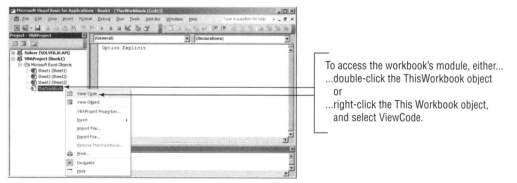

To access the workbook's module, either...
...double-click the ThisWorkbook object
or
...right-click the This Workbook object, and select ViewCode.

FIGURE 12-2

Entering Workbook Event Code

Similar to the worksheet module Code window you saw in Lesson 11, two fields with drop-down arrows are located above the workbook module's Code window. The field on the left is the Object field, and when you click its drop-down arrow, you select the Workbook object item, as shown in Figure 12-3.

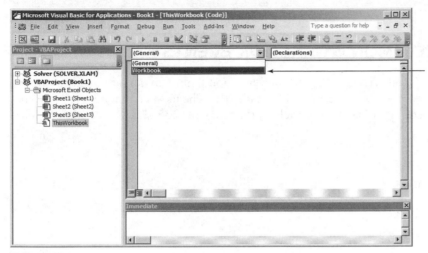

FIGURE 12-3

The field above the workbook module's Code window, and to the right of the Object field, is the Procedure field. Click the Procedure field's drop-down arrow for a list of the workbook-level events available to you, as shown in Figure 12-4.

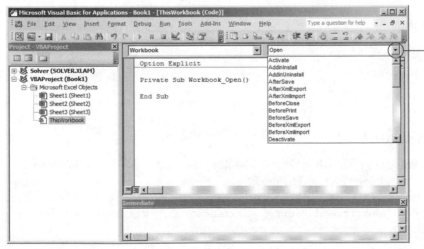

FIGURE 12-4

For convenience, just as with selecting worksheet-level event names, VBA will place the complete workbook-level event statement, with all its arguments and the accompanying End Sub *statement, when you select a workbook-level event name from the Procedure field.*

EXAMPLES OF COMMON WORKBOOK EVENTS

At the workbook level, Excel version 2003 has 28 events, and 8 more than that (mostly associated with pivot tables) for a total of 36 in versions 2007 and 2010. The most commonly used workbook-level events are listed here, with examples of each on the following pages:

➤ Workbook_Open

➤ Workbook_BeforeClose

➤ Workbook_Activate

➤ Workbook_Deactivate

➤ Workbook_SheetChange

➤ Workbook_SheetSelectionChange

➤ Workbook_SheetBeforeDoubleClick

➤ Workbook_SheetBeforeRightClick

➤ Workbook_SheetPivotTableUpdate

➤ Workbook_NewSheet

➤ Workbook_BeforePrint

➤ Workbook_SheetActivate

➤ Workbook_SheetDeactivate

➤ Workbook_BeforeSave

Workbook_Open Event

The Workbook_Open event is triggered when the workbook opens, and is among the most popular and useful of all workbook-level events. The Workbook_Open event is perfect for such tasks as informing users about important features of your workbook, or generating a running list of users who have accessed the workbook, or establishing a particular format setting that would be reset to its original state with the Workbook_BeforeClose event.

Perhaps the users of your workbook would benefit from the Analysis ToolPak add-ins to be installed for their Excel work. You can use the Workbook_Open event to verify if the Analysis ToolPak is installed, and if it isn't, ask the users of your workbook if they would like you to install the Analysis ToolPak add-ins for them.

This procedure uses a Yes/No message box to ask permission (which you should always do before changing another person's computer settings) to install add-ins, and if they click Yes, the Analysis ToolPak add-ins are installed:

```
Private Sub Workbook_Open()
If Not AddIns("Analysis ToolPak").Installed = True Then
Dim myConfirmation As Integer
myConfirmation = _
MsgBox("I notice the Analysis ToolPak add-ins are not installed." & vbCrLf & _
"Would you like me to install them for you now?", _
vbQuestion + vbYesNo, _
"Analysis ToolPak not installed")
If myConfirmation = vbNo Then
MsgBox "The ToolPak add-ins were not installed.", vbInformation, "You clicked No."
Else
AddIns("Analysis ToolPak").Installed = True
AddIns("Analysis ToolPak - VBA").Installed = True
MsgBox "The ToolPak add-ins have been installed.", _
vbInformation, _
"Thanks for confirming."
End If
End If
End Sub
```

Workbook_BeforeClose Event

The `Workbook_BeforeClose` event is triggered just before the workbook closes. This event is often used in conjunction with the `Workbook_Open` event, to set a workbook back to its original state if the `Workbook_Open` event temporarily changed the user's Excel settings.

The following example is one way to apply the `Workbook_BeforeClose` event's versatility. You can tell Excel to save your workbook automatically when you close it, to avoid Excel's prompt that asks you if you want to save your changes.

```
Private Sub Workbook_BeforeClose(Cancel As Boolean)
ThisWorkbook.Save
End Sub
```

Workbook_Activate Event

The `Workbook_Activate` event is triggered when the workbook is activated, such as when the workbook is opened, or when you switch between that workbook and other open workbooks. In this example, the following procedure maximizes the Excel window when you activate the workbook:

```
Private Sub Workbook_Activate()
ActiveWindow.WindowState = xlMaximized
End Sub
```

Workbook_Deactivate Event

The `Workbook_Deactivate` event is triggered when the workbook loses focus, such as when a different Excel workbook is activated or when the workbook is closed. The following example prompts a Message Box to alert you when the workbook is deactivated:

```
Private Sub Workbook_Deactivate()
MsgBox "You are leaving " & Me.Name & "!!", _
vbInformation, _
"Just so you know..."
End Sub
```

Workbook_SheetChange Event

The `Workbook_SheetChange` event is triggered when any cell's contents are changed on any worksheet in the workbook. If you would like to keep a log of the date, time, sheet name, and address of any cell that gets changed, this procedure accomplishes that, by listing information on a worksheet named "Log":

```
Private Sub Workbook_SheetChange(ByVal Sh As Object, ByVal Target As Range)
'The log sheet will hold the record of each sheet change,
'so do not monitor the Log sheet.
If Sh.Name = "Log" Then Exit Sub
'Declare a Long variable for the next available row on the Log sheet.
Dim NextRow As Long
'Assign the row number to the next empty row below that last row of data
'in column A.
NextRow = Worksheets("Log").Cells(Rows.Count, 1).End(xlUp).Row + 1
'In column A, enter the date of the changed cell.
Worksheets("Log").Cells(NextRow, 1).Value = VBA.Date
'In column B, enter the time of the changed cell.
Worksheets("Log").Cells(NextRow, 2).Value = VBA.Time
'In column C, enter the name of the worksheet holding the changed cell.
Worksheets("Log").Cells(NextRow, 3).Value = Sh.Name
'In column D, enter the address of the changed cell.
Worksheets("Log").Cells(NextRow, 4).Value = Target.Address
'Autofit the columns on the Log sheet, to make the information readable.
Worksheets("Log").Columns.AutoFit
End Sub
```

Workbook_SheetSelectionChange Event

The `Workbook_SheetSelectionChange` event is triggered when a different cell is selected on any worksheet in the workbook. In Lesson 11, you saw an example of the `Worksheet_SelectionChange` event whereby the active cell was continuously highlighted. If you are navigating through large ranges of data on your worksheets, such as budgets or financial reports, you might find it useful to visually identify more than just the active cell. The following procedure highlights the entire row and column at each new cell selection:

```
Private Sub Workbook_SheetSelectionChange(ByVal Sh As Object, _
ByVal Target As Range)
Dim myRow As Long, myColumn As Long
myRow = Target.Row
```

```
myColumn = Target.Column
Sh.Cells.Interior.ColorIndex = 0
Sh.Rows(myRow).Interior.Color = vbGreen
Sh.Columns(myColumn).Interior.Color = vbGreen
End Sub
```

Workbook_SheetBeforeDoubleClick Event

The `Workbook_SheetBeforeDoubleClick` event is triggered when a cell on any worksheet is about to be double-clicked. The double-click effect (usually getting into Edit mode) can be canceled with the `Cancel` parameter.

Suppose you have a workbook wherein column A of every worksheet is reserved for the purpose of placing checkmarks in cells. You do not want to deal with embedding possibly hundreds of real checkbox objects, so a checkmark-looking character in a cell would suffice.

You can utilize the `Workbook_DoubleClick` event that would apply only to column A for any worksheet. The following procedure toggles the effect of placing a checkmark in column A. If the cell is empty, a checkmark is entered, and if a checkmark is present when the cell is double-clicked again, the checkmark is removed. As you can see in the code, the "checkmark" is really a lowercase letter "a" formatted in Marlett font.

```
Private Sub Workbook_SheetBeforeDoubleClick(ByVal Sh As Object, _
ByVal Target As Range, Cancel As Boolean)
If Target.Column <> 1 Then Exit Sub
Cancel = True
Target.Font.Name = "Marlett"
Target.HorizontalAlignment = xlCenter
If IsEmpty(Target) = True Then
Target.Value = "a"
Else
Target.Clear
End If
End Sub
```

Workbook_SheetBeforeRightClick Event

The `Workbook_SheetBeforeRightClick` event is triggered when a cell on any worksheet is about to be right-clicked. The right-click effect of the pop-up menu can be canceled with the `Cancel` parameter.

Suppose you want to add a utility to your workbook that would allow you to quickly and easily insert a row above any cell you right-click. A Message Box could ask if you want to insert a row, and if you answer yes, a row would be inserted. The following procedure is an example of how that can be handled:

```
Private Sub Workbook_SheetBeforeRightClick(ByVal Sh As Object, _
ByVal Target As Range, Cancel As Boolean)
If MsgBox("Do you want to insert a row here?", _
vbQuestion + vbYesNo, _
"Please confirm...") = vbYes Then
Cancel = True
ActiveCell.EntireRow.Insert
End If
End Sub
```

Workbook_SheetPivotTableUpdate Event

The `SheetPivotTableUpdate` event monitors all worksheets in the workbook that hold pivot tables. This event code example informs you in real time which worksheet(s) with pivot tables have been updated. Note that the Message Box identifies the worksheet name(s) with the `Sh.Name` expression, which is done by referring to the `Object` argument of `Sh` from the event's set of parameters.

```
Private Sub Workbook_SheetPivotTableUpdate(ByVal Sh As Object, _
ByVal Target As PivotTable)
MsgBox "The pivot table on sheet " & Sh.Name & " was updated.", , "FYI"
End Sub
```

Workbook_NewSheet Event

The `Workbook_NewSheet` event is triggered when a new sheet is added to the workbook. To see this event in action, suppose you do not want to formally protect the workbook, but you want to disallow the addition of any new worksheets. This event procedure promptly deletes a new sheet as soon as it is added, with a message box informing the user that adding new sheets is not permitted:

```
Private Sub Workbook_NewSheet(ByVal Sh As Object)
Dim asn As String
asn = ActiveSheet.Name
Application.EnableEvents = False
Application.DisplayAlerts = False
Sheets(ActiveSheet.Name).Delete
MsgBox "New sheets are not allowed to be added.", vbCritical, "FYI"
Application.DisplayAlerts = True
Application.EnableEvents = True
End Sub
```

Workbook_BeforePrint Event

The `Workbook_BeforePrint` event is triggered before a user attempts to print any portion of the workbook. You can cancel the print job by setting the `Cancel` parameter to True. If you want to ensure that anything printed from that workbook will have the workbook's full name in the footer of every printed page, the following procedure accomplishes that:

```
Private Sub Workbook_BeforePrint(Cancel As Boolean)
Dim sht As Worksheet
For Each sht In ThisWorkbook.Sheets
sht.PageSetup.CenterFooter = ThisWorkbook.FullName
Next sht
End Sub
```

> *When you test the* `Workbook_BeforePrint` *procedure, you can use the* `PrintPreview` *method instead of the* `PrintOut` *method, which can save you costs in paper and printer toner cartridges.*

Workbook_SheetActivate Event

The `Workbook_SheetActivate` event is triggered when a sheet is activated in the workbook. Suppose you want to always return to cell A1 whenever you activate any worksheet, regardless of what cell you had selected the last time you were in that worksheet. The following procedure using the `Application.GoTo` statement does just that:

```
Private Sub Workbook_SheetActivate(ByVal Sh As Object)
If TypeName(Sh) = "Worksheet" Then Application.Goto Range("A1"), True
End Sub
```

> *This example illustrates the distinction between a* `Sheet` *object and a* `Worksheet` *object — they are not necessarily the same things. Excel has several types of* `Sheet` *objects: Worksheets, Chart sheets, Dialog sheets, and the obsolete Macro sheets. In this example, a Chart sheet would create confusion for VBA because Chart sheets do not contain cells. Only worksheets contain cells, which is why the* `TypeName` *of* `Worksheet` *is the only* `Sheet` *object at which this procedure's code is directed.*

Workbook_SheetDeactivate Event

The `Workbook_SheetDeactivate` event is triggered when a sheet loses focus, such as when a different sheet in the workbook is activated. If you have a workbook with tables of data on every worksheet, and you want the tables to be sorted automatically by column A whenever you leave the worksheet, this procedure does that:

```
Private Sub Workbook_SheetDeActivate(ByVal Sh As Object)
If TypeName(Sh) = "Worksheet" Then
Sh.Range("A1").CurrentRegion.Sort Key1:=Sh.Range("A2"), _
Order1:=xlAscending, Header:=xlYes
End If
End Sub
```

Workbook_BeforeSave Event

The `Workbook_BeforeSave` event is triggered just before the workbook is saved. You can set the `Cancel` parameter to True to stop the workbook from being saved.

Suppose you want to limit the time period for a workbook to be saved. The following procedure allows the workbook to be saved only between 9:00 AM and 5:00 PM:

```
Private Sub Workbook_BeforeSave(ByVal SaveAsUI As Boolean, Cancel As Boolean)
If VBA.Time < TimeValue("09:00") _
Or VBA.Time > TimeValue("17:00") Then Cancel = True
End Sub
```

TRY IT

In this lesson you write a `Workbook_BeforePrint` workbook-level event that instructs Excel not to print a particular range of confidential data that resides on a particular worksheet.

Lesson Requirements

To get the sample database files you can download Lesson 12 from the book's website at `www.wrox.com`.

Step-by-Step

1. Open a new workbook and activate Sheet3. To prepare the worksheet for this demonstration, populate range A1:E20 with some sample data by selecting the range, typing the word **Hello**, and pressing Ctrl+Enter.

2. On your keyboard, press Alt+F11 to go to the Visual Basic Editor, and then press Ctrl+R to ensure that the Project Explorer window is visible.

3. Find the name of your workbook in the Project Explorer, and expand the folder named Microsoft Excel Objects.

4. The last item at the bottom of the list of Microsoft Excel Objects is the workbook object, and it is called `ThisWorkbook`. You'll want to access the Code window for the `ThisWorkbook` module, and to do that, you can either double-click the `ThisWorkbook` object name, or right-click it and select View Code.

5. The cursor will be blinking in the Code window of your workbook module. Directly above that, click the down arrow belonging to the Object list, and select Workbook, which will produce the following default lines of code in your workbook module:

   ```
   Private Sub Workbook_Open()

   End Sub
   ```

6. In this example you will be writing a `BeforePrint` procedure, so click the other down arrow above the Code window for the Procedure field, and select `BeforePrint`. VBA will produce these lines of code, which is just what you want:

   ```
   Private Sub Workbook_BeforePrint(Cancel As Boolean)

   End Sub
   ```

7. Though not imperative, unless you are planning to employ the `Workbook_Open` event, there's no reason to keep the default `Private Sub Workbook_Open()` and `End Sub` statements, so go ahead and delete them if you like.

8. In this example, you have confidential data on Sheet3 only, so instruct Excel that it's okay to print anything on any worksheet other than Sheet3:

```
If ActiveSheet.Name <> "Sheet3" Then Exit Sub
```

9. Invoke the `Cancel` argument to halt the print process when an attempt is made to print Sheet3:

```
Cancel = True
```

10. Disable events because you actually will be printing something, but you don't want to re-trigger the `BeforePrint` event while you are already in it:

```
Application.EnableEvents = False
```

11. Your confidential data resides in range B5:D12. Temporarily format that range with three semicolons to make those cells unable to display their contents:

```
Range("B5:D12").NumberFormat = ";;;"
```

12. Print the worksheet:

```
ActiveSheet.PrintOut
```

13. Restore the General format to the confidential range so the cells will be able to show their contents after the print job:

```
Range("B5:D12").NumberFormat = "General"
```

14. Enable events again, now that the print job has been executed:

```
Application.EnableEvents = True
```

15. When completed, the entire procedure will look like this, with comments that have been added to explain each step:

```
Private Sub Workbook_BeforePrint(Cancel As Boolean)
'You have confidential data on Sheet3 only,
'so any other sheet is OK to print anything.
If ActiveSheet.Name <> "Sheet3" Then Exit Sub
'Invoke the Cancel argument to halt the print process.
Cancel = True
'Disable events because you actually will print something
'but you don't want the BeforePrint event to kick in.
Application.EnableEvents = False
'Your confidential data resides in range B5:D12.
'Temporarily format that range with three semicolons
'to make those cells unable to display their contents.
Range("B5:D12").NumberFormat = ";;;"
'Print the worksheet.
```

```
ActiveSheet.PrintOut 'demo with PrintPreview
'Restore the General format to the confidential range
'so the cells will be able to show their contents
'after the print job.
Range("B5:D12").NumberFormat = "General"
'Enable events again, now that the print job has been executed.
Application.EnableEvents = True
End Sub
```

16. Press Alt+Q to return to the worksheet. Test the code by printing Sheet3, noting that the printout will show an empty range of cells, representing the range of confidential data that did not get printed.

 Please select Lesson 12 on the DVD to view the video that accompanies this lesson.

Using Embedded Controls

You've seen many ways to run macros, including using keyboard shortcuts, the Macro dialog box, and the Visual Basic Editor. This lesson shows you how to execute VBA code by clicking a button or other object that you can place onto your worksheet to make your macros easier to run.

WORKING WITH FORMS CONTROLS AND ACTIVEX CONTROLS

A *control* is an object such as a Button, Label, TextBox, OptionButton, or CheckBox that you can place onto a UserForm (covered in Lessons 18, 19, and 20) or embed onto a worksheet. VBA supports these and more controls, which provide an intuitive way for you to run your macros quickly and with minimal effort.

There are two generations of controls. *Forms* controls are the original controls that came with Excel starting with version 5. Forms controls are still fully supported in all later versions of Excel, including Excel 2010. Forms controls are more stable, simpler to use, and more integrated with Excel. For example, you can place a Forms control onto a Chart sheet, but you cannot do that with an ActiveX control.

Generally, ActiveX controls from the Control Toolbox are more flexible with their extensive properties and events. You can customize their appearance, behavior, fonts, and other characteristics. You can also control how different events are responded to when an ActiveX control is associated with those events.

Forms controls have macros that are assigned to them. ActiveX controls run procedures that are based on whatever event(s) they have been programmed to monitor. Not that ActiveX controls look all the more scintillating, but Forms controls have an elementary appearance that will never win them first prize in a beauty contest. But, both kinds of controls serve their purposes well as Microsoft intended, and they are here to stay with Excel for the foreseeable future.

CHOOSING BETWEEN FORMS CONTROLS AND ACTIVEX CONTROLS

The primary differences between the two kinds of controls are in formatting and events. You use Forms controls when you need simple interaction with VBA, such as running a macro by clicking a button. They are also a good choice when you don't need VBA at all, but you want an Option Button or Check Box on your sheet that will be linked to a cell. If you need to color your control, or format its font type, or trigger a procedure based on mouse movement or keyboard activity, ActiveX controls are better.

Be aware that ActiveX controls have a well-deserved reputation for being buggy and not behaving as reliably as do Forms controls. Forms controls will give you minimal problems, if any, but they are limited in what they can do. As you experiment and work with each type, you'll decide which kind of control works best for your purposes.

The Forms Toolbar

The easiest way to access Forms controls is through the Forms toolbar. How you get to the Forms toolbar depends on your version of Excel. For versions prior to Excel 2007, from the worksheet menu, click View ➪ Toolbars ➪ Forms, as shown in Figure 13-1.

The Forms toolbar is like any other toolbar that you can dock at the top or sides of the window, or have floating on the window above the worksheet. Figure 13-2 shows the Forms toolbar and its control icons.

If you are using Excel version 2007 or 2010, the Forms and ActiveX controls are found by clicking the Insert icon on the Developer tab of the Ribbon, as shown in Figure 13-3.

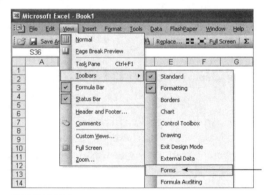

FIGURE 13-1

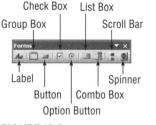

FIGURE 13-2

The Developer tab is a very useful item to place on your Ribbon. See the section entitled "Accessing the VBA Environment" in Lesson 2 for the steps to display the Developer tab.

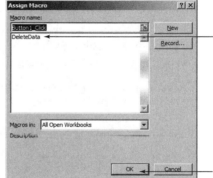

FIGURE 13-3

Buttons

The most commonly used Forms control is the button. When you use a button, you have a macro in mind that you have either already written or will write, which will be attached to the button. The following steps are a common sequence of actions that you will take when using a Forms button:

1. Create the macro that will be attached to the button. Suppose you are negotiating rents, and you need to frequently clear the range C4:F4 on a company budget sheet. The macro you'd write is

   ```
   Sub DeleteData()
   Range("C4:F4").Clear
   End Sub
   ```

2. To make it easy to run that macro, you can assign it to a Forms button. On the Forms toolbar, click the Button icon. Press down your mouse's left button, then draw the button into cell B4. As soon as you do, the Assign Macro dialog box appears, as shown in Figure 13-4.
   Select the macro to be assigned to the button, and click OK.

FIGURE 13-4

3. With your new button selected, click it and delete the entire default caption. Type the caption **Clear Cells** as shown in Figure 13-5.

4. Select any worksheet cell to deselect the button. Click the button to verify that it clears the cells in range of C4:F4, as expected.

	A	B	C	D	E	F	G	H
1	Widgets, Inc. Expense Log							
2								
3			Quarter 1	Quarter 2	Quarter 3	Quarter 4	Total	
4	Rent	Clear Cells	$23,362	$68,531	$66,276	$78,809	$236,978	
5	Utilities		$28,166	$64,728	$99,216	$4,160	$196,270	
6	Payroll		$55,193	$97,457	$24,372	$85,839	$262,861	
7	Office Supplies		$66,540	$78,889	$22,349	$13,606	$181,384	
8	Maintenance		$35,135	$64,505	$36,173	$2,033	$137,846	
9	Landscaping		$14,088	$15,934	$80,263	$27,142	$137,427	
10	Total		$222,484	$390,044	$328,649	$211,589	$1,152,766	
11								

FIGURE 13-5

Using Application.Caller with Forms Controls

One of the cool things about Forms controls is that you can apply a single macro to all of them and gain information about which control was clicked. Once you know which button was clicked, you can take specific action relating to that button.

Expanding on the previous example, suppose you want to place a button on each row of data, so that when you click a button, the cells will be cleared in columns C:F of the row where the button resides. It's obvious that the original macro will apply only to the first button in the Rent row, so here are the steps to have one macro serve many controls:

1. Modify the `DeleteData` macro as follows. For the button that was clicked, the cell holding that button's top-left corner is identified. The macro can now be a customization tool for each individual button to which it is attached.

```
Sub DeleteData()
Dim myRow As Long
myRow = _
ActiveSheet.Buttons(Application.Caller).TopLeftCell.Row
Range(Cells(myRow, 3), Cells(myRow, 6)).Clear
End Sub
```

2. Recall that the original macro name is still attached to that button. Return to your worksheet and right-click the button. Select Copy because you are copying the button and the macro to which it is attached.

3. Select cell B5 and press the Ctrl+V keys. Repeat that step for cells B6, B7, B8, and B9. Your worksheet will resemble Figure 13-6.

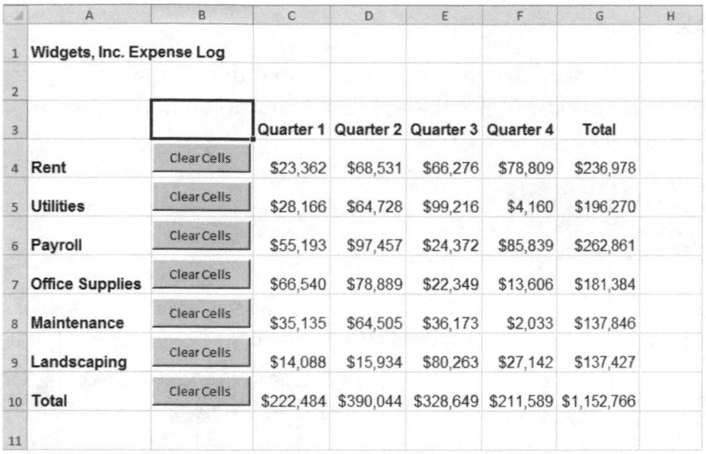

FIGURE 13-6

4. Test the macro by clicking the button on the Office Supplies row. When you click that button, the macro will clear the cells in row 7, columns C:F, as shown in Figure 13-7.

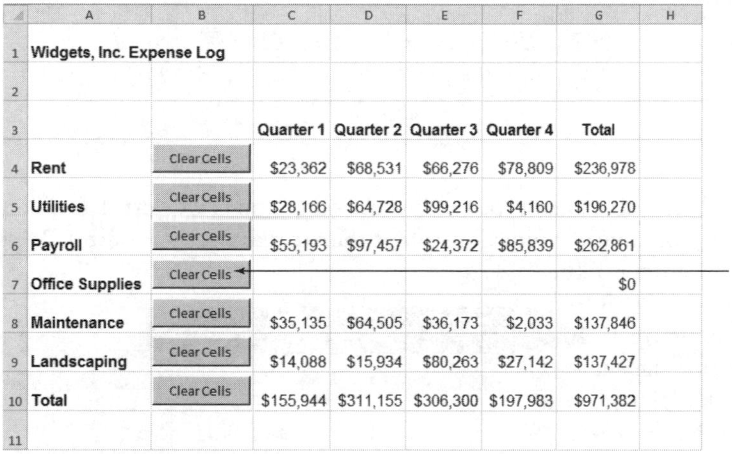

FIGURE 13-7

Attaching a macro to an embedded object is not limited to Forms controls. You can attach a macro to pretty much any Drawing shape or picture that you want to embed onto your worksheet.

The Control Toolbox

Similar to the Forms toolbar, the Control Toolbox can be accessed in versions prior to Excel 2007 from the worksheet menu bar. Click View ➪ Toolbars ➪ Control Toolbox, as shown in Figure 13-8. The Control Toolbox itself is shown in Figure 13-9.

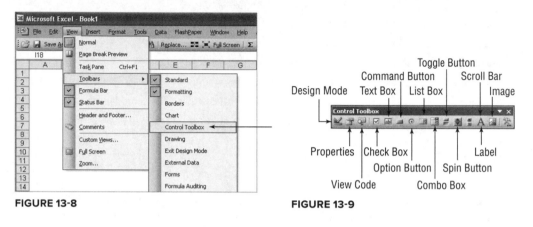

FIGURE 13-8

FIGURE 13-9

> *If you are using version 2007 or 2010, the Forms and ActiveX controls are found by clicking the Insert icon on the Developer tab of the Ribbon, as shown in Figure 13-3.*

More than 100 additional ActiveX controls beyond what you see on the Control Toolbox are available. You might notice an icon named More Controls at the far right of the Control Toolbox toolbar, and in the lower-right corner of the Insert icon in Excel 2007 and 2010. That icon is pointed to in Figure 13-10, and when expanded, reveals the additional ActiveX controls available for you to embed, as indicated in Figure 13-11.

FIGURE 13-10

FIGURE 13-11

> *The odds are you'll never need most of those controls, but it gives you a sense of how much more functionality is available with ActiveX objects.*

CommandButtons

The ActiveX CommandButton is the counterpart to the Forms control button. As with virtually every ActiveX object, the CommandButton has numerous properties through which you can customize its appearance. Unlike Forms controls, an ActiveX object such as a CommandButton responds to event code. There is no such thing as a macro being attached to a CommandButton.

From the Control Toolbox, draw a CommandButton onto your worksheet. Excel defaults to Design Mode, allowing you to work with the ActiveX object you just created. Right-click the CommandButton and select Properties, as shown in Figure 13-12. You can see the Design Mode icon is active.

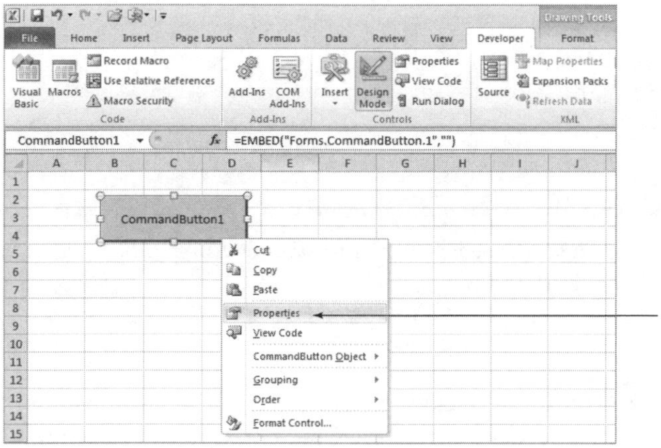

FIGURE 13-12

You will see the Properties window for the CommandButton, where you can modify a number of properties. Change the Caption property of the CommandButton to **CheckBox Checker**, as shown in Figure 13-13.

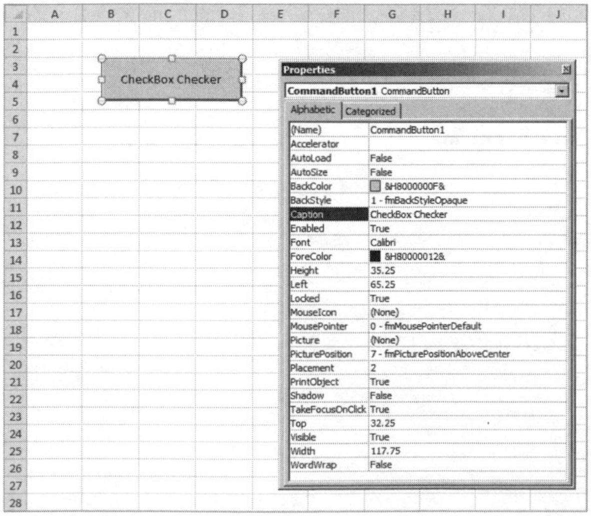

FIGURE 13-13

Draw a Label control and four CheckBoxes from the Control Toolbox below the CommandButton. In Figure 13-14, I changed the Label's caption to Check Your Favorite Activities. I changed each CheckBox's caption to a different leisure activity.

Either double-click the CommandButton, or right-click it and select View Code. Either way, you'll be taken to the worksheet module and the default Click event will be started for you with the following entry:

FIGURE 13-14

```
Private Sub CommandButton1_Click()

End Sub
```

VBA code for embedded ActiveX objects is almost always in the module of the worksheet upon which the objects are embedded.

For this demonstration, when the CommandButton is clicked, it will evaluate every embedded object on the worksheet. When the code comes across an ActiveX CheckBox, it will determine whether the CheckBox is checked. At the end of the procedure, a Message Box will appear, confirming how many (if any) CheckBoxes were checked, and their captions. The entire code will look as follows.

```
Private Sub CommandButton1_Click()
'Evaluate which checkboxes are checked.

'Declare an Integer type variable to help
'count through the CheckBoxes, and an Object
'type variable to identify the kind of ActiveX control
'(checkboxes in this example) that are selected.
Dim intCounter As Integer, xObj As OLEObject
'Declare a String variable to list the captions
'of the selected checkboxes in a message box.
Dim strObj As String

'Start the Integer and String variables.
intCounter = 0
strObj = ""

For Each xObj In ActiveSheet.OLEObjects
If TypeName(xObj.Object) = "CheckBox" Then

If xObj.Object.Value = True Then
intCounter = intCounter + 1
strObj = strObj & xObj.Object.Caption & Chr(10)
End If
```

```
End If
Next xObj

'Advise the user of your findings.
If intCounter = 0 Then
MsgBox _
"There were no CheckBoxes selected.", , _
"Try to get out more often!"

Else
MsgBox _
"You selected " & intCounter & " CheckBox(es):" _
& vbCrLf & vbCrLf & _
strObj, , "Here is what you checked:"

End If

End Sub
```

Leave the VBE and return to the worksheet by pressing the Alt+Q keys. Click the Design Mode button to exit Design Mode. Figure 13-15 shows where the Design Mode icon is on the Developer tab.

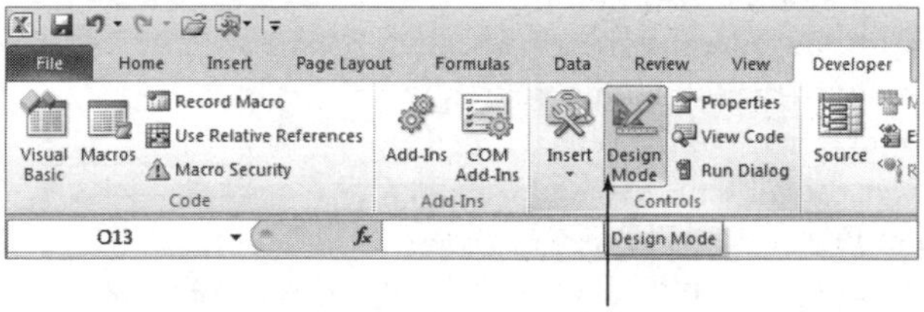

FIGURE 13-15

With Design Mode now off, you can test the `Click` event code for the ActiveX CommandButton. Figure 13-16 shows an example of the confirming Message Box when you click the CommandButton.

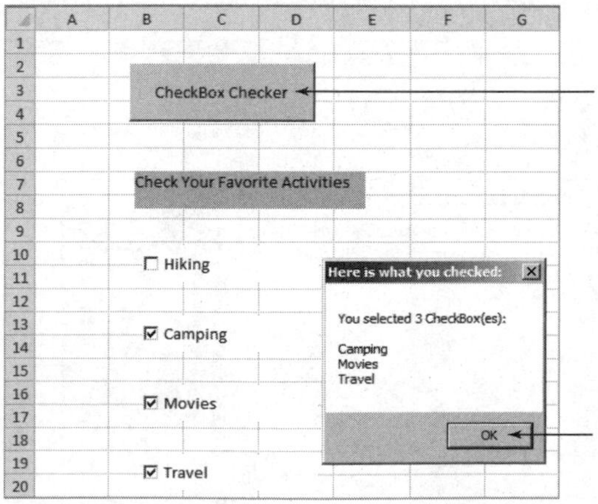

FIGURE 13-16

TRY IT

In this lesson, you attach a macro to a Forms button that will toggle certain columns as being visible or hidden. Along the way, you learn a few tricks about faster methods for entering data into multiple cells.

Lesson Requirements

For this lesson, you place a Forms button on a worksheet that contains a hypothetical table of monthly income activity for a department store's clothing items. A macro will be attached to the button that, when clicked, will toggle columns or rows as being hidden or visible, depending on how you want to see the data. Upon each click of the button, the cycle of views will be to see the entire table's detail, see totals only by clothing item, or see totals only by month. This lesson also includes tips on fast data entry by using the fill handle and shortcut keys. To get the sample database files you can download Lesson 13 from the book's website at www.wrox.com.

Step-by-Step

1. Open Excel and open a new workbook.

2. On your active worksheet, list the months of the year in range A6:A17. You can do this quickly by entering **January** in cell A6, then selecting A6, and pointing your mouse over the fill handle, which is the small black square in the lower-right corner of the selected cell. You know your mouse is hovering over the fill handle when the cursor changes to a crosshairs, as indicated in Figure 13-17. Press your left mouse button onto the fill handle, and drag your mouse down to cell A17 as indicated in Figure 13-18. Release the mouse button, and the 12 months of the year will be filled into range A6:A17 as shown in Figure 13-19.

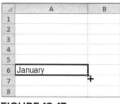

FIGURE 13-17

3. Enter some clothing items into B5:F5.

4. Enter sample numbers in range B6:F17. There is nothing special about the numbers; they are just for demonstration purposes. To enter the numbers quickly as shown in Figure 13-20, do the following:

   ➤ Select range B6:F17.

   ➤ Type the formula
     `= INT(RAND()*1000)`.

   ➤ Press the Ctrl+Enter keys.

   ➤ Press the Ctrl+C keys to copy the range.

   ➤ Right-click somewhere in the range B6:F17, and select Paste Special ➪ Values ➪ OK.

   ➤ Press the Esc key to exit Copy mode.

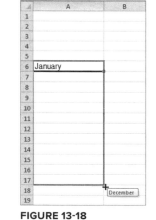

FIGURE 13-18

FIGURE 13-19

5. In cell G5 enter **Total** and in cell A18 enter **Total**.

6. Select the column A header, which will select all of column A. Right-click onto any cell in column A, select Column Width, enter 20, and click OK.

7. Quickly enter Sum functions for all rows and columns. Select range B6:G18, as shown in Figure 13-21, and either double-click the Sum function icon or press the Alt+= keys.

	A	B	C	D	E	F	G	H
1								
2								
3								
4								
5		Jackets	Shoes	Hats	Dresses	Shirts		
6	January	=INT(RAND()*1000)						
7	February							
8	March							
9	April							
10	May							
11	June							
12	July							
13	August							
14	September							
15	October							
16	November							
17	December							
18								
19								

FIGURE 13-20

	A	B	C	D	E	F	G	H
	Sum (Alt+=)		f_x	130				
1								
2								
3								
4								
5		Jackets	Shoes	Hats	Dresses	Shirts	Total	
6	January	$130	$442	$691	$770	$612		
7	February	$669	$320	$834	$695	$687		
8	March	$831	$173	$338	$223	$657		
9	April	$362	$464	$65	$207	$258		
10	May	$652	$278	$127	$348	$300		
11	June	$225	$604	$855	$454	$141		
12	July	$166	$394	$717	$117	$813		
13	August	$927	$283	$569	$113	$780		
14	September	$56	$286	$385	$391	$794		
15	October	$945	$184	$858	$923	$326		
16	November	$440	$778	$220	$39	$899		
17	December	$302	$882	$424	$188	$304		
18	Total							
19								

FIGURE 13-21

8. With range B6:G18 currently selected, right-click anywhere in the selection, select Format Cells, and click the Number tab in the Format Cells dialog box. In the category pane select Currency, set Decimal Places to 0, and click OK as indicated in Figure 13-22. Your final result will resemble Figure 13-23, with different numbers because they were produced with the RAND function, but all good enough for this lesson.

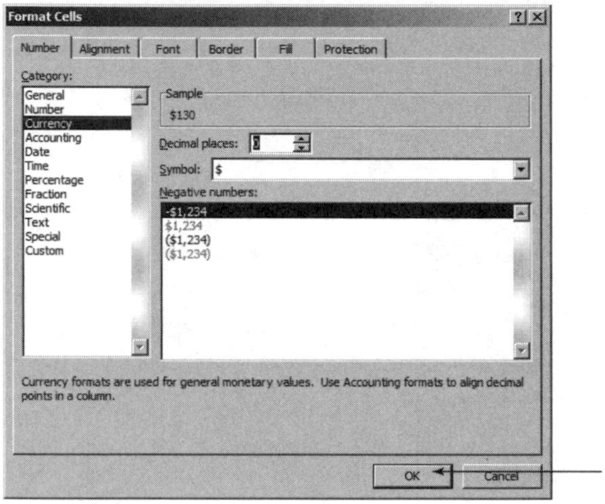

FIGURE 13-22

	A	B	C	D	E	F	G	H
1								
2								
3								
4								
5		Jackets	Shoes	Hats	Dresses	Shirts	Total	
6	January	$130	$442	$691	$770	$612	$2,645	
7	February	$669	$320	$834	$695	$687	$3,205	
8	March	$831	$173	$338	$223	$657	$2,222	
9	April	$362	$464	$65	$207	$258	$1,356	
10	May	$652	$278	$127	$348	$300	$1,705	
11	June	$225	$604	$855	$454	$141	$2,279	
12	July	$166	$394	$717	$117	$813	$2,207	
13	August	$927	$283	$569	$113	$780	$2,672	
14	September	$56	$286	$385	$391	$794	$1,912	
15	October	$945	$184	$858	$923	$326	$3,236	
16	November	$440	$778	$220	$39	$899	$2,376	
17	December	$302	$882	$424	$188	$304	$2,100	
18	Total	$5,705	$5,088	$6,083	$4,468	$6,571	$27,915	
19								

FIGURE 13-23

9. The task at hand is to create a macro that will be attached to a Forms button. Each time you click the button, the macro will toggle to the next of three different views of the table: seeing the entire table's detail, seeing totals only by clothing item, or seeing totals only by month. To get started, press Alt+F11 to go to the Visual Basic Editor.

10. From the VBE menu, click Insert ⇨ Module.

11. In your new module, type **Sub ToggleViews** and press the Enter key. VBA will produce the following two lines of code, with an empty row between them:

```
Sub ToggleViews()

End Sub
```

12. Because the macro will hide and unhide rows and columns, turn off ScreenUpdating to keep the screen from flickering:

```
Application.ScreenUpdating = False
```

13. Open a With structure that uses Application.Caller to identify the Forms button that was clicked:

```
With ActiveSheet.Buttons(Application.Caller)
```

14. Toggle between views based on the button's captions to determine which view is next in the cycle:

```
If .Caption = "SHOW ALL" Then
With Range("A5:G18")
.EntireColumn.Hidden = False
.EntireRow.Hidden = False
End With
.Caption = "MONTH TOTALS"

ElseIf .Caption = "MONTH TOTALS" Then
Range("B:F").EntireColumn.Hidden = True
.Caption = "ITEM TOTALS"

ElseIf .Caption = "ITEM TOTALS" Then
Range("B:F").EntireColumn.Hidden = False
Rows("6:17").Hidden = True
.Caption = "SHOW ALL"

End If 'for evaluating the button caption.
```

15. Close the With structure for Application.Caller:

```
End With
```

16. Turn ScreenUpdating on again:

```
Application.ScreenUpdating = True
```

17. Your entire macro will look like this:

```
Sub ToggleViews()

'Turn off ScreenUpdating.
Application.ScreenUpdating = False

'Open a With structure that uses Application.Caller
'to identify the Forms button that was clicked.
With ActiveSheet.Buttons(Application.Caller)
```

```
'Toggle between views based on the button's captions
'to determine which view is next in the cycle.

If .Caption = "SHOW ALL" Then
With Range("A5:G18")
.EntireColumn.Hidden = False
.EntireRow.Hidden = False
End With
.Caption = "MONTH TOTALS"

ElseIf .Caption = "MONTH TOTALS" Then
Range("B:F").EntireColumn.Hidden = True
.Caption = "ITEM TOTALS"

ElseIf .Caption = "ITEM TOTALS" Then
Range("B:F").EntireColumn.Hidden = False
Rows("6:17").Hidden = True
.Caption = "SHOW ALL"

End If 'for evaluating the button caption.

'Close the With structure for Application.Caller.
End With

'Turn ScreenUpdating on again.
Application.ScreenUpdating = True

End Sub
```

18. Press Alt+Q to return to the worksheet.

19. Draw a Forms button onto your worksheet at the top of column A. When you release the mouse button you'll see the Assign Macro dialog box. Select the macro named ToggleViews and click the OK button as shown in Figure 13-24.

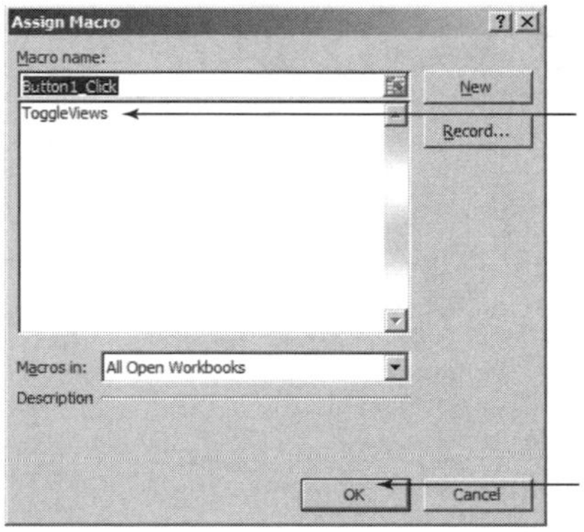

FIGURE 13-24

20. Make sure the button is totally within column A, as indicated in Figure 13-25. Right-click the button and select Edit Text.

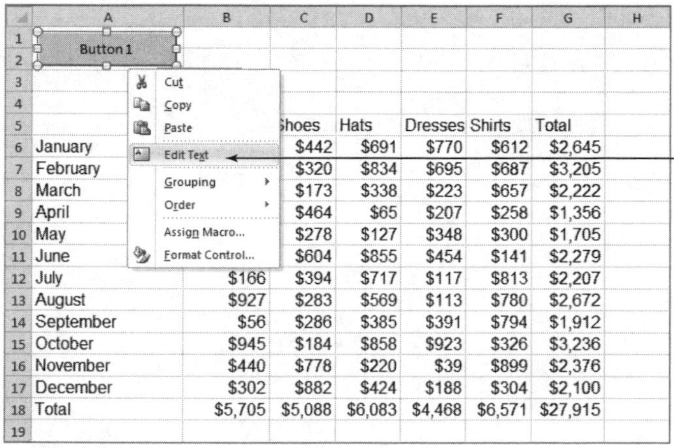

	A	B	C	D	E	F	G	H
1								
2								
3								
4								
5			hoes	Hats	Dresses	Shirts	Total	
6	January		$442	$691	$770	$612	$2,645	
7	February		$320	$834	$695	$687	$3,205	
8	March		$173	$338	$223	$657	$2,222	
9	April		$464	$65	$207	$258	$1,356	
10	May		$278	$127	$348	$300	$1,705	
11	June		$604	$855	$454	$141	$2,279	
12	July	$166	$394	$717	$117	$813	$2,207	
13	August	$927	$283	$569	$113	$780	$2,672	
14	September	$56	$286	$385	$391	$794	$1,912	
15	October	$945	$184	$858	$923	$326	$3,236	
16	November	$440	$778	$220	$39	$899	$2,376	
17	December	$302	$882	$424	$188	$304	$2,100	
18	Total	$5,705	$5,088	$6,083	$4,468	$6,571	$27,915	
19								

FIGURE 13-25

21. Change the button's caption to **SHOW ALL** as seen in Figure 13-26.

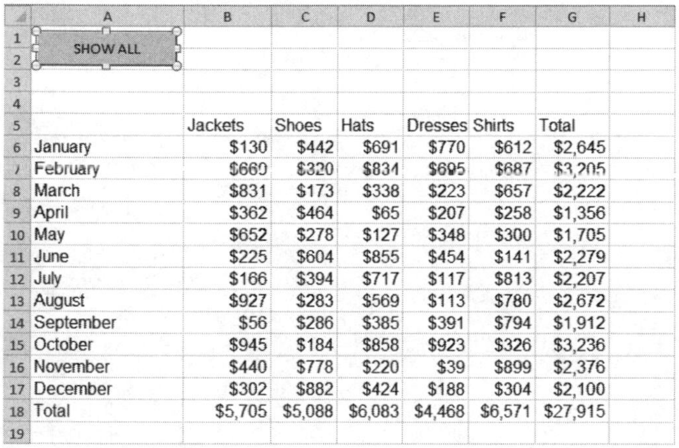

	A	B	C	D	E	F	G	H
1								
2								
3								
4								
5		Jackets	Shoes	Hats	Dresses	Shirts	Total	
6	January	$130	$442	$691	$770	$612	$2,645	
7	February	$660	$320	$834	$695	$687	$3,205	
8	March	$831	$173	$338	$223	$657	$2,222	
9	April	$362	$464	$65	$207	$258	$1,356	
10	May	$652	$278	$127	$348	$300	$1,705	
11	June	$225	$604	$855	$454	$141	$2,279	
12	July	$166	$394	$717	$117	$813	$2,207	
13	August	$927	$283	$569	$113	$780	$2,672	
14	September	$56	$286	$385	$391	$794	$1,912	
15	October	$945	$184	$858	$923	$326	$3,236	
16	November	$440	$778	$220	$39	$899	$2,376	
17	December	$302	$882	$424	$188	$304	$2,100	
18	Total	$5,705	$5,088	$6,083	$4,468	$6,571	$27,915	
19								

FIGURE 13-26

22. Select any cell to deselect the button. Click the button once and nothing will change on the sheet because all the columns and rows are already visible. You'll see that the button's caption changed to MONTH TOTALS. If you click the button again, you'll see the month names listed in column A, and their totals listed in column G. The button's caption will read ITEM TOTALS. Click the button again and you'll see the clothing items named in row 5, and their totals listed in row 18. The button's caption reads SHOW ALL, and if you click the button again, all rows and columns will be shown.

23. You can continue cycling through the table's views in this manner, by clicking the Forms button for each view that you coded into the ToggleViews macro.

 Please select Lesson 13 on the DVD to view the video that accompanies this lesson.

14

Programming Charts

When I started to program Excel in the early 1990s, I remember being impressed with the charting tools that came with Excel. They were very good back then, and today's chart features in Excel are downright awesome, rivaling — and usually surpassing — the charting packages of any software application.

Because you are reading this book, chances are pretty good that you've manually created your share of charts in Excel using the Chart Wizard or by selecting a chart type from the dozens of choices on the Ribbon. You might also have played with the Macro Recorder to do some automation of chart creation. This lesson takes you past the Macro Recorder's capabilities to show how to create and manipulate embedded charts and chart sheets.

The topic of charting is one that can, and does, fill entire books. The myriad of chart types and features that Excel makes available to you goes well beyond the scope of this lesson. What this lesson does is to show you the syntaxes for several methods that work for embedded charts and chart sheets, with a few different features and chart types represented in the programming code. From the VBA examples in this lesson, you can expand your chart programming skills by substituting the chart types and features shown for others that may be more suited to the kinds of charts you want to develop.

> *In the examples, you might notice that the charts being created are declared as a* Chart *type object variable, which makes it easier to refer to the charts when you want to manipulate them in code. In any case, there are two separate object models for charts. For a chart on its own chart sheet, it is a* Chart *object. For a chart embedded on a worksheet, it is a* ChartObject *object. Chart sheets are a member of the workbook's* Charts *collection, and each* ChartObject *on a worksheet is a member of the worksheet's* ChartObjects *collection.*

ADDING A CHART TO A CHART SHEET

As you know, a chart sheet is a special kind of sheet in your workbook that contains only a chart. If the chart is destined to be large and complicated, users often prefer such a chart be on its own sheet so they can view its detail more easily.

Figure 14-1 shows a table of sales by month for a company that will be the source data for this chart example. The table is on Sheet1 and although you can correctly refer to the source range in your code as A1:B13, I prefer using the `CurrentRegion` property to reduce the chances of entering the wrong range reference in my code.

The following macro creates a column chart for a new chart sheet based on the data in Figure 14-1. If the `Location` property of your `Chart` object has not been specified, as it has not been in this macro, your chart will be created in its own chart sheet. The result of this new chart sheet is shown in Figure 14-2.

```
Sub CreateChartSheet()
'Declare your chart type object variable
Dim myChart1 As Chart
'Set your variable to add a chart
Set myChart1 = Charts.Add
'Define the new chart's source data
myChart1.SetSourceData _
Source:=Worksheets("Sheet1").Range("A1").CurrentRegion, _
PlotBy:=xlColumns
'Define the type of chart
myChart1.ChartType = xlColumnClustered
'Delete the legend because it is redundant with the chart title.
ActiveChart.Legend.Delete
End Sub
```

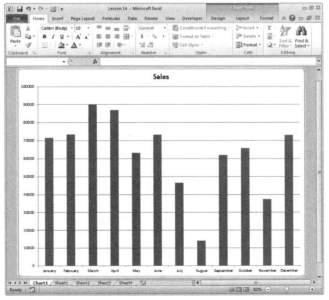

	A	B	C
1	**Month**	**Sales**	
2	January	71605	
3	February	73632	
4	March	90114	
5	April	87041	
6	May	63362	
7	June	73417	
8	July	46648	
9	August	14292	
10	September	62041	
11	October	65849	
12	November	37370	
13	December	73112	
14			

FIGURE 14-1

FIGURE 14-2

> To *change your default type of chart, right-click any chart in your workbook and select Change Chart Type. In the Change Chart Type dialog box, select a chart type, click the Set as Default Chart button, and click the OK button.*

Simply executing the code line `Charts.Add` in the Immediate Window creates a new chart sheet. If the active cell were within a table of data, your default type chart would occupy the new chart sheet, representing the table, or more precisely, the data within the `CurrentRegion` property of the selected cell. If you did not have any data selected at the time, a new chart sheet would still be created, with a blank `Chart` object looking like an empty canvas waiting to be supplied with source data.

DID YOU KNOW...

If the active cell is within a table of data, or you have a range of data selected, and you press the F11 key, a new chart sheet will be added to hold a chart that represents the selected data. Some people find this to be an annoyance because they have no interest in charts and don't even know they touched the F11 key.

If you want to negate the effect of pressing the F11 key, you can place the following `OnKey` procedures into the ThisWorkbook module. Some Excel users who frequently use the F2 key to get into Edit mode nullify the F1 (Help) key in this fashion as well.

```
Private Sub Workbook_Open()
Application.OnKey "{F11}", ""
End Sub

Private Sub Workbook_Activate()
Application.OnKey "{F11}", ""
End Sub

Private Sub Workbook_Deactivate()
Application.OnKey "{F11}"
End Sub

Private Sub Workbook_BeforeClose(Cancel As Boolean)
Application.OnKey "{F11}"
End Sub
```

ADDING AN EMBEDDED CHART TO A WORKSHEET

When you embed a chart onto a worksheet, there is more to consider than when you create a chart for its own chart sheet. When you embed a chart, you need to specify which worksheet you want the chart to be on (handled by the Location property), and where on the worksheet you want the chart to be placed. The following macro is an example of how to place a column chart into range D3:J20 of the active worksheet, close to the source range as shown in Figure 14-3.

```
Sub CreateChartSameSheet()
'Declare an Object variable for the chart
'and for the embedded ChartObject.
Dim myChart1 As Chart, cht1 As ChartObject
'Declare a Range variable to specify what range
'the chart will occupy, and on what worksheet.
Dim rngChart1 As Range, DestinationSheet As String

'The chart will be placed on the active worksheet.
DestinationSheet = ActiveSheet.Name

'Add a new chart
Set myChart1 = Charts.Add

'Specify the chart's location as the active worksheet.
Set myChart1 = _
myChart1.Location _
(Where:=xlLocationAsObject, Name:=DestinationSheet)
'Define the new chart's source data

myChart1.SetSourceData _
Source:=Range("A1").CurrentRegion, PlotBy:=xlColumns

'Define the type of chart, in this case, a Column chart.
myChart1.ChartType = xlColumnClustered

'Activate the chart to identify its ChartObject.
'The (1) assumes this is the first (index #1) chart object
'on the worksheet.
ActiveSheet.ChartObjects(1).Activate
Set cht1 = ActiveChart.Parent

'Specify the range you want the chart to occupy.
Set rngChart1 = Range("D3:J20")
cht1.Left = rngChart1.Left
cht1.Width = rngChart1.Width
cht1.Top = rngChart1.Top
cht1.Height = rngChart1.Height

'Deselect the chart by selecting a cell.
Range("A1").Select
End Sub
```

FIGURE 14-3

One of the best practice items in VBA programming that I mention throughout the book, and you will see posted in newsgroups ad nauseam, is to avoid
selecting or activating objects in your VBA code. In fact that is good advice...
most of the time. Sometimes, you need to select objects to refer reliably to them
or to manipulate them, and the preceding macro demonstrated two examples.
The ChartObject was activated to derive the actual name of the chart. Also,
the macro ended with cell A1 being selected. You could select any cell or any
object, but a cell — any cell — is the safest object to select after creating a new
embedded chart. Any code that is executed after adding a new chart will probably not execute correctly if the chart object is still selected. The most reliable
way to deselect a chart at the end of your macro is to select a cell.

MOVING A CHART

You can change the location of any chart, which you might be familiar with if you've right-clicked
a chart's area and noticed the Move Chart menu item. The following scenarios show how to do this
with VBA.

To move a chart from a chart sheet to a worksheet, select the chart sheet programmatically and
specify the worksheet where you want the chart to be relocated. It's usually a good idea to tell VBA
where on the worksheet you want the chart to go; otherwise, the chart is plopped down on the sheet

wherever VBA decides. That is why the code in the `With` structure specifies that cell C3 be the top-left corner of the relocated chart.

```
Sub ChartSheetToWorksheet()

'Chart1 is the name of the chart sheet.
Sheets("Chart1").Select
'Move the chart to Sheet1
ActiveChart.Location Where:=xlLocationAsObject, Name:="Sheet1"

'Cell C3 is the top left corner location of the chart.
With Worksheets("Sheet1")
ActiveChart.Parent.Left = .Range("C3").Left
ActiveChart.Parent.Top = .Range("C3").Top
End With

'Deselect the chart.
Range("A1").Select

End Sub
```

To move a chart from a worksheet to a chart sheet, you need to determine the name or index number of your chart. If you have only one chart on the sheet, you know that chart's index property is 1, but specifying the chart by its name is a safe way to go. The code is much simpler because a chart sheet can contain only one chart, so you don't need to specify a location on the chart sheet itself.

```
Sub EmbeddedChartToChartSheet()
ActiveSheet.ChartObjects("Chart 1").Activate
ActiveChart.Location Where:=xlLocationAsNewSheet, Name:="Chart1"
End Sub
```

> To determine the name of any embedded chart quickly, select it and you'll see its name in the Name box.

To move an embedded chart from one worksheet to another, it's the same concept of specifying which chart to move, and which worksheet to move it to:

```
Sub EmbeddedChartToAnotherWorksheet()

'Chart 5 is the name of the chart to move to Sheet2.
ActiveSheet.ChartObjects("Chart 14").Activate
ActiveChart.Location Where:=xlLocationAsObject, Name:="Sheet2"

'Cell B6 is the top left corner location of the chart.
With Worksheets("Sheet2")
ActiveChart.Parent.Left = .Range("B6").Left
ActiveChart.Parent.Top = .Range("B6").Top
End With

'Deselect the chart.
Range("A1").Select

End Sub
```

You can quickly move all chart sheets to their own workbook. For example, check out the following example that creates a new workbook and relocates the chart sheets before Sheet1 in that new workbook:

```
Sub ChartSheetsToWorkbook()
'Declare variable for your active workbook name.
Dim myName As String
'Define the name of your workbook.
myName = ActiveWorkbook.Name
'Add a new Excel workbook.
Workbooks.Add 1
'Copy the chart sheets from your source workbook
'to the new workbook.
Workbooks(myName).Charts.Move before:=Sheets(1)
End Sub
```

LOOPING THROUGH ALL EMBEDDED CHARTS

Suppose you want to do something to every embedded chart in your workbook. For example, if some charts were originally created with different background colors, you might want to standardize the look of all charts to have the same color scheme. The following macro shows how to loop through every chart on every worksheet to format the chart area with a standard color of light blue:

```
Sub LoopAllEmbeddedCharts()

'Turn off ScreenUpdating.
Application.ScreenUpdating = False

'Declare variables for worksheet and chart objects.
Dim wks As Worksheet, ChObj As ChartObject

'Open loop for every worksheet.
For Each wks In Worksheets

'Determine if the worksheet has at least one chart.
If wks.ChartObjects.Count > 0 Then

'If the worksheet has a chart, activate the worksheet.
wks.Activate

'Loop through each chart object.
For Each ChObj In ActiveSheet.ChartObjects

'Activate the chart
ChObj.Activate

'Color the chart area blue.
ActiveChart.ChartArea.Interior.ColorIndex = 8

'Deselect the active chart before proceeding to the
'next chart or the next worksheet.
Range("A1").Select
```

```
'Continue and close the loop for every chart on that sheet.
Next ChObj

'Close the If structure if the worksheet had no chart.
End If

'Continue and close the loop for every worksheet.
Next wks

'Turn on ScreenUpdating.
Application.ScreenUpdating = True

End Sub
```

If you have chart sheets to be looped through, the code must be different to take into account the type of sheet to look for, because a chart sheet is a different type of sheet than a worksheet. This macro accomplishes the same task of coloring the chart area, but for charts on chart sheets:

```
Sub LoopAllChartSheets()

'Turn off ScreenUpdating.
Application.ScreenUpdating = False

'Declare an object variable for the Sheets collection.
Dim objSheet As Object

'Loop through all sheets, only looking for a chart sheet.
For Each objSheet In ActiveWorkbook.Sheets
If TypeOf objSheet Is Excel.Chart Then

'Activate the chart sheet.
objSheet.Activate

'Color the chart area blue.
ActiveChart.ChartArea.Interior.ColorIndex = 8

'Close the If structure and move on to the next sheet.
End If
Next objSheet

'Turn on ScreenUpdating.
Application.ScreenUpdating = True

End Sub
```

DELETING CHARTS

To delete all charts on a worksheet, you can execute this code line in the Immediate Window, or as part of a macro:

```
If activesheet.ChartObjects.Count > 0 Then activesheet.ChartObjects.Delete
```

To delete chart sheets, loop through each sheet starting with the last sheet, determine whether the sheet is a chart sheet, and if so, delete it.

This loop starts from the last sheet and moves backward using the Step -1 *statement. It's a wise practice to loop backwards when deleting sheets, rows, or columns. Behind the scenes, VBA relies on the counts of objects in collections, and where the objects are located relative to the others. Deleting objects starting at the end and working your way to the beginning keeps VBA's management of those objects in order.*

```
Sub DeleteChartSheets()

'Turn off ScreenUpdating and the Alerts feature,
'so when you delete a sheet VBA does not warn you.
With Application
.ScreenUpdating = False
.DisplayAlerts = False

'Declare an object variable for the Sheets collection.
Dim objSheet As Object

'Loop through all sheets, only looking for a chart sheet.
'This loop starts from the last sheet and moves backward.
For Each objSheet In ActiveWorkbook.Sheets
If TypeOf objSheet Is Excel.Chart Then objSheet.Delete
Next objSheet

'Turn on ScreenUpdating and DisplayAlerts.
.DisplayAlerts = True
.ScreenUpdating = False
End With

End Sub
```

RENAMING A CHART

As you have surely noticed when creating objects such as charts, pivot tables, or drawing objects, Excel has a refined knack for giving those objects the blandest default names imaginable. Suppose you have three embedded charts on your worksheet. The following macro will change those charts' names to something more meaningful:

```
Sub RenameCharts()
With ActiveSheet
.ChartObjects(1).Name = "Monthly Income"
.ChartObjects(2).Name = "Monthly Expense"
.ChartObjects(3).Name = "Net Profit"
End With
End Sub
```

TRY IT

In this lesson you create an embedded pie chart, position it near the source data, and give each legend key a unique color. The pie will have four slices that will each be given a unique color, and will each display their respective data labels.

Lesson Requirements

To get the sample database files you can download Lesson 14 from the book's website at www.wrox.com.

Step-by-Step

1. Insert a new worksheet and construct the simple table as shown in Figure 14-4.

2. From your worksheet, press Alt+F11 to go to the Visual Basic Editor.

3. From the VBE menu, click Insert ⇨ Module.

4. In your new module, enter the name of this macro, which I am calling `TryItPieChart`. Type **Sub TryItPieChart**, press the Enter key, and VBA will produce the following code:

```
Sub TryItPieChart()

End Sub
```

	A	B	C	D
1	Quarterly Sales			
2				
3	Quarter	Sales	Percent	
4	Quarter 1	$591,254	28%	
5	Quarter 2	$326,589	15%	
6	Quarter 3	$486,234	23%	
7	Quarter 4	$745,698	35%	
8	Total	$2,149,775		
9				

FIGURE 14-4

5. Declare the `ChartObject` variable.

```
Dim chtQuarters As ChartObject
```

6. Set the variable to the chart being added. Position the chart near the source data.

```
Set chtQuarters = _
ActiveSheet.ChartObjects.Add _
(Left:=240, Width:=340, Top:=5, Height:=240)
```

7. Define the range for this pie chart:

```
chtQuarters.Chart.SetSourceData Source:=Range("A3:B7")
```

8. Define the type of chart, which is a pie:

```
chtQuarters.Chart.ChartType = xlPie
```

9. Activate the new chart to work with it:

```
ActiveSheet.ChartObjects(1).Activate
```

10. Color the legend entries to identify each pie piece:

```
With ActiveChart.Legend
.LegendEntries(1).LegendKey.Interior.Color = vbYellow
.LegendEntries(2).LegendKey.Interior.Color = vbCyan
.LegendEntries(3).LegendKey.Interior.Color = vbRed
.LegendEntries(4).LegendKey.Interior.Color = vbGreen
End With
```

11. Add data labels to see the numbers in the pie slices:

```
ActiveChart.SeriesCollection(1).ApplyDataLabels
```

12. Edit the chart title's text.

```
ActiveChart.ChartTitle.Text = "Quarterly Sales"
```

13. Format the legend:

```
ActiveChart.Legend.Select
With Selection.Font
.Name = "Arial"
.FontStyle = "Bold"
.Size = 14
End With
```

14. Deselect the chart by selecting a cell:

```
Range("A1").Select
```

15. Press Alt+Q to return to the worksheet, and test your macro, which in its entirety will look as follows. The result will look like Figure 14-5, with a pie chart settled near the source data.

```
Sub TryItPieChart()

'Declare the ChartObject variable.
Dim chtQuarters As ChartObject

'Set the variable to the chart being added.
'Position the chart near the source data.
Set chtQuarters = _
ActiveSheet.ChartObjects.Add _
(Left:=240, Width:=340, Top:=5, Height:=240)

'Define the range for this pie chart.
chtQuarters.Chart.SetSourceData Source:=Range("A3:B7")

'Define the type of chart, which is a pie.
chtQuarters.Chart.ChartType = xlPie

'Activate the new chart to work with it.
ActiveSheet.ChartObjects(1).Activate
```

```
'Color the legend entries to identify each pie piece.
With ActiveChart.Legend
.LegendEntries(1).LegendKey.Interior.Color = vbYellow
.LegendEntries(2).LegendKey.Interior.Color = vbCyan
.LegendEntries(3).LegendKey.Interior.Color = vbRed
.LegendEntries(4).LegendKey.Interior.Color = vbGreen
End With

'Add data labels to see the numbers in the pie slices.
ActiveChart.SeriesCollection(1).ApplyDataLabels

'Edit the chart title's text
ActiveChart.ChartTitle.Text = "Quarterly Sales"

'Format the legend.
ActiveChart.Legend.Select
With Selection.Font
.Name = "Arial"
.FontStyle = "Bold"
.Size = 14
End With

'Deselect the chart by selecting a cell.
Range("A1").Select

End Sub
```

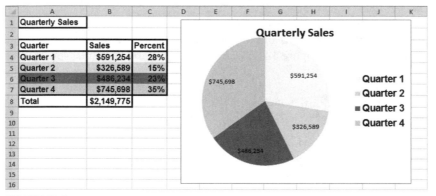

FIGURE 14-5

Please select Lesson 14 on the DVD to view the video that accompanies this lesson.

15

Programming PivotTables and PivotCharts

PivotTables are Excel's most powerful feature. They are an amazing tool that can summarize more than a million rows of data into concise, meaningful reports in a matter of seconds. You can format the reports in many ways, and include an interactive chart to complement the reports at no extra cost of time.

If you are not familiar with PivotTables, you are not alone. Surveys of Excel users worldwide have consistently indicated that far less than half of those surveyed said they use PivotTables, including people who use Excel throughout their entire workday. Because PivotTables are worth becoming familiar with, this lesson starts with an overview of PivotTables and PivotCharts, followed by examples of how to create and manipulate them programmatically with VBA.

CREATING A PIVOTTABLE REPORT

Suppose you manage the clothing sales department for a national department store. You receive tens of thousands of sales records from your stores all over the country, with lists that look similar to Figure 15-1. With lists this large, it's impossible to gain any meaningful insight into trends or marketing opportunities unless you can organize the data in a summarized fashion.

	A	B	C	D	E	F	G
1	Store ID	Region	Item	When	Quantity	Revenue	
2	Store 9	West	Jackets	Quarter 1	1632	6045	
3	Store 3	North	Jackets	Quarter 2	1028	3808	
4	Store 7	West	Pants	Quarter 3	574	2127	
5	Store 6	South	Jackets	Quarter 4	2059	7628	
6	Store 6	South	Shirts	Quarter 1	217	804	
7	Store 8	West	Hats	Quarter 2	116	430	
8	Store 5	South	Jackets	Quarter 3	2179	8074	
9	Store 3	North	Pants	Quarter 4	150	558	
10	Store 1	East	Jackets	Quarter 1	1695	6281	
11	Store 5	South	Jackets	Quarter 2	1595	5908	
12	Store 5	South	Jackets	Quarter 3	2152	7972	
13	Store 5	South	Jackets	Quarter 4	822	3048	
14	Store 4	North	Shirts	Quarter 1	1217	4508	
15	Store 7	West	Shirts	Quarter 2	2007	7434	
16	Store 4	North	Hats	Quarter 3	1767	6548	
17	Store 2	East	Jackets	Quarter 4	440	1632	
18	Store 4	North	Jackets	Quarter 1	1220	4521	
19	Store 5	South	Jackets	Quarter 2	1203	4457	
20	Store 9	West	Jackets	Quarter 3	1244	4609	
21	Store 5	South	Jackets	Quarter 4	1292	4788	
22	Store 3	North	Jackets	Quarter 1	927	3434	
23	Store 1	East	Hats	Quarter 2	2178	8067	
24	Store 5	South	Hats	Quarter 3	1563	5791	
25	Store 5	South	Jackets	Quarter 4	2512	9307	
26	Store 1	East	Jackets	Quarter 1	90	336	
27	Store 3	North	Hats	Quarter 2	545	2020	
28	Store 8	West	Shirts	Quarter 3	2081	7711	
29	Store 4	North	Shirts	Quarter 4	61	229	
30	Store 2	East	Scarves	Quarter 1	2617	9694	
31	Store 6	South	Jackets	Quarter 2	660	2447	
32	Store 6	South	Jackets	Quarter 3	2529	9367	
33	Store 8	West	Jackets	Quarter 4	586	2172	
34	Store 7	West	Jackets	Quarter 1	683	2530	
35	Store 4	North	Pants	Quarter 2	1775	6577	
36	Store 2	East	Hats	Quarter 3	953	3531	

Sheet1 / Sheet2 / Sheet3 / Sheet4

FIGURE 15-1

If you select a single cell anywhere in the list, such as cell E7, which is selected in Figure 15-2, you can create a PivotTable by selecting the Insert tab and clicking the PivotTable icon. The Create PivotTable dialog box will appear, with the Table Range field already filled in, as shown in Figure 15-3. I chose to keep the PivotTable on the same worksheet as the source data, and for the PivotTable's top-left corner to occupy cell H4.

> *When locating a PivotTable on the same worksheet alongside the source table, it's best to have at least one empty column between the source table and your PivotTable. It's also a good idea to leave a few empty rows above the PivotTable to leave room for the Report Filter area (what was called the Page Area in version 2003).*

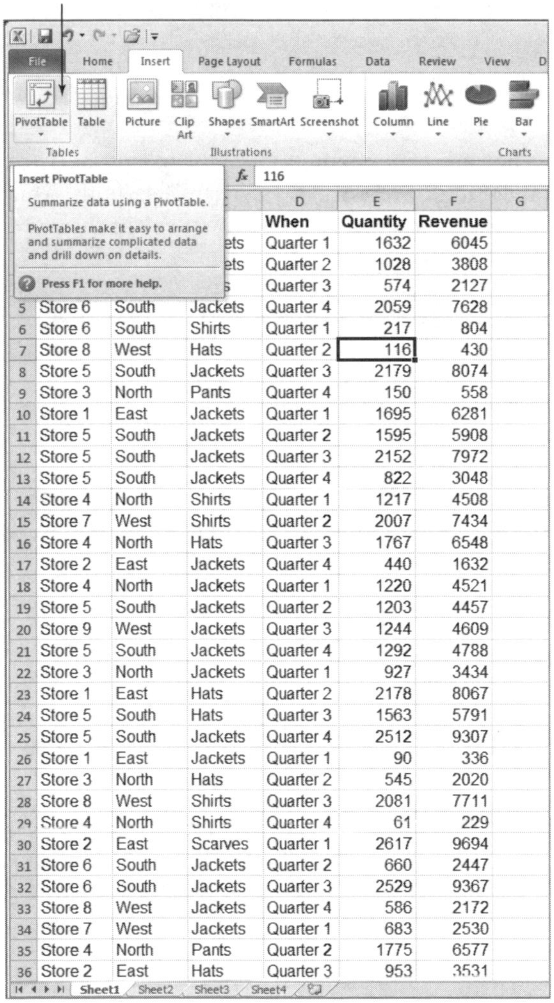

FIGURE 15-2

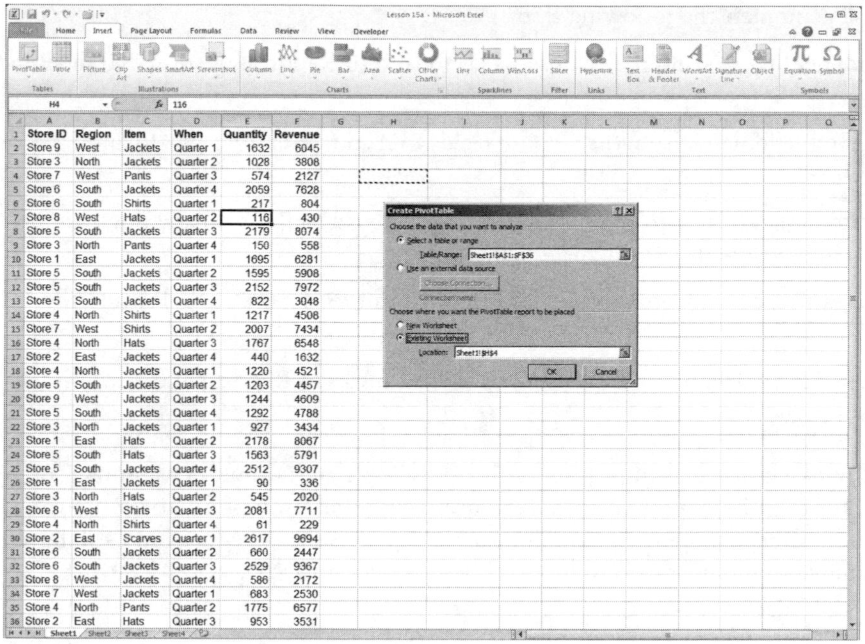

FIGURE 15-3

Using Excel version 2010, when you click the OK button you'll see an image similar to Figure 15-4, with the representation of where the PivotTable will be, and the Field List at the right.

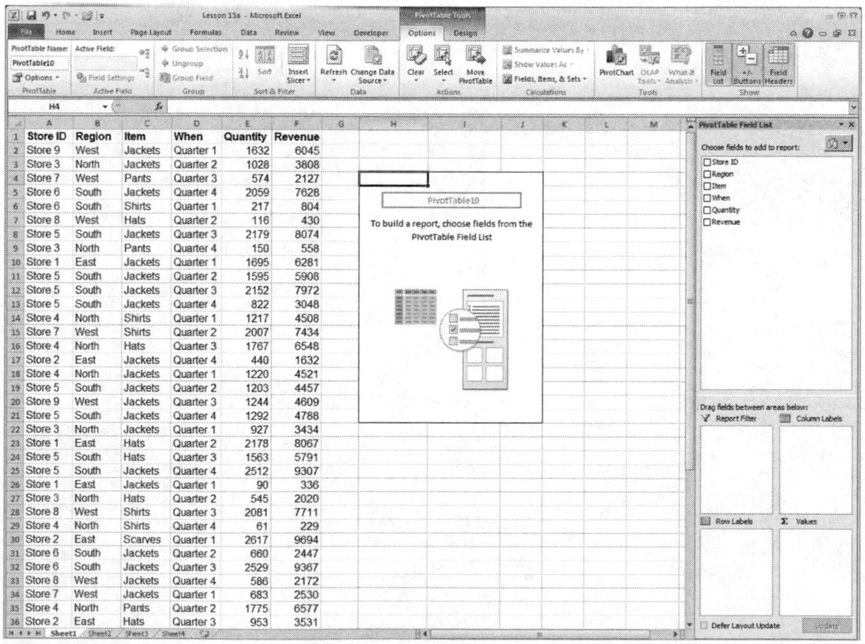

FIGURE 15-4

To create a PivotTable, complete the following steps:

1. Drag the Item field name from the Choose Fields to Add to Report pane down to the Report Filter pane.

2. Drag the Region field name from the Choose Fields to Add to Report pane down to the Row Labels pane.

3. Drag the Store ID field name from the Choose Fields to Add to Report pane down to the Row Labels pane, below the Region field name.

4. Drag the When field name from the Choose Fields to Add to Report pane down to the Column Labels pane.

5. Drag the Revenue field name from the Choose Fields to Add to Report pane down to the Values pane.

Your worksheet will look similar to Figure 15-5, with a PivotTable that shows the summary of Revenue by Quarter for each Region, with each Region showing the detail of its stores' activities. The source list could have been more than a million rows deep, and the process would still have only taken Excel a couple of moments to produce the PivotTable report.

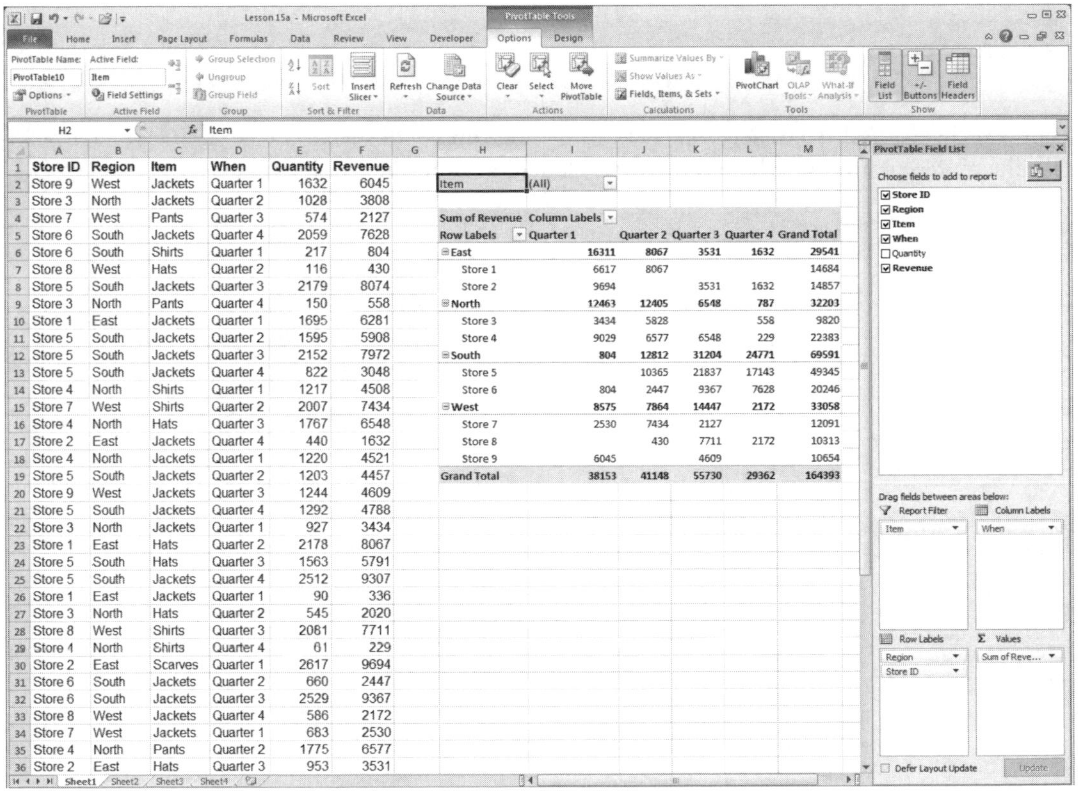

FIGURE 15-5

Hiding the PivotTable Field List

For now, you are done with the PivotTable Field List, so to clear it off your screen, you can click the "X" close button on its title bar, click its Ribbon icon on the PivotTable Tools Option tab, or you can right-click anywhere on the PivotTable area and select Hide Field List, as shown in Figure 15-6. When you want to see the Field List again, click the Field List Ribbon icon, or right-click anywhere on the PivotTable area again and select Show Field List.

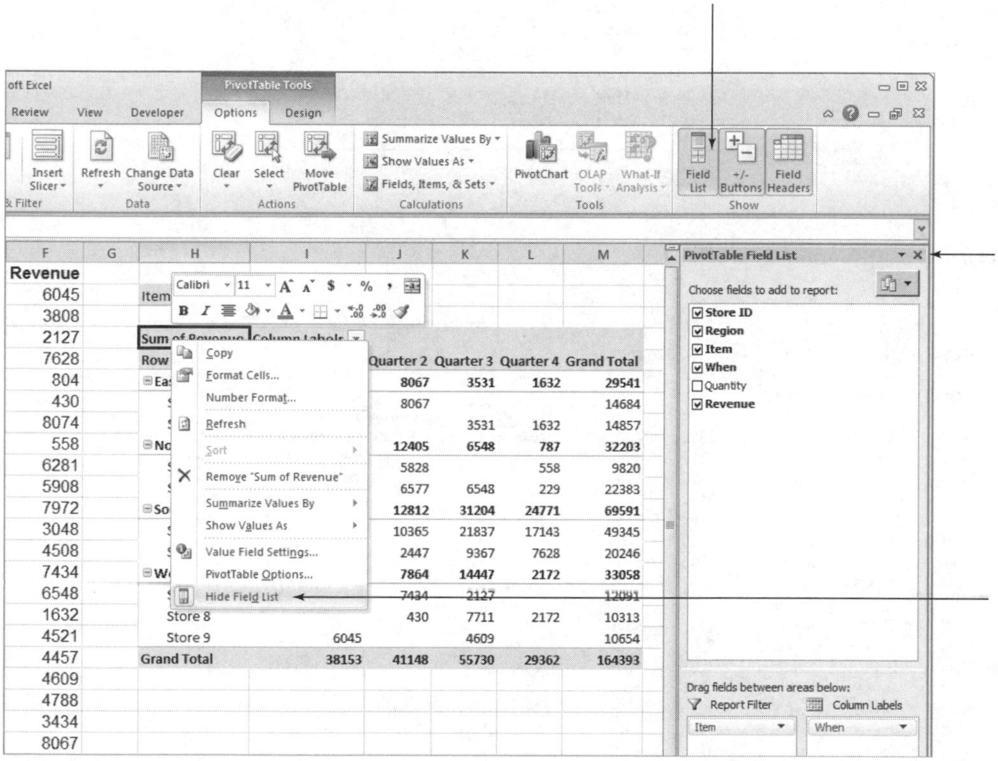

FIGURE 15-6

Using the Report Filter Area

Above the PivotTable's Report area, you see a small filter-looking icon in cell I2, in what is called the Report Filter area. The Item field name was dragged to that area in Step 1 of the process that created this PivotTable. If you click the filter icon (clearly seen in Figure 15-8), you'll see a unique list of clothing items, of which you can select one or several in order to have the PivotTable show only the data relating to the item(s) you select. In Figure 15-7, I selected the Hats item, and in Figure 15-8, you can see how the PivotTable adjusts itself to show only the columns and rows where data is present for the sale of hats.

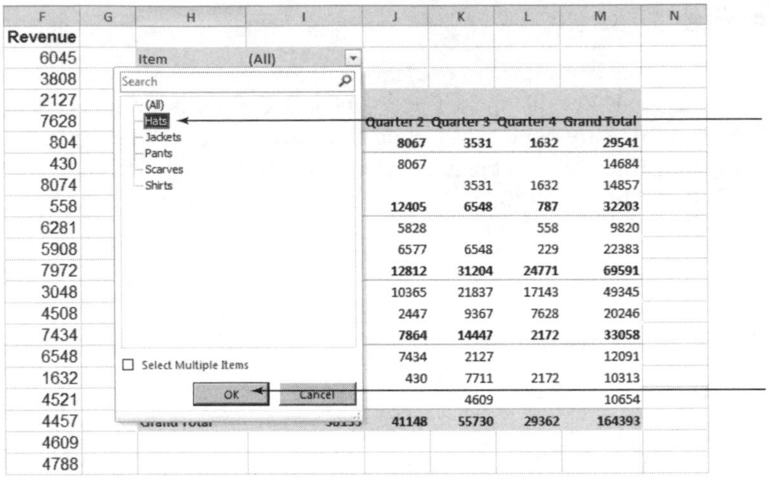

FIGURE 15-7

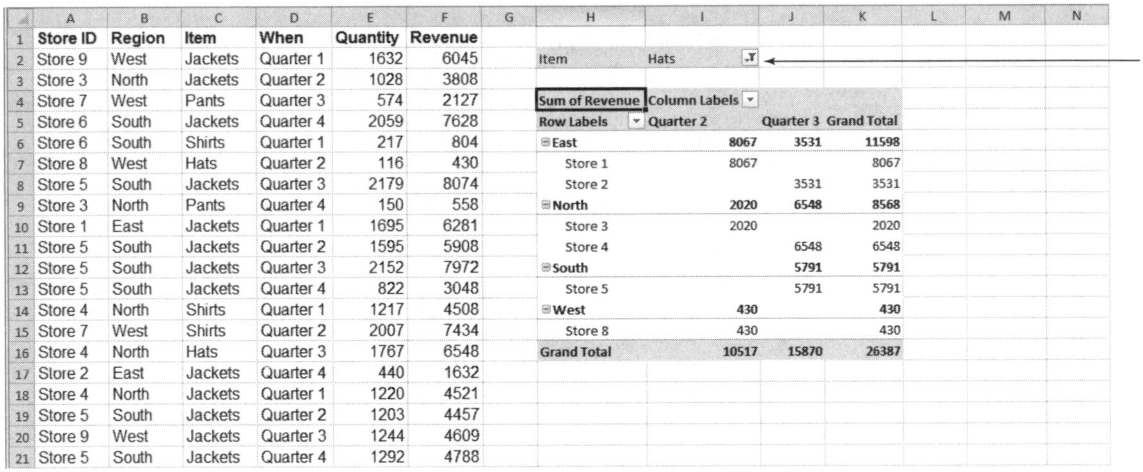

FIGURE 15-8

Formatting Numbers in the Values Area

You can see that the numbers in the PivotTable's Values area are unformatted. As an example of formatting them as Currency, right-click any cell in the Values area and select Value Field Settings as indicated in Figure 15-9. In the Value Field Settings dialog box, click the Number Format button as shown in Figure 15-10.

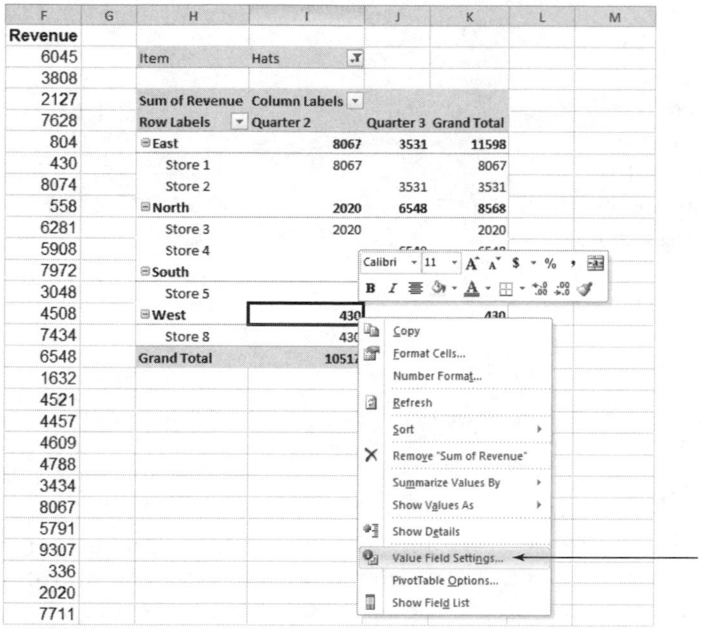

F	G	H	I	J	K	L	M
Revenue							
6045		Item	Hats				
3808							
2127		Sum of Revenue	Column Labels				
7628		Row Labels	Quarter 2	Quarter 3	Grand Total		
804		⊟East	8067	3531	11598		
430		Store 1	8067		8067		
8074		Store 2		3531	3531		
558		⊟North	2020	6548	8568		
6281		Store 3	2020		2020		
5908		Store 4					
7972		⊟South					
3048		Store 5					
4508		⊟West	430		430		
7434		Store 8	430				
6548		Grand Total	10517				
1632							
4521							
4457							
4609							
4788							
3434							
8067							
5791							
9307							
336							
2020							
7711							

FIGURE 15-9

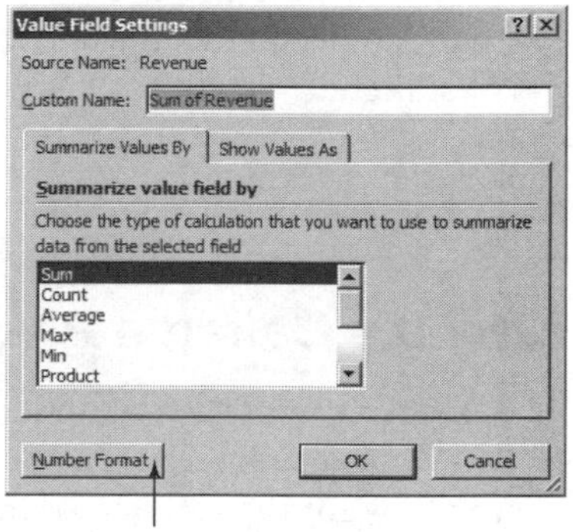

FIGURE 15-10

The familiar Format Cells dialog box will appear next. In Figure 15-11, I selected Currency with the dollar sign symbol and no decimal places. After you click OK here, you then need to click the OK button of the Value Field Settings dialog box, as shown in Figure 15-12.

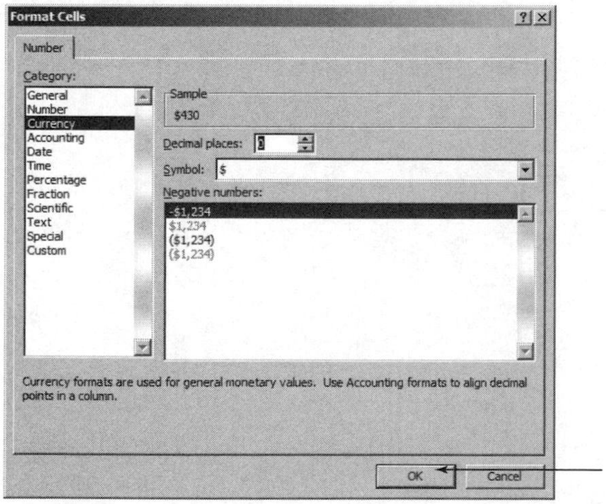

FIGURE 15-11

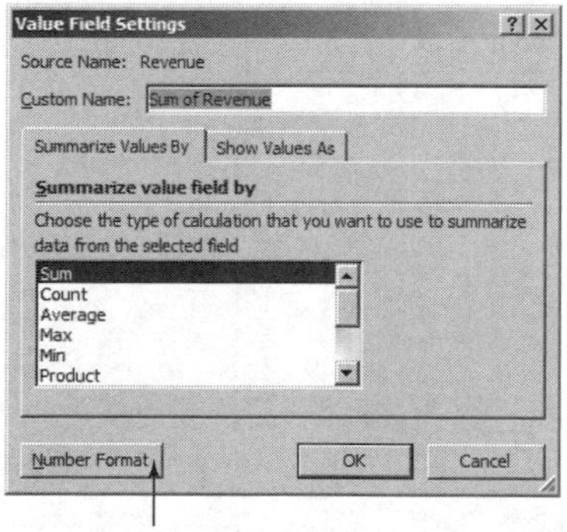

FIGURE 15-12

You will see the cells in the Values area formatted as Currency. Recall that earlier, the item named Hats was selected in the Report Filter area. Go ahead and click the filter icon in cell I2, select the All item, and click OK, as indicated in Figure 15-13. You'll see that the PivotTable report is now fully displayed, with all the Values area cells formatted as Currency, including the cells that had been hidden while the Hats item was filtered.

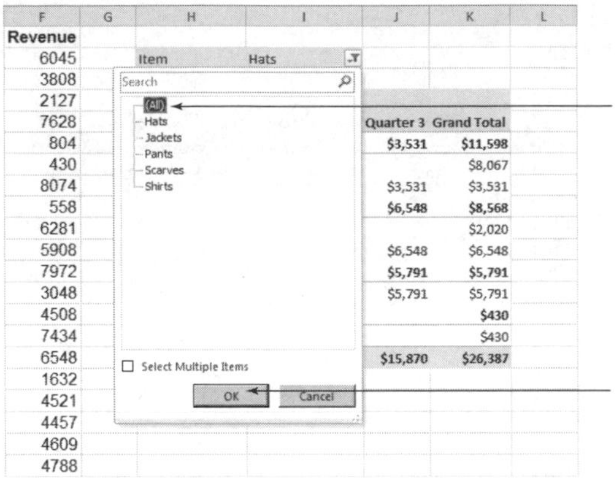

FIGURE 15-13

Why It's Called a PivotTable

One of the most attractive features of a PivotTable is its ability to display the same data in whatever row-and-column arrangement of your field names that you prefer. Just as the essence of a pivot is to allow for the rotation or maneuver from a central point, you can rearrange your source data by varying the location of your field names in the row and column areas of your PivotTable.

For example, since you have summarized the clothing stores by Revenue for each Region by Quarter, you now want to look at the Quantity of each Item that was sold by Region. Reopen the PivotTable Field List and pivot your data by dragging the Item field name out of the Report Filter pane and into the Row Labels pane. Relocate the Regions field into the Column Headers pane. Finally, in the Choose Fields to Add to Report pane, deselect Revenue and select Quantity. Your new PivotTable report will look like Figure 15-14.

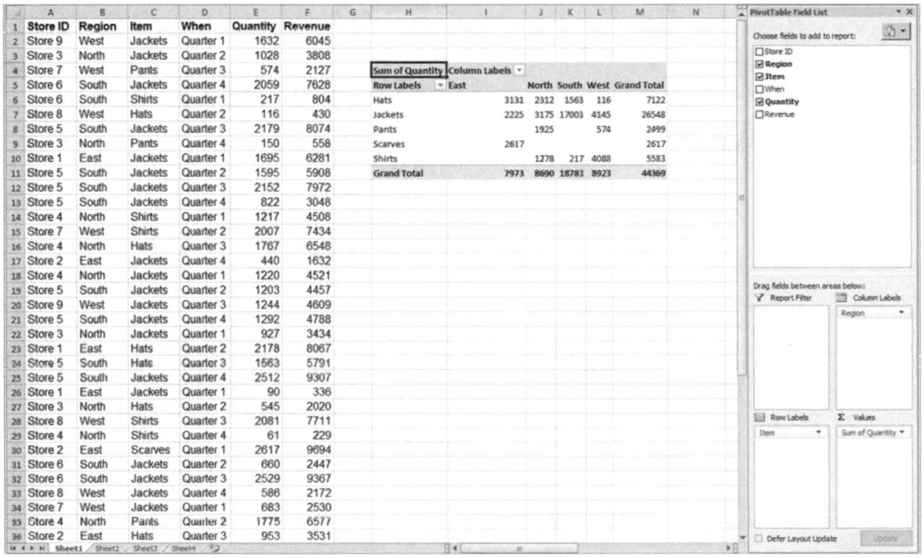

FIGURE 15-14

CREATING A PIVOTCHART

Creating a PivotChart is very easy, only requiring an extra mouse click. You can create a PivotChart using either of two methods. One method is right from the start, when you first indicate to Excel that you want to create a new PivotTable. The other method is to create a PivotChart after you have already created a PivotTable.

In Figure 15-15, notice that you can click the arrow on the lower half of the PivotTable icon on the Ribbon's Insert tab, where an option is there for you to select PivotChart. If you want a PivotChart with your new PivotTable, just select the PivotChart option, and a PivotChart will be created as you build your PivotTable in the PivotTable Field List.

	A		B	C	D	E	F	G
1	Store ID		Region	Item	When	Quantity	Revenue	
2	Store 9		West	Jackets	Quarter 1	1632	6045	
3	Store 3		North	Jackets	Quarter 2	1028	3808	
4	Store 7		West	Pants	Quarter 3	574	2127	
5	Store 6		South	Jackets	Quarter 4	2059	7628	
6	Store 6		South	Shirts	Quarter 1	217	804	
7	Store 8		West	Hats	Quarter 2	116	430	
8	Store 5		South	Jackets	Quarter 3	2179	8074	
9	Store 3		North	Pants	Quarter 4	150	558	
10	Store 1		East	Jackets	Quarter 1	1695	6281	

FIGURE 15-15

If you create a PivotTable and later decide you'd like a PivotChart to go along with it, you can select any cell in the PivotTable, click the Options tab in the PivotTable Tools section of the Ribbon, and click the PivotChart icon as indicated in Figure 15-16. You will see the Insert Chart dialog box appear, where you would select your preferred chart type. In Figure 15-17 I selected the Clustered Column chart type, and then I clicked OK. The result is a PivotChart tied to the PivotTable as shown in Figure 15-18.

F	G	H	I	J	K	L	M	N
Revenue								
6045								
3808								
2127		Sum of Quantity	Column Labels					
7628		Row Labels	East	North	South	West	Grand Total	
804		Hats	3131	2312	1563	116	7122	
430		Jackets	2225	3175	17003	4145	26548	
8074		Pants		1925		574	2499	
558		Scarves	2617				2617	
6281		Shirts		1278	217	4088	5583	
5908		Grand Total	7973	8690	18783	8923	44369	
7972								
3048								

FIGURE 15-16

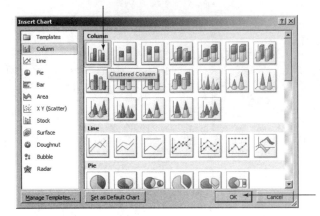

FIGURE 15-17

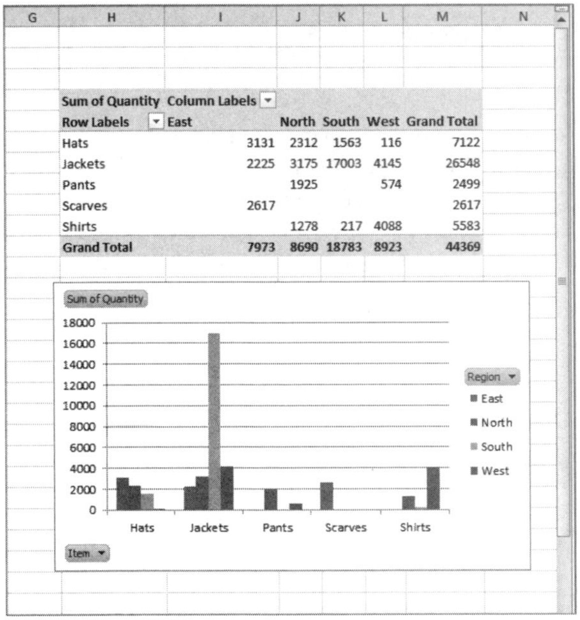

	Sum of Quantity	Column Labels					
	Row Labels	East	North	South	West	Grand Total	
	Hats		3131	2312	1563	116	7122
	Jackets		2225	3175	17003	4145	26548
	Pants			1925		574	2499
	Scarves	2617					2617
	Shirts			1278	217	4088	5583
	Grand Total	7973	8690	18783	8923	44369	

FIGURE 15-18

As you can see, when it comes to PivotCharts, Excel does almost all the grunt work for you. All you need to do is tell Excel that you want a PivotChart, and what type of chart you want, and your chart will be produced with its accompanying PivotTable.

> There is a lot more you can do with PivotCharts and PivotTables, like many other topics, it's one that can fill an entire book. My objective so far in the lesson is to cover the basics of creating and working with PivotTables as a foundation for the VBA examples in the next sections.

PivotCharts are great — they are equipped with Field buttons so you can choose which items in which fields you want to see. Whatever field setting you select on a PivotChart will make the same change to its PivotTable. The following macro will toggle between showing and hiding the Field buttons on your PivotChart:

```
Sub ShowHidePivotChartFieldButtons()
ActiveSheet.ChartObjects(1).Activate
With ActiveChart
.HasPivotFields = Not .HasPivotFields
End With
Range("A1").Select
End Sub
```

UNDERSTANDING PIVOTCACHES

A PivotCache is an object that you do not see, as it is working behind the scenes when a new PivotTable is created directly from the source data. The PivotCache is a container that holds a static copy of the source data in memory.

PivotTables do not summarize data directly from the source data, but rather from the PivotCache that memorized a snapshot of the data. That is why, in the native Excel environment not enhanced with VBA, if you change a piece of existing data in the source data range, the PivotTable report does not reflect that change until you *refresh* the PivotTable.

Figure 15-19 shows the Refresh menu item when you right-click a cell that is part of a PivotTable. The Refresh button actually refreshes the PivotCache.

The PivotCache, though not seen, maintains the source data beforehand in a static go-to container. Keeping the data in PivotCache memory makes pivoting and recalculations a snap, but the downside is extra workbook size and less memory for other tasks.

FIGURE 15-19

When you create a PivotTable manually, Excel does not bother you with the PivotCache details. If you were to create a PivotTable in VBA, you'd need to address the PivotCache issue in code. Suppose you are creating a new PivotTable based on the original source data that has been shown in this lesson. Your first step would be to program VBA to tell Excel four pieces of information:

1. You want to add a PivotCache to the workbook.
2. The location of the source data.
3. Based on items 1 and 2, create the PivotTable.
4. Specify where the PivotTable will be placed.

Assuming that the worksheet holding the source data is the active sheet, and that you want the PivotTable to be located next to the source data, the following single line of code would handle all those instructions:

```
ThisWorkbook.PivotCaches.Add _
(SourceType:=xlDatabase, _
SourceData:=Range("A1").CurrentRegion).CreatePivotTable _
TableDestination:="R4C" & Range("A1").CurrentRegion.Columns.Count + 2
```

> *The notation* `"R4C" & Range("A1").CurrentRegion.Columns.Count + 2` *is translated as the worksheet cell that is on row 4 of the column that is two columns to the right of the last column in the source range. Recall from earlier in the lesson that I recommend placing the top-left corner of the PivotTable on row 4, and with an empty column separating the source data and the new PivotTable.*

The result you get is a PivotTable, but you'd never know by its appearance at the moment — a curious range of four cells that look as if they were formatted for thin borders. In this example, the four cells are in range H4:I5 as shown in Figure 15-20.

	A	B	C	D	E	F	G	H	I	J	K	L	M	N
1	Store ID	Region	Item	When	Quantity	Revenue								
2	Store 9	West	Jackets	Quarter 1	1632	6045								
3	Store 3	North	Jackets	Quarter 2	1028	3808								
4	Store 7	West	Pants	Quarter 3	574	2127								
5	Store 6	South	Jackets	Quarter 4	2059	7628								
6	Store 6	South	Shirts	Quarter 1	217	804								
7	Store 8	West	Hats	Quarter 2	116	430								
8	Store 5	South	Jackets	Quarter 3	2179	8074								
9	Store 3	North	Pants	Quarter 4	150	558								
10	Store 1	East	Jackets	Quarter 1	1695	6281								
11	Store 5	South	Jackets	Quarter 2	1595	5908								
12	Store 5	South	Jackets	Quarter 3	2152	7972								
13	Store 5	South	Jackets	Quarter 4	822	3048								
14	Store 4	North	Shirts	Quarter 1	1217	4508								
15	Store 7	West	Shirts	Quarter 2	2007	7434								
16	Store 4	North	Hats	Quarter 3	1767	6548								
17	Store 2	East	Jackets	Quarter 4	440	1632								
18	Store 4	North	Jackets	Quarter 1	1220	4521								
19	Store 5	South	Jackets	Quarter 2	1203	4457								
20	Store 9	West	Jackets	Quarter 3	1244	4609								
21	Store 5	South	Jackets	Quarter 4	1292	4788								
22	Store 3	North	Jackets	Quarter 1	927	3434								
23	Store 1	East	Hats	Quarter 2	2178	8067								
24	Store 5	South	Hats	Quarter 3	1563	5791								
25	Store 5	South	Jackets	Quarter 4	2512	9307								
26	Store 1	East	Jackets	Quarter 1	90	336								
27	Store 3	North	Hats	Quarter 2	545	2020								
28	Store 8	West	Shirts	Quarter 3	2081	7711								
29	Store 4	North	Shirts	Quarter 4	61	229								
30	Store 2	East	Scarves	Quarter 1	2617	9694								
31	Store 6	South	Jackets	Quarter 2	660	2447								
32	Store 6	South	Jackets	Quarter 3	2529	9367								
33	Store 8	West	Jackets	Quarter 4	586	2172								
34	Store 7	West	Jackets	Quarter 1	683	2530								
35	Store 4	North	Pants	Quarter 2	1775	6577								
36	Store 2	East	Hats	Quarter 3	953	3531								

FIGURE 15-20

The macro is just getting started but I wanted to show you in slow motion what is taking place under the radar when a new PivotTable is created. Actually, with the preceding line of code executed, you could select one of those four cells and the PivotTable Field List would appear, inviting you to drag fields to your desired location as shown in Figure 15-21.

	A	B	C	D	E	F
1	Store ID	Region	Item	When	Quantity	Revenue
2	Store 9	West	Jackets	Quarter 1	1632	6045
3	Store 3	North	Jackets	Quarter 2	1028	3808
4	Store 7	West	Pants	Quarter 3	574	2127
5	Store 6	South	Jackets	Quarter 4	2059	7628
6	Store 6	South	Shirts	Quarter 1	217	804
7	Store 8	West	Hats	Quarter 2	116	430
8	Store 5	South	Jackets	Quarter 3	2179	8074
9	Store 3	North	Pants	Quarter 4	150	558
10	Store 1	East	Jackets	Quarter 1	1695	6281
11	Store 5	South	Jackets	Quarter 2	1595	5908
12	Store 5	South	Jackets	Quarter 3	2152	7972
13	Store 5	South	Jackets	Quarter 4	822	3048
14	Store 4	North	Shirts	Quarter 1	1217	4508
15	Store 7	West	Shirts	Quarter 2	2007	7434
16	Store 4	North	Hats	Quarter 3	1767	6548
17	Store 2	East	Jackets	Quarter 4	440	1632
18	Store 4	North	Jackets	Quarter 1	1220	4521
19	Store 5	South	Jackets	Quarter 2	1203	4457
20	Store 9	West	Jackets	Quarter 3	1244	4609
21	Store 5	South	Jackets	Quarter 4	1292	4788
22	Store 3	North	Jackets	Quarter 1	927	3434
23	Store 1	East	Hats	Quarter 2	2178	8067
24	Store 5	South	Hats	Quarter 3	1563	5791
25	Store 5	South	Jackets	Quarter 4	2512	9307
26	Store 1	East	Jackets	Quarter 1	90	336
27	Store 3	North	Hats	Quarter 2	545	2020
28	Store 8	West	Shirts	Quarter 3	2081	7711
29	Store 4	North	Shirts	Quarter 4	61	229
30	Store 2	East	Scarves	Quarter 1	2617	9694
31	Store 6	South	Jackets	Quarter 2	660	2447
32	Store 6	South	Jackets	Quarter 3	2529	9367
33	Store 8	West	Jackets	Quarter 4	586	2172
34	Store 7	West	Jackets	Quarter 1	683	2530
35	Store 4	North	Pants	Quarter 2	1775	6577
36	Store 2	East	Hats	Quarter 3	953	3531

PivotTable Field List

Choose fields to add to report:
☐ Store ID
☐ Region
☐ Item
☐ When
☐ Quantity
☐ Revenue

Drag fields between areas below:
▽ Report Filter   ▦ Column Labels

▦ Row Labels   Σ Values

☐ Defer Layout Update   Update

FIGURE 15-21

If you want your PivotTable's PivotCache to refresh automatically when a cell in your source list changes, the following Worksheet_Change event will handle that. Note that the code uses the PivotTable's Index property for the first or only PivotTable on the worksheet to be refreshed.

```
Private Sub Worksheet_Change(ByVal Target As Range)
If Intersect(Target, Range("A1").CurrentRegion) Is Nothing _
Or Target.Cells.Count > 1 Then Exit Sub
ActiveSheet.PivotTables(1).PivotCache.Refresh
End Sub
```

MANIPULATING PIVOTFIELDS IN VBA

PivotFields are the row and column areas that you place your field names into, depending on how you want the PivotTable to display your data. The following pieces of VBA code perform the placement of PivotFields as they were for the PivotTable that was manually created earlier in the lesson. Two fields (Region and Store ID) are placed as row labels, and one field (When) is placed as a column label. The Revenue field is placed in the Values area, and the Report Filter area is populated by the Items field.

```
With ActiveSheet.PivotTables(1)

'First (outer) row field
With .PivotFields("Region")
.Orientation = xlRowField
.Position = 1
End With

'Second (inner) row field
With .PivotFields("Store ID")
.Orientation = xlRowField
.Position = 2
End With

'Column field.
With .PivotFields("When")
.Orientation = xlColumnField
.Position = 1
End With

'Report Filter field
With .PivotFields("Item")
.Orientation = xlPageField
.Position = 1
End With

'Revenue in the Values field
.AddDataField ActiveSheet.PivotTables(1).PivotFields("Revenue"), _
"Sum of Amount", xlSum

End With
```

 Be sure to name your PivotFields correctly! They must be spelled the same way in your code as they are in the header cells of your source list. If you misspell the field names in your code, VBA will let you know with a run time error, because the field names you'd be instructing VBA to manipulate do not exist.

MANIPULATING PIVOTITEMS WITH VBA

PivotItems are programmable in PivotTables, and as an example, you can arrange to see just one particular PivotItem in a field. In a PivotTable that was created earlier in the lesson, a Region field was added. Suppose you want to see activity only for the North PivotItem, and hide the South, East, and West PivotItems. The following macro will accomplish that.

```
Sub ShowSingleItem()
Dim objPivotField As PivotField
Dim objPivotItem As PivotItem
Set objPivotField = _
ActiveSheet.PivotTables(1).PivotFields(Index:="Region")
For Each objPivotItem In objPivotField.PivotItems
If objPivotItem.Name = "North" Then
objPivotItem.Visible = True
Else
objPivotItem.Visible = False
End If
Next objPivotItem
End Sub
```

The following macro will show all the PivotItems:

```
Sub ShowAllItems()
Dim objPivotField As PivotField
Dim objPivotItem As PivotItem
Set objPivotField = _
ActiveSheet.PivotTables(1).PivotFields(Index:="Region")
For Each objPivotItem In objPivotField.PivotItems
objPivotItem.Visible = True
Next objPivotItem
End Sub
```

CREATING A PIVOTTABLES COLLECTION

PivotTables are objects for which there is a Collection object, just as there is for worksheets and workbooks. As you might guess, the name of the Collection object for PivotTables is PivotTables, and you can loop through every PivotTable on a worksheet, or throughout the workbook if you need to.

For example, if you have more than one PivotTable on a worksheet and they are tied to the same source list that starts in cell A1, this Worksheet_Change event would refresh all PivotTables on that worksheet automatically when the source data is changed:

```
Private Sub Worksheet_Change(ByVal Target As Range)
If Intersect(Target, Range("A1").CurrentRegion) Is Nothing _
Or Target.Cells.Count > 1 Then Exit Sub
Dim PT As PivotTable
For Each PT In ActiveSheet.PivotTables
PT.RefreshTable
Next PT
End Sub
```

Suppose you have several PivotTables on many different worksheets and you want to be confident that every PivotTable displays the current data from its respective source list. The following `Workbook_Open` procedure will refresh every PivotTable in the workbook when the workbook opens:

```
Private Sub Workbook_Open()
Dim wks As Worksheet, PT As PivotTable
For Each wks In Worksheets
For Each PT In wks.PivotTables
PT.RefreshTable
Next PT
Next wks
End Sub
```

> You can avoid looping through all your PivotTables by using VBA's `RefreshAll` method to refresh all PivotTables at once. The single line of code would be `ActiveWorkbook.RefreshAll`. The `RefreshAll` method also refreshes all external data ranges, such as web queries, for the specified workbook.

You might need to delete all the PivotTables on a worksheet. When you delete a PivotTable, what you are really doing is clearing the cells that are occupied by the PivotTable. The following macro will delete all the PivotTables on the active worksheet:

```
Sub DeleteAllPivotTables()
Dim objPT As PivotTable, iCount As Integer
For iCount = ActiveSheet.PivotTables.Count To 1 Step -1
Set objPT = ActiveSheet.PivotTables(iCount)
objPT.PivotSelect ""
Selection.Clear
Next iCount
End Sub
```

TRY IT

In this lesson, you write a macro that adds a PivotChart to accompany an existing PivotTable. You would like to create a PivotChart that will be located on the worksheet below the PivotTable.

Lesson Requirements

Your worksheet contains a list of source data, and you already have a PivotTable on your worksheet. The worksheet is shown in Figure 15-22 before the PivotChart has been added. To get the sample database files you can download Lesson 15 from the book's website at www.wrox.com.

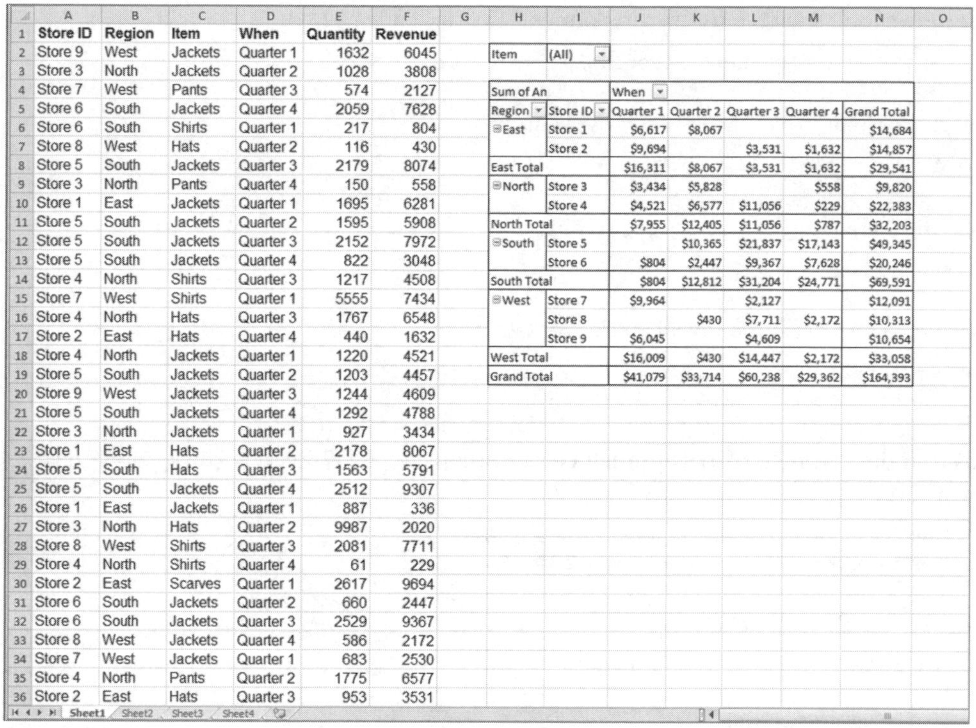

	A	B	C	D	E	F	G	H	I	J	K	L	M	N	O
1	Store ID	Region	Item	When	Quantity	Revenue									
2	Store 9	West	Jackets	Quarter 1	1632	6045		Item	(All)						
3	Store 3	North	Jackets	Quarter 2	1028	3808									
4	Store 7	West	Pants	Quarter 3	574	2127		Sum of An		When					
5	Store 6	South	Jackets	Quarter 4	2059	7628		Region	Store ID	Quarter 1	Quarter 2	Quarter 3	Quarter 4	Grand Total	
6	Store 6	South	Shirts	Quarter 1	217	804		⊟East	Store 1	$6,617	$8,067			$14,684	
7	Store 8	West	Hats	Quarter 2	116	430			Store 2	$9,694		$3,531	$1,632	$14,857	
8	Store 5	South	Jackets	Quarter 3	2179	8074		East Total		$16,311	$8,067	$3,531	$1,632	$29,541	
9	Store 3	North	Pants	Quarter 4	150	558		⊟North	Store 3	$3,434	$5,828		$558	$9,820	
10	Store 1	East	Jackets	Quarter 1	1695	6281			Store 4	$4,521	$6,577	$11,056	$229	$22,383	
11	Store 5	South	Jackets	Quarter 2	1595	5908		North Total		$7,955	$12,405	$11,056	$787	$32,203	
12	Store 5	South	Jackets	Quarter 3	2152	7972		⊟South	Store 5		$10,365	$21,837	$17,143	$49,345	
13	Store 5	South	Jackets	Quarter 4	822	3048			Store 6	$804	$2,447	$9,367	$7,628	$20,246	
14	Store 4	North	Shirts	Quarter 3	1217	4508		South Total		$804	$12,812	$31,204	$24,771	$69,591	
15	Store 7	West	Shirts	Quarter 1	5555	7434		⊟West	Store 7	$9,964		$2,127		$12,091	
16	Store 4	North	Hats	Quarter 3	1767	6548			Store 8		$430	$7,711	$2,172	$10,313	
17	Store 2	East	Hats	Quarter 4	440	1632			Store 9	$6,045		$4,609		$10,654	
18	Store 4	North	Jackets	Quarter 1	1220	4521		West Total		$16,009	$430	$14,447	$2,172	$33,058	
19	Store 5	South	Jackets	Quarter 2	1203	4457		Grand Total		$41,079	$33,714	$60,238	$29,362	$164,393	
20	Store 9	West	Jackets	Quarter 3	1244	4609									
21	Store 5	South	Jackets	Quarter 4	1292	4788									
22	Store 3	North	Jackets	Quarter 1	927	3434									
23	Store 1	East	Hats	Quarter 2	2178	8067									
24	Store 5	South	Hats	Quarter 3	1563	5791									
25	Store 5	South	Jackets	Quarter 4	2512	9307									
26	Store 1	East	Jackets	Quarter 1	887	336									
27	Store 3	North	Hats	Quarter 2	9987	2020									
28	Store 8	West	Shirts	Quarter 3	2081	7711									
29	Store 4	North	Shirts	Quarter 4	61	229									
30	Store 2	East	Scarves	Quarter 1	2617	9694									
31	Store 6	South	Jackets	Quarter 2	660	2447									
32	Store 6	South	Jackets	Quarter 3	2529	9367									
33	Store 8	West	Jackets	Quarter 4	586	2172									
34	Store 7	West	Jackets	Quarter 1	683	2530									
35	Store 4	North	Pants	Quarter 2	1775	6577									
36	Store 2	East	Hats	Quarter 3	953	3531									

Sheet1 / Sheet2 / Sheet3 / Sheet4

FIGURE 15-22

Step-by-Step

1. Activate the worksheet that contains the source data list and PivotTable.

2. Press Alt+F11 to go to the Visual Basic Editor.

3. From the menu bar, click Insert ⇨ Module.

4. In the new module, enter **Sub CreatePivotChart** and press the Enter key. VBA will produce the following lines of code for you:

```
Sub CreatePivotChart()

End Sub
```

5. Turn off ScreenUpdating to help your macro run faster by not refreshing the screen as objects in the code are created and manipulated.

```
Application.ScreenUpdating = False
```

6. Declare an `Object` variable for the existing PivotTable:

```
Dim objPT As PivotTable
```

7. Set the `Object` variable for the first (index #1) PivotTable:

```
Set objPT = ActiveSheet.PivotTables(1)
```

8. Select the PivotTable:

```
objPT.PivotSelect ""
```

9. Add the chart:

```
Charts.Add
```

10. Place the chart onto the PivotTable's worksheet:

```
ActiveChart.Location Where:=xlLocationAsObject, _
Name:=objPT.Parent.Name
```

11. Position the PivotChart so its top-left corner occupies cell H23, a few rows below the PivotTable:

```
ActiveChart.Parent.Left = Range("H23").Left
ActiveChart.Parent.Top = Range("H23").Top
```

12. Deselect the PivotChart:

```
Range("A1").Select
```

13. Turn on ScreenUpdating:

```
Application.ScreenUpdating = True
```

14. When you have completed the macro, it will look as follows:

```
Sub CreatePivotChart()

'Turn off ScreenUpdating.
Application.ScreenUpdating = False

'Declare an Object variable for the existing PivotTable.
Dim objPT As PivotTable
'Set the Object variable for the first (index #1) PivotTable.
 Set objPT = ActiveSheet.PivotTables(1)

'Select the PivotTable.
objPT.PivotSelect ""

' Add the chart.
Charts.Add

'Place it on the PivotTable's worksheet.
ActiveChart.Location Where:=xlLocationAsObject, _
Name:=objPT.Parent.Name
```

```
'Position the PivotChart so its top left corner
'occupies cell H23, a few rows below the PivotTable.
ActiveChart.Parent.Left = Range("H23").Left
ActiveChart.Parent.Top = Range("H23").Top


'Deselect the PivotChart.
Range("A1").Select

'Turn on ScreenUpdating.
Application.ScreenUpdating = True

End Sub
```

15. Press Alt+Q to return to your worksheet and test your macro. Figure 15-23 shows what the worksheet should look like with the PivotChart added right where it was specified in VBA.

	A	B	C	D	E	F	G	H	I	J	K	L	M	N	O
1	Store ID	Region	Item	When	Quantity	Revenue									
2	Store 9	West	Jackets	Quarter 1	1632	6045		Item	(All)						
3	Store 3	North	Jackets	Quarter 2	1028	3808									
4	Store 7	West	Pants	Quarter 3	574	2127		Sum of An		When					
5	Store 6	South	Jackets	Quarter 4	2059	7628		Region	Store ID	Quarter 1	Quarter 2	Quarter 3	Quarter 4	Grand Total	
6	Store 6	South	Shirts	Quarter 1	217	804		East	Store 1	$6,617	$8,067			$14,684	
7	Store 8	West	Hats	Quarter 2	116	430			Store 2	$9,694		$3,531	$1,632	$14,857	
8	Store 5	South	Jackets	Quarter 3	2179	8074		East Total		$16,311	$8,067	$3,531	$1,632	$29,541	
9	Store 3	North	Pants	Quarter 4	150	558		North	Store 3	$3,434	$5,828		$558	$9,820	
10	Store 1	East	Jackets	Quarter 1	1695	6281			Store 4	$4,521	$6,577	$11,056	$229	$22,383	
11	Store 5	South	Jackets	Quarter 2	1595	5908		North Total		$7,955	$12,405	$11,056	$787	$32,203	
12	Store 5	South	Jackets	Quarter 3	2152	7972		South	Store 5		$10,365	$21,837	$17,143	$49,345	
13	Store 5	South	Jackets	Quarter 4	822	3048			Store 6	$804	$2,447	$9,367	$7,628	$20,246	
14	Store 4	North	Shirts	Quarter 3	1217	4508		South Total		$804	$12,812	$31,204	$24,771	$69,591	
15	Store 7	West	Shirts	Quarter 1	5555	7434		West	Store 7	$9,964		$2,127		$12,091	
16	Store 4	North	Hats	Quarter 3	1767	6548			Store 8		$430	$7,711	$2,172	$10,313	
17	Store 2	East	Hats	Quarter 4	440	1632			Store 9	$6,045		$4,609		$10,654	
18	Store 4	North	Jackets	Quarter 1	1220	4521		West Total		$16,009	$430	$14,447	$2,172	$33,058	
19	Store 5	South	Jackets	Quarter 2	1203	4457		Grand Total		$41,079	$33,714	$60,238	$29,362	$164,393	
20	Store 9	West	Jackets	Quarter 3	1244	4609									
21	Store 5	South	Jackets	Quarter 4	1292	4788									
22	Store 3	North	Jackets	Quarter 1	927	3434									
23	Store 1	East	Hats	Quarter 2	2178	8067									
24	Store 5	South	Hats	Quarter 3	1563	5791									
25	Store 5	South	Jackets	Quarter 4	2512	9307									
26	Store 1	East	Jackets	Quarter 1	887	336									
27	Store 3	North	Hats	Quarter 2	9987	2020									
28	Store 8	West	Shirts	Quarter 3	2081	7711									
29	Store 4	North	Shirts	Quarter 4	61	229									
30	Store 2	East	Scarves	Quarter 1	2617	9694									
31	Store 6	South	Jackets	Quarter 2	660	2447									
32	Store 6	South	Jackets	Quarter 3	2529	9367									
33	Store 8	West	Jackets	Quarter 4	586	2172									
34	Store 7	West	Jackets	Quarter 1	683	2530									
35	Store 4	North	Pants	Quarter 2	1775	6577									
36	Store 2	East	Hats	Quarter 3	953	3531									

FIGURE 15-23

Please select Lesson 15 on the DVD to view the video that accompanies this lesson.

16

User Defined Functions

Most Excel users who are not absolute beginners use worksheet functions in their formulas. The most common worksheet function is the SUM function, and there are hundreds more.

Basically, a function performs a calculation or evaluation, and returns a value. Functions used in your VBA expressions act the same way; they do what they are programmed to do, and return a result.

With VBA, you can write ("define") your own custom function that looks, acts, and feels like a built-in function, but with a lot more power and versatility. Once you get the hang of UDFs, you'll wonder how you ever got along without them.

WHAT IS A USER DEFINED FUNCTION?

You are already familiar with many of Excel's built-in worksheet functions such as SUM, AVERAGE, and VLOOKUP, but sometimes you will need to perform calculations or get information that none of Excel's built-in functions can accomplish. A User Defined Function (UDF) is a function in VBA that you create with arguments you specify, to use as a worksheet function or as part of a macro procedure, when a task is otherwise impossible or too cumbersome to achieve with Excel's built-in formulas and functions.

For example, you may need a formula to sum a range of numbers depending on a cell's interior color; or to extract only numbers or letters from an alphanumeric string; or to place an unchanging random number in a cell; or to test whether a particular worksheet exists or another workbook is open. UDFs are an excellent option for handling tasks when regular worksheet functions cannot or should not be used.

Characteristics of User Defined Functions

When used as a worksheet function, the purpose of a UDF is to return a number, string, array, or Boolean (true or false) value to the cell it occupies. UDFs cannot change the Excel environment in any way, meaning they cannot place a value in another cell, or change the interior color of any cell including the cell they are in, or rename a worksheet, or do anything other than return a value to their own cell.

That said, it's important to note that a UDF can be called by a macro. This allows the calling procedure (the macro) to take advantage of the UDF while still retaining the ability to change the Excel environment. This makes your UDF a versatile tool when integrated with macros.

UDFs cannot be composed by the macro recorder. Although in some cases you can record a macro and turn it into a UDF by editing the code, most of the time you will create a UDF by writing the code yourself directly into a standard module.

> *UDFs are always located in a standard module, though they can neither appear in, nor be run from, the Macro dialog. UDFs will not work if placed in any other type of module such as a worksheet, workbook, userform, or class module.*

Whichever way the UDF is called, be aware that it will always compile slower than built-in functions. Avoid reinventing the wheel by using worksheet functions wherever practical, and UDFs for what worksheet functions cannot do.

Anatomy of a UDF

When designing a UDF, it helps to consider three questions:

➤ What is the function's purpose; that is, what do you want it to accomplish?

➤ What arguments, if any, does the function need?

➤ What will the function return as a formula or provide to its caller in a macro?

A UDF always begins with the `Function` statement and ends with the `End Function` statement. Unless you want your function to be visible only to other code in the same module, it's best to declare the function as `Public`, or omit the `Public`/`Private` qualifier altogether, which will default the function's scope to `Public`. Declaring a function as `Public` will also enable the UDF to be listed in the Insert Function dialog.

The general syntax of a UDF is:

```
Function name([argument list]) as type
'VBA statements that make up the Function
[name = returned expression]
End Function
```

> *Function names must begin with a letter, and cannot contain spaces or illegal naming characters such as the slash, colon, comma, bracket, or any arithmetic operator symbols. It's always a good practice to give functions simple, meaningful names, just as you would for a macro.*

After the function's name is the argument list, which is enclosed by parentheses. If there are two or more arguments, each is separated by a comma and a space. Not every UDF will require arguments, but the parentheses are still required immediately after the function name. Following the argument list is the optional (but strongly recommended) specification of the data type, depending on the function's purpose.

Here's an example of a UDF that does not require any arguments. It returns the complete path of the Microsoft Excel program on your computer:

```
Function xlPath() As String
xlPath = Application.Path
End Function
```

On my computer, using Microsoft Office 2010 and entering the formula =xlPath() into a worksheet cell, this UDF returns the path C:\ProgramFiles\Microsoft Office\Office13.

UDF Examples That Solve Common Tasks

User Defined Functions can simplify your work by enabling you to use shorter and more readable formulas. Once you create the UDF, all the user needs to know is the function name and its arguments. User Defined Functions are very useful for handling everyday tasks that you might have thought were impossible to solve by formula. Following are a few examples of UDFs that can solve such tasks.

Sum Numbers in Colored Cells

A question that frequently arises is how to add up the numbers that are only in colored cells of a certain range. If the cells were colored by Conditional Formatting, the solution could be to sum that range of cells based on the condition, such as by using the SUMIF function. However, evaluating the property of a cell, in this case its actual interior color, is more of a challenge because no built-in worksheet function is able to do that.

As an example, Figure 16-1 shows a list of numbers in A2:A15, where some cells are colored gray and some are not. The task is to sum the numbers in gray-colored cells.

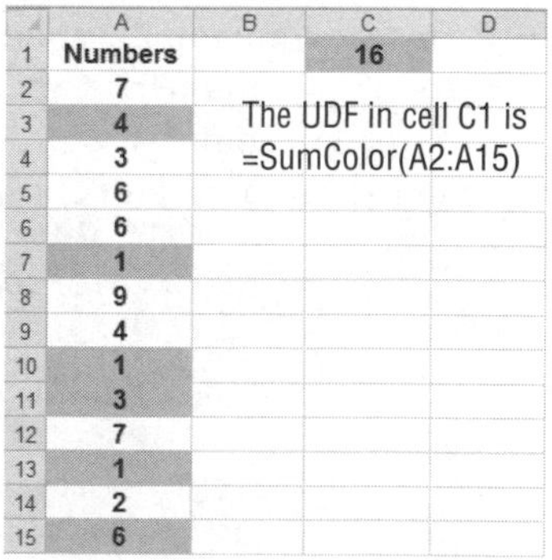

FIGURE 16-1

Outside the range, cell C1 serves the dual purpose of receiving the UDF, and also displaying the color you need to sum by. With this approach, the UDF only needs one argument to specify the range to sum:

```
Function SumColor(RangeToSum As Range) As Long
'Declare the necessary variables.
Dim ColorID As Integer, ColorCell As Range, mySum As Long
'Identify the ColorID variable so you know what color to look for.
ColorID = Range(Application.Caller.Address).Interior.ColorIndex
'Loop through each cell in the range.
For Each ColorCell In RangeToSum
'If the cell's color matches the color we are looking for,
'keep a running subtotal by adding the cell's number value
'to the mySum variable.
If ColorCell.Interior.ColorIndex = ColorID Then mySum = mySum + ColorCell.Value
Next ColorCell
'The cells have all been evaluated, so you can define the SumColor function
'by setting it equal to the mySum variable.
SumColor = mySum
End Function
```

The entry in cell C1 is `=SumColor(A2:A15)`. The UDF loops through each cell in range A2:A15, and along the way keeps a running total with the `mySum` variable when a gray cell is encountered. At the end of the UDF code, the function's name of `SumColor` is set to equal the `mySum` variable, and that enables the UDF to return 16 as the sum of gray-colored cells. Notice that because you were expecting the result to be a whole number, the Long variable type was specified for the function's name.

> This example also demonstrates another useful way to employ the `Application` `.Caller` statement that you first saw in Lesson 13. Here, the object calling the function is cell C1, which was colored gray before the UDF was entered.

Extract Numbers or Letters from an Alphanumeric String

Another common question is how to extract numbers or letters from a string that contains a mixture of alphanumeric characters. If the numbers or letters are all in predictable places or consistently grouped in some way, built-in formulas might do the job. But it gets dicey if the string has an unpredictable mishmash of characters similar to what is in column A in Figure 16-2.

	A	B	C
1	Original string	Numbers extracted	Letters extracted
2	KH5Y3W84A	5384	KHYWA
3	JU83d7x62KBV	83762	JUdxKBV
4	3L4SWc9E179	349179	LSWcE
5			
6			
7	UDF in B2 and copied down is:		UDF in C2 and copied down is:
8			
9	=ExtractNumbers(A2)		=ExtractLetters(A2)
10			

FIGURE 16-2

Following are two similar UDFs, one that extracts just the numbers from an alphanumeric string and one that extracts just the letters. Figure 16-2 shows how the formulas should be entered.

> *Remember that you can copy and paste a UDF just as you can a built-in formula or function. You can also use the fill handle to copy the UDF down.*

```
Function ExtractNumbers(strText As String)
'Declare the necessary variables.
Dim i As Integer, strDbl As String
'Loop through each character in the cell.
For i = 1 To Len(strText)
'If the character is a digit, append it to the strDbl variable.
If IsNumeric(Mid(strText, i, 1)) Then
strDbl = strDbl & Mid(strText, i, 1)
End If
Next i
'Each character in the cell has been evaluated, so you can define the
'ExtractNumbers function by setting it equal to the strDbl variable.
'The purpose of the CDbl function is to coerce the strDbl expression
'into a numeric Double data type.
ExtractNumbers = CDbl(strDbl)
End Function

Function ExtractLetters(strText As String)
'Declare the necessary variables.
Dim x As Integer, strTemp As String
'Loop through each character in the cell.
For x = 1 To Len(strText)
'If the character is not numeric, it must be a letter,
'so append it to the strTemp variable.
If Not IsNumeric(Mid(strText, x, 1)) Then
strTemp = strTemp & Mid(strText, x, 1)
End If
Next x
'Each character in the cell has been evaluated, so you can define the
'ExtractLetters function by setting it equal to the strTemp variable.
ExtractLetters = strTemp
End Function
```

Extract the Address from a Hyperlink

Here is an example of how to return the actual underlying address of a hyperlink. In Figure 16-3, hyperlinks are in column A but the display text in those cells describes the link's destination. This UDF will return the actual hyperlink address; the `"mailto"` portion of the code deals with the possibility of a link being an e-mail address.

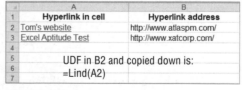

	A	B
1	**Hyperlink in cell**	**Hyperlink address**
2	Tom's website	http://www.atlaspm.com/
3	Excel Aptitude Test	http://www.xatcorp.com/
4		
5	UDF in B2 and copied down is:	
6	=Link(A2)	
7		

FIGURE 16-3

```
Function Link(HyperlinkCell As Range)
Link = Replace(HyperlinkCell.Hyperlinks(1).Address, "mailto:", "")
End Function
```

UDFS AND ERRORS

You might wonder what happens when an error occurs with a UDF. For example, what if the SumColor function is entered into a cell with an illogical range argument address such as =SUMCOLOR(A2:XYZ)? Or, what if a UDF attempts to divide a number by zero?

When a UDF attempts to do what it cannot do, the cell will display a #VALUE! error. Whereas a failed macro will result in a runtime error with an imposing Message Box to announce the error and a debug option to identify the offending code line, such is not the case with a failed UDF. Even though it is a VBA item, a failed UDF will only return the #VALUE! error. With larger UDFs, finding the cause of the error can be a real chore. Therefore, it's a good idea to test each code line in the Immediate window as you write your larger UDFs.

VOLATILE FUNCTIONS

Sometimes, you want a UDF to return a value and then do nothing else until you purposely cause it to recalculate. An example is if you want to produce a random number in a cell but keep that number constant until you decide to change it again, if ever. The worksheet function RAND() will return a random number but it recalculates whenever the worksheet recalculates or any cell in that worksheet is edited. This UDF will return an unchanging (static) random number between 1 and 100:

```
Function StaticRandom() As Double
StaticRandom = Int(Rnd() * 100)
End Function
```

The function entry for the cell is:

```
=StaticRandom()
```

You'll notice that the StaticRandom UDF does not require an argument. Even so, the empty parentheses must immediately follow the function's name in the first code line, and when entering the UDF in a cell, the parentheses must be included as you see in this example.

Now with the StaticRand UDF in its current state, its returned random number will not change unless you purposely call the UDF, such as if you select the cell, press the F2 key, and press Enter, or if you press Ctrl+Alt+F9 to force a calculation on all cells.

If you prefer to have the UDF act as the built-in RAND function would, that is, to recalculate whenever another worksheet formula is recalculated or a cell is edited, you can insert the statement Application.Volatile like so:

```
Function StaticRandom() As Double
Application.Volatile
StaticRandom = Int(Rnd() * 100)
End Function
```

Be aware that if the UDF is used in a lot of cells, Application.Volatile will add to the workbook's overall calculation effort, possibly resulting in longer recalculation times.

The Name of the Active Worksheet and Workbook

A very common request is for a formula to return the name of the active worksheet or workbook. This is a case where a UDF is still a worthy alternative even though there are formulas that can handle this request, and the Application.Volatile statement would be included.

For the worksheet name, this formula is an option but it's not easy to memorize or to enter correctly:

```
=MID(CELL("filename",A1),FIND("]",CELL("filename",A1))+1,32)
```

Although the formula automatically updates itself when a sheet tab name changes, the workbook must be named (saved at least once) or the formula will return a #VALUE! error.

The following code shows a UDF with the Application.Volatile statement that covers all the bases. It updates itself when the worksheet tab changes, and the workbook does not need to be named or saved for the UDF to work. Another advantage is that the formula =SheetName() is easy to remember and to enter:

```
Function SheetName() As String
Application.Volatile
SheetName = ActiveSheet.Name
End Function
```

For the formula that returns the active workbook's name, a lengthier and more difficult one to enter properly is:

```
=MID(CELL("filename",A1),FIND("[",CELL("filename",A1))+1,FIND
("]", CELL("filename",A1))-FIND("[",CELL("filename",A1))-1)
```

The workbook would need to be saved at least once for this formula to work.

The NameWB() function is much easier to remember and enter, and it'll also do the job whether or not the workbook has been saved:

```
= NameWB()
```

Its UDF is:

```
Function NameWB() As String
Application.Volatile
NameWB = ActiveWorkbook.Name
End Function
```

UDFs with Conditional Formatting

One of the less-utilized but powerful applications of a UDF is to combine it with Conditional Formatting. Let's say you want to identify cells that contain a comment in a workbook where the option to show comment indicators is turned off. It's true that cells containing comments fall into the category of `SpecialCells` and you can select them through the Go To Special dialog box, and maybe format the selected comment-containing cells from there. However, you'd need to repeat those steps any time a cell obtains or deletes a comment, and there's no telling if or when that might happen.

A better way to go is with a UDF as the formula rule with Conditional Formatting, to format the comment-containing cells in real time, as comments are added or deleted. For example, place this UDF into a standard module:

```
Public Function TestComment(rng As Range) As Boolean
TestComment = Not rng.Comment Is Nothing
End Function
```

Back onto your worksheet, select the range of interest, in this example starting from cell A1. In the Conditional Formatting dialog (or the New Formatting Rule dialog for Excel versions starting with 2007), enter this formula:

```
=TestComment(A1)
```

Then choose your formatting style, click OK, and all comment-containing cells in that range will be formatted.

Calling Your Function from a Macro

As I mentioned earlier, functions that you create need not only serve as worksheet formulas. A function can also be called by a macro, which does not limit the macro's ability to do whatever needs to be done. In the following code, the `OpenTest` function is set apart from the `OpenOrClosed` macro, which gives you the best of both worlds for testing if a particular workbook is open or closed.

To test by formula if a workbook named "YourWorkbookName.xls" is open or closed, you can enter this in a worksheet cell, which will return TRUE (the workbook is open) or FALSE (the workbook is closed):

```
=OpenTest("YourWorkbookName.xls")
```

To test by macro, you can expand the functionality by asking with a Yes/No message box if you'd like to open that workbook if it is not already open, and open it if Yes is selected, or keep the workbook closed if No is selected. Here's the code:

```
Function OpenTest(wb) As Boolean
'Declare a Workbook variable
Dim wkb As Workbook
```

```
'Employ the On Error Resume Next statement to check for, and bypass,
'a run time error in case the workbook is not open.
On Error Resume Next
Set wkb = Workbooks(wb)
'If there is no error, the workbook is open.
If Err = 0 Then
Err.Clear
OpenTest = True
Else
'An error was raised, meaning the workbook is not open.
OpenTest = False
End If
End Function


Sub OpenOrClosed()
'Declare a string variable that will be the workbook name.
Dim strFileName As String
strFileName = "YourWorkbookName.xls"
'Call the OpenTest UDF to evaluate whether or not the workbook is open.
If OpenTest(strFileName) = True Then
'For demo purposes, this Message Box informs you if the workbook is open.
MsgBox strFileName & " is open.", vbInformation, "FYI..."
Else
'The OpenTest UDF determines that the workbook is closed.
'A Message Box asks if you want to open that workbook.
Dim OpenQuestion As Integer
OpenQuestion = _
MsgBox(strFileName & " is not open, do you want to open it?", _
vbYesNo, _
"Your choice")
'Example code if you answer No, meaning you want to keep the workbook closed.
If OpenQuestion = vbNo Then
MsgBox "No problem, it'll stay closed.", , "You clicked No."
Else
'Example code if you answer Yes, meaning you want to open the workbook.
'You need to tell the macro what the full path is for this workbook,
'so another String type variable is declared for the path.
Dim strFileFullName As String
strFileFullName = "C:\Your\File\Path\" & strFileName
'Open the workbook.
Workbooks.Open Filename:=strFileFullName
End If
End If
End Sub
```

Adding a Description to the Insert Function Dialog

Chances are, the more VBA you learn, the more popular you'll be at your workplace as the Excel go-to person. Soon, if not already, you're building workbooks for other people to use, and it's a nice touch to add a helpful description to your UDFs for the benefit of those other users. The Insert

Function dialog is a good place to help people understand how to enter your UDFs, especially because this dialog is how some users enter functions, and each UDF has its own unique entry requirements.

Figure 16-4 shows a typical Insert Function dialog, where your publicly or non-declared UDFs will appear in the Select a Function pane when the User Defined category is selected. I've selected the `ExtractNumbers` function, but no help is available for someone who has never seen this UDF and would not know how to properly enter the function.

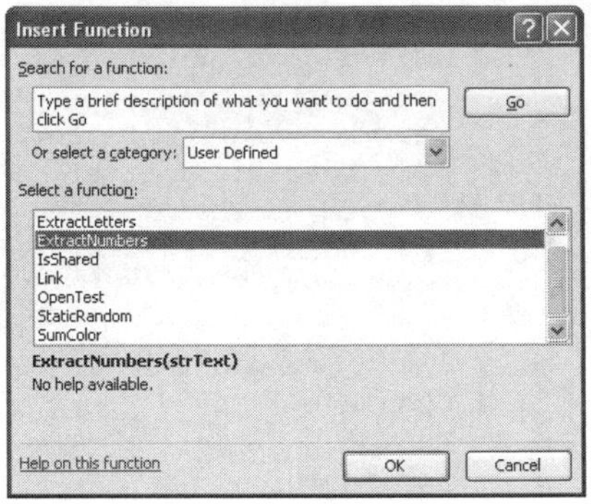

In two easy steps, here's how you can provide a helpful tip for entering a UDF from the Insert Function dialog:

FIGURE 16-4

1. Press Alt+F8 to call the Macro dialog. In the Macro Name field, enter the function name, for example, `ExtractNumbers` as shown in Figure 16-5. Next, click the Options button.

FIGURE 16-5

2. In the Description field of the Macro Options dialog, enter a brief description of how to enter this UDF. As partially shown in Figure 16-6, I entered the following description and confirmed it by clicking OK and exiting the Macro dialog:

```
Example UDF entry:
=ExtractNumbers(A2)
where cell A2 contains the original alphanumeric string.
```

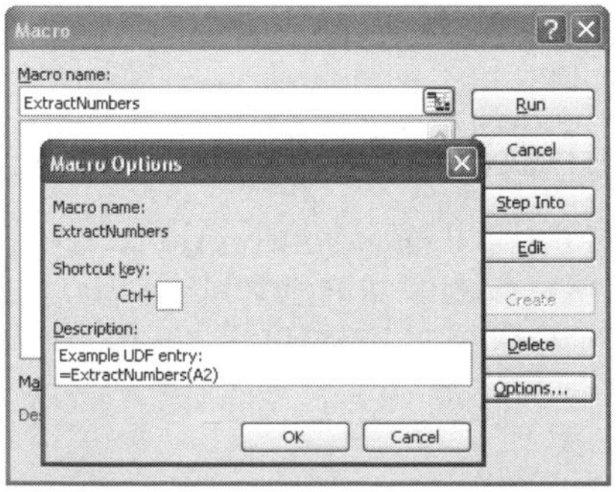

FIGURE 16-6

And that's all there is to it. Now if you go back to the Insert Function dialog and select the `ExtractNumbers` UDF, a description appears as shown in Figure 16-7, providing the users with a useful tip for how to enter the UDF.

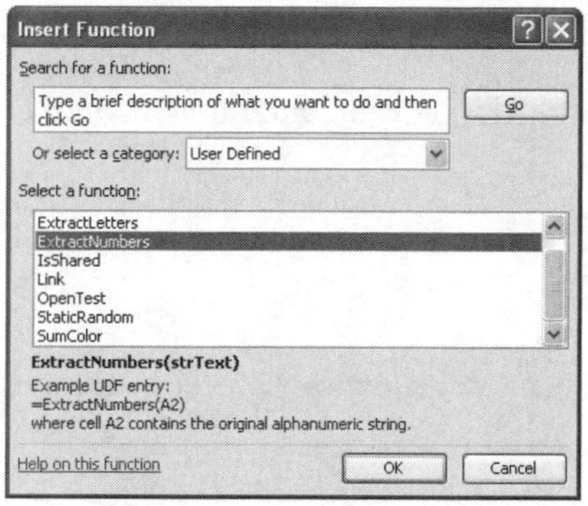

FIGURE 16-7

TRY IT

In this lesson you practice creating a User Defined Function that tests whether a particular cell contains a comment. If so, it returns the text of that comment; if not, it returns "No comment."

Lesson Requirements

To get the sample database files, you can download Lesson 16 from the book's website at www.wrox.com.

Step-by-Step

Create a UDF to examine another cell's comment.

1. From your keyboard press Alt+F11 to get into the VBE, and from the menu bar click Insert ⇨ Module.

2. Enter the function name, declare an argument variable for a `Range` type because a cell will be evaluated, and declare the Function type as `String` because the UDF will return text of some kind. For example:

    ```
    Function GetComment(rng As Range) As String
    ```

3. Declare a `String` type variable to handle either the comment text, or the "No comment" statement. For example:

    ```
    Dim strText As String
    ```

4. Using an `If` structure, evaluate the target cell for the existence of a comment. If there is no comment, define the `strText` variable as "No comment." For example:

```
If rng.Comment Is Nothing Then
strText = "No comment"
```

5. Complete the `If` structure for the condition of the target cell containing a comment. For example:

```
Else
strText = rng.Comment.Text
End If
```

6. Set the name of the Function equal to the `strText` string expression. For example:

```
GetComment = strText
```

7. Close the Function with the `End Function` statement. The entire UDF will look like this:

```
Function GetComment(rng As Range) As String
Dim strText As String
If rng.Comment Is Nothing Then
strText = "No comment"
Else
strText = rng.Comment.Text
End If
GetComment = strText
End Function
```

8. Press Alt+Q to return to the worksheet, test your UDF to evaluate the existence of a comment in cell A1, and return the conditional string with this formula:

```
=GetComment(A1)
```

 Please select Lesson 16 on the DVD to view the video that accompanies this lesson.

17

Debugging Your Code

Despite what you've always heard, there are really *three* sure things in life: death, taxes, and errors in computer programs. There's no avoiding it — errors will happen and they will need to be fixed, whether the length of your VBA programming experience is 10 days or 10 years.

You will need to learn the tools and techniques for debugging your code, so that when things go wrong, you'll be familiar with the resources that are at your disposal for finding and fixing errors. Excel has many good built-in debugging tools. In addition, other techniques exist that you'll learn in this lesson about how to avoid errors in the first place, and, believe it or not, how you can get errors to work for you instead of against you.

WHAT IS DEBUGGING?

A *bug* is an error in your code that can produce erroneous results, or, depending on the nature of the bug, stop the code from executing altogether. In programming, the term *debugging* refers to correcting an error in code, or the process of testing a procedure for the possible existence of bugs that would need to be fixed if found.

YOU CAN DO EVERYTHING RIGHT AND STILL HAVE A BUG

In the next section you'll read about three causes of errors in VBA programming. Actually, there is a fourth cause, which you have absolutely no control over, and that is a bug in a software application itself. This is not in any way a specific reference to a particular software company or to Microsoft. It's a software industry reality that new products are sometimes released with bugs, including known bugs that are deemed to be benign but turn out to be a problem when used with Excel.

continues

(continued)

In your future development projects, you'll encounter many external data storage and management applications that mostly play well with Excel, but sometimes might not when by all rights they should. It's never in any reputable software company's best interests to impose nuisance bugs on its products' users. The point is, if you find that you have all your bases covered and are still scratching your head about an error that has no rhyme or reason, you might have stumbled onto a bug that other users of that product, and especially the software manufacturer, would want to know about.

The process of debugging is a combination of art and science. The science is covered by some terrific debugging tools that come with Excel VBA. The art is owing to the skills and experience you will gain when you build VBA projects with a mindset for anticipating potential minefields based on the intended use, and users, of your projects.

WHAT CAUSES ERRORS?

The world of computer programming enjoys no exemption from Murphy's Law, where if something can go wrong, it will go wrong. Three primary causes of errors can infect your VBA programming code. To avoid errors, your first line of defense is anticipating problems as you write your code, especially considering how the project will be used in real practice. Eventually, however, one of three types of errors will impose their nuisance selves.

One cause is *syntax errors*, such as misspelling a VBA keyword, or not declaring a variable while requiring variable declaration (as was outlined in Lesson 6). This causes a compile error as shown in Figure 17-1, because the `LastRow` variable was not declared in that example. If an error can be classified as friendly, it'd be a compile error because it is VBA's way of telling you what's wrong, and sometimes showing you exactly where the problem is.

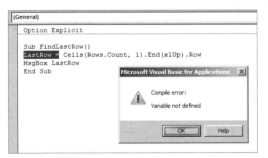

FIGURE 17-1

Another syntax error that can result in a compilation failure is the absence of an `End If`, `End With`, or loop continuation keyword such as `Next` or `Loop`. For example, the macro shown in Figure 17-2 will produce a compile error because it is missing an `End With` statement.

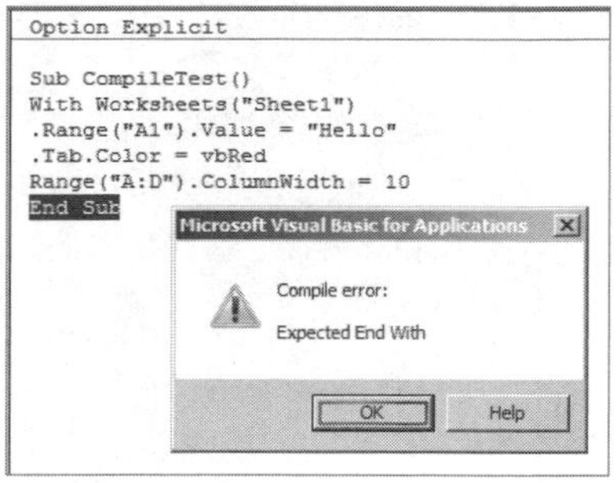

A second cause of errors can be classified as *runtime errors*, because they occur while the macro is running, and usually will stop the procedure dead in its tracks with a runtime error message such as you see in Figure 17-3. Notice the reason for the error: In the Project Explorer window, you can see that the workbook only has three worksheets, named Sheet1, Sheet2, and Sheet3.

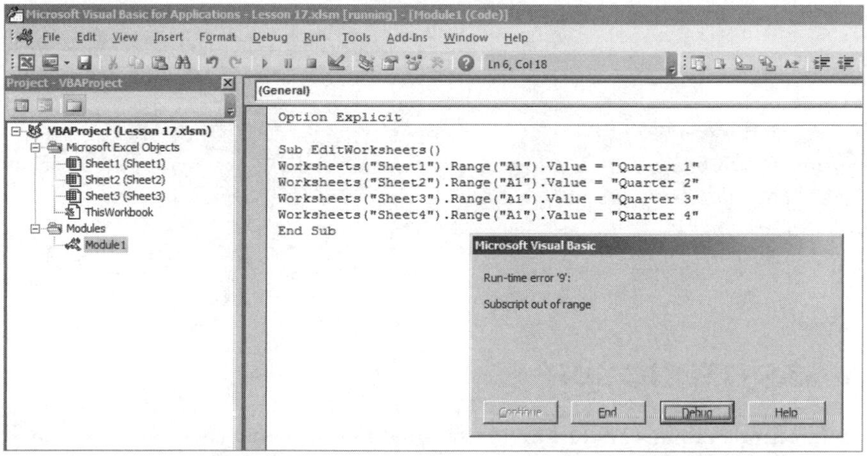

FIGURE 17-2

FIGURE 17-3

The runtime error is VBA's way of protesting that it is being told to do something it cannot do, as in this case because a worksheet does not exist named Sheet4. If the Visual Basic Editor is unprotected, and you click the Debug button on a runtime error message, VBA will take you to the related module and highlight the offending line of code, as shown in Figure 17-4.

The third cause of errors are *logical errors*, and they are the most nefarious, because they come with no message warnings that something is wrong. An example of a logical error is a wrongly coded mathematical calculation that yields incorrect results. Suppose your project is a large VBA effort with macros that calculate financial data that end users and investment clients are depending on for their personal investment strategies. Your macros will run without getting interrupted by compile or runtime errors, but the results are still flawed. People tend not to fix what they think isn't broken, so unless you (or an angry client) discovers the math bug, it can go undetected for a long time, and may never be detected.

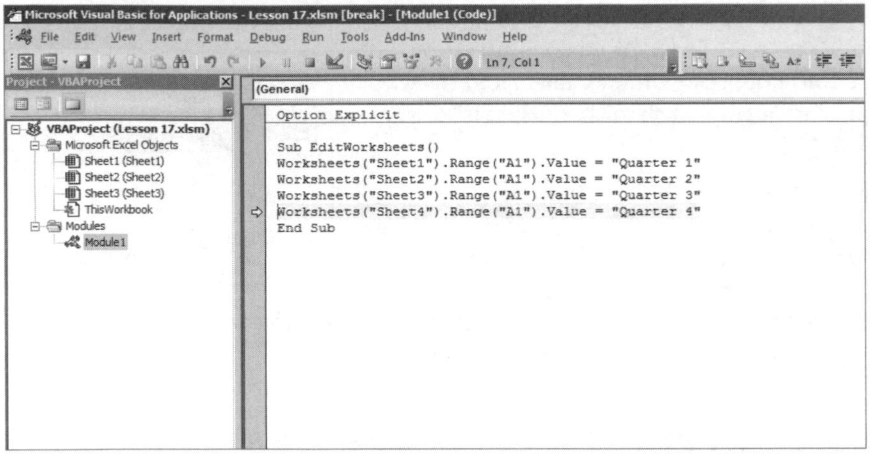

FIGURE 17-4

> *When programming mathematical and logical operations, it's always a good idea to test your code by comparing the output of your VBA results with the output from an independent source.*

WEAPONS OF MASS DEBUGGING

Now that you know what kinds of bugs are lurking in the shadows and how they can bite your code, you can fight back with several excellent debugging tools that are found in the Visual Basic Editor. Your best defense starts with information about the weapons in your debugging arsenal and how they are used.

The Debugging Toolbar

The Debugging toolbar is a handy item to display and keep docked onto your VBE menu bar. To show the Debugging toolbar, from the VBE menu click View ⇨ Toolbars ⇨ Debug as shown in Figure 17-5.

The Debugging toolbar typically contains 13 icons, some of which you are already familiar with. Figure 17-6 shows the toolbar and the names of the icons, and the following sections describe their uses.

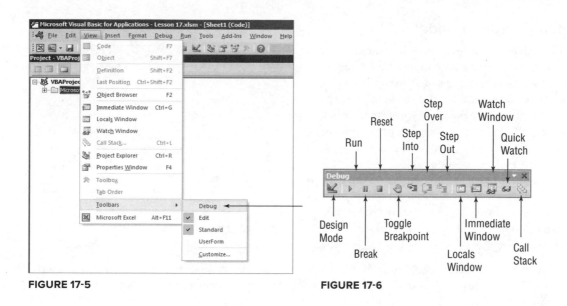

FIGURE 17-5   **FIGURE 17-6**

Design Mode

The Design Mode button turns Design mode on and off in the active workbook. Design mode is the time during which no code from the project is currently running. You can leave Design mode by clicking the Design mode icon again, or by running a macro or using the Immediate window. When you have an ActiveX object on your worksheet, such as a `CommandButton`, Design mode allows you to view the object's properties, or to double-click the object to quickly access its module in the VBE.

Run

Clicking the Run button will have one of two effects. If your cursor happens to be blinking in the Code window within a macro, clicking the Run button, or pressing the F5 key, runs the macro. Otherwise, it will call the Macro dialog box, same as if you were on a worksheet and you pressed the Alt+F8 keys.

Break

Clicking the Break button is the same as pressing the Ctrl+Break keys, which halts macro execution. Break mode is a special mode of operation in the Visual Basic Editor that allows you to run one line of code at a time without having to run the entire macro. Examining one line of code at a time is a way to pinpoint the exact whereabouts of the error. You can edit code in Break mode.

Reset

Clicking the Reset button clears the Call stack and clears the module-level variables. This will end Break mode, end all program execution, and close the Debug window if it is open.

Stepping through Code

On the Debug toolbar, three icons, named Step Into, Step Over, and Step Out, are related to a process known as *stepping* through code. There are times when you'll want to examine each statement in your macro if you suspect a bug is somewhere in your code but you're not sure where. Even large macros can run quickly, so it's difficult, and often impossible, to isolate the specific command that is not executing the way you would have planned. Stepping through your VBA statements allows you to execute one or more lines of code, at your own pace, to see for yourself what every VBA statement is really doing.

	A	B	C	D	E	F
1						
2						
3						
4						
5		Store 1	23499	19974	3525	
6		Store 2	90970	77324	13646	
7		Store 3	94070	79959	14111	
8		Store 4	29592	25153	4439	
9		Store 5	44800	38080	6720	
10		Store 6	54857	46628	8229	
11		Store 7	77402	65791	11611	
12		Store 8	94547	80364	14183	
13		Store 9	83998	71398	12600	
14		Store 10	62688	53284	9404	
15						

FIGURE 17-7

Suppose you oversee a region of 10 hardware stores, and you receive a table of each store's quarterly sales activity. Your table is in a raw form, downloaded into Excel from your company's database, resembling Figure 17-7.

You have a macro such as the one pictured in Figure 17-8 that formats the table and sorts the Net Income column in descending order so you can quickly list the most profitable stores. When you run the macro, you do not get a compile or runtime error, but something still doesn't look right when the macro completes its full execution, as shown in Figure 17-9.

```
Sub StepThroughBreakpointExample()

'Company name
Range("A1").Value = "XYZ Widgets, Inc."

'Quarter header label
Range("A2").Value = "Quarterly Report"

'Call the macro that creates a chart sheet from this data.
Call myChartMaker

'Enter the table headers and bold them.
With Range("B4:E4")
.Value = Array("Store Name", "Gross Sales", "Expenses", "Net Income")
.Font.Bold = True
End With

'Border around the table.
Range("B4:E14").BorderAround Weight:=xlMedium

'Format the numbers to currency and comma separators.
Range("C5:E14").NumberFormat = "$#,##0"

'AutoFit the columns from A:E
Range(Columns(1), Columns(5)).AutoFit

'Sort the table by descending Net Income column E.
With ActiveSheet.Sort
.SortFields.Clear
.SortFields.Add Key:=Range("E5:E13"), _
SortOn:=xlSortOnValues, Order:=xlDescending
.SetRange Range("B5:E13")
.Header = xlYes
.Apply
End With

End Sub
```

FIGURE 17-8

	A	B	C	D	E	F
1	XYZ Widgets, Inc.					
2	Quarterly Report					
3						
4		**Store Name**	**Gross Sales**	**Expenses**	**Net Income**	
5		Store 1	$23,499	$19,974	$3,525	
6		Store 8	$94,547	$80,364	$14,183	
7		Store 3	$94,070	$79,959	$14,111	
8		Store 2	$90,970	$77,324	$13,646	
9		Store 9	$83,998	$71,398	$12,600	
10		Store 7	$77,402	$65,791	$11,611	
11		Store 6	$54,857	$46,628	$8,229	
12		Store 5	$44,800	$38,080	$6,720	
13		Store 4	$29,592	$25,153	$4,439	
14		Store 10	$62,688	$53,284	$9,404	
15						

FIGURE 17-9

Using the Step Into Command

To examine line by line where the problem lies, click your mouse anywhere inside the macro and then click the Step Into button. The macro's Sub line will be highlighted in yellow, indicating to you that it's that particular macro you are about to step into.

> When you "step into" a macro, you are traversing step-by-step (code line by code line), in a single-step process to execute each line in turn.

Click the Step Into button again and the first line of code will be highlighted in yellow, which in this example is Range("A1").Value = "XYZ Widgets, Inc." as shown in Figure 17-10. If you click the Step Into button again, the code line Range("A1").Value = "XYZ Widgets, Inc." will be executed, and the next line of code, Range("A2").Value = "Quarterly Report", will be highlighted in yellow, ready to be executed with your next Step Into command.

Each time you click the Step Into button, the line of code that is highlighted will be executed, and the next line will be highlighted, and so on until you reach the end of the macro. Because you suspect a bug somewhere in the code, you'd be looking at your worksheet after each Step Into command to make sure that what the code is supposed to be doing is what it truly is doing.

In this example, all the cell values and formatting were correctly executed when you stepped into each one, until the very last section of code that executes the Sort method. You find when stepping into that section that the range of cells being sorted is not correct. Your table occupies range B4:E14 but the VBA code is sorting only up to row 13. Your suspicions were correct about the final result on the worksheet looking peculiar, so a quick adjustment is made to the sort range address after you've verified that each of the other lines of code were properly written and being properly executed.

```
Sub StepThroughBreakpointExample()

'Company name
Range("A1").Value = "XYZ Widgets, Inc."

'Quarter header label
Range("A2").Value = "Quarterly Report"

'Call the macro that creates a chart sheet from this data.
Call myChartMaker

'Enter the table headers and bold them.
With Range("B4:E4")
.Value = Array("Store Name", "Gross Sales", "Expenses", "Net Income")
.Font.Bold = True
End With

'Border around the table.
Range("B4:E14").BorderAround Weight:=xlMedium

'Format the numbers to currency and comma separators.
Range("C5:E14").NumberFormat = "$#,##0"

'AutoFit the columns from A:E
Range(Columns(1), Columns(5)).AutoFit

'Sort the table by descending Net Income column E.
With ActiveSheet.Sort
.SortFields.Clear
.SortFields.Add Key:=Range("E5:E13"), _
SortOn:=xlSortOnValues, Order:=xlDescending
.SetRange Range("B5:E13")
.Header = xlYes
.Apply
End With

End Sub
```

FIGURE 17-10

Using the Step Over Command

The Step Over command is similar to the Step Into command, with the difference between the two commands occurring at the point of a call to another macro. You may have noticed in the macro the code line `Call myChartMaker`, where in this hypothetical example the `myChartMaker` macro creates a chart sheet from the table data. Figure 17-11 shows that `Call` statement highlighted during the Step Into process.

In this situation, if you click the Step Over button, the `Call myChartMaker` command will be executed but you will not be taken through it line by line as if it were stepped into. You would prefer to do this when you know for sure that the `myChartMaker` macro works without any problems, and cannot be the cause of whatever bug you are trying to fix in the current macro. The Step Over command will execute the `myChartMaker` macro and the next line of code in your macro will be highlighted for the next Step Into command.

> *Did you notice a tiny arrow in the margin to the left of the macro being stepped into? When a line of code is highlighted during a stepping process, a yellow arrow in the Code window's left margin helps to indicate your place in the process. With your mouse, you can select and drag the arrow upward or downward, dropping it at whichever line of code you want to execute next.*

```
Sub StepThroughBreakpointExample()

'Company name
Range("A1").Value = "XYZ Widgets, Inc."

'Quarter header label
Range("A2").Value = "Quarterly Report"

'Call the macro that creates a chart sheet from this data.
Call myChartMaker

'Enter the table headers and bold them.
With Range("B4:E4")
.Value = Array("Store Name", "Gross Sales", "Expenses", "Net Income")
.Font.Bold = True
End With

'Border around the table.
Range("B4:E14").BorderAround Weight:=xlMedium

'Format the numbers to currency and comma separators.
Range("C5:E14").NumberFormat = "$#,##0"

'AutoFit the columns from A:E
Range(Columns(1), Columns(5)).AutoFit

'Sort the table by descending Net Income column E.
With ActiveSheet.Sort
.SortFields.Clear
.SortFields.Add Key:=Range("E5:E13"), _
SortOn:=xlSortOnValues, Order:=xlDescending
.SetRange Range("B5:E13")
.Header = xlYes
.Apply
End With

End Sub
```

FIGURE 17-11

Using the Step Out Command

The Step Out command executes the remaining lines of code between and including the current highlighted execution point and the End Sub line. You might think by the name Step Out that it refers to simply exiting the Step Into command, but that is not exactly the case. Though it does result in exiting the step through process, it does so by executing the rest of the macro to get to the end. If you want to exit any of the step through process, click the Reset button.

Toggle Breakpoint

One of VBA's convenient features is the ability to set a *breakpoint*, where you can specify a line of code that will be the point up to which the macro would run at full speed. When the macro's execution reaches the breakpoint code line, VBA switches to Break mode and halts the execution process.

> Stepping through your macro is a good way to examine each line of code, but when your macros are hundreds of lines long, a line-by-line examination process is tedious and time consuming. There will be many statements in your code that won't need to be examined, and there's no reason to inch your way to the section of your macro where the error probably resides. This is where breakpoints come in handy.

To set a breakpoint in your code, click your mouse into the line of code where you want the breakpoint to start. Click the Toggle Breakpoint button, or press the F9 key, and the breakpoint will be set at that line. VBA clearly identifies a breakpoint with a large brown dot in the Code window's left margin, and the code line itself is shaded brown.

For example, if you suspect a bug in a macro but you know that the majority of the macro runs without any problems, you can set a breakpoint starting at a section in the program where you want to examine the code more closely. In Figure 17-12, I clicked my mouse into the code line With ActiveSheet.Sort and clicked the Toggle Breakpoint button. If the macro were to be run now, it would execute all lines of code up to, but not including, that breakpoint line. Now, you can step through the subsequent lines of code to verify that each line is doing what you'd expect.

```
Sub StepThroughBreakpointExample()

'Company name
Range("A1").Value = "XYZ Widgets, Inc."

'Quarter header label
Range("A2").Value = "Quarterly Report"

'Call the macro that creates a chart sheet from this data.
Call myChartMaker

'Enter the table headers and bold them.
With Range("B4:E4")
.Value = Array("Store Name", "Gross Sales", "Expenses", "Net Income")
.Font.Bold = True
End With

'Border around the table.
Range("B4:E14").BorderAround Weight:=xlMedium

'Format the numbers to currency and comma separators.
Range("C5:E14").NumberFormat = "$#,##0"

'AutoFit the columns from A:E
Range(Columns(1), Columns(5)).AutoFit

'Sort the table by descending Net Income column E.
With ActiveSheet.Sort
.SortFields.Clear
.SortFields.Add Key:=Range("E5:E13"), _
SortOn:=xlSortOnValues, Order:=xlDescending
.SetRange Range("B5:E13")
.Header = xlYes
.Apply
End With

End Sub
```

FIGURE 17-12

> *You can set a breakpoint only on an executable line. Commented lines in your code, or empty lines, cannot be set as breakpoints.*

True to its name, the Toggle Breakpoint button can be clicked again to clear the current breakpoint with any portion of that line selected, or you can click the large dot in the Code window's margin. You'll notice that if you have already set a breakpoint and you click the Toggle Breakpoint button, or press F9, you will set another breakpoint if you have any other line of code selected. You can set more than one breakpoint, so to quickly clear all breakpoints at once, press the Ctrl+Shift+F9 keys.

Locals Window

The Locals window can help you in situations when you get a runtime error and the offending line of code involves a variable. The Locals window displays the variables and their values for the macro(s) you are currently running.

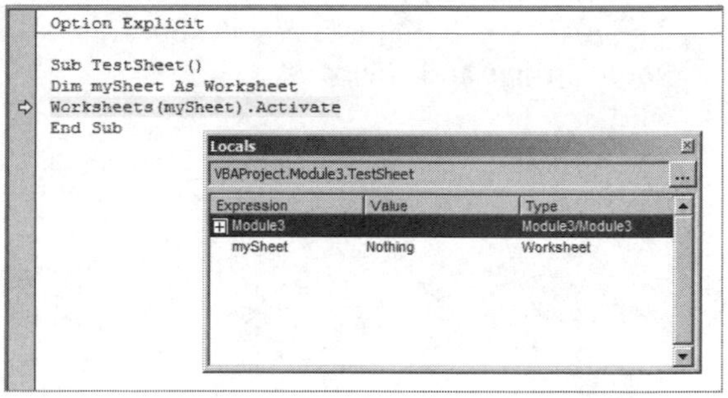

Figure 17-13 shows a very simple macro that attempted to activate a worksheet based on the object variable mySheet. Because that variable was never set with an identifying worksheet, a runtime error occurred because VBA could not determine which sheet the mySheet variable was referring to. While in Break mode in this example, the Locals window shows that mySheet is set to Nothing, telling you that you forgot to include a Set statement for mySheet.

FIGURE 17-13

Immediate Window

The Immediate window allows you to type in or paste a line of VBA code, which will execute when you press the Enter key. To see the Immediate window, you can click its icon button on the Debug toolbar, or from the menu click View ⇨ Immediate Window, or press Ctrl+G.

If it hasn't happened already, you'll soon find yourself using the Immediate window for reasons having nothing to do with errors. The Immediate window is a great way to execute commands quickly without needing to create a formal macro to get the task done, such as in the following examples.

To eliminate leading apostrophes in cell values, which can occur when manually entered or imported from external source data, you can type `Activesheet.UsedRange.Value = Activesheet.UsedRange.Value` and press the Enter key.

To delete hyperlinks but keep the underlying cell value, you can type `ActiveSheet.Hyperlinks .Delete` and press the Enter key.

When querying some fact or condition, precede your statement with a leading question mark. If you want to know the version of Excel you are using, type `? Application.Version` and press the Enter key. As shown in Figure 17-14, when I entered that statement into the Immediate window, the value 14.0 was returned, which is Excel's version 2010.

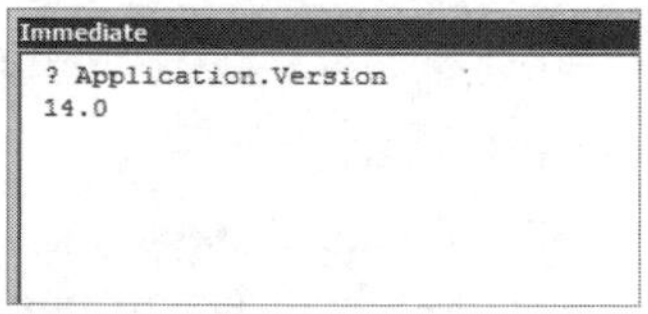

FIGURE 17-14

The point to be made about the Immediate window is that it is a proactive tool. If you are wondering whether a line of code will fail, or whether it will produce the result you have envisioned, you can test that code line in the Immediate window and see the results before taking your chances of putting it into your code.

Watch Window

The Watch window allows you to watch a variable or an expression change as your code executes. You'd normally do this with values that are associated with runtime errors, so you can see at what point the VBA expressions produced a value that might have caused the error.

Select the expression you want to watch, right-click that selection, and choose Add Watch from the pop-up menu. Figure 17-15 shows the process for adding the variable `strValue` to the Watch list. The Add Watch dialog box will appear, as shown by example in Figure 17-16, for you to confirm your settings and click OK.

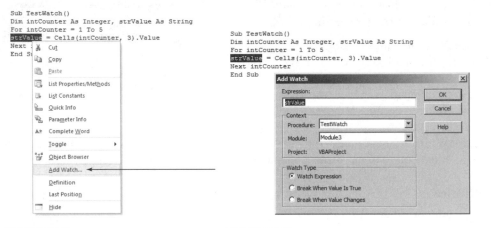

FIGURE 17-15   **FIGURE 17-16**

When you step into code after setting a watch expression, you'll see the expression's value change during execution. Figure 17-17 shows the `strValue` variable's value change with each iteration of the `For Next` loop. Notice that the value at one point in the loop is a number, yet the `strValue` variable was declared as a String type. It's that kind of attention that the Watch window brings to your awareness of what your variables are actually returning, if you suspect a particular expression to be the cause of an error.

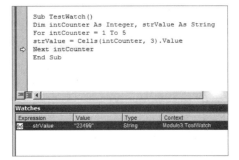

FIGURE 17-17

Quick Watch

The Quick Watch window allows you to get a look at the current value of an expression or variable for which you have not defined a watch expression. While you are in Break mode, select your expression in the module and click the Quick Watch button, or press the Shift+F9 keys. For example, in Figure 17-18, the `intCounter` variable was selected during a step through process, and the Watch window displays 3 in the Value field, indicating that the `For Next` loop is currently in its third iteration.

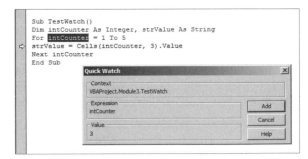

FIGURE 17-18

Call Stack

The Call Stack dialog box shows the list of currently active procedure calls in Break mode. Unless you write macros that involve a maze of calls to other macros, that themselves call other procedures, you won't need the Call Stack dialog box. A word to the wise: Keep your macros simple and limit their procedure calls to a reasonable level, and you won't have to worry about relying on a dialog box to tell you which macro is in error of Break mode.

TRAPPING ERRORS

When you encounter a runtime error and you've figured out the cause, it might be that you need to keep the error-prone code in place because it is such an important component of the larger macro. Actually, you will come across this situation a lot, so you'll need to know how to handle errors programmatically behind the scenes, in a way that the users of your projects will not be bothered by runtime errors.

Error Handler

One of the more common tasks in development projects is to add a worksheet to the workbook. Your project might involve building a report onto a new worksheet, or copying various sections of a master worksheet and pasting those individual sections to their own new worksheets that you create. Say you provide an InputBox for users to enter the name of a worksheet they want to add. What happens if a user already has a worksheet by that name in the workbook? Two worksheets cannot have the same name in the same workbook, but the macro still needs to complete its appointed task.

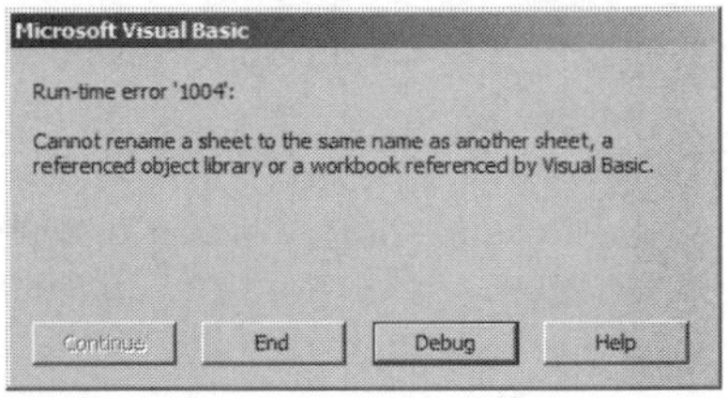

FIGURE 17-19

One approach is using an `On Error GoTo` statement that will trap the error, and point to a certain section in your macro that should be executed next in order to handle the error. Suppose your macro calls for a new worksheet to be added, and named by the user as Sheet3. If a worksheet already exists in the workbook named Sheet3, a 1004 type runtime error message would occur as shown in Figure 17-19.

With the following syntax, you can use an error handler to avoid getting a runtime error message if an attempt is made to give a new worksheet the same name another worksheet already has. In this example macro, the user is provided an InputBox to name the new sheet, and informed if the sheet is added, or if it is not added because duplicate names are not allowed.

```
Sub AddSheetTest()

Dim mySheetName As String
mySheetName = _
InputBox("Enter the worksheet name:", _
"Add and name a new worksheet")

If mySheetName = "" Then Exit Sub

On Error GoTo ErrorHandler
Worksheets.Add.Name = mySheetName
MsgBox _
```

```
"Worksheet " & mySheetName & " was added.", , "Thank you."
Exit Sub

ErrorHandler:
MsgBox _
"A worksheet named " & mySheetName & " already exists.", _
vbCritical, _
"Duplicate sheet names are not allowed."

End Sub
```

Bypassing Errors

My preference for most situations where runtime errors can occur is to avoid the error handler route because the GoTo statement makes the macro more difficult to follow. Using an error bypass approach with the On Error Resume Next statement, you can test for the condition of the Error object, and use an If structure to deal with either possibility.

When it comes to naming a sheet, several considerations need to be monitored:

➤ Does the sheet name already exist in the workbook? Duplicate sheet names are not allowed.

➤ Is the proposed sheet name more than the maximum allowable 31 characters in length?

➤ Are any illegal sheet-naming characters included in the proposed name? Sheet tab names cannot contain the characters /, \, [,], *, ?, or :. If you try to type any of those characters into your sheet tab, Excel will disallow the entry.

The Following macro takes these possibilities into consideration. If all conditions are met, a new sheet is added. If any condition is not met, a new worksheet will not be created and a Message Box will inform you of the reason why.

```
Sub TestSheetCreate()

'Declare String type variables for naming and testing the sheet.
Dim mySheetName As String, mySheetNameTest As String

'Use an InputBox to ask the user to propose a new sheet name.
mySheetName = _
InputBox("Enter the worksheet name:", _
"Add and name a new worksheet")

'Exit if nothing was entered or the Cancel button was clicked.
If mySheetName = "" Then Exit Sub

'Error bypass if the proposed sheet name already exists
'in the workbook.
On Error Resume Next
mySheetNameTest = Worksheets(mySheetName).Name
If Err.Number = 0 Then
MsgBox _
"The sheet named " & mySheetName & " already exists.", _
vbInformation, _
```

```
"A new sheet was not added."
Exit Sub
End If

'If the length of the proposed sheet name exceeds 31 characters,
'disallow the attempt.
If Len(mySheetName) > 31 Then
MsgBox _
"Worksheet tab names cannot exceed 31 characters." & vbCrLf & _
"You entered " & mySheetName & ", which has " & vbCrLf & _
Len(mySheetName) & " characters.", vbInformation, _
"Please use no more than 31 characters."
Exit Sub
End If

'Sheet tab names cannot contain
'the characters /, \, [, ], *, ?, or :.
'Verify that none of these characters
'are present in the cell's entry.
Dim IllegalCharacter(1 To 7) As String, i As Integer
IllegalCharacter(1) = "/"
IllegalCharacter(2) = "\"
IllegalCharacter(3) = "["
IllegalCharacter(4) = "]"
IllegalCharacter(5) = "*"
IllegalCharacter(6) = "?"
IllegalCharacter(7) = ":"
'Loop through each character in the proposed sheet name.
For i = 1 To 7
If InStr(mySheetName, (IllegalCharacter(i))) > 0 Then
MsgBox _
"You included a character that Excel does not allow" & vbCrLf & _
"when naming a sheet. Please re-enter a sheet name" & vbCrLf & _
"without the '" & IllegalCharacter(i) & "' character.", _
vbCritical, _
"Sheet not added."
Exit Sub
End If
Next i

'History is a reserved word, so a sheet cannot be named History.
If UCase(mySheetName) = "HISTORY" Then
MsgBox "A sheet cannot be named " & mySheetName & vbCrLf & _
"because it is a reserved word in Excel.", vbInformation, _
"History is a reserved word."
Exit Sub
End If

'Inform the user that a new sheet has been added.
Worksheets.Add.Name = mySheetName
MsgBox "A new sheet named " & mySheetName & " has been added!", _
vbInformation, _
"Thank you !"

End Sub
```

TRY IT

In this lesson, you create a macro that avoids a runtime error while using the `Find` method to locate a value on your worksheet. If the value is found, its cell address will be displayed in a Message Box.

Lesson Requirements

It is not practical to loop through potentially millions of cells, so the `Find` method is used with an error bypass structure.

If you were to record a macro to find the word Hello on a worksheet, the recorded code would look like this:

```
Cells.Find(What:="Hello", After:=ActiveCell, LookIn:=xlFormulas, _
LookAt:=xlPart, SearchOrder:=xlByRows, SearchDirection:=xlNext, _
MatchCase:=False, SearchFormat:=False).Activate
```

If the word Hello is not found on the worksheet, a runtime error would result because the recorded code is instructing VBA to activate a cell that contains a value that does not exist. The purpose of this lesson is to avoid a runtime error if the value being looked for does not exist on the worksheet. To get the sample database files you can download Lesson 17 from the book's website at www.wrox.com.

Step-by-Step

1. Open a workbook and activate a worksheet that contains a relatively large amount of data. This is an exercise in finding a value if it exists on the worksheet, so the more complex the worksheet, the better.

2. From your worksheet press Alt+F11 to get into the Visual Basic Editor.

3. From the menu bar, click Insert ➪ Module.

4. In your new module, type the name of your macro as **Sub FindTest** and press the Enter key. VBA will display your entry and new macro as follows:

```
Sub FindTest()

End Sub
```

5. For your first line of code, declare a `Variant` type variable for the value you want to locate. In this example, simply call it **varFind**.

```
Dim varFind as Variant
```

6. Declare two more variables, both Long type, for the row and column of the value if it is found:

```
Dim varFindRow As Long, varFindColumn As Long
```

7. Declare a String type variable for the value to be located:

```
Dim FindWhat As String
```

8. Define the FindWhat variable as an InputBox entry:

```
FindWhat = _
InputBox("What do you want to find?", "Find what?")
```

9. If the Cancel button is clicked, or nothing is entered in the InputBox, exit the macro:

```
If FindWhat = "" Then Exit Sub
```

10. Set the varFind variable to the Find method:

```
Set varFind = _
Cells.Find(What:=FindWhat, LookIn:=xlFormulas, lookat:=xlWhole)
```

11. If varFind is Nothing, inform the user that the value being looked for was not found. Also, exit the macro.

```
If varFind Is Nothing Then
MsgBox _
FindWhat& " was not found.", _
vbInformation, _
"No such animal."
Exit Sub

Else
```

12. Define the row and column variables to identify the found cell. Actually, this is not required because varFind, being Variant, would identify the found cell address with varFind.Address. The row and column variables are for demonstration purposes.

```
varFindRow = varFind.Row
varFindColumn = varFind.Column
```

13. A Message Box informs the user that the value was found, and in what cell:

```
MsgBox FindWhat& " was found in cell " & _
Cells(varFindRow, varFindColumn).Address & ".", , "Found"
```

14. Enter the End If statement:

```
End If
```

15. Press Alt+Q to return to the worksheet and test your macro. The entire macro when it is completed will look like this:

```
Sub FindTest()

'Declare a variant type variable for the value to locate.
Dim varFind As Variant
```

```
'Declare two more variables, both Long type, for the row
'and column of the value if it is found.
 Dim varFindRow As Long, varFindColumn As Long

'Declare a String type variable for the value to be located.
Dim FindWhat As String

'Define the FindWhat variable as an InputBox entry.
FindWhat = _
InputBox("What do you want to find?", "Find what?")

'If the Cancel button is clicked, or nothing is entered
'in the InputBox, exit the macro.
If FindWhat = "" Then Exit Sub

'Set the varFind variable to the Find method.
Set varFind = _
Cells.Find(What:=FindWhat, LookIn:=xlFormulas, lookat:=xlWhole)

'If varFind = Nothing, inform the user that the value being
'looked for was not found. Also, exit the macro.
If varFind Is Nothing Then
MsgBox _
FindWhat& " was not found.", _
vbInformation, _
"No such animal."
Exit Sub

Else

'Define the row and column variables to identify the cell.
'Actually this is not required because varFind, being Variant,
'would identify the found cell address with varFind.Address.
'The row and column variables are for demonstration purposes.

varFindRow = varFind.Row: varFindColumn = varFind.Column

'A Message Box informs the user that the value was found,
'and in what cell.
MsgBox FindWhat& " was found in cell " & _
Cells(varFindRow, varFindColumn).Address & ".", , "Found"

End If

End Sub
```

Please select Lesson 17 on the DVD to view the video that accompanies this lesson.

SECTION IV
Advanced Programming Techniques

▶ **LESSON 18:** Creating UserForms

▶ **LESSON 19:** UserForm Controls and Their Functions

▶ **LESSON 20:** Advanced UserForms

▶ **LESSON 21:** Class Modules

▶ **LESSON 22:** Add-ins

▶ **LESSON 23:** Managing External Data

▶ **LESSON 24:** Data Access with ActiveX Data Objects

▶ **LESSON 25:** Not Gone, Not Forgotten

18

Creating UserForms

In previous lessons, you have seen examples of how your workbook can interact with its users to make decisions by employing such methods as InputBoxes and Message Boxes. Although these interactive tools are very useful for the situations they are meant to serve, they have limited usefulness in more complex applications.

Some of your projects will require a more versatile approach to asking for and gathering many kinds of information from the users, all within a dedicated interface that's convenient and easy to use. Perhaps you have seen attempts to accomplish this on a neatly arranged worksheet where certain cells are color-shaded or unprotected for data input, maybe with drop-down lists and embedded check boxes or option buttons. A UserForm in VBA is a more efficient method for collecting and recording such information.

WHAT IS A USERFORM?

A *UserForm* is essentially a custom-built dialog box, but that description does not do justice to the immense complexity and diversity with which UserForms can be built and be made to function. A UserForm is created in the Visual Basic Editor, with controls and associated VBA code, usually meant for the end user to be advised of some information or to enter data, generate reports, or perform some action.

> *Think of UserForms as electronic versions of the different forms you fill out on your computer, such as when you make an online purchase, or with paper and pen in a business office. Some information on most forms is required and some information is optional. A UserForm is a dynamic object, with VBA code working behind the scenes to guide your users toward telling your workbook what it needs to know.*

CREATING A USERFORM

The first step in creating a new UserForm is to insert one into the Visual Basic Editor. To do that, press Alt+F11 to get into the VBE, and select your workbook name in the Project Explorer as shown in Figure 18-1.

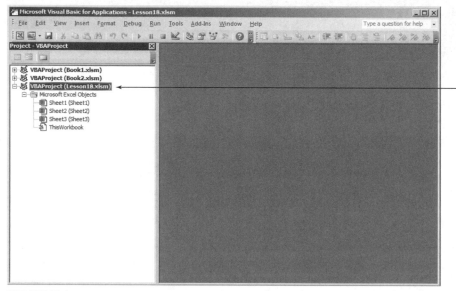

FIGURE 18-1

> Be careful to select the workbook you have in mind before adding a UserForm to it! In Figure 18-1, a couple of other workbooks are open to help make the point that the workbook of interest ("Lesson18.xlsm" in this example) is the workbook selected in the Project Explorer.

With the workbook name selected, from the menu bar click Insert ➪ UserForm as shown in Figure 18-2.

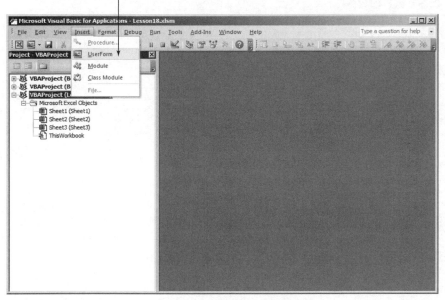

FIGURE 18-2

A new UserForm will appear in its design window as shown in Figure 18-3.

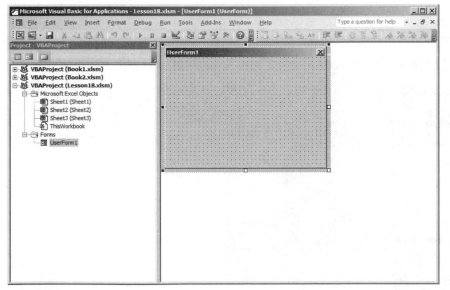

FIGURE 18-3

DESIGNING A USERFORM

UserForms have a wide variety of properties. You can show the Properties window for the UserForm itself, or for any of its controls, by selecting the object and clicking its Properties icon, or clicking View ⇨ Properties Window as shown in Figure 18-4.

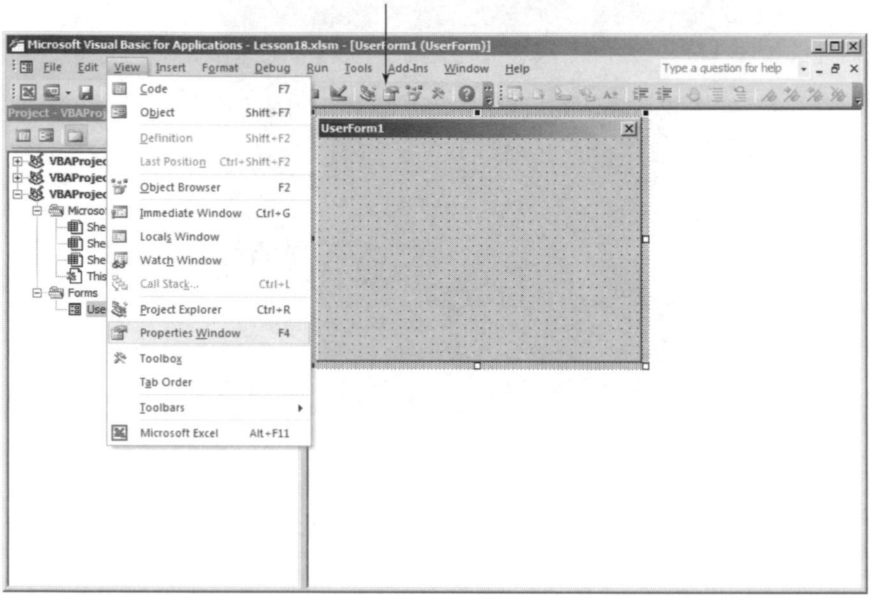

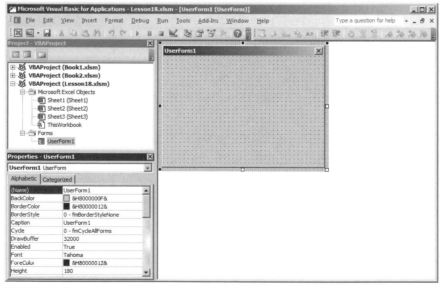

FIGURE 18-4

Below the Project Explorer is where you'll see the Properties window, partially visible in Figure 18-5.

FIGURE 18-5

For the workbook's first UserForm, VBA assigns a default value of "UserForm1" to its Name and Caption properties, as you can see in Figure 18-5. If you were to create a second UserForm, its default Name and Caption properties would be "UserForm2," and so on. To help distinguish between the Name and Caption properties, Figure 18-6 shows where the Name property was changed to "frmEmployees," and the Caption property, which is displayed in the UserForm's title bar, was changed to "Employee Information."

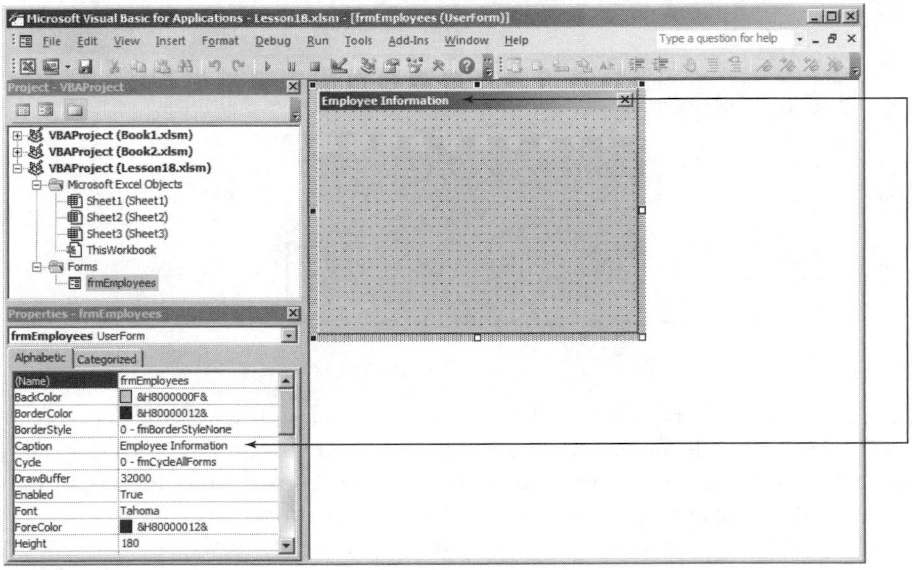

FIGURE 18-6

> When naming UserForms, or any object for that matter, it's best to assign a name that is relevant to the theme of the object. When I name a UserForm, I use the prefix "frm" (for UserForm) followed by a simple, intuitive term (such as "Employees" in this example) that represents the basic idea of the UserForm object.

ADDING CONTROLS TO A USERFORM

A *control* is an object such as a Label, TextBox, OptionButton, or CheckBox, in a UserForm or embedded onto a worksheet that allows users to view or manipulate information. VBA supports these and more controls, which are accessible to you from the VBE Toolbox. To show the Toolbox so you can easily grab whatever controls you want from it, you can click the Toolbox icon, or click View ➪ Toolbox as shown in Figure 18-7.

FIGURE 18-7

The control(s) you place onto your UserForm will depend on its purpose. If you want to design a simple form to gather employee information for your company, you'd at least want to know the employees' names and their titles. It would be useful to display a TextBox to enter the employee name, and then a list of the company's position titles so the user can effortlessly select one. Figure 18-8 shows the Toolbox with the mouse hovering over the Label control icon.

You place a control onto your UserForm by drawing the control onto your UserForm's design area. All you need to do is click whatever Toolbox control icon you're interested in adding to the UserForm, and draw it as you would draw a `Shape` object onto a worksheet. Figure 18-9 shows a Label control that was just drawn, showing its default caption of "Label1."

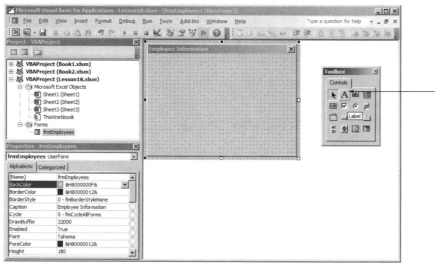

FIGURE 18-8

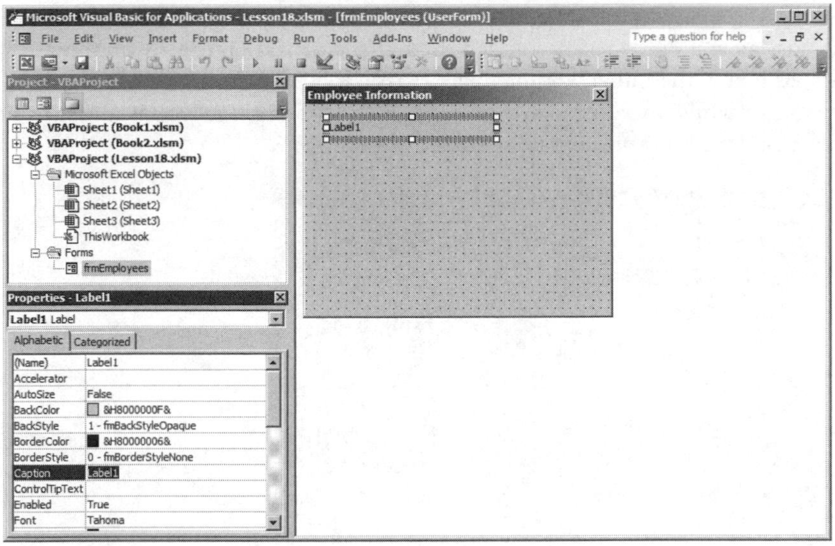

FIGURE 18-9

Notice in Figure 18-9 that the Label's Caption property is selected in the Properties window, so a more meaningful caption can be added to the Label. Because the Label will be directly above the TextBox, and the purpose of the TextBox is to enter an employee name, the Label's caption is changed to "Employee name" as shown in Figure 18-10. Notice further in Figure 18-10 that the TextBox icon is about to be selected in the Toolbox, as you get ready to draw a TextBox control onto the UserForm below the Label.

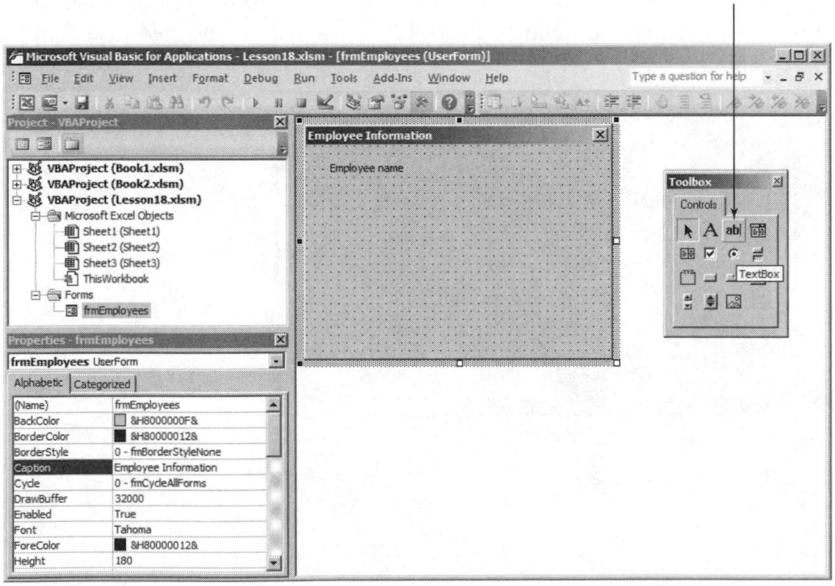

FIGURE 18-10

Once you click the Toolbox's TextBox icon, you add a TextBox control by drawing it onto the UserForm's design area, just as you did when you added the Label control. Figure 18-11 shows the drawn TextBox, positioned below the Label, and having a reasonably sufficient width to accept and display a person's name. Meanwhile, as you can see in Figure 18-11, the Frame icon is about to be selected in preparation for placing a Frame control onto your UserForm.

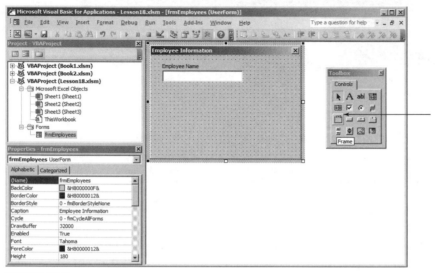

FIGURE 18-11

Figure 18-12 shows your just-drawn Frame control with its default caption of "Frame1." Frames are a good way to group other controls visually by containment, usually with an underlying theme. In the case of this UserForm example, the company's position titles will be contained in such a way that the user can select only one.

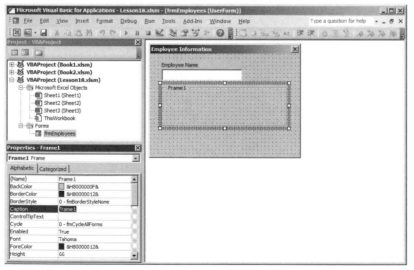

FIGURE 18-12

The caption of a Frame control is an efficient way to describe the purpose of the Frame, just as the Label's caption of "Employee Name" describes the purpose of the TextBox. In Figure 18-12, the Caption property of your new Frame is selected in order to change the meaningless default caption of "Frame1" to a more useful description.

In Figure 18-13, the Frame's default caption of "Frame1" has been changed to "Position Title." Now that the Frame's caption is taken care of, Figure 18-13 also shows that the OptionButton icon in the Toolbox is about to be selected. Because an employee would hold only one particular job position title at a time, a series of OptionButtons can be arranged inside the Frame to represent the company's various position titles, where only one can be selected.

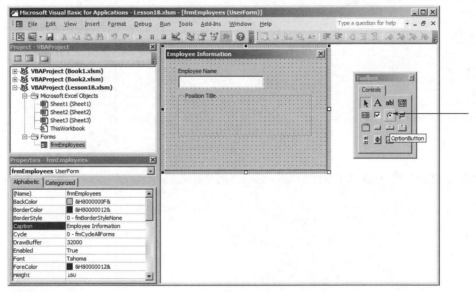

FIGURE 18-13

In this basic UserForm example, Figure 18-14 shows four position titles from which to choose, each as a caption among the four OptionButton controls that were placed inside the Frame. The OptionButtons were added and captioned one at a time. Planning ahead, Figure 18-14 also shows the CommandButton icon in the Toolbox, which is about to be selected in order to add a couple of buttons as the last step in building the UserForm's front-end design.

In Figure 18-15, two CommandButtons have been added, which completes the UserForm's interface design. One of the CommandButtons is captioned OK, which is a common and intuitive caption for users to click their confirmation of data entries. The other CommandButton is a Cancel button to allow users to quit the UserForm altogether, if they so choose.

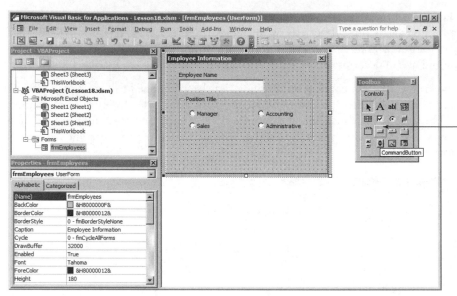

FIGURE 18-14

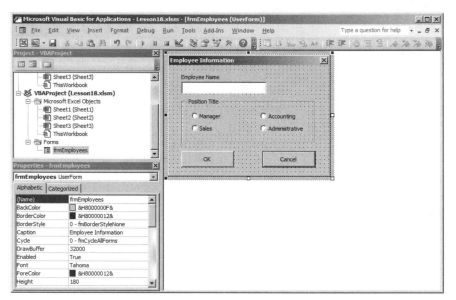

FIGURE 18-15

A standard of proper UserForm design is to always allow your users an escape route out of the UserForm. This is commonly done with a Cancel or Exit button that users can click when they want to leave the form.

SHOWING A USERFORM

To show a UserForm, you execute the VBA Show command in a statement having the syntax *UserFormName.*Show. For example, if you had performed the same steps as you've seen in this lesson to create the frmEmployees UserForm, you may have a simple macro like this to call the UserForm:

```
Sub EmployeeForm()
frmEmployees.Show
End Sub
```

If you'd like to see how the UserForm looks when it is called in the actual worksheet environment, without having to write a formal macro for yourself, you can type **frmEmployees.Show** into the Immediate window and press the Enter key. Figure 18-16 shows how you and your users will see the example UserForm.

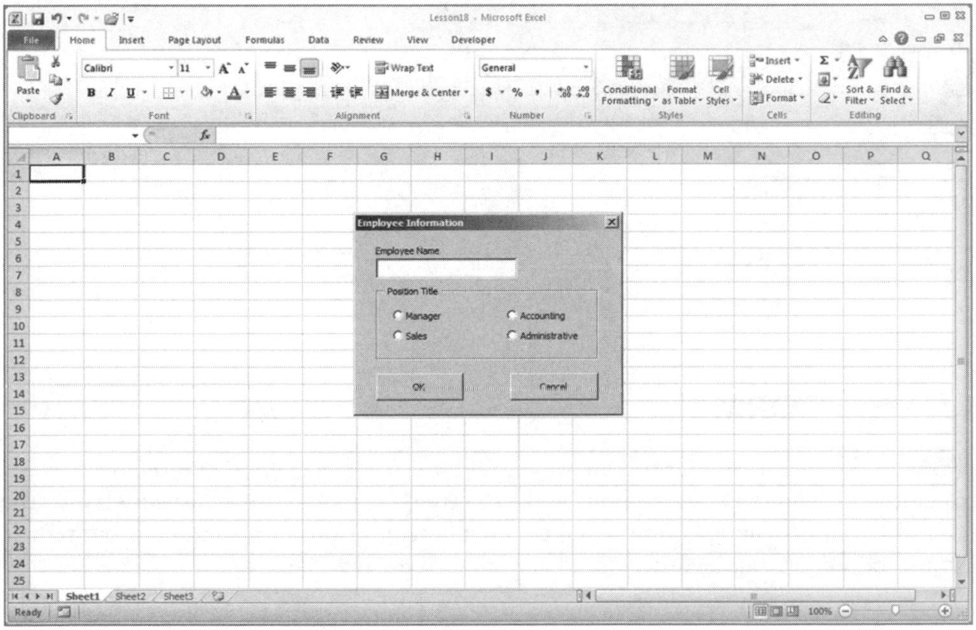

FIGURE 18-16

WHERE DOES THE USERFORM'S CODE GO?

This lesson introduced UserForms and led you through the steps to create a basic form that contains various controls. In Lessons 19 and 20 you see examples of how those and other UserForm controls are programmable with event-driven VBA code.

A UserForm is a class of VBA objects that has its own module. Similar to the notion that each worksheet has its own module, each UserForm you add to your workbook will automatically be created with its own module. Accessing a UserForm's module is easy: In the VBE, you can double-click the UserForm itself in the design pane; or in the Project Explorer, you can right-click the UserForm name and select View Code, as shown in Figure 18-17.

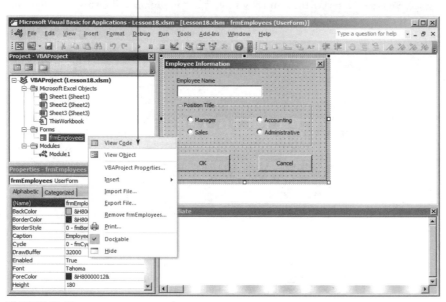

FIGURE 18-17

CLOSING A USERFORM

You have two ways to close a UserForm. One way is with the Unload method and the other way is with the Hide method. Though both methods make the UserForm look as if it has gone away, they each carry out different instructions. This can be a point of confusion for beginning programmers, so it's important to understand the distinction between Unload and Hide.

Unloading a UserForm

When you unload a UserForm, the form closes and its entries are cleared from memory. In most cases, that is what you would want — for the data that was entered to be recorded in some way, or passed to Public variables, and then closed. The statement that unloads a UserForm is simply Unload Me and it is commonly associated with a CommandButton for that purpose, such as the Cancel button that was placed on this lesson's example UserForm.

Suppose you want to unload the UserForm when the Cancel button is clicked. A quick and easy way to do that is to double-click the CommandButton in the UserForm's design, as shown in Figure 18-18.

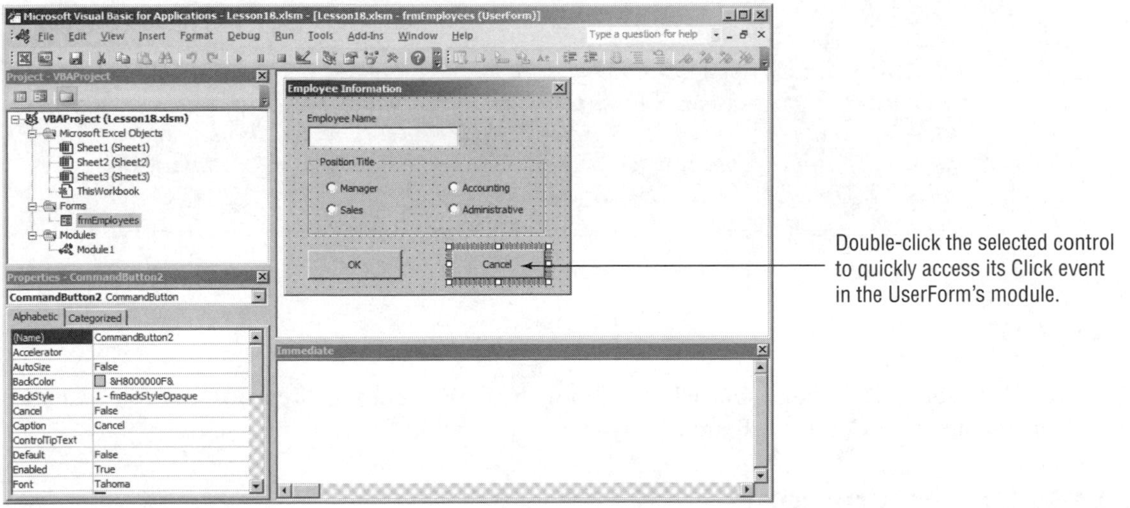

Double-click the selected control to quickly access its Click event in the UserForm's module.

FIGURE 18-18

When you double-click the CommandButton, you will see these lines of code in the UserForm's module:

```
Private Sub CommandButton2_Click()

End Sub
```

To complete the Click procedure, type **Unload Me**. When the Cancel button is clicked, the UserForm will unload — that is, it will close and release from memory the data that was entered — with this Click event for that button:

```
Private Sub CommandButton2_Click()
Unload Me
End Sub
```

Hiding a UserForm

The Hide method makes the UserForm invisible, but the data that was in the UserForm is still there, remaining in memory and able to be viewed when the form is shown again. In some situations you will want this to be the case, such as if you are interacting with two or more UserForms and you want the user to focus on only one form at a time. The statement to hide a UserForm is Me.Hide.

> To summarize the difference between Unload and Hide, the method you choose will depend on why you don't want the UserForm to be seen. Most of the time, you'll want the form cleared from memory, but sometimes, information that was entered into the form needs to be referred to the next time you show the form while the workbook has remained open. Closing the workbook automatically unloads a UserForm only if it was hidden.

TRY IT

In this lesson, you design a simple UserForm with a Label control, a TextBox control, a CheckBox control, and two CommandButton controls.

Lesson Requirements

For this lesson, you practice designing a simple UserForm with various controls to emulate a client profile. To get the sample database files you can download Lesson 18 from the book's website at www.wrox.com.

Step-by-Step

1. Press Alt+F11 to go to the Visual Basic Editor.

2. Select the workbook name in the Project Explorer window, and from the menu at the top of the VBE click Insert ➪ UserForm.

3. Select the UserForm in its design window, and press the F4 key (or click View ➪ Properties Window) to show the Properties window.

4. Change the Name property to **frmClients** and change the Caption property to **Clients**.

5. Size the UserForm by setting its Height property to 240 and its Width property to 190.

6. From the menu at the top of the VBE, click View ➪ Toolbox.

7. From the Toolbox, click the Label control icon and draw a Label across the top of the UserForm. With the Label control selected, change its Caption property to **Company Name**.

8. From the Toolbox, click the TextBox control icon and draw a TextBox directly below the Label.

9. From the Toolbox, click the Label control icon again, and draw a Label a little bit below the TextBox. With that Label control selected, change its Caption property to **Client's business — check all that apply:**.

10. Directly below the Label from Step 9, from the Toolbox, click the CheckBox control icon and draw a CheckBox that is wide enough for you to have its caption property be "Agriculture."

11. Repeat Step 10 four more times, meaning you'll draw a total of five CheckBoxes that are stacked one above the other in a vertical fashion. Change the Caption labels on the four other Checkboxes to **Manufacturing, Medical, Retail,** and **Technology**.

12. From the Toolbox, click the CommandButton icon control and draw a CommandButton in the lower-left corner of your UserForm. Change its Caption property to **OK**.

13. Draw a second CommandButton in the lower-right corner of your UserForm. Change its Caption property to **Cancel**.

14. Take a look at your completed UserForm as it would appear when called. While you are still in the VBE, press Ctrl+G to get into the Immediate Window. Type **frmClients.Show** and press the Enter key. Your UserForm should look like the one shown in Figure 18-19.

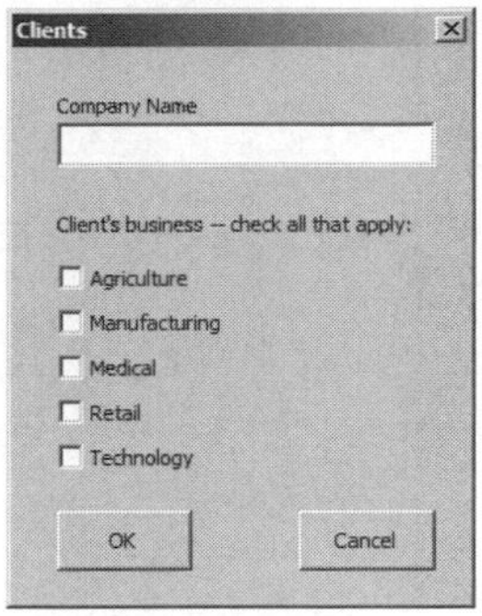

FIGURE 18-19

Please select Lesson 18 on the DVD to view the video that accompanies this lesson.

19

UserForm Controls and Their Functions

UserForms allow you to interact with your users in ways that you can't when using standard Message Boxes, InputBoxes, or controls embedded onto your worksheet. With UserForms, you can control the input of information by validating the kind of data that gets entered, the order in which it is entered, and, if your workbook requires it, the exact location where the information should be stored and how it should be recalled. This lesson leads you through the design of various UserForms, with examples of how to program an assortment of controls that you'll utilize most frequently.

UNDERSTANDING THE FREQUENTLY USED USERFORM CONTROLS

As you saw in Lesson 18, when you add a UserForm to your workbook, the first thing you see is the empty UserForm in its design window, not unlike a blank canvas upon which you'll strategically place your controls. The controls you utilize will depend upon the task at hand, and you'll come across countless sets of circumstances for which a UserForm is the right tool for the job.

Still, you'll find that a core group of frequently used controls can handle most of your UserForm requirements. The fun part is tapping into the events each control supports, in order to create a customizable UserForm that's user-friendly and, most importantly, gets the job done.

> *As you will see in Lesson 20, you are not limited to the relatively few controls shown by default on the Toolbox. Dozens more Toolbox controls are available to you, many of which you'll probably never use, but some you eventually will.*

CommandButtons

The CommandButton is a basic staple of just about any UserForm. The combination of a `Caption` property and `Click` event make CommandButtons an efficient way to convey an objective and then carry it out with a mouse click. And if for no other reason, a Cancel or Exit button is about as basic a need as any form will have.

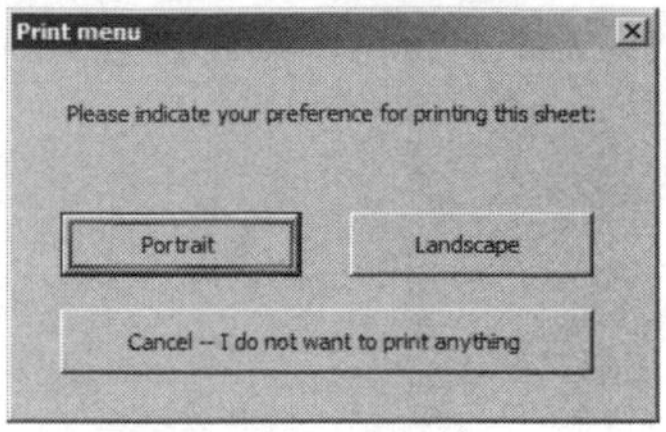

Suppose you want to provide your users with a quick way to print a worksheet in either portrait or landscape orientation. You can make it easy for your users to click a button to indicate their decision, and then just go ahead and execute the print job. Figure 19-1 shows an example of how this may be done, followed by the code behind each of the CommandButtons.

FIGURE 19-1

```
Private Sub cmdPortrait_Click()
With ActiveSheet
.PageSetup.Orientation = xlPortrait
.PrintPreview
End With
End Sub

Private Sub cmdLandscape_Click()
With ActiveSheet
.PageSetup.Orientation = Landscape
.PrintPreview
End With
End Sub

Private Sub cmdCancel_Click()
Unload Me
End Sub
```

> *As you can see in the preceding code, each of the CommandButtons has been named using the prefix "cmd" followed by a notation that gives a clue as to the purpose of the button (see* `cmdPortrait_Click()`, `cmdLandscape_Click()`, *and* `cmdCancel_Click()`). *There is nothing sacred about the "cmd" prefix for CommandButtons, or about the "lbl" prefix when naming Labels, or about any naming prefix for that matter. Still, it's wise to name your controls in some intuitive and consistent way so you and others will recognize the control and its purpose when reviewing your VBA code.*

Labels

You've seen Label controls, such as the examples in Lesson 18, where the Label's Caption property is set to always display the same text. Sometimes, a Label can serve to display dynamic information that is not a static piece of text, and in that case, you'd leave the Caption property empty.

UserForms have an `Initialize` event that is triggered when you call the UserForm, which can help you take action on your UserForm or workbook. Suppose you want to enhance the customized look of your form with a welcome greeting that changes to reflect the time of day. For example, if the UserForm were to be opened in the morning, the message would include the text "Good morning," and so on for the afternoon and evening. The following code achieves that effect, as shown in Figure 19-2.

FIGURE 19-2

```
Private Sub UserForm_Initialize()
Dim TimeOfDay As String
If Time < 0.5 Then
TimeOfDay = "Good Morning !  "
ElseIf Time >= 0.5 And Time < 0.75 Then
TimeOfDay = "Good Afternoon !  "
Else
TimeOfDay = "Good Evening !  "
End If
Label1.Caption = TimeOfDay & "Welcome to the company workbook."
End Sub
```

TIMES IN VBA

Even after studying the preceding code, you might wonder why a number less than .5 translates to morning, why a number greater than or equal to .5 and less than .75 translates to afternoon, and why a number greater than or equal to .75 translates to evening. The reason is that VBA regards a time of day as a completed percentage of the calendar day. For example, 12:00 noon is the halfway mark of a calendar day, and one-half of something can be mathematically represented by the expression .5. The `Time` function in VBA interprets a number less than .5 as morning because by definition, half the day would not yet have completed. Afternoon is between .5 (12:00 noon) and up to just before 6:00 PM, which the `Time` function interprets as .75, being at the three-fourths mark of the 24-hour calendar day. A `Time` number greater than or equal to .75 is evening because it is at or past 6:00 PM and before the `Time` number of 0, which is 12:00 midnight of the next day.

You can also populate a Label's caption from another control's event procedure. Suppose your UserForm provides a CommandButton that when clicked, toggles column C as being visible or hidden, such as with this line of code in the CommandButton's `Click` event:

```
Columns(3).Hidden = Not Columns(3).Hidden
```

> *Columns(3) is another way of expressing* Columns("C:C"). *The "3" refers to C being the third letter in the alphabet, which corresponds to the third column from the left in the worksheet grid. If it were column D, the syntax notation would be* Columns(4) *and so on. There is no schematic advantage to using one style of expression over the other, but I included the numeric expression here so you can be aware of it, and use it in your macros if it feels more intuitive for you to do so.*

It's a good practice when constructing UserForms to give the users an indication that confirms what they've just done. In this example, a Label control can be near the CommandButton that confirms the visible or hidden status of column C, with the following code:

```
Private Sub CommandButton1_Click()
Columns(3).Hidden = Not Columns(3).Hidden
Label1.Caption = "Column C is " & _
IIf(Columns(3).Hidden = True, "hidden", "visible")
End Sub
```

TextBoxes

A TextBox is most commonly used to display information that is entered by a user, or is associated with a cell through the TextBox's ControlSource property, or is entered programmatically, such as to display a calculation result or a piece of data from a worksheet table. You have probably seen TextBoxes when you've entered information on electronic forms, such as when you've entered your name, address, and credit card number when making a purchase online.

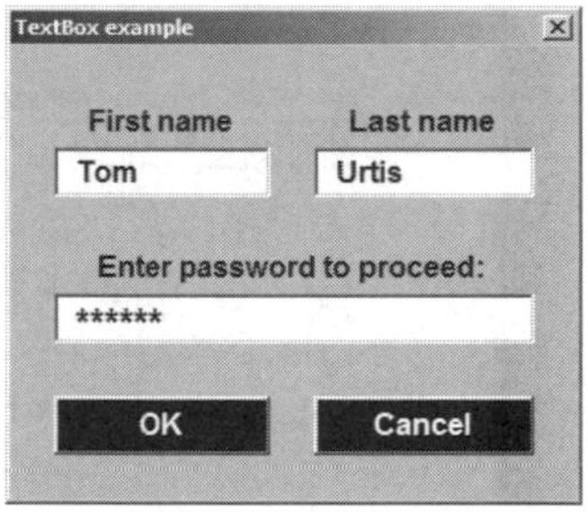

FIGURE 19-3

Figure 19-3 shows a UserForm with three TextBox controls. In this example, I've entered my first and last name, and a password that is represented in the figure as a series of asterisks. UserForms are a good way to greet your user and ask for a password with a TextBox, and with the TextBox's PasswordChar property, you can set any character (in this case an asterisk) to appear instead of the password, so no one else sees the password as it is being typed.

> *Formatting of TextBoxes is limited to the entire TextBox entry. For example, if you want any portion of the TextBox's contents to be bold, the entire contents must be bold.*

Sometimes you will want a TextBox to accept only numeric entries, such as a dollar figure, or a calendar year, or a person's age in years. The following code monitors each keystroke entry into TextBox1, and disallows any character that is not a number. As a courtesy to the user, a message appears to immediately inform the user that an improper character was attempted and disallowed.

```
Private Sub TextBox1_KeyPress(ByVal KeyAscii As MSForms.ReturnInteger)
Select Case KeyAscii
Case 48 To 57
Case Else
KeyAscii = 0
MsgBox "You typed a non-numeric character", _
vbExclamation, _
"Numbers only, please!"
End Select
End Sub
```

> *In the preceding code example, you might not be familiar with the term "ASCII" (pronounced "askee"), which is an acronym for American Standard Code for Information Interchange. Computers can only understand numbers, so a numerical representation is needed for alphanumeric characters and other symbols such as # and @. In the preceding code, numbers 0–9 are recognized by virtue of their ASCII representation of 48–57. If you'd like to see a list of all 255 ASCII and Extended ASCII characters, you can produce it yourself on an Excel worksheet by entering the formula* =CHAR(ROW()) *in cell A1, and copying it down to cell A255. Each cell will hold a character (some characters will not be visible) whose ASCII number will correspond to the cell's row number.*

TextBoxes can display calculated results, and when using numbers for mathematical operations, you'll need to use the Val function, which returns the numbers contained in a TextBox string as a numeric value. Suppose your UserForm contains seven TextBoxes, into which you enter the sales dollars for each day of the week. As shown in Figure 19-4, an eighth TextBox can display the sum of those seven numbers when a CommandButton is clicked, with the following code:

```
Private Sub CommandButton1_Click()
Dim intTextBox As Integer, dblSum As Double
dblSum = 0
For intTextBox = 1 To 7
dblSum = dblSum + Val(Controls("TextBox" & intTextBox).Value)
Next intTextBox
TextBox8.Value = Format(dblSum, "#,###")
End Sub
```

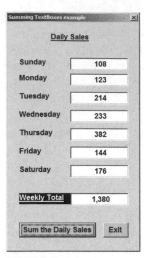

FIGURE 19-4

ListBoxes

A ListBox displays a list of items and lets you select one or more. ListBoxes are fairly versatile in their display of information, and their options for allowing you to select one, many, or all listed items.

Suppose you want to list all 12 months of the year, so any particular month can be selected to perhaps run a report for income and expenses during that month. You might also want the flexibility to run a single report that includes activity for any combinations of months. The ListBox control is an excellent choice because its MultiSelect property can be set to allow just one item, or multiple items, to be selected. Figure 19-5 shows an example of how you can control the way the items appear with the ListStyle property, and selection options for your ListBox (allow only one, or more than one item to be selected) with the MultiSelect property.

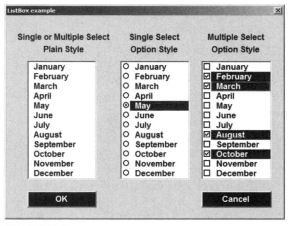

FIGURE 19-5

There are two common methods by which a ListBox is populated with items. In the preceding example, the 12 months of the year could be listed on a worksheet, say on Sheet2 in range A1:A12. To have the ListBox display the list of months, you can enter Sheet2!A1:A12 as the RowSource property for that ListBox.

In many cases, however, you'll want to populate your ListBox without having to store the items on a worksheet. The UserForm's Initialize event is perfect for populating your ListBox with a dynamic or static list of items. Suppose you want to list the names of various countries. The following code does that using the AddItem method in the UserForm's Initialize event, which you can easily append when you want to add or omit a country name.

```
Private Sub UserForm_Initialize()
With ListBox1
.AddItem "England"
.AddItem "Spain"
.AddItem "France"
.AddItem "Japan"
.AddItem "Australia"
.AddItem "United States"
End With
End Sub
```

> *When you programmatically populate a ListBox (or, as you'll see, a ComboBox), be sure to clear the control's RowSource property or you will get a runtime error when you call (initialize) the UserForm.*

The following code lists all the visible worksheets in your workbook, and excludes the worksheets that are hidden:

```
Private Sub UserForm_Initialize()
With ListBox1
.Clear
Dim wks As Worksheet
For Each wks In Worksheets
If wks.Visible = xlSheetVisible Then .AddItem wks.Name
Next wks
End With
End Sub
```

ListBoxes support many events, and using the Click event, for example, this code activates the worksheet whose name you click, with the ListBox's MultiSelect property set to 0 - fmMultiSelectSingle:

```
Private Sub ListBox1_Click()
Worksheets(ListBox1.Value).Activate
End Sub
```

ComboBoxes

A ComboBox combines the features of a ListBox and a TextBox, in that you can select an item from its drop-down list, or you can type an item into the ComboBox that is not included in its list. Most of the time, you'll use the ComboBox the same way you'd use Data Validation, where a drop-down arrow is visible for revealing the list of items that are available for selection.

> *If you want to limit the ComboBox to only accept items from the drop-down list, set its Style property to* 2 - fmStyleDropDownList.

ComboBoxes allow only one item to be selected; you cannot select multiple items in a ComboBox the way you can with a ListBox. However, ComboBoxes are populated much the same way as ListBoxes, with a RowSource property and an AddItem method.

Suppose you want to guide the users of your workbook to select a year that is within three years — past or future — of the current year. The following code could accomplish that, with Figure 19-6 showing the ComboBox's list after the drop-down arrow was clicked, assuming the current year is 2011:

```
Private Sub UserForm_Initialize()
With ComboBox1
.Clear
Dim iYear As Integer, jYear As Integer
jYear = Format(Date, "YYYY")
For iYear = 1 To 7
ComboBox1.AddItem jYear - 3
jYear = jYear + 1
Next iYear
End With
End Sub
```

FIGURE 19-6

As with a ListBox, if the items needed to populate the ComboBox are listed on a worksheet, it does not mean you must refer to them with the RowSource property. You can leave the RowSource property empty, and populate the ComboBox (same concept applies to a ListBox) with the following code example, assuming the values are listed in range A1:A8 with no blank cells in that range:

```
Private Sub UserForm_Initialize()
ComboBox1.List = Range("A1:A8").Value
End Sub
```

> *If you want the first item in the drop-down list to be automatically visible in your ComboBox, you can add the following line before the* End Sub *line, assuming the ComboBox is named ComboBox1:*
>
> ComboBox1.ListIndex = 0

Sometimes you'll need to populate the ComboBox (or ListBox) with items listed in a range that also contains blank cells. Figure 19-7 shows how horrible that will make the drop-down list look, if the ComboBox was attempted to be populated with the line of code `ComboBox1.List = Range("A1:A8").Value`.

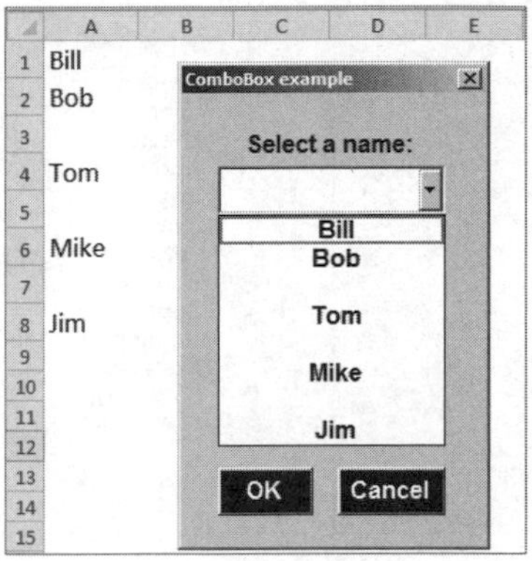

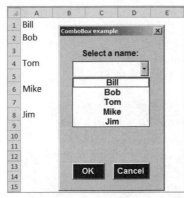

FIGURE 19-7

Much nicer looking is Figure 19-8, which shows empty spaces in its drop-down list even though empty cells exist among the list of names. The code to do that is shown here, which uses the LEN function to disregard cells that have no value in them.

```
Private Sub UserForm_Initialize()
Dim LastRow As Long, cboCell As Range
LastRow = Cells(Rows.Count, 1).End(xlUp).Row
For Each cboCell In Range("A1:A" & LastRow)
If Len(cboCell) > 0 Then ComboBox1.AddItem cboCell.Value
Next cboCell
End Sub
```

FIGURE 19-8

CheckBoxes

A CheckBox on your UserForm can serve one of two purposes: to provide users with an option that is of the Yes/No variety, without a superfluous Message Box to present the option, or to provide a pair of OptionButtons (covered in the next section). Simply, a single CheckBox is inferred to mean Yes or OK if it is checked, and No if it is not checked.

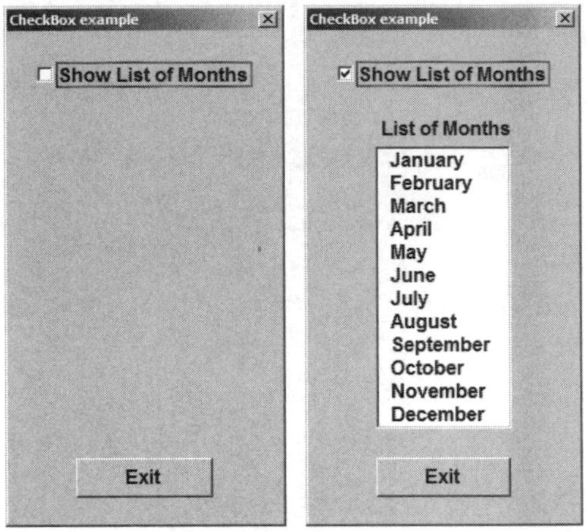

As you develop more complex UserForms, you will want to provide your users with convenient options for viewing — or not viewing — interface objects that might be irrelevant to them in some cases, and useful in others. For example, Figure 19-9 shows the same UserForm in two situations, where the user can check or uncheck the CheckBox captioned Show List of Months. If the CheckBox is unchecked, neither the ListBox nor the Label above it will be visible, but if the CheckBox is checked, those controls do appear. The code associated with the CheckBox follows.

FIGURE 19-9

```
Private Sub CheckBox1_Click()
With CheckBox1

If .Value = True Then
Label1.Visible = True
ListBox1.Visible = True

Else

Label1.Visible = False
ListBox1.Visible = False
End If

End With
End Sub
```

> *Users appreciate having a say as to what they see on a form, which helps give them some control over the form's navigation process. However, as the workbook's developer, your primary objective is to design a smart form. In this example, if the selection of a month name is a mandatory action in the UserForm's overall process, you would not consider building in the option of hiding a ListBox of month names. You'll often see a single CheckBox on a UserForm when a simple preference is to be indicated, such as including a header on all printed pages, or performing the same action on all worksheets.*

Another popular use of CheckBoxes is to provide the user with several options at the same time. Figure 19-10 shows a UserForm that asks for users to indicate which regions a company report should include. When the OK button is clicked, you can assign variables to each CheckBox that was checked, and incorporate those variables later in a VBA decision process that recognizes only the checked regions. One way to accomplish that is to loop through each CheckBox and identify the selected CheckBox(es), as shown in the following code.

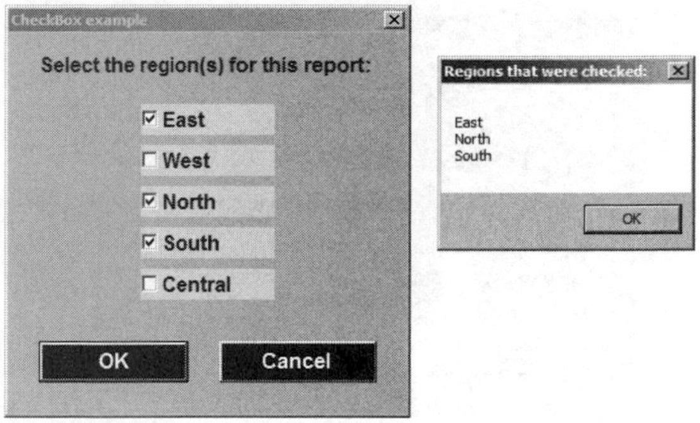

FIGURE 19-10

```
Private Sub cmdOK_Click()
'Declare an Integer type variable for the five CheckBoxes.
Dim intCheckBox As Integer
'Declare a String type variable for the list of selected Checkboxes.
Dim strCheckBoxNames As String
'Open a For next loop to examine each of the 5 CheckBoxes.
For intCheckBox = 1 To 5
'If the CheckBox is selected, meaning its value is True,
'build the strCheckBoxNames string with the caption of the
'selected CheckBox, followed by a Chr(10) new line character
'for readability in the confirming MsgBox.
If Controls("CheckBox" & intCheckBox).Value = True Then
strCheckBoxNames = strCheckBoxNames & _
Controls("CheckBox" & intCheckBox).Caption & Chr(10)
End If
'Continue the loop until all 5 CheckBoxes have been examined.
Next intCheckBox
'Display a Message Box to advise the users what they selected.
MsgBox strCheckBoxNames, , "Regions that were checked:"
End Sub
```

OptionButtons

An OptionButton is used when you want the user to select one choice from a group of optional choices. You would use a group of OptionButtons to show the single item that was selected among the group's set of choices. For example, on a college application form, in the gender section, an applicant could select only Male or Female.

In Figure 19-11, a menu for running a financial report might ask the user to select the month of activity upon which the report should be based. A group of 12 OptionButtons limits the user to only one selection. Each OptionButton's caption property was filled in with the name of a month.

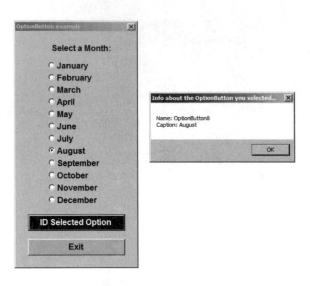

FIGURE 19-11

Figure 19-11 shows that the month of August was selected, and in real practice, you'd identify that selection in your code with a variable that refers to the selected month name, and produces the report for that month. One way to do that is to loop through each of the OptionButtons and stop when you encounter the selected OptionButton whose value would be True.

To help make the point, there is a button on the form with the caption "ID Selected Option," and when you click the button, a Message Box appears, telling you the name of the selected OptionButton and its caption. The following code examines the OptionButtons' status and then produces the Message Box:

```
Private Sub CommandButton1_Click()
Dim intOption As Integer, optName As String, optCaption As String
For intOption = 1 To 12
If Controls("OptionButton" & intOption) = True Then
optName = Controls("OptionButton" & intOption).Name
optCaption = Controls("OptionButton" & intOption).Caption
MsgBox _
"Name: " & optName & vbCrLf & _
"Caption: " & optCaption, , _
"Info about the OptionButton you selected:"
Exit For
End If
Next intOption
End Sub
```

OptionButtons have a useful property called `GroupName` that you should be aware of. In Figure 19-11, a simple UserForm lists 12 OptionButtons, all with the same objective of eliciting a selection for a particular month. But what if your UserForm has other sections for user options that require OptionButtons, such as to select a day of the week, or a print orientation preference of Landscape or Portrait? You'll find many reasons to apply OptionButtons to your UserForms, and you will need each set of options to be a mutually exclusive group.

You have two ways to create a group of mutually exclusive OptionButton controls. You can place the group inside a Frame (a control that is covered in the next section), or you can use the `GroupName` property of the related OptionButtons to group them together. In Figure 19-12, the OptionButtons have been selected in the UserForm's design window, and the `GroupName` property has been defined with the name "Months."

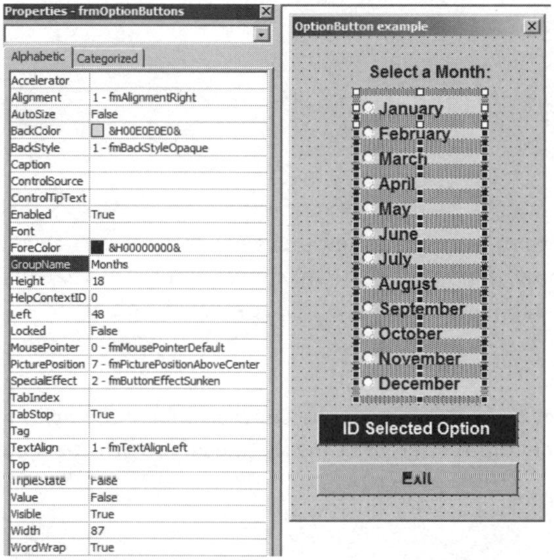

FIGURE 19-12

> *Whether organized by* `GroupName` *or a Frame control, clicking an OptionButton sets its value to True and automatically sets the other OptionButtons in the group (or in the Frame) to False.*

Frames

Frame controls group related controls together, to provide an organized look and feel when the UserForm calls for many controls. Figure 19-13 illustrates an example of employing a Frame.

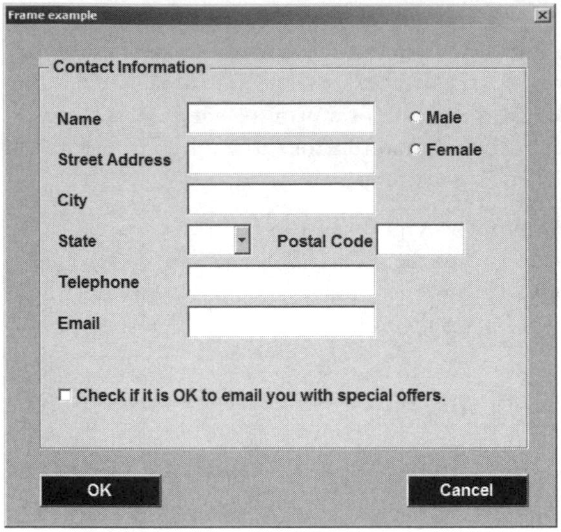

FIGURE 19-13

When you place controls within a Frame control, manipulating the Frame's properties can affect all the controls inside the Frame. For example, assuming the Frame control shown in Figure 19-13 is named Frame1, this line of code would hide that frame along with all the controls inside it:

```
Frame1.Visible= False
```

Sometimes you will want your Frame to be visible, but you want all the controls inside the Frame to be temporarily disabled. You can disable the Frame and render its controls unusable with the following line of code:

```
Frame1.Enabled = False
```

If you test that for yourself, you'll see a curious result, which is the controls inside the Frame are not "grayed out" but are essentially disabled, because they are rendered useless by virtue of the Frame being disabled. The controls themselves appear to be enabled and that can fool your users into wondering what's wrong with perfectly good looking controls that do not respond to any keystrokes or mouse clicks.

If you want to disable the actual controls inside the Frame, and make them look disabled, you must loop through each of the controls inside the Frame with the following example code. Note that this code will not disable Frame1, only the controls inside it.

```
Dim FrmControl As Control
For Each FrmControl In Frame1.Controls
FrmControl.Enabled = False
Next FrmControl
```

Naturally, to enable a control that's been disabled, change the `False` statement to `True`, which you can handle in a separate procedure, or in one single procedure with a line of code that toggles the `Enabled` property using the `Not` statement. The following example shows how to do this:

```
Private Sub CommandButton4_Click()
Dim FrmControl As Control
For Each FrmControl In Frame1.Controls
FrmControl.Enabled = Not FrmControl.Enabled
Next FrmControl
End Sub
```

MultiPages

A MultiPage control is like having a set of tabbed folders that each contain information and controls that would be too voluminous to fit comfortably within the UserForm's interface. Figure 19-14 shows an example of how a MultiPage control can come in handy when a lot of information is being sought from the workbook's users about their viewing preferences.

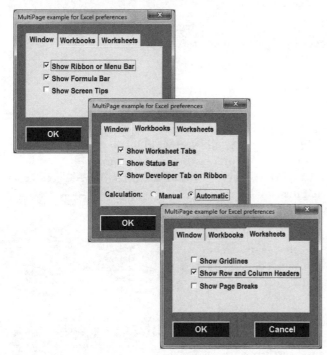

FIGURE 19-14

The MultiPage control has a collection of `Page` objects that are each dedicated to a theme. You can right-click a tab to add a new page, delete the page you right-clicked, rename the page's caption, or move the page. MultiPage controls are a terrific way to maximize the space on your UserForm with a smart, organized look and feel.

TRY IT

In this lesson, you design a UserForm with several controls, including a ListBox that is populated dynamically with the ability to select multiple items.

Lesson Requirements

To get the sample database files you can download Lesson 19 from the book's website at www.wrox.com.

Step-by-Step

1. Open a new workbook and activate Sheet1.

2. In column A, enter the items in the cells as you see them displayed in Figure 19-15.

3. Press Alt+F11 to get into the Visual Basic Editor.

4. Select your workbook name in the Project Explorer, and from the menu bar click Insert ⇨ UserForm and accept its default name of UserForm1.

5. Change the UserForm's caption property to **Shopping List**.

6. Select the UserForm in its design window, and if the Toolbox is not visible, click View ⇨ Toolbox.

7. Draw a ListBox on the UserForm and accept its default name of ListBox1. Set its `MultiSelect` property to **1 - fmMultiSelectMulti.8.** Draw a CommandButton on the UserForm below the ListBox and accept its default name of CommandButton1. Change its caption property to **Transfer selected items to Sheet2 column E.**

8. Draw another CommandButton on the UserForm below the first CommandButton, and change its caption property to **Exit**. That completes the design of the UserForm, which should resemble Figure 19-16 when it is called.

9. Double-click the UserForm, which will take you to its module. Type the code under the UserForm's `Initialize` event that populates the ListBox with items in column A of Sheet1, ignoring the empty cells.

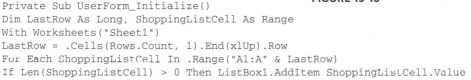

FIGURE 19-15

FIGURE 19-16

```
Private Sub UserForm_Initialize()
Dim LastRow As Long, ShoppingListCell As Range
With Worksheets("Sheet1")
LastRow = .Cells(Rows.Count, 1).End(xlUp).Row
For Each ShoppingListCell In .Range("A1:A" & LastRow)
If Len(ShoppingListCell) > 0 Then ListBox1.AddItem ShoppingListCell.Value
```

```
Next ShoppingListCell
End With
End Sub
```

10. While in the UserForm's module, type the code for CommandButton2 that is the Exit button:

```
Private Sub CommandButton2_Click()
Unload Me
End Sub
```

11. Immediately above the Code window are two drop-down lists. Click the drop-down arrow at the left belonging to the Object field, and select CommandButton1. That will place these two statements in the UserForm's module:

```
Private Sub CommandButton1_Click()

End Sub
```

12. For the first line of code in the CommandButton1 Click event, open a With structure for Sheet2, which is the destination sheet for selected items:

```
With Worksheets("Sheet2")
```

13. Declare variables for ListBox items and NextRow:

```
Dim intItem As Integer, NextRow As Long
```

14. Clear column E of Sheet2 to start your shopping list with a clean slate:

```
.Columns(5).Clear
```

15. Put a header in cell E1 of Sheet2, to start the list:

```
.Range("E1").Value = "Shopping List"
```

16. Define the NextRow variable as 2, because column E was just cleared and the Shopping List header is in cell E1 with nothing below it:

```
NextRow = 2
```

17. Loop through all items in ListBox1 and if any are selected, list them in turn in column E of Sheet2:

```
For intItem = 0 To ListBox1.ListCount - 1
If ListBox1.Selected(intItem) = True Then
.Range("E" & NextRow).Value = ListBox1.List(intItem)
```

18. Add **1** to the NextRow variable to prepare for the next selected item:

```
NextRow = NextRow + 1
End If
```

19. Continue the loop until all ListBox items have been examined:

```
Next intItem
```

20.   Close the `With` structure for Sheet2:

```
End With
```

21.   Your final CommandButton1 code will look like this:

```
Private Sub CommandButton1_Click()
'Open a With structure for Sheet2
With Worksheets("Sheet2")

'Declare variables for ListBox items and NextRow
Dim intItem As Integer, NextRow As Long
'Clear column E of Sheet2
.Columns(5).Clear
'Put a header in cell E1
.Range("E1").Value = "Shopping List"
'Define the NextRow variable as 2
'because column E was just cleared and the Shopping List
'header is in cell E1 with nothing below it.
NextRow = 2

'Loop through all items in ListBox 1 and if any are selected,
'list them in turn in column E of Sheet2.
For intItem = 0 To ListBox1.ListCount - 1
If ListBox1.Selected(intItem) = True Then
.Range("E" & NextRow).Value = ListBox1.List(intItem)
'Add 1 to the NextRow variable to prepare for the next selected item.
NextRow = NextRow + 1
End If
'Continue the loop until all ListBox items have been examined.
Next intItem
'Close the With structure for Sheet2.
End With
End Sub
```

Please select Lesson 19 on the DVD to view the video that accompanies this lesson.

20

Advanced UserForms

Lesson 18 introduced you to UserForms and showed how to add controls to your form. Lesson 19 provided several examples of UserForms with frequently used controls to help you gather and store information. This lesson takes an expanded look at how you can get more out of UserForms by tapping into their capacity for supporting some interesting and useful operations.

THE USERFORM TOOLBAR

In the Visual Basic Editor, there's a handy toolbar for working with UserForms, aptly named the UserForm toolbar, shown in Figure 20-1. To display it in the VBE, from the menu bar click View ➪ Toolbars ➪ UserForm.

The UserForm toolbar has eight features:

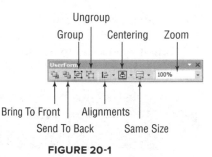

FIGURE 20-1

➤ **Bring to Front** — Brings the selected control to the front of the other controls.

➤ **Send to Back** — Sends the selected control to the back of the other controls.

➤ **Group** — Groups the selected controls.

➤ **Ungroup** — Ungroups the selected grouped controls.

➤ **Alignments** — The small drop-down arrow to the right of the Alignments icon provides options for aligning the selected controls by their Rights, Lefts, Centers, Tops, Middles, Bottoms, and To Grid.

➤ **Centering** — Centers the selected controls horizontally or vertically on the UserForm.

➤ **Same Size** — Sizes the selected controls to be of the same Height, Width, or Both.

➤ **Zoom** — Displays the UserForm as a zoomed percentage of its normal size.

> If you're working in a UserForm module and you forget the names of controls, and you've selected the Require Variable Declaration option (on the Editor tab when you click Tools ➪ Options in the VBE) type **Me** followed by a dot. You'll see a list of all the methods and properties for the UserForm, including the list of control names belonging to the UserForm.

MODAL VERSUS MODELESS

Beginning with Excel version 2000, UserForms became equipped with a new property called *ShowModal*. When a UserForm's ShowModal property is set to True, that is, when it is shown as Modal, it means that while the UserForm is visible, you cannot select a worksheet cell, or another worksheet tab, or any of the Ribbon or menu icons until you close the UserForm. Most of the time, this is what you will want — for the UserForm to command all focus and attention while it is visible.

At times your project will benefit from the ability to select cells and generally to navigate worksheets while a UserForm is visible. When that's what you need, call the UserForm by specifying the ShowModal property as False, for example:

```
Sub ShowUserForm1()
UserForm1.Show vbModeless
End Sub
```

The preceding code line can also be written as UserForm1.Show 0. The default setting for the ShowModal property is vbModal (or the numeral 1), which you don't need to specify when calling a UserForm if you want it to be Modal. The code line UserForm1.Show vbModal, or UserForm1.Show 1, or (which you have typically been using all along) UserForm1.Show will show the UserForm as Modal.

> Here's a neat trick that might interest you. When you call a UserForm as Modeless, the UserForm will be the active object and an extra mouse click is required to actually activate the worksheet. If you want the worksheet itself to be the active object without manual intervention, add the line AppActivate ("Microsoft Excel") *below the* Show *line; here is a full macro example:*

```
Sub ShowUserForm2()
UserForm2.Show vbModeless
AppActivate ("Microsoft Excel")
End Sub
```

DISABLING THE USERFORM'S CLOSE BUTTON

Some of your UserForms might require input before the user can proceed further. To enforce user input, you can disable the Close button, usually located at the far right of the UserForm's title bar. This is not an everyday happenstance but when your project requires input at a critical point in a process, you will need a way to keep the UserForm active until the required information is input.

UserForms have a `QueryClose` event that can help you control such situations. In Figure 20-2, a Message Box appears if the "X" Close button was clicked in an attempt to close the UserForm without selecting a name from the drop-down list. The code associated with that follows Figure 20-2.

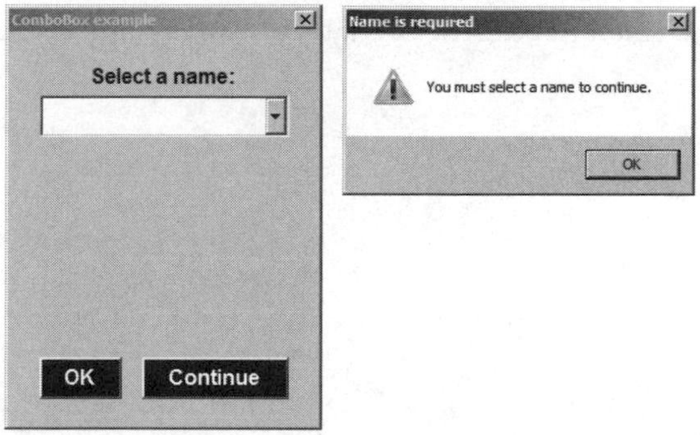

FIGURE 20-2

```
Private Sub UserForm_QueryClose _
(Cancel As Integer, CloseMode As Integer)
'Prevents use of the Close button
'if a name has not been selected.
If CloseMode = vbFormControlMenu Then
If Len(ComboBox1.Value) = 0 Then
Cancel = True
MsgBox _
"You must select a name to continue.", _
vbExclamation, _
"Name is required"
'Set Focus to the ComboBox for the user.
ComboBox1.SetFocus
End If
End If
End Sub
```

Keep in mind that you'll want to monitor the input requirement through the other controls on the UserForm as well. The following example is associated with the Continue button:

```
Private Sub cmdContinue_Click()
If Len(ComboBox1.Value) = 0 Then
MsgBox _
"You must select a name to continue.", _
vbExclamation, _
"Name is required"
'Set Focus to the ComboBox for the user.
ComboBox1.SetFocus
Exit Sub
Else
Unload Me
End If
End Sub
```

MAXIMIZING YOUR USERFORM'S SIZE

If you want to fill the screen with just your UserForm and nothing else, the following code in the `Initialize` event can help you do that. Be aware that some adjustment to the code might be needed with the `Zoom` property, in case the UserForm is so small to begin with that its fully expanded size exceeds the window's Zoom capacity.

```
Private Sub UserForm_Initialize()
With Application
.WindowState = xlMaximized
Zoom = Int(.Width / Me.Width * 100)
Width = .Width
Height = .Height
End With
End Sub
```

> *You don't need to settle for the UserForm loading in the center of your screen. You can specify the location, such as with the following example that shows the UserForm in the top-left corner of the screen:*
>
> ```
> Private Sub UserForm_Initialize()
> Me.StartUpPosition = 0
> Me.Top = Application.Top
> Me.Left = Application.Left
> End Sub
> ```

SELECTING AND DISPLAYING PHOTOGRAPHS ON A USERFORM

An Image control helps you display a graphic object, such as a picture, on a UserForm. You have three ways to place a picture onto an Image file — two are manual methods and one is a VBA method.

Suppose you have a picture file on your computer, such as your company's logo, that you want to show for a customized look on your UserForm. You can use VBA's `LoadPicture` method to load the picture file onto the Image control when you call the UserForm, with the following example:

```
Private Sub UserForm_Initialize()
Image1.Picture = LoadPicture("C:\CompanyPictures\CompanyLogo.jpg")
End Sub
```

This method works great, so long as the picture file exists in that folder path for every computer on which the UserForm will ever be opened, which is not likely. As you develop UserForms for others' use outside a shared network environment, you'll want to manually load a picture onto an Image control, and forego the VBA route.

You can manually load an Image control in two ways. In the UserForm's design window, place the Image control where you want it on the UserForm. Activate the Image control's Properties window and locate the `Picture` property. Placing your cursor inside the `Picture` property will expose a small ellipsis button, as shown in Figure 20-3. Click that button to show the Load Picture dialog box. From the LoadPicture dialog box, navigate to the picture file you want to load, select it, and click the Open button.

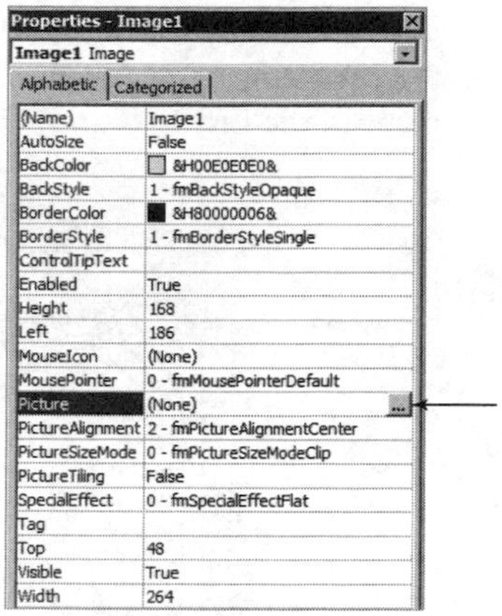

The other manual alternative is even simpler. After you've added your Image control, select your `Picture` object and press Ctrl+C to place it onto the clipboard. Select the Image control on the UserForm, select its `Picture` property in the Properties window, click inside the `Picture` property, and press Ctrl+V to paste the picture into the Image control.

FIGURE 20-3

UNLOADING A USERFORM AUTOMATICALLY

Have you ever wanted to show a UserForm for a limited period of time, and then unload it without user intervention? UserForms need not serve the sole purpose of user input. Sometimes they can be opportunistically employed as a mechanism for a specialized greeting, or, if tastefully designed, an informative splash screen.

Personally, I do not appreciate most of the splash screens I see when opening various software applications; many look like cheap advertisements that waste the user's time. However, a nice opening welcome message to customize the look and feel of your workbook can be a good thing if designed well, but do keep the visible time to a maximum of five seconds — any longer than that is an annoyance.

Call the UserForm as you normally would. The following code goes into the UserForm module, in this example for a five-second appearance:

```
Private Sub UserForm_Activate()
Application.Wait (Now + TimeValue("0:00:05"))
Unload Me
End Sub
```

PRE-SORTING THE LISTBOX AND COMBOBOX ITEMS

Suppose you want to import a list of items into your ListBox (or ComboBox) such as a list of cities in range A1:A20 as shown in Figure 20-4. You can do that easily with this event code for a ListBox:

```
Private Sub UserForm_Initialize()
ListBox1.List = Range("A1:A20").Value
End Sub
```

Lists tend to be easier to work with when they are alphabetized. To handle that seamlessly for the user, the following amendment to the preceding code is a series of loops with variables that examine each element in the ListBox, and sorts it in ascending alphabetical order. The result is shown in Figure 20-4.

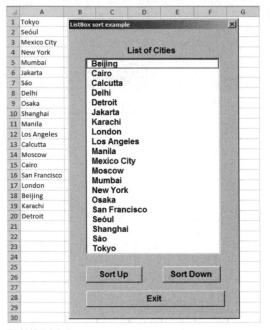

FIGURE 20-4

```
Private Sub UserForm_Initialize()
ListBox1.List = Range("A1:A20").Value
Dim x As Integer, y As Integer, z As String
With ListBox1
For x = 0 To .ListCount - 2
For y = x + 1 To .ListCount - 1
If .List(x) > .List(y) Then
z = .List(y)
.List(y) = .List(x)
.List(x) = z
End If
Next y
Next x
End With
End Sub
```

Notice two additional CommandButtons near the bottom of the UserForm. One is captioned Sort Up and the other is captioned Sort Down. Users appreciate the ability to customize the look of their interface. If it is easier for some people to read a list from Z to A, and others from A to Z, so be it. The following code shows an example of how each button, when clicked, will sort the ListBox. First, ascending:

```
Private Sub cmdSortUp_Click()
Dim x As Integer, y As Integer, z As String
'Sort ascending
With ListBox1
For x = 0 To .ListCount - 2
For y = x + 1 To .ListCount - 1
If .List(x) > .List(y) Then
z = .List(y)
.List(y) = .List(x)
.List(x) = z
End If
Next y
Next x
End With
End Sub
```

Then, descending:

```
Private Sub cmdSortDown_Click()
Dim x As Integer, y As Integer, z As String
'Sort descending
With ListBox1
For x = 0 To .ListCount - 2
For y = x + 1 To .ListCount - 1
If .List(x) < .List(y) Then
z = .List(y)
.List(y) = .List(x)
.List(x) = z
End If
Next y
Next x
End With
End Sub
```

If you were to do this in real practice, you'd eliminate the redundancy of declaring the same variables for each event, and instead publicly declare them once.

POPULATING LISTBOXES AND COMBOBOXES WITH UNIQUE ITEMS

As often as not, when you load a ListBox or ComboBox with a source list of items from a worksheet, the range will be dynamic, meaning the length of the list will vary. Also, chances are pretty good that the source list will contain duplicate entries, and there is no need to place more than one unique item in a ListBox or ComboBox.

In Figure 20-5, column A contains a list of clothing items that were sold in a department store. A unique list of these items was compiled in a ComboBox as shown in Figure 20-5, with the following code to demonstrate how to populate the ComboBox in this manner when the length of the source list is not known, and some cells in the source list might have no entry.

	A	B	C	D	E	F
1	Items Sold	How many sold	Unique List in ComboBox example			
2	Jackets	32				
3	Socks	37	Unique List of Items Sold			
4	Skirts	53				
5	Jackets	17				
6	Shoes	31	Jackets			
7	Socks	23	Socks			
8	Hats	72	Skirts			
9	Shoes	49	Shoes			
10	Jackets	22	Hats			
11	Pants	67	Pants			
12	Socks	73	Dresses			
13	Hats	40				
14	Pants	89				
15	Hats	96				
16	Skirts	98	Exit			
17	Dresses	30				
18	Pants	55				
19	Dresses	10				
20	Skirts	99				
21	Socks	65				
22	Dresses	63				
23	Socks	33				
24	Jackets	62				
25	Shoes	71				

FIGURE 20-5

```
Private Sub UserForm_Initialize()
'Declare variables for a Collection and cell range.
Dim myCollection As Collection, cell As Range

'Error bypass to set a new collection.
On Error Resume Next
Set myCollection = New Collection

'Open a With structure for the ComboBox
With ComboBox1
'Clear the ComboBox
.Clear

'Open a For Next loop to examine every cell starting with A2
'and down to the last used cell in column A.
For Each cell In Range("A2:A" & Cells(Rows.Count, 1).End(xlUp).Row)

'If the cell is not blank...
If Len(cell) <> 0 Then
'Clear the possible error for a Collection
'possibly not having been established yet.
Err.Clear
'Add the cell's value to the Collection.
myCollection.Add cell.Value, cell.Value
'If there is no error, that is, if the value does not
```

```
'already exist in the Collection, add the item to the ComboBox.
If Err.Number = 0 Then .AddItem cell.Value
End If

'Loop to the next cell.
Next cell

'Close the With structure for the ComboBox.
End With
End Sub
```

> *If you want the first item in the ComboBox's list to be visible when the UserForm is called, add this line before the* End Sub *line:*
>
> ```
> ComboBox1.ListIndex = 0
> ```

To expand a bit on the possible usefulness of listing unique items in a ComboBox, see the example in Figure 20-6, where two Label controls were added (named Label2 and Label3) to the right of the ComboBox. When the ComboBox value is changed with the following code, Label2's caption reflects the value item, and Label3's caption sums the items sold in column B for the item that was selected in the ComboBox.

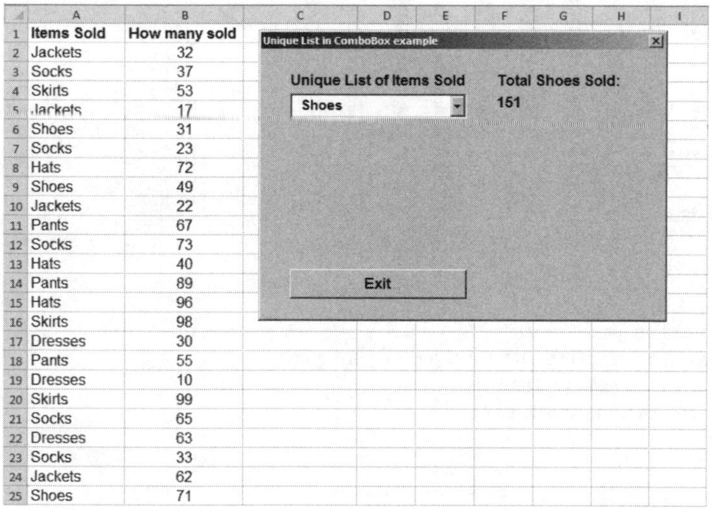

FIGURE 20-6

```
Private Sub ComboBox1_Change()
Label2.Caption = _
"Total " & ComboBox1.Value & " Sold:"
Label3.Caption = _
WorksheetFunction.SumIf(Columns(1), ComboBox1.Value, Columns(2))
End Sub
```

DISPLAY A REAL-TIME CHART IN A USERFORM

Earlier in this lesson you saw how to load a picture into an Image control. You can also create a temporary graphic file on the fly, load that file into a UserForm's Image control, and delete the temporary graphic file, all with the user being none the wiser.

Figure 20-7 shows a list of cities, ranked by their approximate population. Elsewhere in the workbook is a Chart sheet named Chart1 with a bar chart of this city population data. You can represent the Chart1 sheet's chart in real time by exporting its image as a .gif file and loading it onto an Image control when the UserForm is called. Figure 20-7 shows the result and following that is the Initialize event code that handles this task.

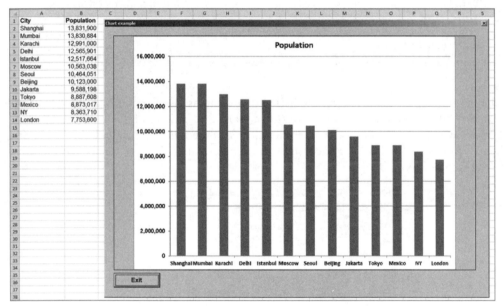

FIGURE 20-7

```
Private Sub UserForm_Initialize()
ActiveWorkbook.Charts("Chart1").Export "CityPopulation.gif"
Image1.Picture = LoadPicture("CityPopulation.gif")
Image1.PictureSizeMode = fmPictureSizeModeZoom
Kill "CityPopulation.gif"
End Sub
```

> *You can print a UserForm, even if it is not open, with the following line:*
>
> ```
> UserForm1.PrintForm
> ```

TRY IT

In this lesson you build a UserForm to browse the Internet.

Lesson Requirements

For this lesson, you design a UserForm to have the basic functionality of a web browser, including the ability to navigate to the websites of your choice, go backward and forward to websites, and set the initial website when the UserForm is initialized. To get the sample database files you can download Lesson 20 from the book's website at www.wrox.com.

Step-by-Step

1. Open a new workbook and press Alt+F11 to get into the Visual Basic Editor.

2. If the Project Explorer window is not visible, press Ctrl+R, and if the Properties window is not visible, press the F4 key.

3. In the Project Explorer window, select your workbook name, and from the menu bar click Insert ⇨ UserForm.

4. In the Properties window for that UserForm, accept the default Name property of UserForm1, set the Height property to **540** and the Width property to **852**.

5. Click the Toolbox icon, or from the menu bar click View ⇨ Toolbox.

6. Draw a TextBox near the upper-left corner of the UserForm. Accept the default Name property of TextBox1, set its Height property to **24**, and its Width property to **252**.

7. Draw four CommandButtons along the top of the UserForm to the right of the TextBox. Each CommandButton should be the same size, with its Height property set at **24** and its Width property set at **120**.

8. Name the first CommandButton **cmdNavigate** and label its Caption property as **Navigate**. Set its Default property to True.

9. Name the second CommandButton **cmdBack** and label its Caption property as **Back**.

10. Name the third CommandButton **cmdForward** and label its Caption property as **Forward**.

11. Name the fourth CommandButton **cmdExit** and label its Caption property as **Exit**.

12. The final control you'll place onto your UserForm is a WebBrowser, and chances are its icon is not on your Toolbox's Cover tab. If that's the case, right-click the Cover tab and select Additional Controls as shown in Figure 20-8.

FIGURE 20-8

13. Scroll down the list of available controls and select Microsoft Web Browser as shown in Figure 20-9. Click OK and that will place the WebBrowser icon on your Toolbox's Cover tab as shown in the lower-left corner of Figure 20-10.

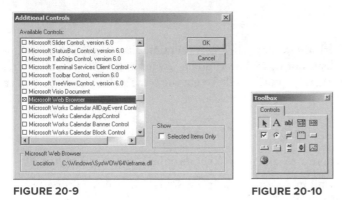

FIGURE 20-9   **FIGURE 20-10**

14. Click to select the WebBrowser icon on the Toolbox just as you would with any control, and draw a WebBrowser control onto the open area of the UserForm. Accept the default Name property of WebBrowser1, and then set its Height property to **450** and its Width property to **816**. This completes the design of the UserForm, which in the VBE will look like Figure 20-11.

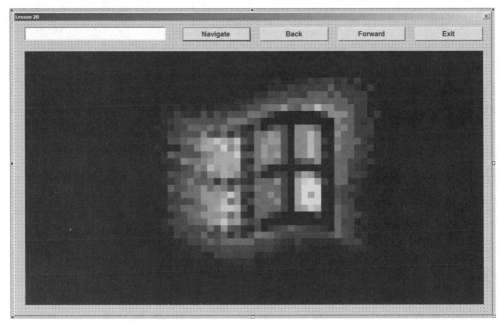

FIGURE 20-11

15. The code associated with this UserForm is surprisingly simple. Double-click the UserForm to access its module. In the Object drop-down list, select UserForm and in the Procedure drop-down list select Initialize. The `Initialize` event is a single line of code that tells the WebBrowser which website to navigate to when the UserForm initializes, similar to the homepage setting on your web browser. In this example, I entered the website for wrox.com. Here is the entire `Initialize` event with that navigation command:

```
Private Sub UserForm_Initialize()
WebBrowser1.Navigate "http://www.wrox.com"
End Sub
```

16. You have an Exit button named `cmdExit`, so use the `Unload Me` command for that:

```
Private Sub cmdExit_Click()
Unload Me
End Sub
```

17. Regarding the CommandButton for navigation, the process will start by the user entering a website address in the TextBox. The user can then either click the cmdNavigate button, or press the Enter key because you set the Default property to True for the cmdNavigate button in Step 8. Thinking ahead for more convenience, you can structure the cmdNavigate's `Click` event to assume that all web addresses start with "http://www.", which will save the user time and effort by just entering the web address's domain name. For example, instead of entering http://www.somewhere.com in the TextBox, a user need only enter somewhere.com with this code for the cmdNavigate button:

```
Private Sub cmdNavigate_Click()
WebBrowser1.Navigate "http://www." & TextBox1.Text
End Sub
```

18. All that's left are the two buttons for Back and Forward, easily handled with the WebBrowser control's `GoBack` and `GoForward` methods. For both methods, `On Error Resume Next` is utilized to avoid a run time error if the browsing session is at its starting or ending point when the cmdBack or cmdForward button is clicked. Here is the code for `GoBack`:

```
Private Sub cmdBack_Click()
On Error Resume Next
WebBrowser1.GoBack
Err.Clear
End Sub
```

Here is `GoForward`:

```
Private Sub cmdForward_Click()
On Error Resume Next
WebBrowser1.GoForward
Err.Clear
End Sub
```

19. When you call the UserForm, Figure 20-12 shows an example that is similar to what you will see.

FIGURE 20-12

Please select Lesson 20 on the DVD to view the video that accompanies this lesson.

21

Class Modules

Class modules — the very name has caused many an Excel VBA programmer to turn away from the topic as if it doesn't or shouldn't exist. For some reason, the use of class modules is not a skill held by many otherwise knowledgeable VBA programmers, despite the power and flexibility class modules can provide to your workbook projects.

Class modules are not rocket science, but they are a different kind of VBA animal that takes some extra attention to grasp. I want to express three objectives in this lesson:

> ➤ Explain what classes and class modules are.

> ➤ Describe what class modules can do for you.

> ➤ Provide examples of class modules applied to UserForm and embedded worksheet controls.

Here is an opportunity for you to set yourself apart from the VBA crowd and learn a valuable skill that has actually been available in Excel since Office 97. Though you won't need class modules for most of your projects, you'll learn how to recognize when the time is right to use class modules, and most importantly, how to program them.

WHAT IS A CLASS?

A *class* is the formalized definition of an object that you create. Your first reaction might be to wonder why you'd ever need to create yet another object in Excel, which seemingly has no shortage of objects. Actually, you normally don't *need* to, but there will be times when your workbook will be better off if you do.

> It's easy to get lost on any new topic if the emphasis on learning it is based on definitions and theory. That is why most of this lesson relies on real-world examples to show what class modules are all about. Though kept to a minimum, the definitions and theory in this lesson are useful for you to gain a perspective on class modules. If you don't fully comprehend all definitions the first time around, don't worry — the VBA examples will be your biggest ally in helping you understand the process of developing class modules.

A new class (as in classification) is like a blueprint for your created object and its properties, methods, and events. In Lesson 16 you learned about User Defined Functions; where class modules are concerned, you can think of a class as a user-defined model for an object that you create. You'll see examples later in the lesson that will help clarify the theory.

WHAT IS A CLASS MODULE?

A class module is a special module in the Visual Basic Editor whose purpose is to hold VBA code that defines classes. A class module looks like any other kind of module you have seen, and in its own way acts like one, too. For example, whereas the code for worksheet event procedures goes into worksheet modules, the code for creating and defining classes goes into class modules.

You create a class module in the VBE by clicking Insert ➪ Class Module from the menu bar as shown in Figure 21-1. A class module is created with the default name of Class1 as shown in Figure 21-2.

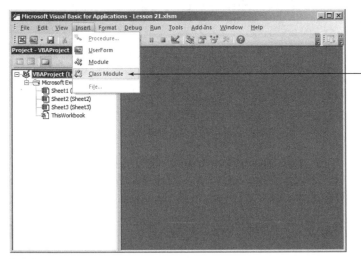

FIGURE 21-1

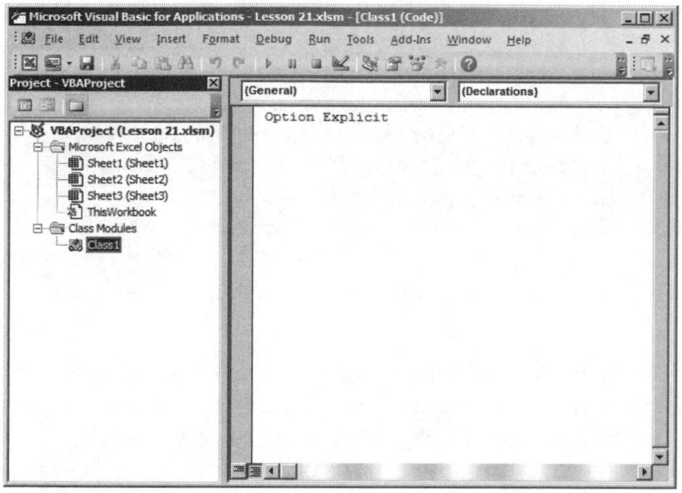

FIGURE 21-2

> There is a one-to-one relationship between a class and a class module. A class module provides for only one class to be defined. If you need to define three classes in your workbook, you'll need three class modules, one for each class. For example, suppose you have several CheckBox controls on your UserForm, and you want to color the CheckBoxes green when they are checked, and red when they are unchecked. Instead of coding this functionality for every CheckBox's Click event, you can use a class module that groups all the CheckBoxes as a single collection object. That way, all CheckBoxes respond to the same Click event, with one VBA class procedure. If you also want some (or all) of the CommandButtons on a UserForm in that same workbook to respond to, say, a MouseMove event, you'd create another class module for that.

CREATING YOUR OWN OBJECTS

I started this lesson saying that many VBA programmers have avoided the topic of class modules, and it wouldn't surprise me if a primary culprit is VBA's intentionally vague concept of class objects. Seeing actual VBA examples of class modules in everyday situations is the best way to pick up the concept of class objects.

> *Here's the theoretical synopsis: A class is defined in a class module, and you can think of a class as a blueprint or template for an object. In the context of class modules, the term* object *can be almost any object in Excel whose functionality you want to expand. This concept becomes clearer with VBA examples you'll see in this lesson dealing with controls that are embedded in a worksheet, or are placed onto UserForms. You can have those controls all respond to one single event, instead of needing to write numerous redundant procedures for each control.*

As you'll see, a class module only serves the purpose of holding the code that defines (but does not create) a class object. In some other module that is not a class module, such as a UserForm module or workbook module (depending on the task you are solving), you can declare a variable of the class type and create an instance of that class (known as *instantiating* the class) with the New keyword. Upon instantiation, your declared variable becomes an object whose events, properties, and methods are defined by your code in the class module.

AN IMPORTANT BENEFIT OF CLASS MODULES

Suppose you have a UserForm with 12 TextBoxes, into which a dollar figure for budgeted expenses is to be entered for each month of the year, as in the example shown in Figure 21-3.

It's important that only numbers are entered, so you want to validate every TextBox entry to be numeric, while disallowing entry of an alphabetic letter, symbol, or any character other than a number. The following example can handle that for TextBox1 in the UserForm module:

```
Private Sub TextBox1_KeyPress _
(ByVal KeyAscii As MSForms.ReturnInteger)
Select Case KeyAscii
Case 48 To 57 'numbers 0-9
Case Else
KeyAscii = 0
MsgBox "You entered a non-numeric character.", _
vbCritical, _
"Numbers only please!"
End Select
End Sub
```

FIGURE 21-3

You can maybe get away with the redundancy of writing 12 separate events to monitor the entries in each TextBox. But what happens if your project requires 100 TextBoxes, or if the numeric validation process expands to allow decimals or negative numbers? You'd have to do a lot of updates for each TextBox, and the volume of redundant code will create a bad design that's destined for human error and runtime failure.

If you insert a class module instead, you can define an object that would be a group of 12 TextBoxes. You can name your group object TxtGroup and declare it as a TextBox type variable. There is nothing special about the variable name TxtGroup. I chose it because the idea is to group TextBoxes, but whatever object variable name makes sense to you will work just as well.

The following VBA declaration statement is a common example that gets placed at the top of your class module. It defines the class object, and includes the WithEvents keyword, which exposes the events associated with TextBoxes:

```
Public WithEvents TxtGroup As MSForms.TextBox
```

Now that you have defined the TxtGroup variable as a TextBox type object, you can invoke it to handle the same KeyPress event that you might have written individually for all 12 TextBoxes. As shown in the following code, you now use the TxtGroup object to have VBA recognize the KeyPress event triggered by keyboard data entry upon any one of the 12 TextBoxes in your TxtGroup object. The code to handle an event for all 12 TextBoxes is the same for TxtGroup as it is for TextBox1, except for the name of the object.

```
Private Sub TxtGroup_KeyPress _
(ByVal KeyAscii As MSForms.ReturnInteger)
Select Case KeyAscii
Case 48 To 57 'numbers 0-9
Case Else
KeyAscii = 0
MsgBox "You entered a non-numeric character.", _
vbCritical, _
"Numbers only please!"
End Select
End Sub
```

Keep in mind that, so far, all you have done is define the object, but it still exists only as a concept. The next step is to create your defined object (formally known as *instantiating* it) to make it a working object that responds to events, and becomes associated with methods and properties. At this moment, with the UserForm created and the class module selected with the preceding code in it, your work in the class module is complete. Your VBE window will look similar to Figure 21-4.

The final step is to go into the UserForm module and instantiate the TxtGroup object that will be a group of 12 TextBoxes. At the top of the UserForm module, declare a variable for 12 TextBoxes to instantiate the TxtGroup class object, with the New keyword for the Class1 module name:

```
Dim txtBoxes(1 To 12) As New Class1
```

Using the Initialize event, declare an Integer type variable that will assist in looping through the 12 TextBoxes. Set each TextBox as a member of the TxtGroup class.

```
Private Sub UserForm_Initialize()
Dim intCounterTextBox As Integer
For intCounterTextBox = 1 To 12
Set txtBoxes(intCounterTextBox).TxtGroup = _
Controls("TextBox" & intCounterTextBox)
Next intCounterTextBox
End Sub
```

Your entire coding process relating to the class module is complete, and it is quite a bit shorter than all the code you'd have amassed if you coded the KeyPress event for every TextBox! If you were to open the UserForm and attempt a non-numeric character in any of the 12 TextBoxes, that character would be disallowed and the Message Box would appear, looking like Figure 21-5.

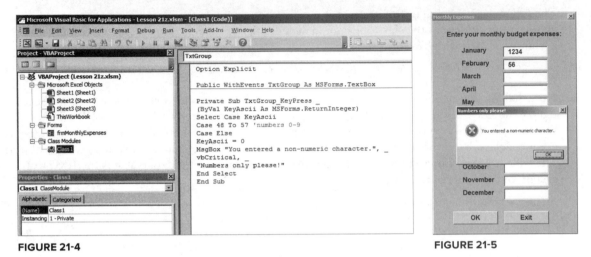

FIGURE 21-4   **FIGURE 21-5**

CREATING COLLECTIONS

In the preceding example, you created a class for 12 TextBoxes. You knew ahead of time the number of TextBoxes was 12 because there was a TextBox for each of the 12 calendar months. The question becomes, what do you do if the count of inclusive TextBoxes is not known? What if your project is so wide in scope that TextBoxes are being frequently added and subtracted from the UserForm, and you don't want to keep modifying the code with every change in TextBox count?

The answer is, you create a *collection* of TextBoxes by looping through all the controls in the UserForm. Then, when a TextBox is encountered in the loop, it is automatically added to the collection, which is then transferred to the class object. Assuming the event code you placed in the class module has not changed, all that needs to be adjusted is the code in the UserForm module using the previous example. The first item of business is to prepare a declaration statement at the top of the module that does not specify a count of TextBox names, such as the following example:

```
Dim TxtGroup() As New Class1
```

Next, the following code in the UserForm's Initialize event will wrap up all the TextBoxes into one array package using the ReDim Preserve keywords. This method does not depend on how many TextBoxes are embedded on Sheet1; it simply collects all the ones into the TxtGroup object that it finds.

```
Private Sub UserForm_Initialize()
Dim intCounterTextBox As Integer, ctl As Control
intCounterTextBox = 0
For Each ctl In Controls
If TypeName(ctl) = "TextBox" Then
intCounterTextBox = intCounterTextBox + 1
```

```
ReDim Preserve TxtGroup(1 To intCounterTextBox)
Set TxtGroup(intCounterTextBox).TxtGroup = ctl
End If
Next ctl
End Sub
```

CLASS MODULES FOR EMBEDDED OBJECTS

So far, UserForms have been the backdrop for objects in a class module. You can also create a class of objects embedded on worksheets, such as charts, pivot tables, and ActiveX controls. In the case of ActiveX controls, it's worth mentioning a syntax difference when referring to them.

Suppose you have an unknown number of CommandButtons on Sheet1 and you want to create a class module to determine which button was clicked, without having to program every CommandButton's `Click` event. This example of code in a class module named Class1 demonstrates how to extract the name, caption, and address of the cell being touched by the top-left corner of the CommandButton object. Figure 21-6 shows the Message Box that appears when you click one of the CommandButtons.

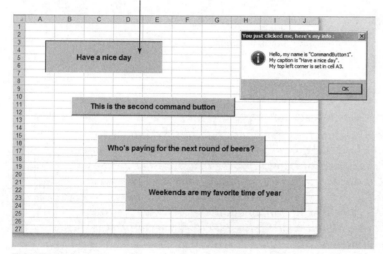

FIGURE 21-6

```
Public WithEvents cmdButtonGroup As CommandButton

Private Sub cmdButtonGroup_Click()
MsgBox _
"Hello, my name is ''" & _
cmdButtonGroup.Name & "''." & vbCrLf & _
"My caption is ''" & _
cmdButtonGroup.Caption & "''." & vbCrLf & _
"My top left corner is set in cell " & _
cmdButtonGroup.TopLeftCell.Address(0, 0) & ".", _
64, "You just clicked me, here's my info :"
End Sub
```

You can also tap into other events in the same class module. All that's required is that you use the same class object (cmdButtonGroup in this example), and that the event is supported by the object. With CommandButtons, the MouseOver event can help you identify which button you are hovering your mouse over by shading it orange, while all other CommandButtons on the sheet are colored gray.

> *I used hex codes in this example for the buttons'* BackColor *property, to show how you'd use hex in code to refer to colors. These hex values are always shown in the Properties window of ActiveX controls for* BackColor *and* ForeColor *properties, and I personally find them very reliable in VBA code with any version of Excel.*

```
Private Sub cmdButtonGroup_MouseMove _
(ByVal Button As Integer, _
ByVal Shift As Integer, _
ByVal X As Single, _
ByVal Y As Single)
Dim myBtn As Object
For Each myBtn In ActiveSheet.OLEObjects
If TypeName(myBtn.Object) = "CommandButton" Then _
myBtn.Object.BackColor = &HC0C0C0 'turn all to gray
Next
cmdButtonGroup.BackColor = &H80FF& 'orange
End Sub
```

> *As you can probably tell, despite the appearance of differently shaped CommandButtons with comical captions, the larger point of this example is that you can capture various properties of class objects, assign them to a variable, and utilize that variable information in other macros, or even as part of the class module's event code. For example, in real practice, you don't need or want a Message Box to pop up and tell you which button you just clicked; you already know that. If, for example, your project is such that the CommandButtons' captions have a word or phrase to be used as a criterion for automatically filtering a table of data, this application of flexible class module coding will save you a lot of work.*

For embedded ActiveX controls, you can instantiate the collection of OLE objects, in this example for CommandButtons, with the following code that goes into the ThisWorkbook module. Be sure to place this example declaration statement at the top of the ThisWorkbook module:

```
Dim cmdButtonHandler() As New Class1
```

Finally, utilize the Open event to collect the CommandButtons that are only on Sheet1. Notice the references to the OLEObject and OLEObjects keywords when dealing with embedded ActiveX controls.

```
Private Sub Workbook_Open()
Dim cmdButtonQuantity As Integer, MYcmdButton As OLEObject
cmdButtonQuantity = 0
With ThisWorkbook
For Each MYcmdButton In .Worksheets("Sheet1").OLEObjects
If TypeName(MYcmdButton.Object) = "CommandButton" Then
cmdButtonQuantity = cmdButtonQuantity + 1
ReDim Preserve cmdButtonHandler(1 To cmdButtonQuantity)
Set cmdButtonHandler(cmdButtonQuantity).cmdButtonGroup _
= MYcmdButton.Object
End If
Next MYcmdButton
End With
End Sub
```

Not all controls recognize the same event types though, so you'd need to set a class event that the object type can recognize.

There is another technique using the Collection keyword for grouping the same types of objects into a class. In this example, Sheet1 has a number of embedded CheckBox controls, and you want to write one small piece of VBA code that will apply to all CheckBoxes.

The visual effect you want is for any CheckBox on Sheet1 to be shaded black if it is checked, and white if it is unchecked. Figure 21-7 shows the differences in color shading depending on the status of the CheckBoxes.

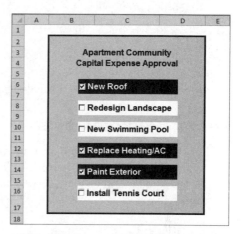

FIGURE 21-7

The code to do this is surprisingly minimal. Insert a new class module, and assuming it is named Class2 because you already have a Class1 module established, this code will go into the Class2 module:

```
Public WithEvents grpCBX As MSForms.CheckBox

Private Sub grpCBX_Click()
With grpCBX
If .Value = True Then

.BackColor = &H0&      'Black background
.ForeColor = &HFFFFFF  'While font
Else

.BackColor = &HFFFFFF  'White background
.ForeColor = &H0&      'Black font
End If
End With
End Sub
```

The rest of the code goes into the ThisWorkbook module. It instantiates the `grpCBX` object and is refreshed each time the workbook opens by utilizing the `Workbook_Open` event.

```
Public myControls As Collection


Private Sub Workbook_Open()
Dim oleCtl As OLEObject, ctl As Class2
Set myControls = New Collection
For Each oleCtl In Worksheets("Sheet1").OLEObjects
If TypeOf oleCtl.Object Is MSForms.CheckBox Then
Set ctl = New Class1
Set ctl.grpCBX = oleCtl.Object
myControls.Add ctl
End If
Next
End Sub
```

TRY IT

In this lesson you create a class module to handle the `Click` event of some of the OptionButtons on a UserForm, purposely not involving all OptionButtons in the class.

Lesson Requirements

For this lesson, you design a simple UserForm with eight OptionButtons, of which only five will be a part of a class module that identifies which OptionButton by name and caption was clicked. To get the sample database files, you can download Lesson 21 from the book's website at http://www.wrox.com/.

Step-by-Step

1. Open a new workbook.

2. Press Alt+F11 to get into the Visual Basic Editor.

3. From the menu bar, click Insert ➪ UserForm, and size the UserForm to a Height of **200** and a Width of **400**.

4. Draw a Label control near the top-left corner of your UserForm, and caption it as **OptionButtons In Class Module**.

5. Draw a Label control near the top-right corner of your UserForm and caption it as **Other OptionButtons**. Figure 21-8 shows how your UserForm should look so far.

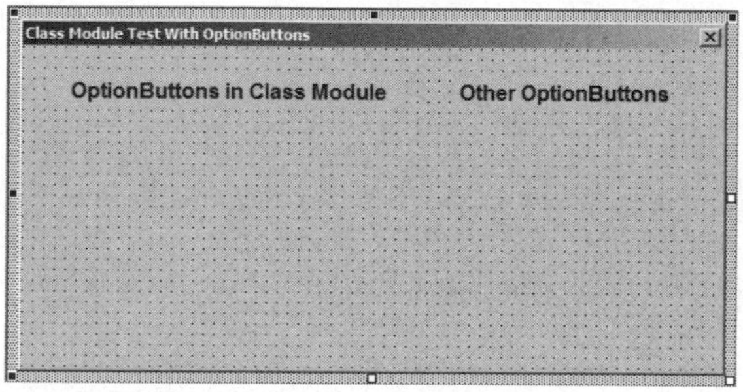

FIGURE 21-8

6. Under the first Label control, draw a vertical column of five OptionButtons. A fast way to do this is to draw one OptionButton, and then copy and paste it four times. Change the captions of those five OptionButtons to **Apples**, **Bananas**, **Peaches**, **Grapes**, and **Oranges**, as shown in Figure 21-9.

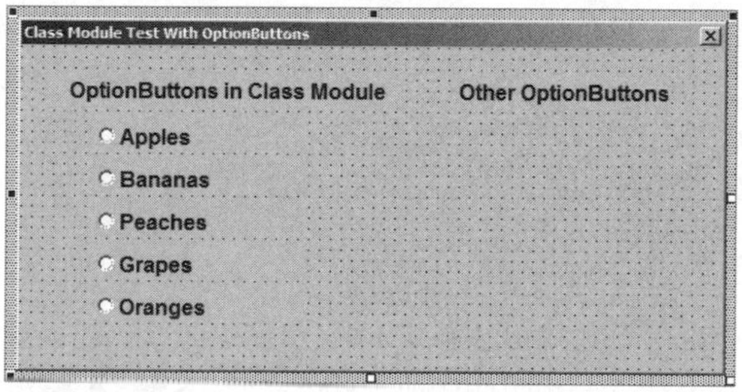

FIGURE 21-9

7. Paste three more OptionButtons below the second Label control. Change the captions of those three OptionButtons to Plums, Pears, and Tangerines. You now have eight OptionButtons on your UserForm, all with different captions that are the names of fruits. The actual VBA names of the eight OptionButtons have not changed — they all are still named by default as OptionButton1, OptionButton2, and so on, to OptionButton8. For example, if you were to select the OptionButton that is captioned Oranges, you would see in its Properties window that it is named OptionButton5. Figure 21-10 shows how your UserForm looks at this point.

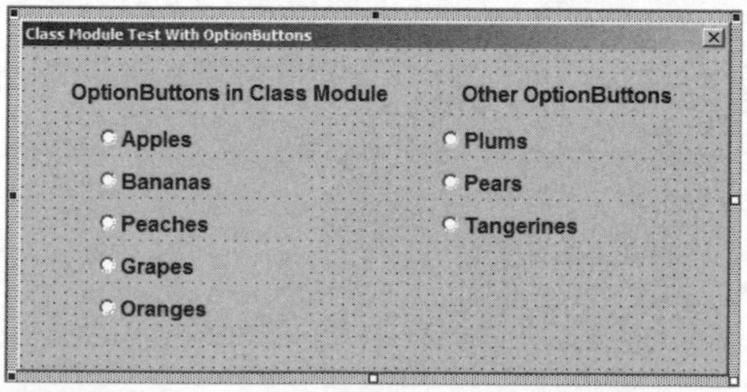

FIGURE 21-10

8. Draw a CommandButton in the lower-right corner of the UserForm. Name it **cmdExit** and caption it as **Exit**.

9. Double-click the `cmdExit` button, which will take you into the UserForm's module, with the `cmdExit` button's `Click` event ready for your code. Type **Unload Me**, and your UserForm module in the VBE will look like Figure 21-11.

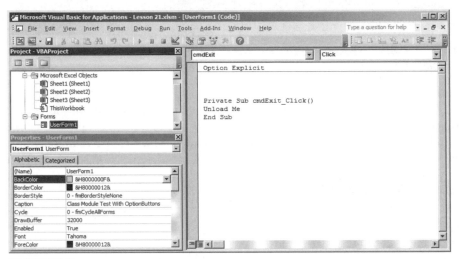

FIGURE 21-11

10. Insert a class module. From the menu bar, click Insert ⇨ Class Module and accept the default name of Class1. Your cursor will be blinking in the Class1 module's Code window.

11. The purpose of this particular class module is to capture an event that is associated with OptionButton controls. At the top of the Class1 module, publicly declare a variable that refers to the group of OptionButtons you will involve in the class module code. In that same statement, expose the events associated with OptionButtons using the `WithEvents` keyword. The following statement accomplishes this task:

```
Public WithEvents OptGroup As msforms.OptionButton
```

> *There is nothing special about the* `OptGroup` *variable name; you can give your class module variable whatever name makes sense to you. What makes sense to me is that I am grouping some OptionButton controls for a demonstration, so* `OptGroup` *is an intuitive name.*

12. To demonstrate the point of this lesson, you can use the `Click` event for your `OptGroup` class. A Message Box will display the name and caption of the OptionButton that was clicked if that OptionButton is included in the class. Figure 21-12 shows how the VBE will look after inputting the following class module code.

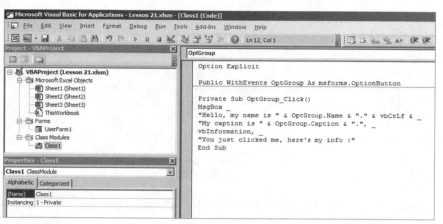

FIGURE 21-12

```
Private Sub OptGroup_Click()
MsgBox _
"Hello, my name is " & OptGroup.Name & "." & vbCrLf & _
"My caption is " & OptGroup.Caption & ".", _
vbInformation, _
"You just clicked me, here's my info :"
End Sub
```

If this were an actual workbook project, you would not need a Message Box to tell you which OptionButton was just clicked. More realistically, you might assign a String type variable to the selected OptGroup.Caption if that caption string is needed as part of an operation elsewhere in your project.

13. Return to the UserForm module. At the top of the module, identify which OptionButtons you want to be grouped into the OptGroup class. For this example, the first five OptionButtons will be grouped, so create an instance of the OptGroup class with the New keyword for the Class1 module name:

```
Dim optButtons(1 To 5) As New Class1
```

14. The UserForm's Initialize event is a good opportunity to do the actual grouping of the five OptionButtons. From the Object drop-down list select UserForm, and in the Procedure drop-down list select Initialize. VBA will enter the UserForm_Initialize and End Sub statements with an empty space between the two lines, as follows:

```
Private Sub UserForm_Initialize()

End Sub
```

15. Declare an Integer type variable that will help loop through the five OptionButtons that will become a part of the class module:

```
Dim intCounterOptionButton As Integer
```

16. Open a For Next loop to loop through the five OptionButtons:

```
For intCounterOptionButton = 1 To 5
```

17. Set each of the five OptionButtons as members of the OptGroup class:

```
Set optButtons(intCounterOptionButton).OptGroup = _
Controls("OptionButton" & intCounterOptionButton)
```

18. Continue and close the For Next loop with the Next statement:

```
Next intCounterOptionButton
```

19. All of your coding is complete. The entire UserForm module contains the following VBA code:

```
Option Explicit

Dim optButtons(1 To 5) As New Class1

Private Sub UserForm_Initialize()
Dim intCounterOptionButton As Integer
For intCounterOptionButton = 1 To 5
Set optButtons(intCounterOptionButton).OptGroup = _
Controls("OptionButton" & intCounterOptionButton)
Next intCounterOptionButton
End Sub

Private Sub cmdExit_Click()
Unload Me
End Sub
```

20. Test your class module by showing the UserForm. Press Ctrl+G to open the Immediate window, type the statement **UserForm1.Show**, and then press the Enter key.

21. Click any of the five OptionButtons on the left to display the Message Box that identifies the name and caption of the OptionButton you click. In Figure 21-13 I clicked OptionButton4, having the caption Grapes. The OptionButtons on the right side of the UserForm are not included in the class, and if clicked will not invoke a Message Box.

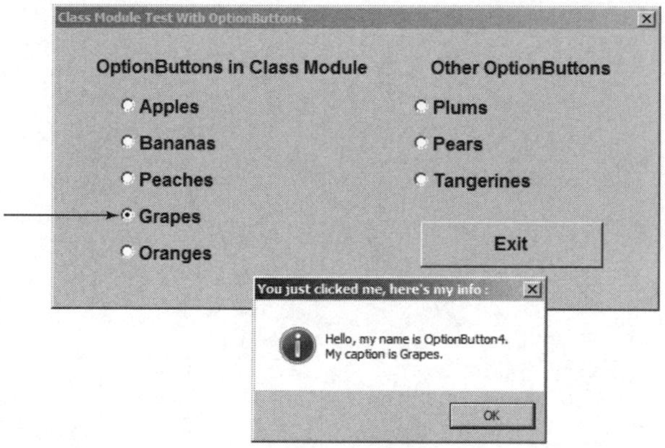

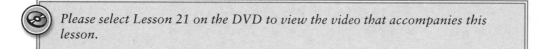

FIGURE 21-13

Please select Lesson 21 on the DVD to view the video that accompanies this lesson.

Add-Ins

Add-ins are a useful feature in Excel, considered by many Excel developers to be an indispensable tool when distributing their custom projects to a wider audience. Anyone can create an add-in — it's the kind of thing that's easy to do once you know how. This lesson discusses the concept of add-ins and how to incorporate them into your Excel projects.

> *This lesson discusses standard Excel add-ins. Two other types of add-ins exist that are not developed with VBA and are not discussed in this lesson. One of the other types is called* COM *add-ins, developed with languages such as Visual Basic, C++, and J++ that support Component Object Model components. The other type is* DLL *add-ins, which are Windows files known as Dynamic Link Library files.*

WHAT IS AN EXCEL ADD-IN?

An Excel add-in is a special type of Excel workbook that has been converted to an add-in file. There is no magic to the add-in conversion process, but after you create an add-in file, you'll notice its unique characteristics:

➤ The file extension is .xla for Excel versions prior to 2007, and .xlam for Excel versions 2007 and 2010.

➤ Add-ins are always hidden; you do not open and view them as you would an Excel workbook.

➤ You cannot show sheets of any kind belonging to the add-in file.

➤ The add-in file is not recognized as an open workbook in the Workbooks collection.

WHY CREATE AN EXCEL ADD-IN?

Add-ins commonly use VBA macros, event procedures, User Defined Functions, and UserForms to make everyday tasks faster and easier to accomplish. Many Excel users don't find the need to create an add-in, but here are some reasons why you might want to:

➤ Add-in files are hidden and therefore provide seamless integration to open Excel workbooks. Novice Excel users won't need to worry about opening an add-in once it's been loaded, and they won't wonder about an extra open Excel file because add-ins cannot be seen or unhidden.

➤ Even if the macro security is set to its most restrictive level, the VBA programming for an installed add-in can still run.

➤ Add-ins open automatically when Excel starts.

➤ The custom feature(s) contained within the add-in file are usually available to any of the open workbooks.

➤ The programming code is contained in the add-in file itself, and does not travel with the workbooks that use it. This gives you more control over how the file is distributed and who can access its code.

➤ Where add-ins really shine is in their ability to perform actions on several objects, such as cells or sheets, that if done manually would be cumbersome, time-consuming, and require some knowledge of Excel for the user to complete. Novice Excel users will especially appreciate the ease of clicking a button to do tasks that they might not know how to do manually, or might not know the most efficient methods by which to handle those tasks quickly.

CREATING AN ADD-IN

You create an Excel add-in file manually, but you make its features available by using VBA. To create an add-in, the first thing you do is open a new workbook. Because you'll be adding VBA code that will become the add-in's functionality, you'll want to test and retest your code before releasing the add-in for others to use. I mention this obvious point because if your add-in deals with manipulating worksheets in the active file, you'll need to observe the code's effect on those worksheets to make sure everything is working properly. Once you convert the workbook to an add-in, you'll no longer be able to view the worksheets, so you'll want to construct and test all your code before converting your workbook as an add-in.

PLAN AHEAD FOR BEST RESULTS

Any workbook can be converted to an add-in file, but not every workbook after it is created is a good candidate as an add-in. When I create an add-in, I know in advance what features I want the add-in to have, and what kind of code to avoid. This is important, because the add-in file is a hidden workbook that cannot contain code for activating a sheet or a range of cells.

You are allowed to write data to your add-in file, but you cannot activate the add-in file at any time. If you want to keep any data you've written to the add-in file, you'll need to save the file in the `Workbook_BeforeClose` event, because when an add-in closes, it does not prompt the user to save unsaved changes.

Suppose you want to create an add-in that offers the options to hide, unhide, protect, or unprotect multiple worksheets. A novice Excel user might perform these tasks one sheet at a time — quite an undertaking if the workbook contains dozens or hundreds of worksheets, and the tasks are a frequent chore.

In your new workbook that is destined to become an add-in, press the Alt+F11 keys to go to the Visual Basic Editor. From the VBE menu bar, click Insert ➪ UserForm. If the Properties window is not visible, press the F4 key. Follow these steps to create the add-in:

1. Select your new UserForm in its design area. In the Properties window, name the UserForm **frmSheetManager**, enter its caption as **Sheet Manager**, and set its Height property to **210** and its Width property to **276**.

2. Place the following controls on your UserForm:

➤ A Label control near the top, setting its Width property to **228**, and its Caption property to **Please select your action**.

➤ An OptionButton control below the Label control, keeping the default name `OptionButton1`, setting its BackColor property to white, its Width property to **228**, and its Caption property to **Unhide all sheets**.

➤ A second OptionButton control below `OptionButton1`, keeping the default name `OptionButton2`, setting its BackColor property to white, its Width property to **228**, and its Caption property to **Hide all sheets except active sheet**.

➤ A third OptionButton control below `OptionButton2`, keeping the default name `OptionButton3`, setting its BackColor property to white, its Width property to **228**, and its Caption property to **Protect all sheets**.

➤ A fourth OptionButton control below `OptionButton3`, keeping the default name `OptionButton3`, setting its BackColor property to white, its Width property to **228**, and its Caption property to **Unprotect all sheets**.

➤ A CommandButton near the bottom-left corner of the UserForm, setting its Name property to **cmdOK**, and its Caption property to **OK**.

➤ A CommandButton near the bottom-right corner of the UserForm, setting its Name property to **cmdExit**, and its Caption property to **Exit**.

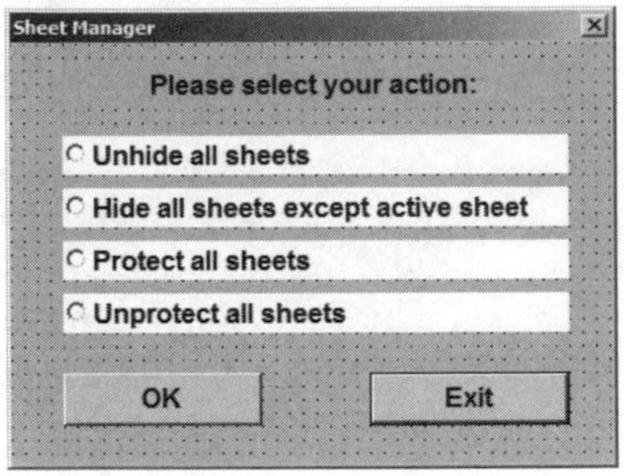

FIGURE 22-1

Your UserForm will end up looking like Figure 22-1.

The design work is complete for your UserForm. In the UserForm module, enter the following code, which is mostly triggered by the cmdOK button's Click event. The requested task will be performed depending on whichever OptionButton was selected.

```
Private Sub cmdOK_Click()

'Declare an Integer type variable to help loop
'through the worksheets.
Dim intSheet As Integer

'Open a Select Case structure to evaluate each OptionButton.
Select Case True

'If OptionButton1 was selected:
'Unhide all sheets.
Case OptionButton1.Value = True
For intSheet = 1 To Sheets.Count
Sheets(intSheet).Visible = xlSheetVisible
Next intSheet

'If OptionButton2 was selected:
'Hide all sheets except active sheet.
Case OptionButton2.Value = True
For intSheet = 1 To Sheets.Count
If Sheets(intSheet).Name <> ActiveSheet.Name Then
Sheets(intSheet).Visible = xlSheetHidden
End If
Next intSheet

'If OptionButton3 was selected:
'Protect all sheets.
Case OptionButton3.Value = True
For intSheet = 1 To Sheets.Count
Sheets(intSheet).Protect
Next intSheet

'If OptionButton4 was selected:
'Unprotect all sheets.
Case OptionButton4.Value = True
For intSheet = 1 To Sheets.Count
Sheets(intSheet).Unprotect
Next intSheet
```

```
'If no OptionButton was selected:
Case Else
MsgBox "No Action option was selected", , _
"Please select an option"

'Close the Select Case structure.
End Select

End Sub


Private Sub cmdExit_Click()
Unload Me
End Sub
```

Create a small macro to call the UserForm. From the VBE menu bar, click Insert ➪ Module and enter the following macro:

```
Private Sub SheetManager()
frmSheetmanager.Show
End Sub
```

After completing the VBA functionality that your add-in will provide to its users, it's almost time to convert the workbook to an add-in. There is an additional step you can take to add a description to the file's Properties information. It's purely optional that you do this, but it's a good habit to get into because it will help the add-in's users know what the add-in does.

The process for accessing the file's Properties information depends on your version of Excel. To access the Properties dialog box in Excel versions prior to 2007, click File ➪ Properties from the worksheet menu bar as shown in Figure 22-2. In the Properties dialog box, some fields may already be entered for you by default. As you will see later in this lesson, the most useful information to enter is the Title and Comments fields, as indicated in Figure 22-3.

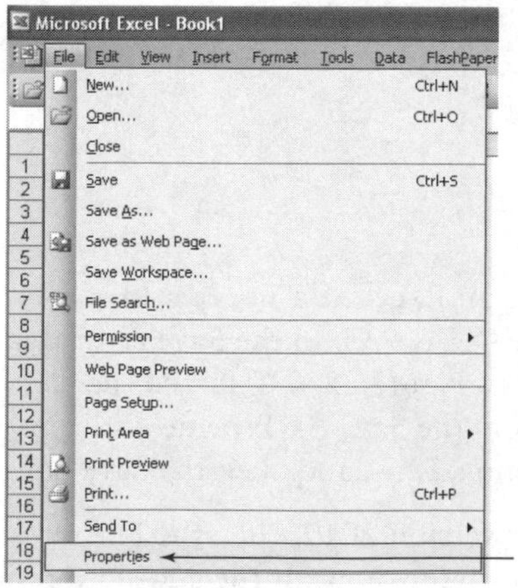

FIGURE 22-2

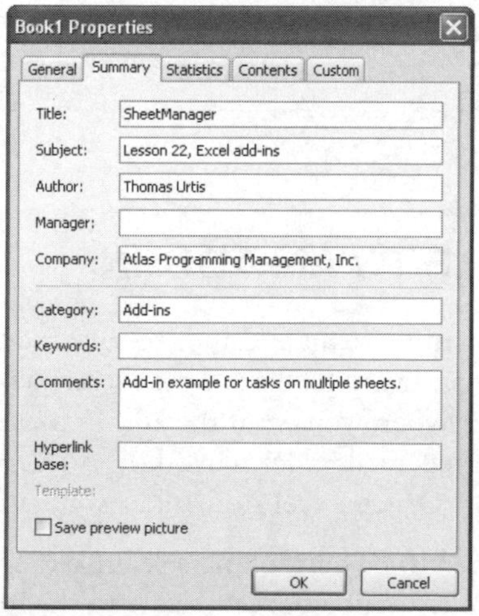

FIGURE 22-3

To reach the Properties information in Excel version 2007, click the round Office button near the top-left corner of your window. You will see a vertical pane on the left side of the window. Click Prepare, and then in the pane on the right, click Properties, as shown in Figure 22-4.

To reach the Properties information in Excel version 2010, click the File tab on the Ribbon, and in the vertical pane at the left, click Info. At the far right, you will see a Properties label with a drop-down arrow. As indicated in Figure 22-5, selecting the Advanced Properties item in the drop-down list displays the Properties dialog box.

FIGURE 22-4

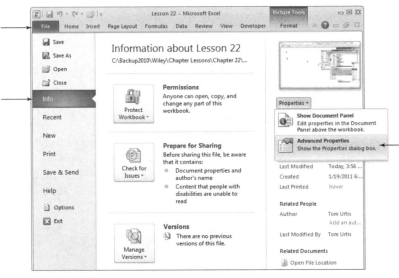

FIGURE 22-5

CONVERTING A FILE TO AN ADD-IN

The easiest way to convert a file to an add-in is to save the file as an Excel Add-in type. In versions of Excel prior to 2007, from the worksheet menu click File ⇨ Save As. In the Save As dialog box, navigate to the folder where you want the add-in to reside. In Figure 22-6, I named the file `SheetManager`, and I created a subfolder named `My Addins`. From the Save As Type field's drop-down list, select Microsoft Office Excel Add-In, as shown in Figure 22-6, and click the Save button.

For version 2007, click the Office button and select Save As. For version 2010, click the File tab and select Save As. In the Save As dialog box, navigate to the folder where you want the add-in to reside, and give the file a name. As shown in Figure 22-7, select Excel Add-In from the Save As Type drop-down list and click the Save button.

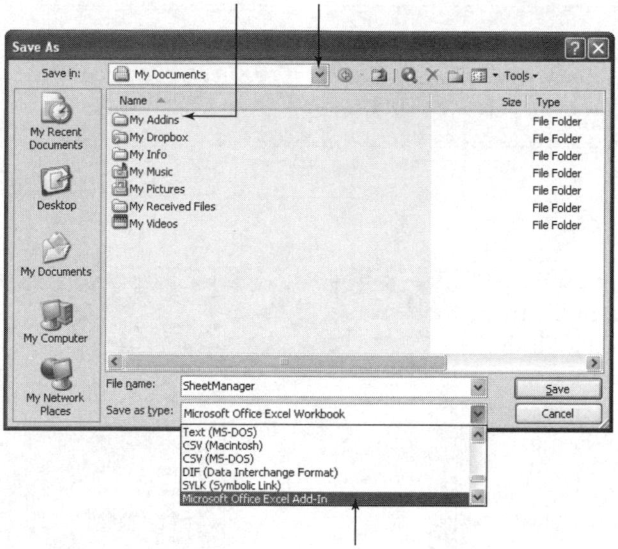

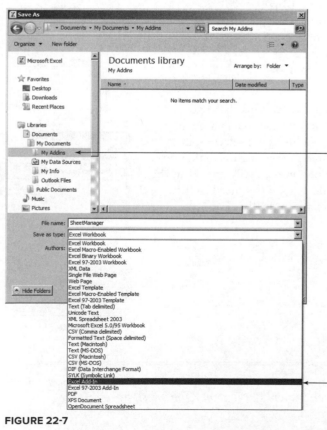

FIGURE 22-6

FIGURE 22-7

> *While saving a file as an add-in, you must have a worksheet be the active sheet.*
> *If by chance you have a chart sheet in your file and it is the active sheet, the Save*
> *As Type drop-down list won't include an Add-in file type.*

INSTALLING AN ADD-IN

If your add-in is being distributed to other users, the first thing you do is to deliver the add-in file to them in some way, such as by e-mail, or on a Flash drive if by hand delivery. In any case, your users would save the add-in file to whatever folder they prefer, similar to how you saved your add-in file into a folder on your computer.

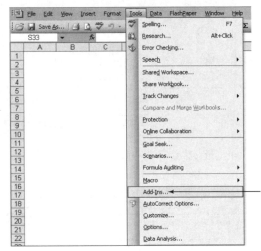

FIGURE 22-8

The easiest way to install an add-in is to use the Add-Ins dialog box, which you can do from any open workbook. In versions of Excel prior to 2007, from the worksheet menu click Tools ⇨ Add-Ins as shown in Figure 22-8. In versions 2007 and 2010, click the Developer tab on the Ribbon, and select the Add-Ins icon as shown in Figure 22-9. An example of the Add-Ins dialog box is shown in Figure 22-10.

The Add-Ins dialog box shows a list of all the add-ins that Excel is aware of. An add-in is open if a checkmark is next to its name in the list. You'll notice in Figure 22-10 that no add-ins are selected, and that the SheetManager add-in is not listed in the Add-Ins dialog box. When a new add-in is created, it does not automatically appear in the Add-Ins dialog box. To install a new add-in, you first need to list it in the Add-Ins dialog box, and then select it in the list.

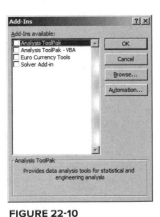

FIGURE 22-10

FIGURE 22-9

> *The Developer tab is a very useful item to place on your Ribbon. See the section*
> *named "Accessing the VBA Environment" in Lesson 2 for the steps to display*
> *the Developer tab.*

> *A quick way to open the Add-Ins dialog box from any version of Excel is to press the Alt+TI keys — that is, hold down the Alt key and with your other hand press the T key and the I key. If you prefer to work with a mouse instead of the keyboard, and you prefer not to show the Developer tab, you can access the Add-Ins dialog box another way. In Excel version 2007, click the Office button, then click the Excel Options button. In Excel version 2010, click the File tab, click the Options menu item, and select the Add-Ins menu item. At the bottom of the window, select Excel Add-Ins from the Manage drop-down list, and click the Go button.*

To include an add-in on the Add-Ins list, click the Browse button on the Add-Ins dialog box. Navigate to the folder where you saved the add-in file, select the filename, and click OK to exit the Browse dialog box as indicated in Figure 22-11.

You now will see your selected file listed in the Add-Ins dialog box. By default, Excel places a checkmark next to the selected add-in's name. If you don't want the add-in to be open — that is, for its features to be available to you — simply deselect the add-in by unchecking the box next to its name.

If and when you do select your new add-in, you and the users of that add-in will appreciate the extra time you spent in the Properties window before you converted the original file to an add-in. Notice that the selected add-in's filename and comments appear at the bottom of the Add-Ins dialog box, informing the user what the add-in does. In any case, now that you've listed the add-in file, click the OK button to exit the Add-Ins dialog box as indicated in Figure 22-12.

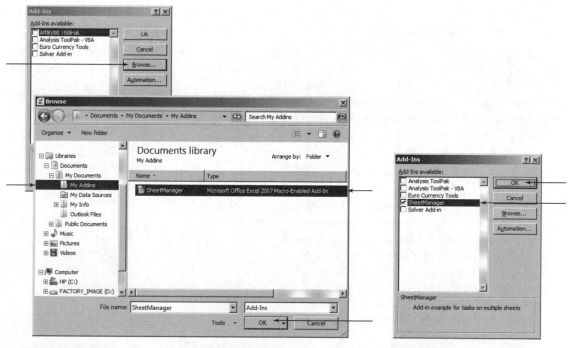

FIGURE 22-11

FIGURE 22-12

WHERE DID THOSE OTHER ADD-INS COME FROM?

Even before you created your first add-in, you saw there were already some add-ins listed in the Add-Ins dialog box. Excel ships with four available add-ins; they are not open until you select them in the Add-Ins dialog box. The four add-ins are:

➤ The Analysis ToolPak add-in, which provides an expanded set of analysis tools not available in standard worksheet functions and features

➤ The Analysis ToolPak VBA add-in, which provides an expanded set of functions for your VBA programming code

➤ The Euro Currency Tools add-in is a tool for converting and formatting the euro currency

➤ The Solver add-in is a what-if analysis tool that attempts to find an optimal value for a formula in one cell while considering constraints placed on the values in other cells

CREATING A USER INTERFACE FOR YOUR ADD-IN

Now that the add-in has been created and installed, you need to provide your users with the ability to access the functionality. As it stands right now, all that's happened is the add-in is available behind the scenes. However, because the `SheetManager` add-in's functionality is tied to a UserForm, you'll need to establish a way for users to click a link of some kind that calls the UserForm.

Before the Ribbon came along, a custom worksheet menu item was created using the `CommandBar` object. For this example, I named the menu item SheetManager, and it appears on the Tools menu. The good news is, Excel versions 2007 and 2010 still support `CommandBars`, and you can use the same code to achieve a user-friendly custom menu interface that is compatible with every version of Excel starting with Excel 97.

For versions of Excel prior to 2007, a menu item named Sheet Manager will appear in the Tools menu, as shown in Figure 22-13. For versions 2007 and 2010, the menu item named Sheet Manager will be displayed in the Menu Commands section of a new tab on the Ribbon named Add-Ins. The Add-Ins tab appears when you apply custom add-in code. In any case, clicking the Sheet Manager menu item executes the macro that calls the UserForm, as shown in Figure 22-14.

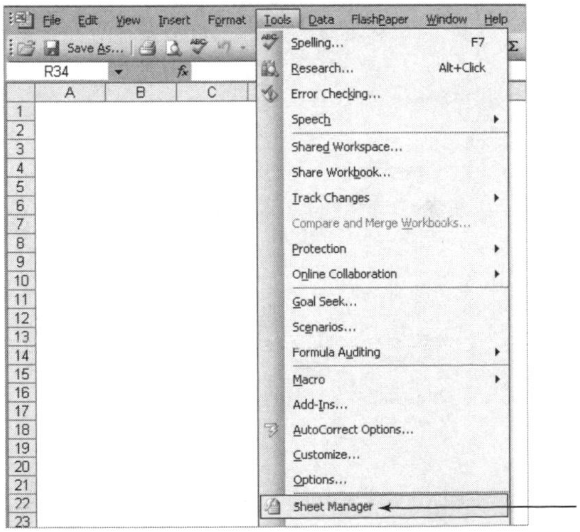

FIGURE 22-13

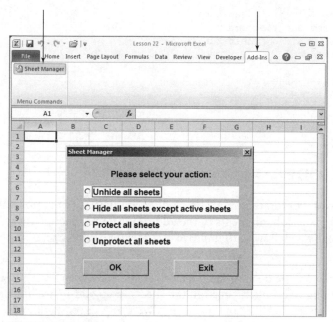

FIGURE 22-14

The following event code, found in the ThisWorkbook module of the add-in file, establishes the custom user interface:

```
Private Sub Workbook_Open()

'Declare a CBC variable for the custom menu item.
Dim objCmdControl As CommandBarControl
'The custom menu item will be named "Sheet Manager"
'and it will go onto the Tools menu for versions before 2007.
Set objCmdControl = _
Application.CommandBars("Worksheet Menu Bar") _
.Controls("Tools").Controls.Add

'For the new menu item, give it a meaningful caption,
'help it to clearly stand out by starting a BeginGroup.
'The OnAction method will call the UserForm.
'The Face ID is a small icon next to the menu item
'that is optional, but adds a feeling of customization.
With objCmdControl
.Caption = "Sheet Manager"
.BeginGroup = True
.OnAction = "SheetManager"
.FaceId = 144
End With

End Sub
```

```
Private Sub Workbook_BeforeClose(Cancel As Boolean)
'Delete the custom menu item from the Tools menu.
'The error bypass is for cases when the "Sheet Manager"
'item is not listed on the Tools menu.
On Error Resume Next
Application.CommandBars("Worksheet Menu Bar") _
.Controls("Tools").Controls("Sheet Manager").Delete
Err.Clear
End Sub
```

CHANGING THE ADD-IN'S CODE

You'll find that some of your add-ins are a work in progress. Users will enjoy the ease of performing add-in tasks, and you'll be requested to make enhancements to the add-in for more functionality. As you pick up more VBA programming skills, you'll want to improve your original code by making edits for speed and efficiency.

Any changes you make to your add-in file will be done in the Visual Basic Editor. Open your add-in file and all you will see is an empty-looking Excel file because all the sheets in an add-in are hidden and cannot be viewed. Press Alt+F11 to go to the VBE, and just as if it were any Excel workbook, make whatever changes to the code you need to make. When you are done, save your changes in the VBE and close the add-in file.

> For add-ins that you distribute to other users, you'll want to protect the code from being inadvertently changed or viewed by others. The process for protecting your add-in code is the same as with any Excel workbook, and that is to lock and protect the project in the Visual Basic Editor. The steps to do this are discussed in Lesson 4, in the section "Locking and Protecting the VBE."

CLOSING ADD-INS

As you saw in the section "Changing the Add-in's Code," you can open an add-in file, but you might like to know how to close an add-in file, because it cannot be closed the same way you close a workbook. You have three ways to close an add-in file:

➤ Deselect (uncheck) the add-in's name in the Add-Ins dialog box.

➤ Go into the VBE and press Ctrl+G to ensure that the Immediate window is open. In the Immediate window, enter a line of code that closes the add-in file and press Enter. An example of such code for the SheetManager add-in is as follows:

```
Workbooks("SheetManager.xlam").Close
```

➤ Close Excel, which closes all files, including add-ins.

REMOVING AN ADD-IN FROM THE ADD-INS LIST

At some point in the future, you might want to remove the add-in from the list of available add-ins in the Add-Ins dialog box, if the add-in is outdated or you just don't need it anymore. To accomplish this is an example of how science meets art, because Excel does not have a built-in way to remove an add-in's name from the list. Here are the steps to make this happen:

1. Close Excel.

2. Open Windows Explorer and navigate to the folder that holds your add-in file.

3. Select the add-in filename, and without opening the file, either change its name, or drag the file to a different folder, or, if you really no longer need the add-in, delete the file altogether.

FIGURE 22-15

4. Open Excel, and when you do, you'll receive a message telling you that the add-in file cannot be found. Click the OK button as indicated in Figure 22-15.

5. Open the Add-Ins dialog box and uncheck the name of the add-in you want to remove. Excel reminds you that the file cannot be found, and asks for confirmation that you want to delete the file from the list of available add-ins. Click the Yes button as indicated in Figure 22-16.

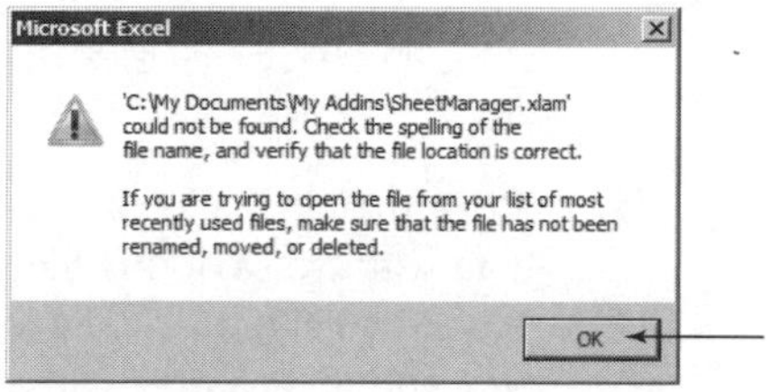

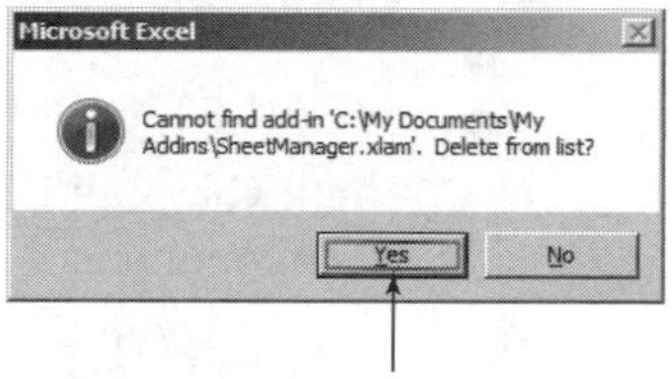

FIGURE 22-16

TRY IT

In this lesson, you create and install an add-in that contains a User Defined Function to return the text of another cell's comment.

Lesson Requirements

For this lesson, you create an add-in to return the text of comments in other cells, and you test the add-in by installing it onto a workbook that has comments in worksheet cells. To get the sample database files you can download Lesson 22 from the book's website at www.wrox.com.

Step-by-Step

1. Open a new workbook.

2. Go to the Properties window. In the Title field enter **Comment Text** and in the Comments field enter `Return text of comments in other cells`.

3. Exit the Properties window and press the Alt+F11 keys to go into the Visual Basic Editor.

4. From the menu bar in the VBE, click Insert ⇨ Module. Copy the following User Defined Function into the module:

```
Function GetComment(rng As Range) As String
Dim strText As String
If rng.Comment Is Nothing Then
strText = "No comment"
Else
strText = rng.Comment.Text
End If
GetComment = strText
End Function
```

5. Press the Ctrl+S keys to display the Save As dialog box. Navigate to the folder into which you want to save this file. Name the file **CommentText** and select Excel Add-In in the Save As Type field, as indicated in Figure 22-17. Click the Save button, which will convert this workbook as a new add-in file named `CommentText.xlam`.

6. Close Excel.

7. Restart Excel and open a new workbook.

8. Right-click cell B2 of the active worksheet, and select Insert Comment. Enter some text in your comment.

9. Select cell G1.

10. Press Alt+TI to show the Add-Ins dialog box.

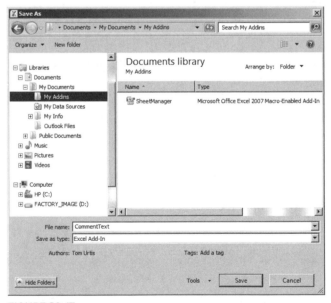

FIGURE 22-17

11. Click the Browse button and navigate to the folder where you saved the `CommentText` add-in file. Select the `CommentText` file, and click OK. Your Add-Ins dialog box will look like Figure 22-18, with the `CommentText` add-in loaded. Recall that the file is named `CommentText` but the add-in dialog box shows it as Comment Text, and also shows the description of the add-in, because that is the information you entered in Step 2 about the add-in file in its Properties dialog box. Click the OK button to exit the Add-Ins dialog box.

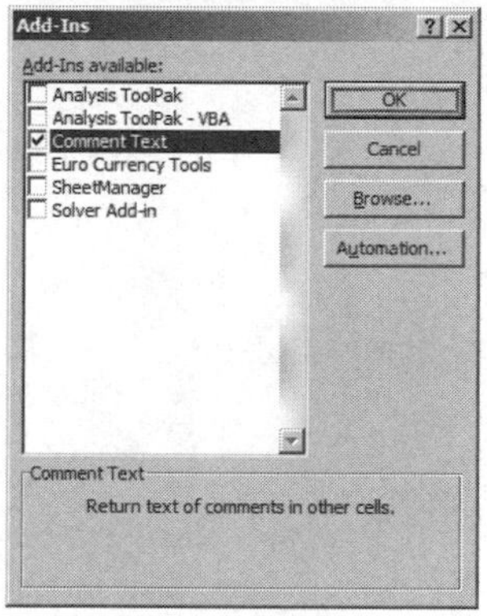

FIGURE 22-18

12. In cell G1, enter the User Defined Function **=GetComment(B1)** and press the Enter key. Copy the formula down to cell G2. You will see that the UDF returned "No comment" in cell G1 because no comment exists in cell B1. However, you did enter a comment into cell B2 in Step 8, so the UDF in cell G2 returns the text of the comment from cell B2. Your worksheet will look similar to Figure 22-19.

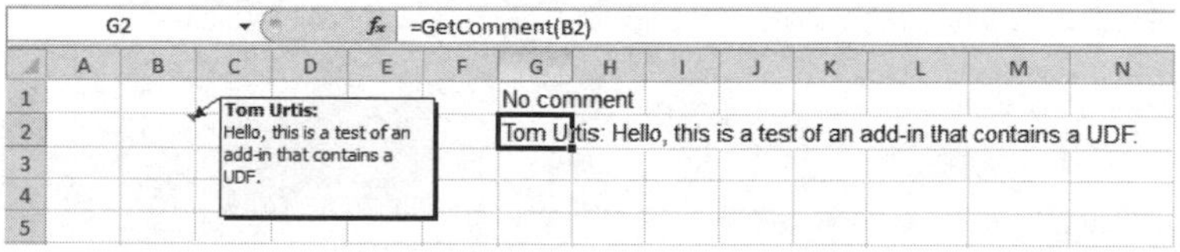

FIGURE 22-19

13. Note that the workbook you are looking at does not contain the `GetComment` UDF code. You can utilize that UDF because its code belongs to the `CommentText` add-in file that you installed for the active workbook.

Please select Lesson 22 on the DVD to view the video that accompanies this lesson.

Managing External Data

One of the most versatile and useful benefits of Excel is its ability to import data from external sources. In Lessons 26–30 you will see examples of sharing data back and forth with other Microsoft Office applications from Excel.

Prior to Excel 97, the data that a person would be working with was entered into Excel manually. An Excel workbook was essentially a self-contained object that produced and stored its own data, having almost no contact with the outside world except for the person working in the project.

Starting with Office 97, Microsoft has been devoted to providing more and better tools for importing and exporting data to the Internet, database programs, and text-related software applications. Excel leads the way in this effort among all Office applications. In this lesson, you learn how to use VBA to share data between Excel and other external sources, including Access, the Internet, and text files.

CREATING QUERYTABLES FROM WEB QUERIES

The Internet as we know it has only been around since the mid 1990s, not that long ago really, but it's hard to imagine what life would be like today without the World Wide Web. The public's desire is only increasing for access to the galaxy of information that is stored on the Web. With each new release of its Office suite, Microsoft has improved the capacity of its applications to interact with web-based information.

> *When you connect Excel to an external source such as the Internet, you add a QueryTable to your worksheet. Objects that can connect to external data sources include a cell range, an Excel table, a pivot table, a text file, and a Web query. In this case, you are adding a QueryTable to a worksheet because you are querying the Web for information that will be displayed on your worksheet.*

Suppose you are interested in monitoring the stock prices of a half-dozen or so technology companies. If you want to avoid the monotony of going to a financial website and entering the same stock symbols every time, you can automate the process with a Web query, and refresh the data anytime you like.

When you build a Web query, you need to tell Excel what website to extract the information from, and the cell address on the destination sheet where you want the QueryTable to be located. Some background information about URLs and their parameters might be helpful for you to understand what is going on.

If you open your Web browser and enter the URL `http://money.cnn.com/quote/quote .html?symb=YHOO,GOOG`, you will reach a site that provides a table of stock quotes for Yahoo and Google. With this URL, you are essentially passing URL parameters that allow you to pass information such as search criteria to a website. In this case, the URL parameters being used are the symbols for Yahoo (YHOO) and Google (GOOG).

The following macro places the QueryTable on cell A1, and points to one of the bevy of websites out there that provide current stock quotes. For demonstration purposes, I chose a few companies that are all headquartered in Silicon Valley where I live. The stock symbols of those companies are the criteria that will apply URL parameters through the code to gather the stock quote information that will populate the QueryTable. Figure 23-1 shows what the result looked like when I ran this macro in January 2011.

```
Sub ImportStocks()

'Declare variables for destination worksheet,
'and two halves of the connection string:
'one half for the URL, and the other half for
'the quotes, to make it easier for you to edit.
Dim wsDestination As Worksheet
Dim strURL As String, strStocks As String

'Set the destination worksheet; here it is Sheet2.
Set wsDestination = Worksheets("Sheet2")

'Define the URL for getting your stock quotes.
'There are many websites where you can do this.
strURL = "http://money.cnn.com/quote/quote.html?symb="

'Define your stocks of interest. I only selected these
'as an example because they are silicon valley businesses
'near where I live and run my Excel development company.
strStocks = "AAPL,CSCO,EBAY,GOOG,INTC,ORCL,YHOO"

'My preference is to activate the destination worksheet
'and select cell A1.
Application.Goto wsDestination.Range("A1"), True

'Clear the cells in the worksheet so you know the data
'being imported will not be confused with other data
'you may have imported previously and not yet deleted.
Cells.Clear
```

```
'Add your QueryTable with the connection string
'and other useful methods you see in the With structure.
With wsDestination.QueryTables.Add _
(Connection:="URL;" & strURL & strStocks, _
Destination:=Range("$A$1"))
.BackgroundQuery = True
.SaveData = True
.AdjustColumnWidth = True
.WebSelectionType = xlSpecifiedTables
.WebFormatting = xlWebFormattingNone
.WebTables = """wsod_multiquoteTable"""
.Refresh BackgroundQuery:=False
End With

'Release object variable memory.
Set wsDestination = Nothing

End Sub
```

	A	B	C	D	E	F	G	H
1	Stocks							
2	Company	Price	Change	% Change	P/E	Volume	YTD change	
3	AAPL Apple Inc	343.85	2.45	0.72%	19.2	3.3K	6.60%	
4	CSCO Cisco Systems Inc	21.42	-0.12	-0.56%	15.6	65.5M	5.88%	
5	EBAY eBay Inc	31.06	0.1525	0.49%	22.8	13.1M	11.62%	
6	GOOG Google Inc	616.5	-3.41	-0.55%	23.4	2.0M	3.79%	
7	INTC Intel Corp	21.75	0.2	0.93%	10.6	2.0K	3.42%	
8	ORCL Oracle Corp	32.56	0.27	0.84%	24.3	21.5M	4.03%	
9	YHOO Yahoo! Inc	15.57	-0.4475	-2.79%	20.2	49.7M	-6.36%	
10								

FIGURE 23-1

With the worksheet active, you can refresh the data by right-clicking cell A1 and selecting Refresh, as shown in Figure 23-2. Alternatively, you can execute the VBA expression `Range("A1").QueryTable .Refresh` in the Immediate window or in a macro. Each time you refresh the data, you see the most recent version of the information in the data source, including any changes that were made to the data.

FIGURE 23-2

> *Does your Web query take too long to refresh? You can cancel the Refresh
> method if it's running longer than you want to wait with this block of code:*
>
> ```
> If Application.Wait(Now + TimeValue("0:00:10")) Then
> With Worksheets(1).QueryTables(1)
> If .Refreshing Then .CancelRefresh
> End With
> End If
> ```

While on the subject of corporate performance, the following macro opens a `.csv` file for you,
depending on which stock symbol you are searching for, and copies several years of historical stock
price activity to Sheet3 of your workbook:

```
Sub ImportHistory()
Dim strStockSymbol As String
Dim strURL1 As String, strURL2 As String

'Download the past years' stock price activity.
strURL1 = "http://ichart.finance.yahoo.com/table.csv?s="
strURL2 = "&d=2&e=18&f=2010&g=d&a=2&b=13&c=1986&ignore=.csv"
strStockSymbol = "EBAY"
Workbooks.Open Filename:=strURL1 & strStockSymbol & strURL2

'Copy data from the csv file to your worksheet.
Range("A1").CurrentRegion.Copy _
ThisWorkbook.Worksheets("Sheet3").Range("A1")

'Close the csv file without saving it.
ActiveWorkbook.Close False

'Autofit the columns.
Columns.AutoFit
End Sub
```

There may be times when you are composing Web queries for other people to use. Before they try
running your macros, seeing as an Internet connection is required for the code to perform, it might
be a good idea to programmatically verify that the user has an Internet connection. You can place
the following procedures into a new standard module, and if no Internet connection exists, it would
be wise to use this code to halt any web-related activity your project may involve.

> *The strange-looking Public Declaration Function is not VBA code. It is
> Applications Programming Interface, or API, which is the programming language
> of the Microsoft Windows operating system. If you are wondering why API is being
> used in this example, the reason is that the task at hand is a query about Internet
> connectivity, which is a computer-wide issue that is not related specifically to any
> one application, including Excel. In your programming travels, you will see API
> being used with VBA for controlling objects that are related to Windows, such as
> manipulating the task bar or returning the name of the computer.*

```
Private Declare Function IsNetworkAlive Lib "Sensapi" _
   (lpdwFlags As Long) As Long

Sub IsConnection()
If IsNetworkAlive(lngAlive) = 1 Then
MsgBox "You are connected to the internet."
Else
MsgBox "Connection to the internet not found."
End If
End Sub
```

> *There is another example in the Try It section that leads you in a step-by-step process of creating a Web query.*

CREATING A QUERYTABLE FOR ACCESS

In upcoming lessons you learn about importing and exporting data between Excel and Access, using VBA and a technology called Structured Query Language, or SQL. Because this lesson deals with external data, you might be interested to know how to quickly, albeit manually, import an Access table directly to your worksheet.

Click the Data tab on the Ribbon, and find the Get External Data section at the far left. Click the left-most icon that is labeled From Access as shown in Figure 23-3.

You will see the Select Data Source dialog box. Navigate to the folder holding your Access database, select the folder, and also select the name of the database file. Click the Open button as shown in Figure 23-4.

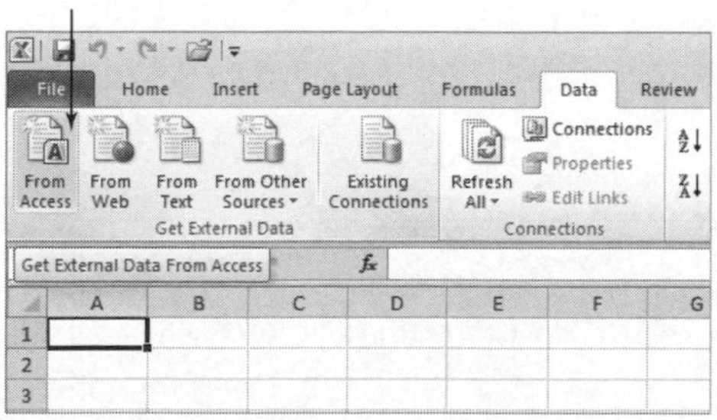

FIGURE 23-3

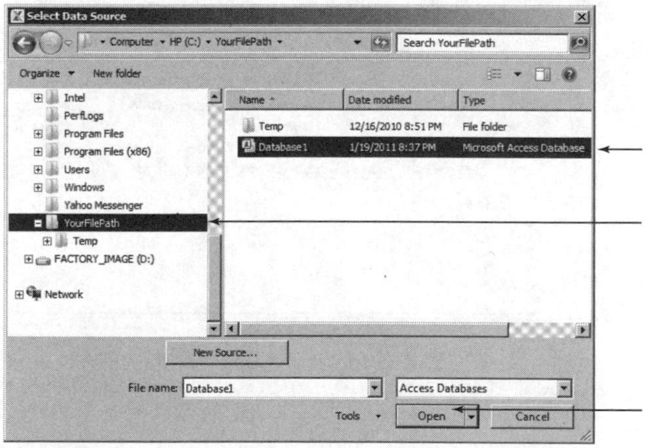

FIGURE 23-4

The Select Table dialog box will appear, so all you need to do is click to select the name of the table, and then click the OK button as shown in Figure 23-5. After that, the Import dialog box will appear. I chose to keep the imported table as a Table format, placed onto my worksheet, starting in cell A1 as shown in Figure 23-6. Your Access table will load onto your worksheet as shown in Figure 23-7, with the top row having AutoFilter buttons to help you with your future searches.

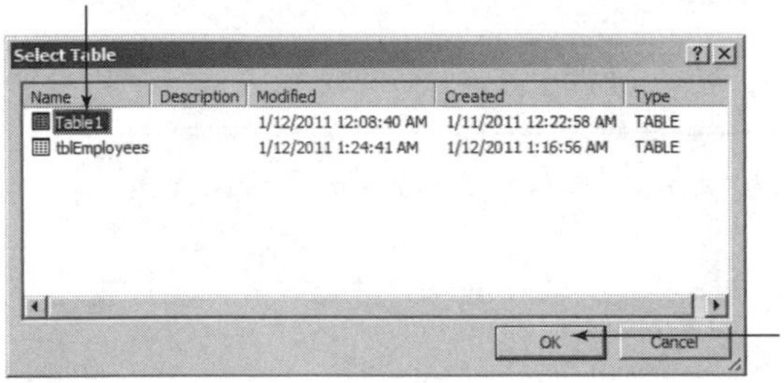

FIGURE 23-5

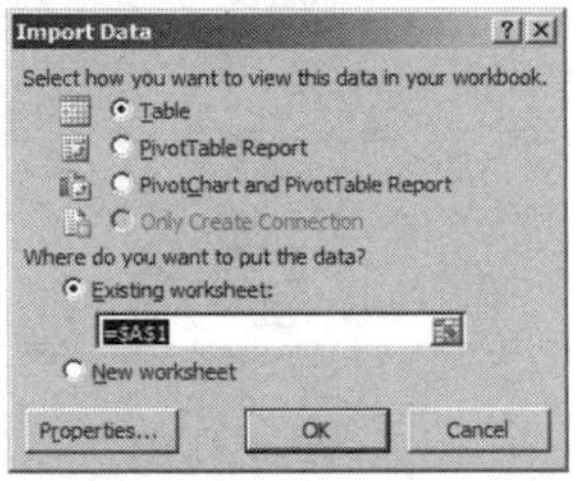

FIGURE 23-6

	A	B	C	D	E	F	G	H	I	J
1	ID	Name	Region	Weekday	Month	Item	Color	Count	Original	
2	1	Tom	North	Monday	January	Widgets	Red	507	1	
3	2	Mike	West	Tuesday	February	Witches	Purple	23	2	
4	3	Jim	East	Wednesday	March	Wombats	Blue	116	3	
5	4	Tom	South	Thursday	April	Warlocks	Red	618	4	
6	5	Mike	West	Friday	May	Widgets	Green	712	5	
7	6	Mary	South	Saturday	June	Warlocks	Blue	714	6	
8	7	Bill	West	Sunday	July	Wallabees	Yellow	600	7	
9	8	Bob	East	Monday	August	Witches	Blue	654	8	
10	9	Tom	North	Tuesday	September	Widgets	Red	644	9	
11	10	Mike	North	Wednesday	October	Warlocks	Purple	570	10	
12	11	Jim	West	Thursday	November	Wallabees	Purple	148	11	
13	12	Tom	East	Friday	December	Warlocks	Yellow	822	12	
14	13	Mike	West	Saturday	January	Wombats	Black	562	13	
15	14	Jim	East	Sunday	February	Warlocks	Red	456	14	
16	15	Nancy	North	Monday	March	Witches	Red	323	15	
17	16	Zelda	West	Tuesday	April	Widgets	Green	183	16	
18	17	William	South	Wednesday	May	Warlocks	Blue	728	17	
19	18	Mary	West	Thursday	June	Warlocks	Black	910	18	
20	19	Bill	East	Friday	July	Wombats	Black	898	19	
21	20	Bob	West	Saturday	August	Warlocks	Yellow	240	20	
22	21	Tom	South	Sunday	September	Witches	Black	871	21	
23	22	Mike	South	Monday	October	Witches	Blue	892	22	
24	23	Jim	West	Tuesday	November	Wombats	Black	66	23	

FIGURE 23-7

> The Select Table dialog box may contain tables and queries, and you can import data from either of them. You might want to be aware that Parameter queries will not appear in this dialog box.

USING TEXT FILES TO STORE EXTERNAL DATA

Hail the text file, the true foot soldier interface for transferring information between two or more otherwise disparate platforms. In the modern age of computing, it's always been the text file that could be relied on for one application downloading its information in a comma-delimited or fixed-length file, and another application like Excel being able to accept the data.

Text files are not pretty, they are almost never formatted, and they are not easy to read. But when all else fails, they come through and are fairly easy to program. The following examples show how text files can help you in your everyday work.

Suppose you want Excel to add a new record to a text file that records the date and time a particular Excel workbook was saved. In the folder YourFilePath is a text file named LogFile.txt. The following VBA code goes into the ThisWorkbook module of the Excel file you are monitoring:

```
Private Sub Workbook_BeforeSave(ByVal SaveAsUI As Boolean, Cancel As Boolean)
Dim intCounter As Integer, myFileName As String
myFileName = "C:\YourFilePath\LogFile.txt"
intCounter = FreeFile
Open myFileName For Append As #intCounter
Write #intCounter, ThisWorkbook.FullName, Now, Application.UserName
Close #intCounter
End Sub
```

This macro will create four new text files, naming each with the prefix MyFile, followed by a number suffix in order from 1 to 4. For example, the first file will be named MyFile001.txt, the second file will be named MyFile002.txt, and so on. The starting number of 1 is derived by the code line For intCounter = 1 to 4. If you wanted to create four new text files starting with the name MyFile038.txt, you'd establish the starting number of 38 by specifying it with the line of code For intCounter = 38 to 41.

```
Sub CreateTextFiles()
Dim intCounter As Integer, strFile As String
For intCounter = 1 To 4
strFile = "MyFile" & Format(intCounter, "000")
strFile = "C:\YourFilePath\" & strFile & ".txt"
Open strFile For Output As #1
Close
Next intCounter
End Sub
```

The following macro will copy the text of your comments in your worksheet's used range into a text file, where they will be listed along with the cell values in that range. This is a very fast macro.

```
Sub Comment2Text()
Dim cmt As Comment, rng As Range
Dim iRow As Long, iCol As Long
Dim strText As String
```

```
Set rng = Range("A1").CurrentRegion
Open "C:\YourFilePath\YourFileName.txt" For Output As #1
For iRow = 1 To rng.Rows.Count
For iCol = 1 To rng.Columns.Count
If Not Cells(iRow, iCol).Comment Is Nothing Then
strText = strText & Cells(iRow, iCol).Text & _
     "(" & Cells(iRow, iCol).Comment.Text & ")" & ";"

Else

strText = strText & Cells(iRow, iCol).Text & ";"
End If
Next iCol
strText = Left(strText, Len(strText) - 1)
Print #1, strText
strText = ""
Next iRow
Close
End Sub
```

If you want to know how many lines a particular text file has, this macro will tell you:

```
Sub Test1()
Dim MyObject As Object, LineCount As Variant
Set MyObject = _
CreateObject("Scripting.FileSystemObject")
With MyObject.OpenTextFile("C:\YourFilePath\YourFileName.txt", 1)
LineCount = Split(.ReadAll, vbNewLine)
End With
MsgBox UBound(LineCount) - LBound(LineCount) + 1
End Sub
```

Export each sheet in this workbook as a text file, with each file named as the sheet tab name. Text file macros compile very quickly.

```
Sub TextExport()
Dim rng As Range
Dim iWks As Integer, LRow As Long, iCol As Long
Dim sTxt As String, sPath As String
sPath = "C:\YourFilePath\"

For iWks = 1 To Worksheets.Count
Open sPath & Worksheets(iWks).Name & ".txt" For Output As #1
Set rng = Worksheets(iWks).Range("A1").CurrentRegion
For LRow = 1 To rng.Rows.Count
For iCol = 1 To rng.Columns.Count
sTxt = sTxt & Worksheets(iWks).Cells(LRow, iCol).Value & vbTab
Next iCol
Print #1, Left(sTxt, Len(sTxt) - 1)
sTxt = ""
```

```
Next LRow
Close #1
Next iWks
MsgBox "The text files can be found in " & Left(sPath, Len(sPath) - 1)
End Sub
```

If you would like to see a text file's contents in a Message Box, you can use the following code.

```
Sub GetTextMessage()
Dim sTxt As String, sText As String, sPath As String
sPath = "C:\YourFilePath\YourFileName.txt"

If Dir(sPath) = "" Then
MsgBox "File was not found."
Exit Sub
End If

Close
Open sPath For Input As #1
Do Until EOF(1)
Line Input #1, sTxt
sText = sText & sTxt & vbLf
Loop
Close
sText = Left(sText, Len(sText) - 1)
MsgBox sText
End Sub
```

Suppose you want to save the contents of cell A1 on Sheet1 as a text file. The following example shows how that can be done:

```
Sub SaveCellValue()
Open "C:\YourFilePath\YourFileName.txt" For Append As #1
Print #1, Sheets("Sheet1").Range("A1").Value
Close #1
End Sub
```

Finally, this macro demonstrates how to delete a text file if it exists, and replace it with a new text file of the same name. If the text file does not exist, the macro will create a new text file.

```
Sub DeleteAndCreate()
Dim strFile As String, intFactor As Integer
On Error Resume Next
strFile = "C:\YourFilePath\YourFileName.txt"
Kill strFile
Err.Clear
intFactor = FreeFile
Open strFile For Output Access Write As #intFactor
Close #intFactor
End Sub
```

TRY IT

What is today's date, and what is the current time of day? In this lesson you create a Web query to import a display of the current day and time for several North American time zones.

Lesson Requirements

For this lesson, you access the website to the United States Naval Observatory, where the day and time are recorded on the Master Clock of the United States Navy. To get the sample database files you can download Lesson 23 from the book's website at www.wrox.com.

Step-by-Step

1. Open a new workbook.

2. From your worksheet, press Alt+F11 to go to the Visual Basic Editor.

3. From the menu bar in the VBE, click Insert ⇨ Module.

4. In your new module, type **Sub TimeAfterTime** and press the Enter key. VBA will produce the following two lines of code, separated by an empty line:

    ```
    Sub TimeAfterTime()

    End Sub
    ```

5. Open a With structure for the destination worksheet:

    ```
    With Worksheets("Sheet1")
    ```

6. Declare a String type variable for the website address:

    ```
    Dim strURL As String
    ```

7. Define the website address from which the information will be imported to your worksheet:

    ```
    strURL = _
    "http://tycho.usno.navy.mil/cgi-bin/timer.pl"
    ```

8. For consistency, I prefer to activate the worksheet that will receive the web data. Cell A1 is a convenient cell to start with:

    ```
    Application.Goto .Range("A1"), True
    ```

9. Clear the cells in the worksheet so you know the data being imported will not be confused with other data you may have imported previously and not yet deleted:

    ```
    Cells.Clear
    ```

10. Open a `With` structure for the `Add` method of your new QueryTable. The connection, URL, destination sheet, and other information that follows must be specified.

```
With .QueryTables.Add _
(Connection:="URL;" &strURL, Destination:=.Range("A1"))
.BackgroundQuery = True
.TablesOnlyFromHTML = False
.Refresh BackgroundQuery:=False
.SaveData = True
```

11. Close the `With` structure of the QueryTable's `Add` method:

```
End With
```

12. Close the `With` structure for the destination worksheet:

```
End With
```

13. Your entire macro will look as follows:

```
Sub TimeAfterTime()

'Open a With structure for the destination worksheet.
With Worksheets("Sheet1")

'Declare a String type variable for the website address.
Dim strURL As String
'Define the website address, from which the information
'will be imported to your worksheet.
strURL = _
"http://tycho.usno.navy.mil/cgi-bin/timer.pl"

'For consistency, I prefer to activate the worksheet
'that will receive the web data.
'Cell A1 is a convenient cell to situate yourself.
Application.Goto .Range("A1"), True

'Clear the cells in the worksheet so you know the data
'being imported will not be confused with other data
'you may have imported previously and not yet deleted.
Cells.Clear

'Open a With structure for the Add method of your new
'QueryTable. The connection, URL, and destination sheet,
'and other information that follows, must be specified.
With .QueryTables.Add _
(Connection:="URL;" &strURL, Destination:=.Range("A1"))
.BackgroundQuery = True
.TablesOnlyFromHTML = False
.Refresh BackgroundQuery:=False
.SaveData = True
```

```
'Close the With structure of the QueryTable's Add method.
End With

'Close the With structure for the destination worksheet.
End With

End Sub
```

14. Press Alt+Q to return to the worksheet.

15. You can test the macro by pressing Alt+F8 to display the Macro dialog box as shown in Figure 23-8. Run the macro named TimeAfterTime. The result will resemble Figure 23-9.

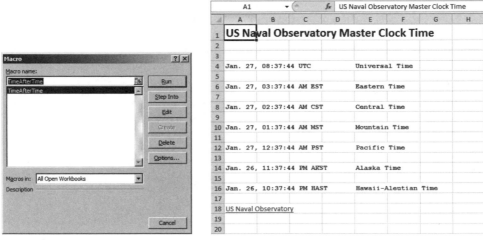

FIGURE 23-8   **FIGURE 23-9**

Please select Lesson 23 on the DVD to view the video that accompanies this lesson.

24

Data Access with ActiveX Data Objects

The topic of data access has become one of the most intensive forces in driving the recent development of commercial software applications. Data storage and search engine companies have become the face of the worldwide voracious demand for accessing information.

Excel is without peer in its powerful features for calculating and analyzing data, and in its ability to produce customized reports in an instant with VBA. For users who deal with extremely large volumes of source data, Excel can still fall short as a data storage application. Microsoft has built Excel with some robust methods for importing external data into your workbooks, making Excel a terrific front-end application that analyzes data it does not need to store.

INTRODUCING ADO

ADO is an acronym for ActiveX Data Objects, which is the technology Microsoft recommends for accessing data in external databases. Excel's spreadsheets, being tabular row and column objects, share common features with database tables, providing a natural environment for data to be transferred between Excel and relational databases.

From Excel, using ADO you can

➤ Connect to most any external database in the Windows operating system, as long as that database has, as many do, an ODBC (Open Database Connectivity) or OLE DB (Object Linking and Embedding Database) driver.

➤ Add, delete, and edit records from a database to your workbook, or from your workbook to a database.

➤ Query data to return a recordset, allowing you to import some or all records from a database table directly to your worksheet, for whatever analysis you want to perform, just as if the data was already in Excel.

DEFINITIONS OF DATABASE TERMS

Because this lesson introduces concepts for external data access, there is more descriptive theory about databases than actual code examples. In Lesson 29, you'll see several working examples of how Excel utilizes ADO and SQL in conjunction with Access databases. If you are unfamiliar with database terminology, the following definitions for common database terms might help you throughout this lesson.

A database is an organized collection of related information.

DAO (Data Access Objects) is a library of objects and their associated methods and properties that can be used to represent objects in databases, enabling Excel to interact directly with databases through VBA.

DBMS is an abbreviation for database management system. Popular examples of database management systems include dBASE, Paradox, and Microsoft Access.

A field is a column in a list such as in an Excel worksheet or Access database that describes a characteristic about records, such as first name or city.

ODBC (Open Database Connectivity) is a database standard that enables a program to connect to and manipulate a data source, allowing a single user to access many different databases.

A primary key is one or more fields that determine the uniqueness of each record in a database.

A query is a series of statements written in Structured Query Language to specify the tables and fields you want to work with that add, modify, remove, or return data from a database.

A record is a row of data in a table.

A recordset is one or more records (rows) of data derived from a table.

A relational database is a collection of data items organized as a set of formally described tables from which data can be accessed or reassembled in many ways.

Prior to ADO, Microsoft's primary recommended tool for accessing external data was an interface called DAO, or Data Access Objects. The DAO interface has become all but obsolete due to its limitations as compared to ADO, though DAO is still supported by ADO. The two technologies share many of the same code syntaxes but they are not the same in terms of flexibility and performance. You still do have a choice between the two, but you'll be much better served by ADO, which is why it is covered in this book.

With entire books devoted to database integration with ADO, there is much more complexity to the topic than this lesson is meant to cover. The best way to start becoming familiar with ADO is to examine the three primary tools in its object model: the `Connection` object, the `Recordset` object, and the `Command` object.

The Connection Object

The `Connection` object establishes a path that connects Excel and the database. With ADO from Excel, you normally issue commands that pass information back and forth through the `Connection` object. Among the key methods belonging to the `Connection` object are `Open`, which establishes the database connection, and `Close`, which closes the connection. The `Connection` object's `ConnectionString` property defines how to connect to the database.

Connecting to the database is accomplished with the `Provider` keyword. The following line of code is a common syntax for Excel versions 2007 and 2010:

```
Provider = "Microsoft.ACE.OLEDB.12.0;Data Source= _
C:\YourFilePath\Database1.accdb";Persist Security Info=False;"
```

In versions of Excel prior to 2007, the Provider would have been specified as the Microsoft Jet database engine of Access:

```
Provider = "Microsoft.Jet.OLEDB.4.0;" & _
"Data Source=C:\YourFilePath\Database1.accdb; Extended Properties=Excel 8.0;"
```

Or, depending on the circumstance, more simply:

```
Provider = "Microsoft.Jet.OLEDB.4.0"
```

> *When working with databases, you almost always connect to them, meaning you do not open them in a way you'd open a Word document if you were working with Word from Excel. The* Connection *object is like a conduit between Excel and your database.*

The Recordset Object

The `Recordset` object is probably the most commonly used object in ADO. When you instruct ADO to retrieve a single record or the entire count of records from a database table, you use the `Recordset` object to do that.

Among the key members of the `Recordset` object are the following:

> ➤ The `ActiveConnection` property, which is a connection string or a `Connection` object that identifies the connection being used to access the database. As with this property for the `Command` object, where `objRecordset` and `objConnection` are object variables, the `ActiveConnection` syntax is
>
> ```
> Set objRecordset.ActiveConnection = objConnection
> ```

➤ The `Open` method opens the `Recordset` object so you can access the data. Its syntax is

```
recordset.Open Source, ActiveConnection, CursorType, LockType, Options
```

Note that the `Source` argument is often a string that names the table from which the recordset should be retrieved.

➤ The `Close` method closes an open `Recordset` object. With the `Recordset` object declared as `dbRecordset`, the syntax for `Close` would be

```
dbRecordset.Close
```

The Command Object

The `Command` object holds information about the kind of task being run, which is usually related to action queries in Access, or procedures in SQL, which are described in the next section. A `Command` object can also return a list of data records, and is most often run with a combination of parameters, of which there are more than this lesson can possibly cover.

The `Command` object has three important properties:

➤ The `ActiveConnection` property, which, like the `ActiveConnection` property for the `Recordset` object, is a connection string or a `Connection` object that identifies the connection being used to access the database. For example, this syntax assigns a `Connection` object to the `ActiveConnection` property, where `objRecordset` and `objConnection` are object variables:

```
Set objRecordset.ActiveConnection = objConnection
```

➤ The `CommandText` property, which sets the command that will be executed by the database, and will usually be an SQL string.

➤ The `CommandType` property, which tells the database how to interpret and execute the `CommandText`'s instructions.

AN INTRODUCTION TO STRUCTURED QUERY LANGUAGE (SQL)

Structured Query Language (SQL) is a database language used in querying, updating, and managing relational databases. SQL is used to communicate with the vast majority of databases that are commonly in use today.

Structured Query Language is a complex language in response to the rigid nature of table design in relational database construction. This lesson covers SQL's four basic operations of SELECT, INSERT, UPDATE, and DELETE. As a reminder of what I mentioned at the beginning of this lesson, you'll find several examples of these operations in Lesson 29 that show how to work with Access from Excel.

> You'll notice that SQL statements such as SELECT and INSERT are shown in upper case. This is a standard SQL programming practice and a good habit to get into from the start. The SQL code examples you'll see in this book are relatively small, but SQL code can be very large and complex. SQL is easier to read when its statements are shown in upper case, distinguishing them from the clauses of code with which they are associated.

The SELECT Statement

The SELECT statement retrieves data in the form of one or more rows (records) from one or more tables. The SELECT statement is probably SQL's most commonly used operation, because it tells the data source what field(s) you want to return from what table(s).

If you want to retrieve all columns and all rows from the Vendors table, the expression in SQL would be as follows:

```
SELECT *
FROM Vendors
```

Sometimes you might not want to retrieve all columns. The following example will retrieve the State column from the Vendors table, if you want to know the count of your vendors per state.

```
SELECT State
FROM Vendors
```

If you want to see a list of vendors and the names of their contact people, but only for vendors in California, the following example would accomplish that. Note that the literal string criterion California is in single quotes, which is SQL's required syntax.

```
SELECT VendorName, ContactName
FROM Vendors
WHERE State 'California'
```

If you want to retrieve the previous recordset by having it already sorted by the VendorName field, you could add the ORDER BY statement and specify the field name as follows:

```
SELECT VendorName, ContactName
FROM Vendors
WHERE State 'California'
ORDER BY VendorName
```

The INSERT Statement

The INSERT statement adds a new row (record) to a table. You need to specify the name of the table where the row will be added. You may optionally omit the field names from the INSERT statement but it is advisable that you name them anyway because it will help you to see that the values you are entering are in the same order as the field names.

An example of using INSERT is this fictional pair of statements that respectively place the values 5432, Doe, John, Male into a table named Employees, for fields named EmployeeID, LastName, FirstName, and Gender.

```
INSERT INTO EmployeeID (EmployeeID, LastName, FirstName, Gender)
VALUES ('5432', 'Doe', 'John', 'Male')
```

> *It's standard SQL programming practice to enter the statements in upper case. It is mandatory SQL programming practice to place the string literal* VALUES *within single quotes, just as you see it here.*

If you had opted to enter the preceding SQL code without naming each field, the syntax example for that same procedure would have been as follows:

```
INSERT INTO EmployeeID
VALUES ('5432', 'Doe', 'John', 'Male')
```

The UPDATE Statement

The UPDATE statement allows you to change the values in one or more columns (fields) in a table. UPDATE is most commonly used to modify the value of a specific record that you identify with the WHERE clause. You also need to specify each column you want to change, and what each column's new value should be.

The following example shows how you could update the contact name of one of your company's vendors in the ContactName column of the Vendors table. You need to be careful to specify the WHERE clause so that only one record is changed, and that it is the correct record.

In the Vendors table, you have a field named VendorID that lists unique vendor identification numbers. The vendor name itself is Widgets, Inc. but that is not as important as its vendor identification number. Suppose that the vendor identification number for Widgets, Inc. is 1234. The new contact name is John Doe, executed with these three statements in SQL:

```
UPDATE Vendors
SET ContactName = 'John Doe'
WHERE VendorID = '1234'
```

If the ContactName field had many empty (referred to as *Null*) values, and you wanted to fill those empty spaces with the word Unknown, the following example would accomplish that:

```
UPDATE Vendors
SET ContactName = 'Unknown'
WHERE ContactName IS NULL
```

The DELETE Statement

The DELETE statement deletes one or more rows from a table. If you want to delete the vendor named Widgets, Inc., you would use the WHERE statement to specify which value in which column should identify the record for Widgets, Inc. The VendorID column is the perfect column for this task because a large company might have two vendors with the same name.

The following SQL statements would delete the record from the Vendors table that has the value 1234 in the VendorID column:

```
DELETE FROM Vendors
WHERE VendorID = '1234'
```

> ⊗ *Make absolutely certain you specify the* WHERE *clause, because if you do not, every row from the Vendors table would be deleted. If an empty table is what you want, this fictional sequence would accomplish that:*
>
> ```
> DELETE FROM Vendors
> ```
>
> *Odds are, you don't want an empty table with all rows deleted from it. The kicker is, after the rows are deleted, you cannot undo that action as you can in Excel. Unless you are good friends with an experienced database programmer who might (or might not) be able to recover your unintentionally deleted rows, take heed and always specify the* WHERE *clause in your SQL* DELETE *actions.*

TRY IT

This lesson introduced the fundamentals of ADO and SQL. You will see several examples in Lesson 29 of VBA macros that show how to program ADO with SQL to interact with Access databases from Excel.

Here is a way to get a head start on the instruction in Lesson 29 — become familiar with database tables. Open Access and create a new database. Create a new table and enter some fictional data such as a mailing list with fields for FirstName, LastName, StreetAddress, City, State, Country, and Postal Code. Make a dozen or so entries and get a feel for navigating and editing a database table. For example, Figure 24-1 shows a table in Access being populated with hypothetical employee information, such as you might see in a company's personnel database.

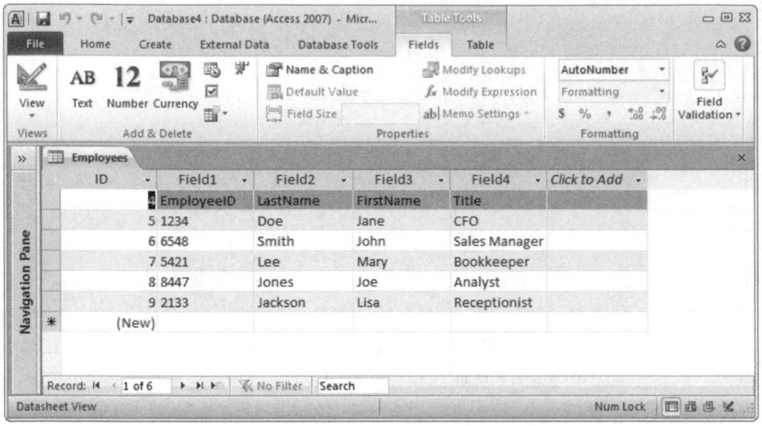

FIGURE 24-1

You'll notice an important distinction between an Access table and an Excel worksheet. Database tables do not have row headers as numbers, or columns designated by letters. Columns (called *fields* in a database environment) rely on being identified by their field headers such as FirstName, LastName, and so on. Rows (called *records*) rely on being identified by one or more *key* fields, or certain properties of other fields such as being empty (*Null*) or having date entries between a start date and end date.

You might also want to surf the Web for sites that list SQL objects and their associated properties and methods. Keep in mind that SQL's capacity for database interaction goes far beyond what you'll need it to do for your Excel projects, so stick with the basics for now when perusing SQL instructional material.

25

Not Gone, Not Forgotten

With each release of Excel, Microsoft typically introduces new features that are meant to help make it easier and more productive to work with your spreadsheets. Over the course of Excel's evolution, older features that were state of the art in their day have been cast aside for newer ways of doing things. Some of those older features are still supported in all versions of Excel, and although they've been largely forgotten, they can still be very useful in some development circumstances.

This lesson looks at two almost-forgotten features: 5.0 dialog sheets and XLM Get.Cell functions. You'll also see examples of the SendKeys method, which is not so much outdated as it is misunderstood. Each of these features can claim its useful place among your collection of VBA tools.

USING DIALOG SHEETS

In Lessons 18, 19, and 20 you learned about UserForms, which first arrived on the Excel scene with ActiveX controls in Office 97. The precursor to UserForms was an interface built from a type of sheet called a *5.0 dialog sheet*, which was used in versions Excel 5 and Excel 95. Dialog sheets served the purpose of constructing a customized dialog box that that has almost entirely been superseded by UserForms and their more programmable ActiveX controls.

I like dialog sheets, even in this modern era of Excel VBA. The dialog sheet is a hidden gem that's been mostly a forgotten art, which makes it look like a special feature when used in the right circumstances.

I am not recommending that you forego UserForms for dialog sheets, but dialog sheets do have several advantages that merit their worth, for example:

➤ Dialog sheets utilize only Forms controls which, unlike ActiveX controls, are fully integrated with Excel and do not cause as many VBA programming errors.

➤ You may come across older workbooks with dialog sheets, so it's a good idea to at least be familiar with them as you would any Excel object.

➤ Dialog sheets are created on the fly, and then deleted automatically, which means the workbook has less overhead without a UserForm hanging around for its next infrequent appearance.

➤ Dialog sheets are fully supported in all versions of Excel up to and including Excel 2010, having backwards compatibility with earlier versions of Excel.

➤ Dialog sheets are a history lesson in the evolution of Excel, providing a sense as to what gave rise to the modern-day UserForm.

➤ Dialog sheets have the intangible "wow" factor; you can program and display a custom UserForm-like dialog box without building a UserForm, with your users appreciating the simple, straightforward design.

What Does a Dialog Sheet Look Like?

When I use dialog sheets, only the dialog box (called the *DialogFrame*) is seen by the user, not the dialog sheet itself. If you'd like to see a dialog sheet, right-click any worksheet tab. From the pop-up menu, select Insert, and on the General tab of the Insert dialog box, select MS Excel 5.0 Dialog. Click OK and you'll insert a dialog sheet that looks like Figure 25-1.

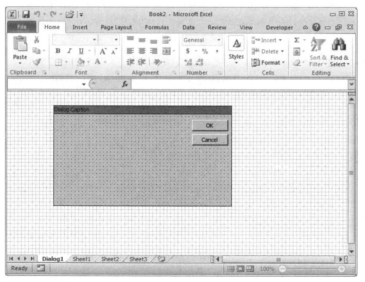

FIGURE 25-1

You can also insert a dialog sheet programmatically, by executing this code line in the Immediate window:

```
ActiveWorkbook.Sheets.Add Type:=xlDialogSheet
```

One look at a dialog sheet and you can see the reason to avoid showing it; they are not pleasant-looking objects. However, what the dialog sheet lacks in attractiveness is compensated for by its ease of integration with Excel due to its use of Forms controls, to help make custom dialog boxes a valuable part of your VBA programming skill set.

> *A downside to dialog sheets is the volume of code they require for being produced, designed, and discarded. The amount of code can be visually daunting at first, but please do not get discouraged. You have already seen most of the kind of code that's involved. The only difference is, unlike a UserForm where you manually draw controls onto the form and then assign code to them, with dialog sheets you are positioning the controls programmatically and assigning their associated code all at the same time. There are notes at each step to explain what's going on.*

You might be surprised at what you can do with dialog sheets. They can produce customized dialog boxes that resemble UserForms in their basic functionality, but they are actually dialog boxes within which you place Forms controls such as Buttons, DropDowns, Option Buttons, Labels, and Edit Boxes. Figure 25-2 shows examples of a few custom dialog boxes that I created using dialog sheets.

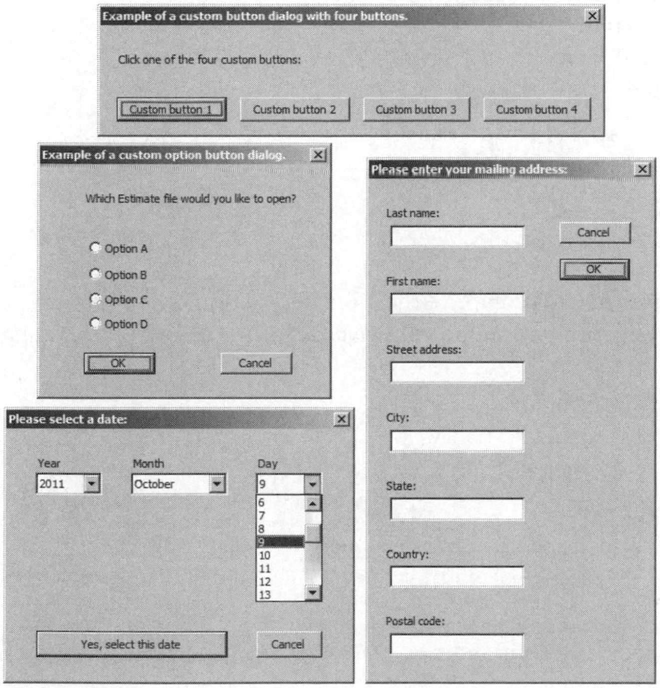

FIGURE 25-2

Option to Show Message Only Once

To see a dialog sheet in action, suppose you maintain an inventory of clothing items and their retail prices, such as shown in Figure 25-3. The prices are important and not meant to be changed without some thought.

If you want to be made aware that a price was changed, you can easily implement a `Worksheet_Change` procedure that informs you of a change having been made in range B2:B10. You might eventually get tired of being constantly reminded if you make changes often, so a built-in utility for turning off the advisement would be nice.

FIGURE 25-3

In Figure 25-4, you see that the price of Jackets was just changed from $65 to $57, and there is your dialog box, dutifully telling you what you already know. If you check the box next to Do Not Show This Message Again, you won't see that dialog box again after making changes to range B2:B10, for the rest of the time the workbook is open.

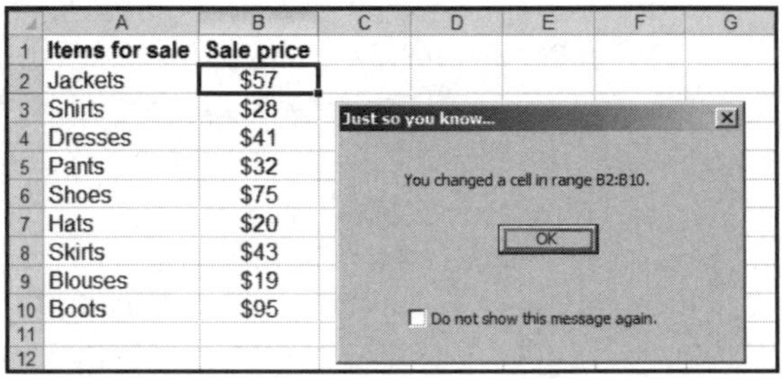

FIGURE 25-4

The following examples of VBA code are what make this possible without a UserForm. First, because this is a `Worksheet_Change` event, place this procedure in the worksheet's module:

```
Private Sub Worksheet_Change(ByVal Target As Range)
If Intersect(Target, Range("B2:B10")) Is Nothing _
Or Target.Cells.Count > 1 Then Exit Sub
Run "MsgBoxShowOnceOption"
End Sub
```

In a standard module, the following three macros comprise the VBA instructions. The primary macro is named `MsgBoxShowOnceOption`, with two supporting macros for the `Check Box` evaluation and the dialog sheet deletion.

```
'Declare Public variables because several modules are involved.
Public dlgShowMessageOnce As DialogSheet
Public blnMessage As Boolean

Private Sub MsgBoxShowOnceOption()
'This macro creates a fresh dialog sheet named "ShowOnce",
'to produce a dialog box that the user can set to stop being shown.

'If the checkbox was checked to not show the message,
'the Boolean variable blnMessage is False, so exit sub.
If blnMessage = False Then Exit Sub

'Declare and define a variable name for the dialog.
Dim strDialogName As String
strDialogName = "ShowOnce"
```

```
'Set ScreenUpdating to False.
Application.ScreenUpdating = False

'Delete the dialog sheet if by chance it exists.
'It will be added in the next step.
On Error Resume Next
Application.DisplayAlerts = False
ActiveWorkbook.DialogSheets(strDialogName).Delete
Application.DisplayAlerts = True
Err.Clear

'Create and name the new dialog sheet, then hide it.
Set dlgShowMessageOnce = ActiveWorkbook.DialogSheets.Add
With dlgShowMessageOnce
.Name = strDialogName
.Visible = xlSheetHidden

'Size the dialog sheet frame (the dialog box you will actually see),
'and give its title bar a meaningful caption.
With .DialogFrame
.Height = 130
.Width = 210
.Caption = "Just so you know..."
End With

'Hide the Cancel default button that comes with dialog sheets,
'as the checkbox is the key to halting the showing of the dialog.
.Buttons("Button 3").Visible = False

'Add a Label at the top of the dialog, distance from
'Left, Top, Width, Height.
.Labels.Add 100, 50, 180, 18
'Caption the Label.
.Labels(1).Caption = "You changed a cell in range B2:B10."

'Position the dialog's default OK button.
With .Buttons("Button 2")
.Visible = True
.Left = 150
.Top = 80
End With

'Add the checkbox with caption, distance from
'Left, Top, Width, Height.
.CheckBoxes.Add 100, 120, 140, 18
With .CheckBoxes(1)
.Caption = "Do not show this message again."
.OnAction = "myCheckBox"
End With

'Set ScreenUpdating to True.
Application.ScreenUpdating = True

If .Show = False Then
'The X Cancel button was clicked on the title bar so delete the dialog sheet.
Application.DisplayAlerts = False
```

```
            .Delete
            Application.DisplayAlerts = True
            End If

            End With 'for the dialog frame.
            End Sub

            Private Sub myCheckBox()
            'If the checkbox is checked (Value = 1) set the Boolean variable to False,
            'otherwise set it to True.
            If dlgShowMessageOnce.CheckBoxes(Application.Caller).Value = 1 Then
            blnMessage = False
            Else
            blnMessage = True
            End If
            End Sub
            'Delete the dialog sheet if it exists.
            Private Sub DeleteDialog()
            With Application
            .ScreenUpdating = False
            .DisplayAlerts = False
            On Error Resume Next
            DialogSheets("ShowOnce").Delete
            Err.Clear
            .DisplayAlerts = True
            .ScreenUpdating = True
            End With
            End Sub
```

A final piece of precautionary code I install in the ThisWorkbook module is to make sure that if the workbook is opened, closed, activated, or deactivated, the custom dialog sheet is deleted if it exists. Sometimes, at a critical moment such as a power failure or some odd circumstance, the dialog sheet might exist in the workbook, and you just want to make sure you cover your bases with no extra dialog sheets having accumulated when you open the workbook again. These workbook-level procedures handle the task of monitoring the proper absence of an unwanted dialog sheet.

```
            'As a precaution, delete the dialog sheet if by chance it exists
            'when the workbook is opened, closed, activated, or deactivated.
            'The default Boolean value is True.

            Private Sub Workbook_Open()
            Run "DeleteDialog"
            blnMessage = True
            End Sub

            Private Sub Workbook_Activate()
            Run "DeleteDialog"
            End Sub

            Private Sub Workbook_Deactivate()
            Run "DeleteDialog"
            End Sub
```

```
Private Sub Workbook_BeforeClose(Cancel As Boolean)
Run "DeleteDialog"
blnMessage = True
ThisWorkbook.Save
End Sub
```

USING XLM GET.CELL FUNCTIONS

Get.Cell is a function from the Excel 4.0 Macro Language (XLM) that returns information about the formatting, location, or contents of a cell. The syntax of the Get.Cell function is *Get.Cell(num, cell reference)*, where the num argument may be one of 66 numbers that correspond to the piece of information being sought.

As an example of how you can benefit from a Get.Cell function, suppose you have a worksheet that contains formulas, text, and empty cells. You can apply Conditional Formatting to the range with the Get.Cell function and its number 48 number argument, which evaluates a cell for the existence of a formula. The following steps lead you through the process, and when completed, your cells will be conditionally formatted in real time to reflect the existence of a formula, or a constant value, or nothing.

1. Press the Ctrl+F3 keys to insert a new name.

2. Depending on the version of Excel you are using, in the Names in Workbook field or the Name field, enter the word **Formulas**. (You can enter most any name you want, but to keep it simple just call it Formulas.)

3. In the Refers To field near the bottom of the dialog box, enter **=GET.CELL(48,INDIRECT("rc",0))**.

4. Click Add, then click OK.

5. Select the range of cells on your worksheet that you want to conditionally format. For this example, select cell A1 to the last row and column of your choice.

6. Open the Conditional Formatting dialog box. If you are using a version prior to Excel 2007, from the menu bar click Format ➪ Conditional Formatting, and select Formula Is from the drop-down menu. If you are using a later version, click the Home tab on the Ribbon, click the Conditional Formatting icon, and click New Rule ➪ Use a Formula to Determine Which Cells to Format.

7. The first Conditional Formatting formula to be entered is **=Formulas**. After that, select your fill color for formula-containing cells and click OK.

8. While still in the Conditional Formatting dialog box, click the Add button.

9. Enter a second formula for text-containing cells, which is **=AND(LEN(A1)>0,ISTEXT("rc"))**.

10. Click the Format button, select the kind of formatting you want for cells containing constants, and then click OK. Click OK again to exit the Conditional Formatting dialog box.

Now, formula-containing cells will be shaded the color you specified in step 7, constant-containing cells will be formatted as you specified in step 10, and empty cells will have no Conditional Formatting. Microsoft has a downloadable help file for Excel 4.0 macros at this address:

```
http://support.microsoft.com/default.aspx?scid=KB;EN-US;Q128185&ID=KB;
EN-US;Q128185&FR=1.
```

USING THE SENDKEYS METHOD

The `Application.SendKeys` method sends keystrokes through VBA to the active application. The term "active application" plays a key role in understanding when and when not to use `SendKeys`. You'll encounter some situations where `SendKeys` is the only viable alternative, and other situations where `SendKeys` should not be used.

Executing a `SendKeys` command is a way of programmatically pressing the keys on your keyboard. If, as a service of convenience to the users of your workbook, they need to perform an edit by appending some text to the existing value, you can get them started with this set of `SendKeys`, which has the effect of double-clicking the cell and having the cursor blinking at the end of the current value:

```
SendKeys "{F2}"
SendKeys "{End}"
```

This use of `SendKeys` should normally pose no problem. `SendKeys` gets more of a bad rap than it should because when executed in rapid-fire succession in loops or upon inactive applications, which is an ill-advised programming practice, the code compilation process cannot catch up with the execution process after a time, and errors result when the intended window or object of interest is not the proper focus. In the preceding example, the use of `SendKeys` is fine because it's just one command in a small macro for a cell that is already selected.

`SendKeys` is a better approach in the case of showing DataForms because the `ShowDataForm` command will error if the source data's header row starts on a row below row 2 (that is, row 3 or below), where rows 1 and 2 are empty. The `Application.SendKeys "%DO"` command will call the DataForm regardless of what row the source data starts on. Error traps and conditional statements for data starting on row 1 or row 3 are superfluous when a simple `SendKeys` command can handle the situation right then and there, whatever the first row of source data.

> *You may be curious about the syntax for* `SendKeys`. *The keys for Alt, Ctrl, and Shift are represented by the characters %, ^, and +, respectively. For example, the expression "%c" means Alt+C; "^C" means Ctrl+C (which means copy); and "+C" means Shift+C. The Enter key is represented by the tilde (~) character, and keys such as Home, End, and Tab are represented by* `SendKeys` *as* {Home},{End}, *and* {Tab}.

As a further example, this will take you to the last row of the DataForm, assuming column B is a part of its source table:

```
Cells(Rows.Count, 2).End(xlUp).Select
SendKeys "%DO"
```

Finally, the following pair of code lines will open the DataForm and get you ready for entering the next record. This example also shows how the Select statement has its place as well; sometimes it's okay to select a cell when working with it.

```
Cells(Rows.Count, 2).End(xlUp).Select
SendKeys "%DO%W"
```

SendKeys is as safe as any other method when used with common sense for awareness in your coding as to what application and window are active at the point of execution. You see another example of SendKeys in the Try It section.

TRY IT

In this lesson, you compose a short Worksheet_Selection procedure that uses the SendKeys method to automatically expand the drop-down list of a cell containing Data Validation.

Lesson Requirements

Using the SendKeys method with the Worksheet_Selection event, if a worksheet cell has Data Validation, make the Data Validation drop-down list appear automatically when the cell is selected. If the cell is not validated, the SendKeys instruction is bypassed. To get the sample database files you can download Lesson 25 from the book's website at www.wrox.com.

Step-by-Step

1. On a new worksheet, select cell C3 and establish Data Validation to allow a list, such as the seven days of the week. Be sure that the In-Cell Dropdown option is selected on the Settings tab of the Data Validation dialog.

2. Select any cell other than C3 on that worksheet.

3. Right-click the worksheet tab and select View Code.

4. In the Object drop-down list, select Worksheet. By default, the Worksheet_Selection event line and its accompanying End Sub line will appear in the worksheet module, which will look like this:

```
Private Sub Worksheet_SelectionChange(ByVal Target As Range)

End Sub
```

5. For the first line of code, instruct VBA to do nothing if more than one cell is selected. The code will be of value only when one cell at a time is selected.

```
If Target.Cells.Count> 1 Then Exit Sub
```

6. Declare a `Variant` type variable that will verify the Data Validation Type in the selected cell:

```
Dim dvCell As Variant
```

7. Insert an error bypass with the `On Error Resume Next` statement to avoid a runtime error when a selected cell does not contain Data Validation:

```
On Error Resume Next
```

8. Assign the Data Validation Type to the variable:

```
dvCell = Target.Validation.Type
```

9. If there is no VBA runtime error, that is, if the selected cell contains Data Validation, execute the `SendKeys` method that simulates the keyboard action of pressing the Alt and Down Arrow keys. The optional True keyword refers to the Wait argument of SendKeys, for VBA to wait until the SendKeys action is completed before executing the next line of code.

```
If Err = 0 Then SendKeys "%{down}", True
```

10. Clear the `Error` object in case a runtime error did occur:

```
Err.Clear
```

11. The entire `Worksheet_Selection` procedure will look as follows:

```
Private Sub Worksheet_SelectionChange(ByVal Target As Range)
If Target.Cells.Count> 1 Then Exit Sub
Dim dvCell As Variant
On Error Resume Next
dvCell = Target.Validation.Type
If Err = 0 Then SendKeys "%{down}", True
Err.Clear
End Sub
```

12. Press Alt+Q to return to your worksheet. Select a few cells, then select cell C3. When you do so, its Data Validation drop-down list will appear, as shown in Figure 25-5.

	A	B	C	D	E
1					
2			**Enter a weekday:**		
3					
4			Sunday		
5			Monday		
			Tuesday		
6			Wednesday		
7			Thursday		
			Friday		
8			Saturday		
9					
10					

FIGURE 25-5

 Please select Lesson 25 on the DVD to view the video that accompanies this lesson.

SECTION V
Interacting with Other Office Applications

▶ **LESSON 26:** Overview of Office Automation from Excel

▶ **LESSON 27:** Working with Word from Excel

▶ **LESSON 28:** Working with Outlook from Excel

▶ **LESSON 29:** Working with Access from Excel

▶ **LESSON 30:** Working with PowerPoint from Excel

26

Overview of Office Automation from Excel

As you may recall from Lesson 1, Visual Basic for Applications is a programming language created by Microsoft to automate operations in applications that support it, such as Excel. VBA is also the language that manipulates Microsoft Office applications in Access, Word, PowerPoint, and Outlook. So far, the focus of this book has been on running VBA from Excel, for the purpose of acting directly upon Excel in some way.

This section shows how to control other Office applications from Excel, using the same VBA programming language with which you are now familiar, but using a different set of methods and statements with which those other Office applications are familiar. The reasons for interacting with other Office applications might not be for the purpose of changing your Excel workbook application, but they will always be for the purpose of making your workbook projects more robust, versatile, and easier to use when the situation calls for it.

WHY AUTOMATE ANOTHER APPLICATION?

In the dawn of this modern era of personal computers, it was rare that two or more separate applications were able to communicate with each other. For two applications to share the same information, you usually had to retype the information manually into the other application that needed it. Today, thanks to the advances of drag and drop, and copy and paste, it has become a simple matter to share data across many applications.

The business of Excel is to perform calculations and analyze data. You can enter and edit text in Excel, but it is not a word processor. You can build data tables and compare their information, but Excel is not a relational database application. You can create charts and graphics in Excel but they cannot be presented in a sophisticated slide show format. You can send a workbook through e-mail but Excel cannot manage your calendar or incoming e-mails the way an e-mail client can.

You get the idea — sooner or later you'll need to perform some kind of operation that another application was especially made to handle. This lesson lays the groundwork for you to understand Office automation from Excel, and the theory behind some best practices in doing so.

UNDERSTANDING OFFICE AUTOMATION

Where VBA is concerned, the only difference between Excel, Word, Access, PowerPoint, and Outlook lies in their object models. Each of these applications can access another's object model, so long as the target application has been properly installed on the host computer. Controlling one Office application from another becomes a simple matter of knowing how to link to the object model of the Office application you want to control.

The term "automation" is an Office programmer's way of referring to the VBA technology that provides the ability to manipulate another application's objects. Though VBA is the common language among Office applications, the respective object models differ in their objects' names, methods, and properties. Both Excel and Word have a `Range` object but with different properties. Excel has a `Workbooks` object, which is the counterpart to PowerPoint's `Presentations` object.

For Excel to access another Office application's object model, a connection needs to be established to that target application. Two options for doing this exist: one option is called *early binding*, and the other option is called *late binding*. The term "binding" refers to the verification that an object exists, and that the command to manipulate that object's methods and properties is valid.

Early Binding

With early binding, a reference is established with the target application's object library before you write your macro, so that the application's objects, methods, and properties can be accessed in your code. For example, if you are using Office 2010 and you want to write a macro to open Word and edit a document, you would first need to establish a reference to the Microsoft Word 14.0 Object Library. To do that, you can go to the Visual Basic Editor, and from the menu bar click Tools ⇨ References and scroll to select the reference, as shown in Figure 26-1.

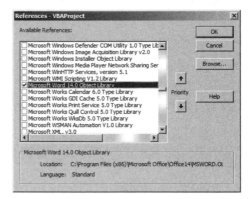

FIGURE 26-1

VBA sees versions of Microsoft Office as numbers, not names. For example, VBA knows Office 2003 as version 11, Office 2007 as version 12, and Office 2010 as version 14 (Microsoft knowingly skipped number 13). Therefore, if you are working with Office 2007 at home, you'd have Word 12 listed in your VBA References, but if you are using Office 2010 at work, you'd see Word 14 listed.

Once you have established the proper reference, you can write a macro using early binding that will, for example, open a Word document in Office 2010. Suppose you already have a Word document named `myWordDoc.docx` that you keep in the path C:\Your\File\Path\. This macro will open that document, using early binding:

```
Sub EarlyBindingTest()
Dim wdapp As Word.Application, wddoc As Word.Document
Set wdapp = New Word.Application
wdapp.Visible = True
Set wddoc = wdapp.Documents.Open(Filename:="C:\Your\File\Path\myWordDoc.docx")
End Sub
```

When you attempt to run this macro, you would immediately know if you did not properly establish the Word 14.0 library reference, because you would be prompted by a compile error message, as shown in Figure 26-2.

As you compose a macro using early binding, you will have the benefit of VBA's IntelliSense feature, where objects and properties pop up as you type your code's object references. And, macros with early binding run faster than macros performing the same task with late binding, because a reference has already been established to the target application's objects, methods, and properties.

FIGURE 26-2

> *If your macro runs without errors but you don't see a Word document, or you don't even see Word on your task bar, it could be that you really did create a new instance of Word, but it is not visible. In the Immediate window, type* `Word.Application.Visible = True` *and press Enter.*

So then, why would you ever *not* want to use early binding? Actually, there is a very good reason why not: the referenced object (Word 14.0 in this example) must exist on the computer. If it does not exist, an error will occur such as shown in Figure 26-2.

The concern is, unless you are composing your Office automation macros to be run on a system that you know for a fact will (a) be installed with the target application, and (b) will have the proper object library reference established in advance, chances are pretty good the macro will fail using early binding. And with new Office versions being released every few years, when you upgrade your Office version you will need to edit all the macros in which you utilized early binding that will then be referring to an outdated earlier version.

Late Binding

With late binding, you declare an object variable that refers to the target application, just as you would with early binding. However, instead of setting the variable to a specific (in this case) Word object, you create an object called a Word application.

If you use late binding, you do not use Tools ⇨ References to set a reference because you do not know which Word object library version will be on a user's machine. Instead, you use code to create the object. The following macro named `LateBindingTest` accomplishes the same task as the `EarlyBindingTest`, by opening a specific Word document:

```
Sub LateBindingTest()
Dim WdApp As Object, wddoc As Object
Set WdApp = CreateObject("Word.Application")
WdApp.Visible = True
Set wddoc = WdApp.Documents.Open(Filename:="C:\Your\File\Path\myWordDoc.docx")
End Sub
```

In a nutshell, when you declare a variable `As Object` and set it as `CreateObject`, VBA doesn't know whether the object is a cell, a worksheet, a Word application, or any other object. The code goes through a series of tests behind the scenes until it finds the correct application for the use intended by your code. That's the essential reason why late binding takes longer to execute.

Which One Is Better?

For my money, even with moderately sized macros, the extra seconds of run time due to late binding make up for the headaches of trying to accommodate every version of your target Office application, from 2000 through 2010. You will find that the VBA skills you are acquiring will lead to composing macros that others will use, and you'll never know what Office versions are installed on users' systems. People have varying opinions on the merits of early versus late binding, so consider the pros and cons of both methods to decide which approach is best for you.

TRY IT

In this lesson, you compose a macro using late binding that opens a Presentation file in PowerPoint.

Lesson Requirements

For this lesson, you first create a PowerPoint presentation, name that file PowerPointExample1, and save it into the folder path C:\Your\File\Path\. You'll compose a macro that will open the PowerPoint file, taking into consideration that the Office version is unknown, so the late binding method will be utilized.

Step-by-Step

1. Open a new workbook and press Alt+F11 to go to the Visual Basic Editor.

2. From the menu at the top of the VBE, click Insert ⇨ Module.

3. In the module you just created, type **Sub OpenPowerPoint** and press Enter. VBA will automatically place a pair of empty parentheses at the end of the `Sub` line, followed by an empty line, and the `End Sub` line below that. Your macro will look like this so far:

```
Sub OpenPowerPoint()

End Sub
```

4. Declare variables for the file path, the PowerPoint file name, and the file extension. The reason for the variable extension is that starting with Office version 2007, PowerPoint file extensions are commonly .pptx or .pptm. Prior to 2007, the extension for PowerPoint files was simply .ppt.

```
Dim myPath As String, myFileName As String, myExtension As String
```

5. Define the variables for myPath and myFileName:

```
myPath = "C:\Your\File\Path\"
myFileName = "PowerPointExample1"
```

6. Use an If structure to define the extension String variable. Note the Val statement, which ensures the Office application version is regarded as a number for the logical evaluation of being less than or equal to version 11, which is Office 2003.

```
If Val(Application.Version) <= 11 Then
myExtension = ".ppt"
Else
myExtension = ".pptx"
End If
```

7. Declare the PowerPoint application object and set it using the CreateObject method for late binding:

```
Dim appPPT As Object
Set appPPT = CreateObject("PowerPoint.Application")
```

8. When opening other applications, don't forget to make them visible:

```
appPPT.Visible = True
```

9. Compose the Open statement for PowerPoint that combines the myPath, myFileName, and myExtension variables:

```
appPPT.Presentations.Open Filename:=myPath & myFileName & myExtension
```

10. When completed, the macro will look like this, with comments that have been added to explain each step:

```
Sub OpenPowerPoint()
'Declare variables for path, file name and file extension.
Dim myPath As String, myFileName As String, myExtension As String
'Define the myPath and myFileName variables.
myPath = "C:\Your\File\Path\"
myFileName = "PowerPointExample1"
'Using an If structure and depending on the host computer's Office version,
'define the extension of the PowerPoint file.
If Val(Application.Version) = 11 Then
myExtension = ".ppt"
Else
myExtension = ".pptx"
End If
```

```
'Declare a variable for what will be the PowerPoint object.
'Set the object to late binding by using the CreateObject method.
Dim appPPT As Object
Set appPPT = CreateObject("PowerPoint.Application")
'Make sure you include the command to make the application visible.
appPPT.Visible = True
'Open the PowerPoint file.
appPPT.Presentations.Open Filename:=myPath & myFileName & myExtension
End Sub
```

11. Press Alt+Q to return to the worksheet. Press Alt+F8 to show the macro dialog box, and test the macro by selecting the macro name and clicking the Run button.

To get the sample database files, you can download Lesson 26 from the book's website at www.wrox.com.

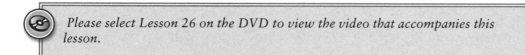

Please select Lesson 26 on the DVD to view the video that accompanies this lesson.

Working with Word from Excel

With the ubiquitous presence of Microsoft Office, a common task is to create and maintain documents in Microsoft Word that either accompany, or include as part of their narrative content, data and information from Excel workbooks. From your own experience, you have probably seen situations that call for information from Word documents to be appended, printed, or exported from Word into your Excel workbook.

Word and Excel work very well together in sharing data across their respective applications. These tasks can be automated with VBA macros right from Excel, to provide your workbook projects with robust and user-friendly methods of integrating data with Word.

ACTIVATING A WORD DOCUMENT

In Lesson 26, you saw a macro named `LateBindingTest` that opens a Word document named `myWordDoc.docx`. However, with the everyday world being what it is, a seemingly simple task like activating a Word document involves a few considerations:

➤ Word might not be open.

➤ Word is open but the document itself is not open.

➤ The Word document is already open.

➤ The Word document you want to open does not exist.

For such tasks that have multiple considerations, the "divide and conquer" approach is a good way to cover your bases. If you take each consideration in turn, you can craft a single macro to handle the entire process seamlessly.

Activating the Word Application

The basic premise of activating Word is that you must tell Excel you are leaving it altogether, for a totally different application destination. The GetObject function is a reliable way to do this, as shown in the following macro:

```
Sub ActivateWord()
Dim wdApp As Object
Set wdApp = GetObject(, "Word.Application")
wdApp.Activate
End Sub
```

The GetObjectfunction has two arguments, the first of which is an optional *pathname* argument that tells VBA where to look for a specified object. Because the pathname is not specified (which it need not be because it is optional), GetObject activates Word, because Word.Application is the object being specified in the second argument.

But what if Word is not open? If you try running the ActivateWord macro without Word being open, a runtime error will occur because VBA is being told to activate an object that is not able to be activated. You need to insert an error bypass in your macro to tell VBA to activate Word *only* if Word is open, and to open and then activate Word *only* if Word is closed.

You can accomplish this with the On Error Resume Next statement that monitors runtime error number 429, which is the VBA error number that occurs with the GetObject function if Word is not open. In that case, VBA will open a new instance of Word, as shown in the following modified ActivateWord macro:

```
Sub ActivateWord()
Dim wdApp As Object
On Error Resume Next
Set wdApp = GetObject(, "Word.Application")
If Err.Number = 429 Then
Err.Clear
Set wdApp = CreateObject("Word.Application")
wdApp.Visible = True
End If
wdApp.Activate
End Sub
```

Opening and Activating a Word Document

Now that you have Word open, it's reasonable to assume that the next item on your agenda is to open an existing Word document, or to create a new Word document. If the plan is to open an existing document, a wise programming practice is to account for the possibility that the document does not exist in the specified folder path.

> *You never know — files get deleted, or have their names changed, or get moved from one folder to another. A VBA runtime error will eventually come back to bite you when a command is given to open a file having an unrecognized name or location.*

For demonstration purposes, say you maintain a Word document named `myWordDoc.docx` in the folder path C:\Your\File\Path\. Before you attempt to open the document, check the directory to make sure it resides in the expected folder path. If the Word document is not where your macro thinks it should be, you'll want to exit the macro with a Message Box informing the user why the process could not be completed.

Finally, your macro will need to keep its eyes on the prize: the Word document that might already be open if Word was already open. A lot to remember but that's what macros are for…tell them once and they do what they're told. Here is the complete modification of the `ActivateWord` macro that wraps it all up into a single package:

```
Sub ActivateWord()

'Declare Object variables for the Word application and document.
Dim WdApp As Object, wddoc As Object
'Declare a String variable for the example document's
'name and folder path.
Dim strDocName As String

'On Error statement if Word is not already open.
On Error Resume Next
'Activate Word if it is already open.
Set WdApp = GetObject(, "Word.Application")
If Err.Number = 429 Then
Err.Clear
'Create a Word application if Word is not already open.
Set WdApp = CreateObject("Word.Application")
End If
'Make sure the Word application is visible.
WdApp.Visible = True

'Define the strDocName String variable.
strDocName = "C:\Your\File\Path\myWordDoc.docx"

'Check the directory for the presence of the document
'name in the folder path.
'If it is not recognized, inform the user of that
'fact and exit the macro.
If Dir(strDocName) = "" Then
MsgBox "The file myWordDoc.docx" & vbCrLf & _
"was not found in the folder path" & vbCrLf & _
"C:\Your\File\Path\.", _
vbExclamation, _
"Sorry, that document name does not exist."
Exit Sub
End If

'Activate the Word application.
WdApp.Activate
'Set the Object variable for the Word document's full
'name and folder path.
Set wddoc = WdApp.Documents(strDocName)
'If the Word document is not already open, then open it.
If wddoc Is Nothing Then Set wddoc = WdApp.Documents.Open(strDocName)
```

```
'The document is open, so activate it.
wddoc.Activate

'Release the system memory that was reserved for the two
'Object variables.
Set wddoc = Nothing
Set WdApp = Nothing

End Sub
```

CREATING A NEW WORD DOCUMENT

You can easily create a new Word document from scratch with the statement

```
WdApp.Documents.Add
```

You'll typically create a new Word document for the purpose of holding some kind of narrative or data, which means you'll want to save your new document. Tapping into many of the same processes that were covered in the `ActivateWord` macro, here is an example of a macro that creates and saves a new Word document:

```
Sub CreateWordDoc()

'Declare Object variables for the Word application
'and new document.
Dim objWordApp As Object, objWordDoc As Object

'On Error statement if Word is not already open.
On Error Resume Next
'Activate Word if it is already open.
Set objWordApp = GetObject(, "Word.Application")
If Err.Number = 429 Then
Err.Clear
'Create a Word application if Word is not already open.
Set objWordApp = CreateObject("Word.Application")
End If

'Make sure the Word application is visible.
objWordApp.Visible = True

'Activate the Word application.
objWordApp.Activate

'Create your new Word document.
Set objWordDoc = objWordApp.Documents.Add
'Save your new Word document in a folder path.
objWordDoc.SaveAs "C:\Your\File\Path\myNewWordDoc.docx"

'Release the system memory that was reserved for the
'two Object variables.
Set objWordApp = Nothing
Set objWordDoc = Nothing

End Sub
```

COPYING AN EXCEL RANGE TO A WORD DOCUMENT

Suppose you have a table of data in your Excel workbook on Sheet1 in range A1:H25. You want to export the table into an existing Word document named myWordDoc.docx, which you know exists and you know is closed. To make it interesting, say the task calls for the following set of actions:

1. Open Word.

2. Open myWordDoc.docx.

3. Export the data table from Excel into the myWordDoc.docx document.

4. Save myWordDoc.docx.

5. Close myWordDoc.docx.

The following macro accomplishes this task very quickly. Note that you can copy a worksheet's used range or current region of a cell; you do not need to refer to a specific range address as this example does.

```
Sub ExportFromExcelToWord()
'Turn off ScreenUpdating
Application.ScreenUpdating = False
'Copy the Excel range to be exported.
Worksheets("Sheet1").Range("A1:H25").Copy
'Declare object variables.
Dim WdApp As Object, wddoc As Object
'Open Word
Set WdApp = CreateObject("Word.Application")
'Open the Word document that will accept the exported data.
Set wddoc - WdApp.Documents.Open(Filename:="C:\Your\File\Path\myWordDoc.docx")
'Paste the copied date from Excel to the Word document.
wddoc.Range.Paste
'Close the Word document and save changes
wddoc.Close savechanges:=True
'Quit the Word application.
WdApp.Quit
'Set the Object variables to Nothing to release system memory.
Set wddoc = Nothing
Set WdApp = Nothing
'Exit Copy mode
Application.CutCopyMode = False
'Turn ScreenUpdating back on.
Application.ScreenUpdating = True
End Sub
```

PRINTING A WORD DOCUMENT FROM EXCEL

To print a Word document, you can use the PrintOut method to print the entire document, or only a portion of the document if you so choose. The following macro shows an example of opening and printing a Word document:

```
Sub PrintWordDoc()
'Declare object variables.
```

```
Dim WdApp As Object, wddoc As Object
'Open Word
Set WdApp = CreateObject("Word.Application")
'Open the Word document to be printed.
Set wddoc = WdApp.Documents.Open(Filename:="C:\Your\File\Path\myWordDoc.docx")
'Print the entire Word document.
WdApp.ActiveDocument.PrintOut
'Give the print job 5 seconds to complete before closing Word.
Application.Wait Now + TimeSerial(0, 0, 5)
'Close the Word document, no need to save changes.
wddoc.Close savechanges:=False
'Quit the Word application.
WdApp.Quit
'Set the Object variables to Nothing to release system memory.
Set wddoc = Nothing
Set WdApp = Nothing
End Sub
```

> *You might have noticed that this macro, and a couple of others in this lesson, do not include the statement to make the Word application visible. It's easy to forget that you have an open application if you cannot see it. The point to be made is, do remember to include the* Close *and* Quit *statements in your macros when opening applications. Otherwise, you'll get read-only messages, and then error messages when rerunning the macro, which to VBA will be interpreted as an attempt to re-open a file that is already open.*

If you want to print only a portion of the Word document, for example only page 2, then in the preceding PrintWordDoc macro, substitute the statement

```
WdApp.ActiveDocument.PrintOut
```

with

```
WdApp.ActiveDocument.PrintOut pages:="2"
```

IMPORTING A WORD DOCUMENT TO EXCEL

There may be times when you want to import some text from Word into Excel. Admittedly this is not a common task, because Excel cells are not meant to serve as word processing instruments for extensive amounts of text. But because it's possible, here's a macro that opens a Word document, copies the second paragraph, and pastes that text into cell A1 of Sheet1:

```
Sub ImportToExcelFromWord()
'Declare object variables.
Dim WdApp As Object, wddoc As Object
'Open Word
Set WdApp = CreateObject("Word.Application")
```

```
'Open the Word document
Set wddoc = WdApp.Documents.Open(Filename:="C:\Your\File\Path\myWordDoc.docx")
'Copy paragraph 2
wddoc.Paragraphs(2).Range.Copy
'Activate your workbook and go to the paste destination of Sheet1 cell A1.
Application.GotoThisWorkbook.Worksheets("Sheet1").Range("A1")
'Paste paragraph 2 from the Word document.
ActiveSheet.Paste
'Close the Word document, no need to save changes.
wddoc.Close Savechanges:=False
'Quit the Word application.
WdApp.Quit
'Set the Object variables to Nothing to release system memory.
Set wddoc = Nothing
Set WdApp = Nothing
End Sub
```

TRY IT

In this lesson, you write a macro that asks for the name of a Word document and opens that Word document if it exists in a particular folder.

Lesson Requirements

For this lesson, you write a macro that uses an InputBox to ask for the name of a Word document to be opened from a predetermined folder path. If the Word document exists, it is opened, but if it does not exist, the user is advised of that. To get the sample database files you can download Lesson 27 from the book's website at www.wrox.com.

Step-by-Step

1. From any worksheet in your Excel workbook, press Alt+F11 to go to the Visual Basic Editor.

2. From the VBE menu, click Insert ⇨ Module.

3. In the module you just created, type **Sub OpenRequestedWordDoc** and press Enter. VBA will automatically place a pair of empty parentheses at the end of the Sub line, followed by an empty line, and the End Sub line below that. Your macro will look like this so far:

   ```
   Sub OpenRequestedWordDoc()

   End Sub
   ```

4. Declare a String type variable for the predetermined folder path:

   ```
   Dim myPath As String
   ```

5. Define the String type variable for the example folder path:

   ```
   myPath = "C:\Your\File\Path\"
   ```

6. Declare a `String` type variable for the anticipated `InputBox` entry:

```
Dim myFileName As String
```

7. Show the `InputBox` to ask the user for the name of the Word document to be opened from the predetermined folder path:

```
myFileName = InputBox _
("Enter the full Word document name to be opened" & Chr(10) & _
"from the folder path " & myPath & ":", _
"What file name with extension do you wish to open?", _
"YourDocumentName.docx")
```

8. Exit the macro if nothing is entered or if the Cancel button is clicked:

```
If myFileName = "" Then Exit Sub
```

9. Declare a `String` type variable for the combined folder path and document name:

```
Dim myDocName As String
```

10. Define the `String` type variable for the combined folder path and document name:

```
myDocName = myPath & myFileName
```

11. Check to see if the Word document name exists in the folder path. If it does not, advise the user and exit the macro.

```
If Dir(myDocName) = "" Then
MsgBox "The file " & myFileName & vbCrLf & _
"was not found in the folder path" & vbCrLf & _
myPath & ".", _
vbExclamation, _
"No such animal."
Exit Sub
End If
```

12. At this point, the Word document is determined to exist in the folder. Declare `Object` variables for the Word application and the Word document:

```
Dim appWord As Object, wdDoc As Object
```

13. Using late binding in this example, create a Word application:

```
Set appWord = CreateObject("Word.Application")
```

14. Make the created Word application visible:

```
appWord.Visible = True
```

15. Open the requested Word document name:

```
Set wdDoc = appWord.Documents.Open(myDocName)
```

16. Release the reserved memory in VBA for the declared `Object` type variables now that they have served their purpose and are no longer needed:

```
Set wdDoc = Nothing
Set appWord = Nothing
```

17. Go ahead and test your macro, which will look like this in its entirety:

```
Sub OpenRequestedWordDoc()

'Declare a String variable for the predetermined folder path.
Dim myPath As String
'Define the String variable with the example folder path.
myPath = "C:\Your\File\Path\"

'Declare a String variable for the anticipated InputBox entry.
Dim myFileName As String

'Show the InputBox to ask the user for the name of the Word
'document they want to open from the predetermined folder path.
myFileName = InputBox _
("Enter the full Word document name to be opened" & Chr(10) & _
"from the folder path " & myPath & ":", _
"What file name with extension do you wish to open?", _
"YourDocumentName.docx")

'Exit the macro if nothing is entered or the Cancel button is clicked.
If myFileName = "" Then Exit Sub

'Declare a String variable for the combined folder path
'and document name.
Dim myDocName As String
'Define the String variable for the combined folder path
'and document name.
myDocName = myPath & myFileName

'Check to see if the Word document name actually exists
'in the folder path.
'If it does not, then advise the user and exit the macro.
If Dir(myDocName) = "" Then
MsgBox "The file " & myFileName & vbCrLf & _
"was not found in the folder path" & vbCrLf & _
myPath & ".", _
vbExclamation, _
"No such animal."
Exit Sub
End If

'At this point, the Word document is determined to exist
'in the folder.
'Declare Object variables for the Word application and
'the Word document.
Dim appWord As Object, wdDoc As Object
```

```
'Using late binding in this example, create a Word application.
Set appWord = CreateObject("Word.Application")
'Make the created Word application visible.
appWord.Visible = True
'Open the requested Word document name.
Set wdDoc = appWord.Documents.Open(myDocName)
'Release the reserved memory in VBA for the declared Object variables
'now that they have served their purpose and are no longer needed.
Set wdDoc = Nothing
Set appWord = Nothing

End Sub
```

 Please select Lesson 27 on the DVD to view the video that accompanies this lesson.

28

Working with Outlook from Excel

Microsoft Outlook is the e-mail client application that is included in Microsoft's Office suite. In addition to e-mail management, Outlook also provides personal information management capabilities with its Calendar, Contacts, and Task Manager features. Each of these components in Outlook can be controlled from Excel with VBA.

> *With all the competing e-mail clients to choose from, Outlook continues to be far and away the world's most popularly used e-mail application. Chances are pretty good that Outlook is your e-mail client at work or at home, or it is being used by the recipients of e-mails you send.*

OPENING OUTLOOK

Before diving into the programming of Outlook from Excel, it's important to be aware of a particular design distinction of Outlook that is different than Excel, Word, Access, or PowerPoint. Unlike those other Office applications for which you can create multiple instances, Microsoft designed Outlook, when serving as a default e-mail client, to provide for only one instance to be open at a time.

> *As with any application, ways exist to circumvent Outlook's resistance to multiple open instances, but why anyone would want to force that is beyond me. When it comes to handling e-mails, tasks, and calendars, it's just common sense to have only a single instance of Outlook open at any one time.*

The following macro first checks to see if Outlook is already open, and if so, Outlook is activated. If Outlook happens to be closed, an Outlook application is created using the late binding method.

```
Sub OpenOutlook()

'Declare and establish the Object variables for Outlook.
Dim objOutlook As Object
Dim objNameSpace As Object
Dim objInbox As Object
Set objOutlook = CreateObject("Outlook.Application")
Set objNameSpace = objOutlook.GetNamespace("MAPI")
Set objInbox = objNameSpace.Folders(1)

'Activate Outlook if it is already open, or display Outlook's
'application object interface if it is closed.
On Error Resume Next
AppActivate ("Outlook")
If Err.Number <> 0 Then objInbox.Display
Err.Clear

End Sub
```

> The `CreateObject` *method provides an optional second argument for applications residing on a server, for example:* `Set objOutlook = CreateObject("Outlook.Application", "")`.

COMPOSING AN E-MAIL IN OUTLOOK FROM EXCEL

Most of the time, when you open Excel, whether manually or with VBA, it's for the purpose of doing something, such as to receive or send e-mails, but also to update your calendar or manage your task list. Building upon the previous code that opens or activates Outlook, this section explains how to compose and send a complete e-mail message.

Creating a MailItem Object

Where VBA is concerned, `MailItem` is an Outlook object that you know (no doubt all too well) as a typical e-mail message that arrives in your Inbox. The `MailItem` object is made up of the familiar fields "To," "CC," and "Subject." The other components of the `MailItem` object are the "Body" where you type the text of your message; an optional level of Importance; and maybe an attachment.

When you want to compose an e-mail with VBA, you declare a variable for the `MailItem` object and set it as a created item of the Outlook application object. For example, the following macro would create an e-mail message:

```
Sub SendEmail()
'Declare and establish the Object variables for Outlook.
Dim objOutlook As Object
Dim objNameSpace As Object
```

```
Dim objInbox As Object
Set objOutlook = CreateObject("Outlook.Application")
Set objNameSpace = objOutlook.GetNamespace("MAPI")
Set objInbox = objNameSpace.Folders(1)

'Activate Outlook if it is already open, or display Outlook's
'application object interface if it is closed.
On Error Resume Next
AppActivate ("Outlook")
If Err.Number <> 0 Then objInbox.Display
Err.Clear


Dim objMailItem As Object
Set objMailItem = objOutlook.CreateItem(1)
With objMailItem
.To = "someone@somewhere.com"
.CC = "anyone@anywhere.com"
.Subject = "Testing my email code"
.Importance = 1 'Sets it as Normal importance (Low = 0 and High = 2)
.Body = "Hello, this is a test. Have a nice day."
.Attachments.Add "C:\Your\File\Path\YourFileName.xlsx"
.Display 'Change to Send if you don't want to review the email before sending.
End With

End Sub
```

> *A couple of FYIs: The* `Importance` *property is optional; you don't need to include it. If you do include it as I did with this example, the "1" is a reference to Normal Importance. Low Importance would be "0" and High Importance would be "2." Also, in all the e-mail examples in this lesson, "Display" is utilized rather than "Send," so that when you test these examples, you can actually see the resulting* `MailItem` *object.*

Transferring an Excel Range to the Body of Your E-mail

In the preceding example of composing a `MailItem` object, the body of the e-mail message was hard-entered into the macro, with this statement:

```
.Body = "Hello, this is a test. Have a nice day."
```

You might be interested to know that you can represent a range of worksheet data in the body of an e-mail message. One way to accomplish that is to loop through the cells and create a text string, with a line break character to simulate each row item. Figure 28-1 shows a simple list that will be referred to in this example.

	A	B	C
1	Employee Names		
2	Mary		
3	Jane		
4	Jack		
5	Mike		
6	Stan		
7	Dana		
8	Adam		
9	Lisa		
10	Steven		
11			
12			

FIGURE 28-1

To copy the list, declare a `String` variable for the text values as you loop through each cell in the list, and declare `Long` variables for the count of rows and columns in the range you are copying. In this example it is a single column being copied. However, the range you want to copy might have an unknown number of rows and columns to be represented in your e-mail. The following example takes into consideration a dynamic range based on the `CurrentRegion` property of cell A1:

```
Dim strtext As String
Dim xRow As Long, xColumn As Long
For xRow = 1 To Range("A1").CurrentRegion.Rows.Count
For xColumn = 1 To Range("A1").CurrentRegion.Columns.Count
strtext = strtext & " " & Range("A1").Cells(xRow, xColumn).Value
Next xColumn
strtext = strtext & Chr(10)
Next xRow
```

Putting It All Together

The following macro ties together all the previous code examples in this lesson. Figure 28-2 shows what your e-mail would look like in Outlook 2010 after running the macro named `ExampleEmail`.

```
Sub ExampleEmail()

'Declare and establish the Object variables for Outlook.
Dim objOutlook As Object
Dim objNameSpace As Object
Dim objInbox As Object
Dim objMailItem As Object
Set objOutlook = CreateObject("Outlook.Application")
Set objNameSpace = objOutlook.GetNamespace("MAPI")
Set objInbox = objNameSpace.Folders(1)
Set objMailItem = objOutlook.CreateItem(0)

'Declare a String variable for the worksheet data.
Dim strtext As String
'Declare Long variables for the range's Row and Columns.
Dim xRow As Long, xColumn As Long

'Build the string that is the text inside the range
'you want to represent in the Body of the email.
For xRow = 1 To Range("A1").CurrentRegion.Rows.Count
For xColumn = 1 To Range("A1").CurrentRegion.Columns.Count
strtext = strtext & " " & Range("A1").Cells(xRow, xColumn).Value
Next xColumn
strtext = strtext & Chr(10)
Next xRow

'Activate or open Outlook.
On Error Resume Next
AppActivate ("Outlook")
If Err.Number <> 0 Then objInbox.Display
Err.Clear
```

```
'Create your MailItem email object.
With objMailItem
.To = "someone@somewhere.com"
.CC = "anyone@anywhere.com"
.Subject = "Testing my email code"
.Importance = 1
.Body = _
"Hello, attached is a workbook, and below is a list of employee names." _
& Chr(10) & Chr(10) & strtext
.Attachments.Add "C:\Your\File\Path\YourFileName.xlsx"
.Display
End With

'Release object variables from system memory.
Set objOutlook = Nothing
Set objNameSpace = Nothing
Set objInbox = Nothing
Set objMailItem = Nothing

End Sub
```

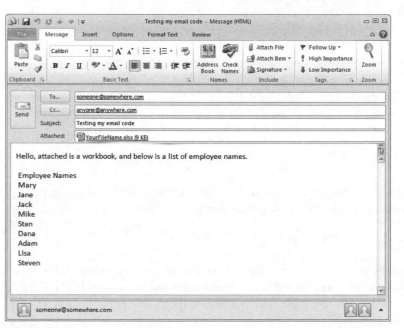

FIGURE 28-2

Before testing the ExampleEmail *macro, you'll probably need to modify the folder path and filename of the attachment. If you want to test the macro without attaching a file, you can simply delete or comment out the* Attachments.Add *statement.*

E-MAILING A SINGLE WORKSHEET

You can e-mail a single worksheet using `SendMail` with Microsoft Outlook. The following macro copies the active worksheet and sends it as the lone worksheet in its own workbook:

```
Sub EmailSingleSheet()
ActiveSheet.Copy
On Error Resume Next
ActiveWorkbook.SendMail "someone@anywhere.com", "Test of single sheet"
Err.Clear
ActiveWorkbook.Close False
End Sub
```

> `SendMail` *can send a single worksheet as an attachment by housing that worksheet in its own workbook and e-mailing it.* `SendMail` *does not require specifying a Simple Mail Transport Protocol (SMTP) server; it sends the mail using your installed mail system. This has the advantage of bypassing much of the Outlook-related code you've seen, but it comes with disadvantages, such as limited ability to attach files, and no available CC argument.*

> *A worksheet in Excel cannot exist on its own; a worksheet must be housed in a parent Excel workbook.*

TRY IT

In this lesson, you write a macro in Excel that creates an e-mail in Microsoft Outlook for multiple recipients and attaches the active Excel workbook to that e-mail.

Lesson Requirements

With recipient e-mail addresses already listed in column A, you write a macro in Excel that creates an e-mail in Microsoft Outlook that attaches the active workbook, and populates the "To" field with all the recipients' names. To get the sample database files you can download Lesson 28 from the book's website at `www.wrox.com`.

Step-by-Step

1. In column A of your worksheet, list a few sample recipient names. For example:

    ➤   In cell A1 enter **no_one@nowhere.com**

    ➤   In cell A2 enter **anyone@anywhere.com**

    ➤   In cell A3 enter **someone@somewhere.com**

2. Press Alt+F11 to go to the Visual Basic Editor.

3. From the menu at the top of the VBE, click Insert ⇨ Module.

4. In the module you just created, type **Sub EmailAttachmentRecipients** and press Enter. VBA will automatically place a pair of empty parentheses at the end of the Sub line, followed by an empty line, and the End Sub line below that. Your macro will look like this so far:

```
Sub EmailAttachmentRecipients ()

End Sub
```

5. Declare and establish the Object variables for Outlook:

```
Dim objOutlook As Object
Dim objNameSpace As Object
Dim objInbox As Object
Dim objMailItem As Object
Set objOutlook = CreateObject("Outlook.Application")
Set objNameSpace = objOutlook.GetNamespace("MAPI")
Set objInbox = objNameSpace.Folders(1)
Set objMailItem = objOutlook.CreateItem(0)
```

6. Declare a String variable for the recipient list, and a Long variable for the count of cells in column A that contain e-mail addresses:

```
Dim strTo As String
Dim i As Integer
strTo = ""
i = 1
```

7. Loop through the recipient e-mail addresses you entered from Step 1, in order to build a continuous string where each recipient address is separated by a semicolon and a space, just as it would appear in an Outlook "To" field:

```
Do
strTo = strTo & Cells(i, 1).Value & "; "
i = i + 1
Loop Until IsEmpty(Cells(i, 1))
'Remove the last two characters from the string,
'which are an unneeded semicolon and space.
strTo = Mid(strTo, 1, Len(strTo) - 2)
```

8. Display the e-mail message:

```
With objMailItem
.To = strTo
.Subject = "Test of multiple recipients"
.Body = "Hello everyone, this is a test of multiple recipients with a workbook
attachment."
.Attachments.Add ActiveWorkbook.FullName
.Display 'Change to Send
End With
```

> ⊗ *The active workbook you are attaching must be an actual workbook that has been named and saved, or the code line* `.Attachments.Add ActiveWorkbook .FullName` *will fail.*

9. Release object variables from system memory:

```
Set objOutlook = Nothing
Set objNameSpace = Nothing
Set objInbox = Nothing
Set objMailItem = Nothing
```

10. When your macro is complete, it should look like this:

```
Sub EmailAttachmentRecipients()

'Declare and establish the Object variables for Outlook.
Dim objOutlook As Object
Dim objNameSpace As Object
Dim objInbox As Object
Dim objMailItem As Object
Set objOutlook = CreateObject("Outlook.Application")
Set objNameSpace = objOutlook.GetNamespace("MAPI")
Set objInbox = objNameSpace.Folders(1)
Set objMailItem = objOutlook.CreateItem(0)

'Declare a String variable for the recipient list,
'and a Long variable for the count of cells in column A
'that contain email addresses.
Dim strTo As String
Dim i As Integer
strTo = ""
i = 1

'Loop through the recipient email addresses you entered from Step 1,
'in order to build a continuous string where each recipient address
'is separated by a semicolon and a space, just as it would appear
'in an Outlook "To" field.
Do
strTo = strTo & Cells(i, 1).Value & "; "
i = i + 1
Loop Until IsEmpty(Cells(i, 1))
'Remove the last two characters from the string,
'which are an unneeded semicolon and space.
strTo = Mid(strTo, 1, Len(strTo) - 2)

'Display the email message, including the attachment of the active workbook.
With objMailItem
.To = strTo
.Subject = "Test of multiple recipients"
.Body = "Hello everyone, this is a test of multiple recipients with a workbook
attachment."
```

```
.Attachments.Add ActiveWorkbook.FullName
.Display 'Change to Send
End With

'Release object variables from system memory.
Set objOutlook = Nothing
Set objNameSpace = Nothing
Set objInbox = Nothing
Set objMailItem = Nothing

End Sub
```

11. Press Alt+Q to return to the worksheet. Press Alt+F8 to show the macro dialog box, and test the macro by selecting the macro name and clicking the Run button.

 Please select Lesson 28 on the DVD to view the video that accompanies this lesson.

Working with Access from Excel

As terrific a product as Excel is, there will likely come a point when the volume of data you are working with will exceed Excel's capacity for storing records. Even with more than one million available rows starting with version 2007, some projects require a larger data management platform with Microsoft Access. If you plan to develop projects for business clients, sooner or later you'll encounter a client that uses Access for its relational database capabilities.

Using Excel VBA with the storage capabilities of an Access relational database is a powerful combination for front-end data management. This lesson offers examples for adding, retrieving, and updating records in Access data tables from the familiar comfort of your Excel workbook.

ADDING A RECORD TO AN ACCESS TABLE

Among the more common actions you'll do when interacting with Access from Excel is to transfer records from an Excel worksheet to an Access database table, and vice versa. Suppose there is an Access database named `Database1.accdb` that contains a table named Table1 that has eight fields. In Sheet4 of your Excel workbook, you amass records during the day that are added to Table1 at the end of the workday.

> *A reference to the Microsoft ActiveX Data Objects 2.8 Library is required for the code in this lesson to run. Before attempting to run the macros, get into the VBE and from the menu, click Tools ➪ References. Navigate to the reference for Microsoft ActiveX Data Objects 2.8 Library (or the highest Objects Library number you see), select it as indicated in Figure 29-1, and click OK.*

To automate the daily task of transferring the day's records from Excel to Access, you would maintain the Excel table with the fields in the same order as they are found in Table1 of the Access database. The following Excel macro would accomplish this task.

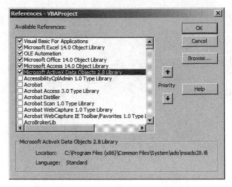

FIGURE 29-1

```
Sub ExcelToAccess()

'Declare variables
Dim dbConnection As ADODB.Connection
Dim dbFileName As String
Dim dbRecordset As ADODB.Recordset
Dim xRow As Long, xColumn As Long
Dim LastRow As Long

'Go to the worksheet containing the records you want to transfer.
Worksheets("Sheet4").Activate
'Determine the last row of data based on column A.
LastRow = Cells(Rows.Count, 1).End(xlUp).Row

'Create the connection to the database.
Set dbConnection = New ADODB.Connection
'Define the database file name
dbFileName = "C:\YourFilePath\Database1.accdb"

'Define the Provider and open the connection.
With dbConnection
.Provider = "Microsoft.ACE.OLEDB.12.0;Data Source=" & dbFileName & _
";Persist Security Info=False;"
.Open dbFileName
End With

'Create the recordset
Set dbRecordset = New ADODB.Recordset
dbRecordset.CursorLocation = adUseServer
dbRecordset.Open Source:="Table1", _
ActiveConnection:=dbConnection, _
CursorType:=adOpenDynamic, _
LockType:=adLockOptimistic, _
Options:=adCmdTable

'Load the records from Excel to Access, by looping through the rows and columns.
'Assume row 1 is the header row, so start at row 2.
For xRow = 2 To LastRow
dbRecordset.AddNew
'Assume this is an 8-column (field) table starting with column A.
For xColumn = 1 To 8
dbRecordset(Cells(1, xColumn).Value) = Cells(xRow, xColumn).Value
```

> *The preceding line of code will fail, and result in a run time error, if any field in your Excel table contains data that is in conflict with the specified data type of its corresponding field in the Access table. For example, if the second field in your Access table is specified to be a Number data type, and in your Excel worksheet, column B has a text value in it, the macro will fail at this point because a text value is attempting to be placed into an Access field meant to accept only numbers.*

```
Next xColumn
dbRecordset.Update
Next xRow

'Close the connections.
dbRecordset.Close
dbConnection.Close

'Release Object variable memory.
Set dbRecordset = Nothing
Set dbConnection = Nothing

'Optional
'Clear the range of data (the records) you just transferred.
'Range("A2:H" & LastRow).ClearContents

End Sub
```

> *You are probably aware that beginning with the release of Office 97, extensions changed for Microsoft's applications. For example, Excel workbooks that had the extension* .xls *now are either* .xlsx *or* .xlsm. *Access extensions also changed, from* .mdb *to* .accdb, *as shown in the preceding macro.*
>
> *Take note of the version(s) of Excel and Access when the time comes to implement this code. Especially, the* Provider *line in the code is*
>
> ```
> .Provider = "Microsoft.ACE.OLEDB.12.0;Data Source=" & dbFileName &
> _
> ";Persist Security Info=False;".
> ```
>
> *Had this been a version of Office prior to 2007, that same line might have been*
>
> ```
> .Provider = "Microsoft.Jet.OLEDB.4.0"
> ```
>
> *or*
>
> ```
> .Provider = "Microsoft.Jet.OLEDB.4.0;" & "Data Source=" _
> & dbFileName & ";" & "Extended Properties=Excel 8.0;".
> ```

WHAT IF YOU WANT TO OPEN AN ACCESS DATABASE FILE ONLY FROM EXCEL?

A common theme you'll notice with the examples in this lesson is that Excel is acting upon the Access files by connecting to them, rather than by opening and closing them as you saw in the lessons for working with Word and Outlook. You will rarely need Excel to open an Access database just for the sake of opening it.

If the situation should arise where you do need to open an Access database from Excel, the following example is what I use. It works by incorporating a ShellExecute command in conjunction with the declaration of the ShellExecute function in the Microsoft Windows programming language Applications Programming Interface, or API. The subject of API can easily fill a large book, but in brief, ShellExecute in API performs an operation on a specified file. In this case, the specified file is the one you want to open (named "Database1.accdb" in the hypothetical directory path "C:\YourFilePath"), and the operation is to open that database file, using the parameters in the declaration statement. This code is placed in a standard Excel VBA module just as any macro would be, and works with Windows versions from XP through Windows 7.

```
Private Declare Function ShellExecute _
Lib "shell32.dll" Alias "ShellExecuteA" _
(ByVal hwnd As Long, ByVal lpOperation As String, _
ByVal lpFile As String, ByVal lpParameters As String, _
ByVal lpDirectory As String, ByVal nShowCmd As Long) _
As Long

Sub OpenAccessDB()
Call ShellExecute(0, "Open", "Database1.accdb", "", _
"C:\YourFilePath\", 1)
End Sub
```

EXPORTING AN ACCESS TABLE TO AN EXCEL SPREADSHEET

As mentioned earlier, you will commonly need to import a table from an Access database into an Excel worksheet, to take advantage of Excel's versatile formatting and data manipulation capabilities. To export the database's Table1 data, you define the recordset while passing an SQL string to the connection. In this example, the entire count of records in Table1 will be copied to Sheet2 in your Excel workbook:

```
Sub AccessToExcel()

'Declare variables.
Dim dbConnection As ADODB.Connection
Dim dbRecordset As ADODB.Recordset
Dim dbFileName As String
Dim strSQL As String
Dim DestinationSheet As Worksheet
```

```vba
'Set the assignments to the Object variables.
Set dbConnection = New ADODB.Connection
Set dbRecordset = New ADODB.Recordset
Set DestinationSheet = Worksheets("Sheet2")

'Define the Access database path and name.
dbFileName = "C:\YourFilePath\Database1.accdb"
'Define the Provider for post-2007 database files.
dbConnection.Provider = "Microsoft.ACE.OLEDB.12.0;Data Source=" _
& dbFileName & ";Persist Security Info=False;"

'Use SQL's SELECT and FROM statements for importing Table1.
strSQL = "SELECT Table1.* FROM Table1;"

'Clear the destination worksheet.
DestinationSheet.Cells.Clear

With dbConnection
'Open the connection.
.Open
'The purpose of this line is to disconnect the recordset.
.CursorLocation = adUseClient
End With

With dbRecordset
'Create the recordset.
.Open strSQL, dbConnection
'Disconnect the recordset.
Set .ActiveConnection = Nothing
End With

'Copy the Table1 recordset to Sheet2 starting in cell A2.
'Row 1 contains headers that will be populated at the next step.
DestinationSheet.Range("A2").CopyFromRecordset dbRecordset

'Reinstate field headers (assumes a 4-column table).
'Note that the ID field will also transfer into column A,
'so you can optionally delete column A.
DestinationSheet.Range("A1:E1").Value = _
Array("ID", "Header1", "Header2", "Header3", "Header4")

'Close the recordset.
dbRecordset.Close
'Close the connection.
dbConnection.Close

'Release Object variable memory.
Set dbRecordset = Nothing
Set dbConnection = Nothing
Set DestinationSheet = Nothing

End Sub
```

CREATING A NEW TABLE IN ACCESS

Suppose you are managing a project that involves both Excel and Access, and you need to add a new table to the Access database. You can do that with the following macro, and from there if need be, using the first macro in this lesson named `ExcelToAccess`, you can transfer any records you may have accumulated for that new table.

In this example, you create a simple three-field table that will maintain a company's Employee Identification Number, which will be a Primary Field, and the employees' last names and first names. The new table is named tblEmployees, and it is added to the `Database1.accdb` file that's been the subject of this lesson. Figure 29-2 shows `Database1.accdb` with the new table added after running the following macro named `CreateAccessTable`.

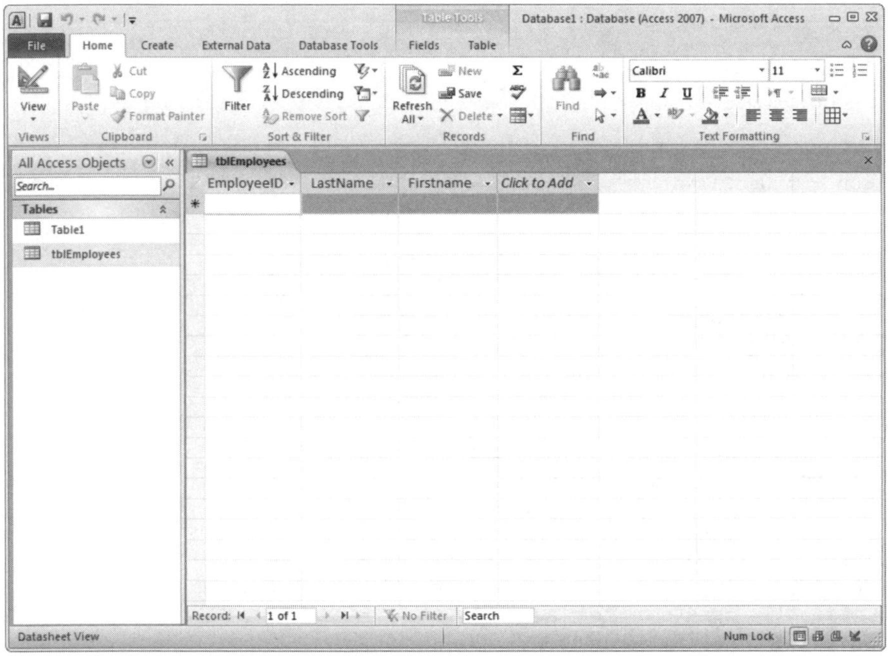

FIGURE 29-2

```
Sub CreateAccessTable()
'Create a three-column table in an existing Access database:
'EmployeeID
'LastName
'FirstName

'Declare variables
Dim dbConnection As ADODB.Connection
Dim dbCommand As ADODB.Command
Dim dbFileName As String

'Define the Access database path and name.
dbFileName = "C:\YourFilePath\Database1.accdb"
```

```
'Set the assignment to open the connection.
Set dbConnection = New ADODB.Connection

'Define the Provider and open the connection.
With dbConnection
.Provider = "Microsoft.ACE.OLEDB.12.0;Data Source=" & dbFileName & _
";Persist Security Info=False;"
.Open dbFileName
End With

'Set the Command variables.
Set dbCommand = New ADODB.Command
Set dbCommand.ActiveConnection = dbConnection

'Create the table, which will be named tblEmployees.
dbCommand.CommandText = _
"CREATE TABLE tblEmployees (EmployeeID Char(10) " & _
"Primary Key, LastName text, FirstName text)"

'Execute the command to create the table.
dbCommand.Execute , , adCmdText

'Release Object variable memory.
Set dbCommand = Nothing
Set dbConnection = Nothing

End Sub
```

> The text *reference following the field names in the* CommandText *is to advise Access that the field's data type will be text. As you may know with Access tables, other field types are Memo, Number, Date/Time, Currency, Yes/No, OLE Object, Hyperlink, and Attachment.*

TRY IT

In this lesson, you write a macro that adds a new field to an existing table in an Access database.

Lesson Requirements

For this lesson, you maintain an Access database named Database1.accdb. In that database is a table named tblEmployees. You discover that a new field is required to be added to that table, which will record the middle names of employees. The data type of the new field will be Text. To get the sample database files, you can download Lesson 29 from the book's website at www.wrox.com/.

Step-by-Step

1. In your Excel workbook, press Alt+F11 to go to the Visual Basic Editor.

2. From the VBE menu, click Insert ⇨ Module.

3. In the new module, type the name of your macro, which will be **AddNewField**. VBA will automatically place a pair of parentheses after the macro name, followed by an empty line, followed by the End Sub statement. Your code will look as follows:

   ```
   Sub AddNewField()

   End Sub
   ```

4. Similar to what you have seen in this lesson's macros, declare three variables: one for the ADO connection, one for the ADO command, and one for the full path and name of the Access database you are working with:

   ```
   Dim dbConnection As ADODB.Connection
   Dim dbCommand As ADODB.Command
   Dim dbFileName As String
   ```

5. Define the Access database path and name:

   ```
   dbFileName = "C:\YourFilePath\Database1.accdb"
   ```

6. Set the assignment to open the connection:

   ```
   Set dbConnection = New ADODB.Connection
   ```

7. Define the Provider and open the connection:

   ```
   With dbConnection
   .Provider = "Microsoft.ACE.OLEDB.12.0;Data Source=" & dbFileName & _
   ";Persist Security Info=False;"
   .Open dbFileName
   End With
   ```

8. Set the Command variables:

   ```
   Set dbCommand = New ADODB.Command
   Set dbCommand.ActiveConnection = dbConnection
   ```

9. Establish the command that adds a field for a middle name:

   ```
   dbCommand.CommandText = _
   "ALTER TABLE tblEmployees Add Column MiddleName text)"
   ```

10. Execute the command to create the new field:

    ```
    dbCommand.Execute , , adCmdText
    ```

11. Release Object variable memory:

    ```
    Set dbCommand = Nothing
    Set dbConnection = Nothing
    ```

12. Examine the `Database1.accdb` file to confirm the existence of your new field for a middle name. Figure 29-3 shows what you should see, and the following code shows the complete macro.

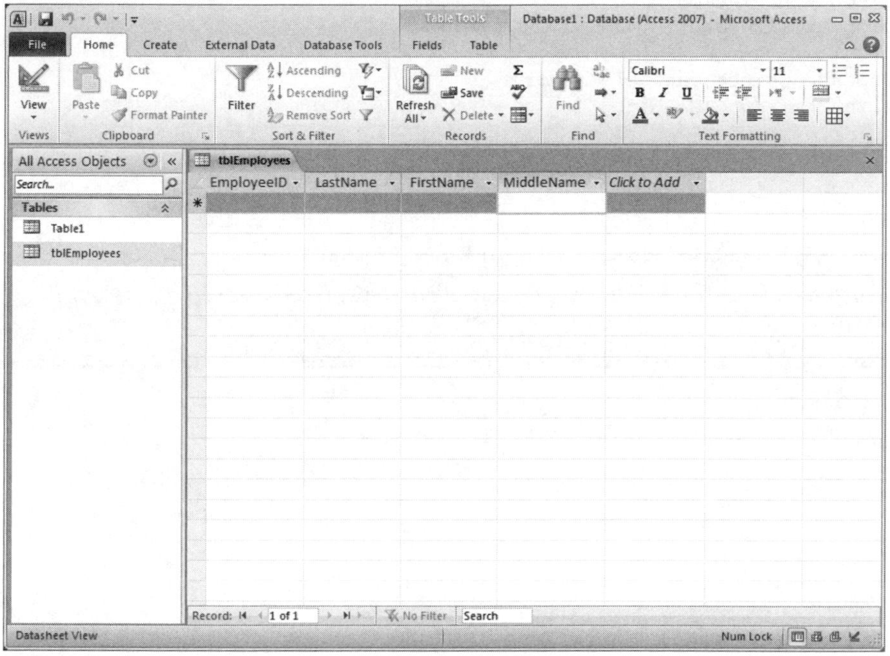

FIGURE 29-3

```
Sub AddNewField()

'Declare variables
Dim dbConnection As ADODB.Connection
Dim dbCommand As ADODB.Command
Dim dbFileName As String

'Define the Access database path and name.
dbFileName = "C:\YourFilePath\Database1.accdb"

'Set the assignment to open the connection.
Set dbConnection = New ADODB.Connection

'Define the Provider and open the connection.
With dbConnection
.Provider = "Microsoft.ACE.OLEDB.12.0;Data Source=" & dbFileName & _
";Persist Security Info=False;"
.Open dbFileName
End With

'Set the Command variables.
Set dbCommand = New ADODB.Command
Set dbCommand.ActiveConnection = dbConnection
```

```
'Establish the command that adds a field for a middle name.
dbCommand.CommandText = _
"ALTER TABLE tblEmployees Add Column MiddleName text)"

'Execute the command to create the new field.
dbCommand.Execute , , adCmdText

'Release Object variable memory.
Set dbCommand = Nothing
Set dbConnection = Nothing

End Sub
```

 Please select Lesson 29 on the DVD to view the video that accompanies this lesson.

30

Working with PowerPoint from Excel

With each new release of its Office suite, Microsoft has made it increasingly easier to share information between applications. Copying data from Excel, such as a worksheet range or chart, and pasting it into a PowerPoint slide is as simple as copying and pasting from Excel into a Word document.

Still, PowerPoint is a unique animal in that its primary purpose is not to manipulate data but to display images of data for presentation purposes. When you need to transfer data from Excel to PowerPoint, such as a chart or a range of cells, I recommend you use VBA's CopyPicture method, which will paste an image of the data — not the data itself — into PowerPoint.

CREATING A NEW POWERPOINT PRESENTATION

Creating a new PowerPoint presentation file is an uncomplicated process; all you do is follow the usual steps for creating the PowerPoint application and then add a presentation with the expression Presentations.Add. Here's an example from start to finish, ending up with a new presentation file and an initial slide:

```
Sub CreateNewPresentation()

'Declare Object variables for the PowerPoint application
'and for the PowerPoint presentation file.
Dim ppApp As Object, ppPres As Object
'Declare Object variable for a PowerPoint slide.
Dim ppSlide As Object

'Open PowerPoint
Set ppApp = CreateObject("PowerPoint.Application")
'Make the PowerPoint application visible.
ppApp.Visible = msoTrue
```

```
'Create a new Presentation and add a slide.
Set ppPres = ppApp.Presentations.Add
With ppPres.Slides

'11 is the numeric Constant for ppLayoutTitleOnly.
'The Constant is used with late binding.
Set ppSlide = .Add(.Count + 1, 11)
End With

'Save your new file.
ppPres.SaveAs Filename:=ThisWorkbook.Path & "\CreateTest.pptx"

'Release system memory reserved for the Object variables.
Set ppApp = Nothing
Set ppPres = Nothing
Set ppSlide = Nothing

End Sub
```

COPYING A WORKSHEET RANGE TO A POWERPOINT SLIDE

Now that you have just created a PowerPoint presentation file, while it's still open, suppose you want to copy a worksheet range into that presentation's first slide. The following macro uses an `InputBox` for the user to select a range to be copied.

> *Please note that this macro relies on the PowerPoint presentation file to be open. The code will not copy an Excel worksheet range to a closed PowerPoint presentation.*

One consideration to monitor is the selected size of a range, as you can see in the code. My column and row limitations are just for example purposes. Whatever limit, if any, that you decide, the objective should be to place a clear, concise image on the slide.

```
Sub CopyRange()

'Declare a Range type variable
Dim rng As Range
'Use an Application InputBox to have the user select the desired range.
'Exit the macro if the user cancels.
On Error Resume Next
Set rng = Application.InputBox("Select a range to be copied:", Type:=8)
If Err.Number<> 0 Then
Err.Clear
MsgBox "You did not enter a range.", vbInformation, "Cancelled"
Exit Sub
End If

'Monitor the size of the range so an unreasonably large range is not attempted.
If rng.Columns.Count> 6 Or rng.Rows.Count> 20 Then
MsgBox "You selected a range that is too large." & vbCrLf & _
```

```
"Please select a range that has no more than" & vbCrLf & _
"6 columns and/or 20 rows.", vbCritical, "Range too large"
Exit Sub
End If

'Declare variables.

Dim ppApp As Object, ppPres As Object, ppSlide As Object


'Assign the PowerPoint application you are working in to the ppApp variable.
Set ppApp = GetObject(, "Powerpoint.Application")
'Assign the presentation file you are working in.
Set ppPres = ppApp.ActivePresentation
Set ppSlide = ppPres.Slides(ppApp.ActiveWindow.Selection.SlideRange.SlideIndex)
'Copy the range as a picture
rng.CopyPicture Appearance:=xlScreen, Format:=xlPicture
'Paste the picture of the range onto the slide.
ppSlide.Shapes.Paste.Select

'Align the range picture to be centered in the slide.
With ppApp.ActiveWindow.Selection.ShapeRange
.Align msoAlignCenters, msoTrue
.Align msoAlignMiddles, msoTrue
End With

'Release system memory reserved for the Object variables.
Set rng = Nothing
Set ppApp = Nothing
Set ppPres = Nothing
Set ppSlide = Nothing

End Sub
```

COPYING CHART SHEETS TO POWERPOINT SLIDES

The Try It section of this lesson discusses how to copy an embedded chart into PowerPoint. If you have a choice between copying embedded charts or chart sheets, choose embedded charts — they provide you with greater control over how well they can be sized to fit a PowerPoint slide. This is because the ChartObject object is the container for an embedded chart, and it has properties that you can control for height, width, and location (where you can place it on the worksheet). Charts on chart sheets do not allow you to control their size.

Sometimes you won't have a choice, such as when a project calls for chart sheets to be copied into PowerPoint, and that is what the following macro accomplishes. To take things a step further, this macro:

1. Creates a new PowerPoint presentation.

2. Adds an initial title slide.

3. Loops through all chart sheets, and with each one, copies its image and pastes it into a new slide.

4. Places a header title on each slide, then populates it with the chart name and formats the text.

5. Saves the file.

```
Sub CopyChartSheets()

'Declare Object variables for the PowerPoint application
'and for the PowerPoint presentation file.
Dim ppApp As Object, pptPres As Object
'Declare Object variable for a PowerPoint slide.
Dim pptSlide As Object
'Declare variables for the Charts you will copy.
Dim ch As Chart
'Declare an Integer type variable for a running count of slides
'as each chart sheet is added to the new presentation file.
Dim SlideCount As Integer

'Open PowerPoint
Set ppApp = CreateObject("PowerPoint.Application")
'Make the PowerPoint application visible.
ppApp.Visible = msoTrue

'Create a new Presentation and add a title slide.
Set pptPres = ppApp.Presentations.Add
With pptPres.Slides
Set pptSlide = .Add(.Count + 1, 11)
End With
pptSlide.Shapes.Title.TextFrame.TextRange.Text = "Chart sheet copy test"

'Open a for Next loop to place each chart sheet in a slide.
For Each ch In ThisWorkbook.Charts
ch.CopyPicture Appearance:=xlScreen, Format:=xlPicture, Size:=xlScreen

'Add a new slide.
SlideCount = pptPres.Slides.Count

Set pptSlide = pptPres.Slides.Add(SlideCount + 1, 11)


ppApp.ActiveWindow.View.GotoSlide pptSlide.SlideIndex

'Paste and select the chart picture.
pptSlide.Shapes.Paste.Select
'Align the chart to be centered in the slide.
With ppApp.ActiveWindow.Selection.ShapeRange
.Align msoAlignCenters, msoTrue
.Align msoAlignMiddles, msoTrue
End With

'Set the position of the slide's header label.
With ppApp.ActiveWindow.Selection
.SlideRange.Shapes.AddLabel _
(msoTextOrientationHorizontal, 300, 20, 500, 50).Select
.ShapeRange.TextFrame.WordWrap = msoFalse

'Format the header label.
With .ShapeRange.TextFrame.TextRange
```

```
                   .Characters(Start:=1, Length:=0).Select
                   .Text = "This is " & ch.Name
                   With .Font
                   .Name = "Arial"
                   .Size = 12
                   .Bold = msoTrue
                   End With
                   End With

                   End With

                   'Continue the loop until all chart sheets have been copied.
                   Next ch

                   'End the macro by activating the first slide.
                   ppApp.ActiveWindow.View.GotoSlide 1

                   'Save your new file.
                   pptPres.SaveAs Filename:=ThisWorkbook.Path & "\ChartSheetTest.pptx"

                   'Relase system memory reserved for the Object variables.
                   Set ppApp = Nothing
                   Set pptSlide = Nothing
                   Set pptPres = Nothing
                   Set ppApp = Nothing

                   End Sub
```

RUNNING A POWERPOINT PRESENTATION FROM EXCEL

Running a PowerPoint presentation from Excel provides a dynamic effect to your Excel project. Unlike Word, Outlook, or Access, just opening a presentation file in PowerPoint is not enough if you want to show what that file contains. You can cycle through the slides with the `slideshowsettings.Run` statement. Notice the `With` structure that demonstrates a method of setting the amount of time (three seconds of the `advancetime` property in this example) that each slide will be shown, without affecting the user's local PowerPoint slide transition settings.

```
          Sub PowerPointSlideshow()

          'Declare Object variables for the PowerPoint application
          'and for the PowerPoint presentation file.
          Dim ppApp As Object, ppPres As Object
          'Declare String variables for folder path and name of file.
          Dim strFilePath As String, strFileName As String
          'Define the String variables with the directory path and name.
          strFilePath = "C:\Your\File\Path\"
          strFileName = "PowerPointExample1.pptx"

          'Verify if the path and filename really exist.
          'If not, exit the macro and advise the user.
          If Dir(strFilePath & strFileName) = "" Then
          MsgBox _
```

```
"The PowerPoint file " & strFileName & vbCrLf & _
"does not exist in the folder path" & vbCrLf & _
strFilePath & ".", _
vbInformation, "No such animal."
Exit Sub
End If

'Open PowerPoint
Set ppApp = CreateObject("PowerPoint.Application")
'Make the PowerPoint application visible.
ppApp.Visible = msoTrue
'Open the PowerPoint presentation you want to run.
Set ppPres = ppApp.Presentations.Open(strFilePath & strFileName)

'Establish the amount of time each slide should be shown,
'which in this example is 3 seconds.
With ppPres.slides.Range.slideshowtransition
.advanceontime = True
.advancetime = 3
End With

'Run the PowerPoint presentation.
ppPres.slideshowsettings.Run

'When the presentation is completed, have VBA regard it as saved
'so you are not prompted to save the presentation when you close it.
ppPres.Saved = True
'Quit Powerpoint (optional)
'ppApp.Quit

'Release memory taken from the Object variables.
Set ppPres = Nothing
Set ppApp = Nothing

End Sub
```

TRY IT

In this lesson, you copy an embedded chart to an empty slide in an open PowerPoint presentation.

Lesson Requirements

With a PowerPoint presentation open, you copy an embedded chart from your Excel workbook and paste its picture image into an empty slide. To get the sample database files you can download Lesson 30 from the book's website at www.wrox.com.

Step-by-Step

1. From your workbook, press Alt+F11 to go to the Visual Basic Editor.

2. From the menu at the top of the VBE, click Insert ⇨ Module.

3. In the module you just created, type **Sub CopyEmbeddedChart** and press Enter. VBA will automatically place a pair of empty parentheses at the end of the `Sub` line, followed by an empty line, and the `End Sub` line below that. Your macro will look like this so far:

```
Sub CopyEmbeddedChart()

End Sub
```

4. This example assumes you have PowerPoint open, with your destination presentation file open. Declare variables for the PowerPoint application, presentation filename, and `Slide` object:

```
Dim ppApp As Object, ppPres As Object, ppSlide As Object
```

5. For this example, you want to copy the first chart on your worksheet. Programmatically select the chart by its index number 1:

```
ActiveSheet.ChartObjects(1).Select
```

6. Establish the identity of the open PowerPoint application:

```
Set ppApp = GetObject(, "Powerpoint.Application")
```

7. Establish the identity of the open PowerPoint presentation:

```
Set ppPres = ppApp.ActivePresentation
```

8. Establish a reference to the next available slide:

```
Set ppSlide = ppPres.Slides(ppApp.ActiveWindow.Selection.SlideRange.SlideIndex)
```

9. Copy the selected chart:

```
ActiveChart.CopyPicture Appearance:=xlScreen, Size:=xlScreen, Format:=xlPicture
```

10. Paste the chart into the PowerPoint slide:

```
ppSlide.Shapes.Paste.Select
```

11. Align the chart picture to be centered in the slide:

```
With ppApp.ActiveWindow.Selection.ShapeRange
.Align msoAlignCenters, msoTrue
.Align msoAlignMiddles, msoTrue
End With
```

12. Deselect the selected chart:

```
Range("A1").Select
```

13. Release system memory reserved for the `Object` variables:

```
Set ppApp = Nothing
Set ppPres = Nothing
Set ppSlide = Nothing
```

14. When completed, the macro will look like this, with comments that have been added to explain each step:

```
Sub CopyEmbeddedChart()

'This example assumes you have PowerPoint open,
'with your destination presentation file open.
'Declare variables for the PowerPoint application,
'presentation filename, and Slide object.

Dim ppApp As Object, ppPres As Object, ppSlide As Object


'For this example, you want to copy the first chart on your worksheet.
'Select the chart by its index number one.
ActiveSheet.ChartObjects(1).Select

'Establish the identity of the open PowerPoint application.
Set ppApp = GetObject(, "Powerpoint.Application")

'Establish the identity of the open PowerPoint presentation.
Set ppPres = ppApp.ActivePresentation

'Establish a reference to the next available slide.
Set ppSlide = ppPres.Slides(ppApp.ActiveWindow.Selection.SlideRange.SlideIndex)

'Copy the selected chart.
ActiveChart.CopyPicture Appearance:=xlScreen, Size:=xlScreen, Format:=xlPicture

'Paste the chart into the PowerPoint slide.
ppSlide.Shapes.Paste.Select

'Align the range picture to be centered in the slide.
With ppApp.ActiveWindow.Selection.ShapeRange
.Align msoAlignCenters, msoTrue
.Align msoAlignMiddles, msoTrue
End With

'Deselect the selected chart.
Range("A1").Select

'Release system memory reserved for the Object variables.
Set ppApp = Nothing
Set ppPres = Nothing
Set ppSlide = Nothing

End Sub
```

15. Press Alt+Q to return to the worksheet. Press Alt+F8 to show the macro dialog box, and test the macro by selecting the macro name and clicking the Run button.

> *Please select Lesson 30 on the DVD to view the video that accompanies this lesson.*

APPENDIX

What's on the DVD?

This appendix provides you with information on the contents of the DVD that accompanies this book. For the latest and greatest information, please refer to the ReadMe file located at the root of the DVD. Here is what you will find in this appendix:

➤ System Requirements

➤ Using the DVD

➤ What's on the DVD

➤ Troubleshooting

SYSTEM REQUIREMENTS

Most reasonably up-to-date computers with a DVD drive should be able to play the screencasts that are included on the DVD. You may also find an Internet connection helpful for downloading updates to this book.

If your computer doesn't meet the following requirements, then you may have some problems using the software:

➤ PC running Windows XP, Windows Vista, Windows 7, or later

➤ A processor running at 1.6GHz or faster

➤ An Internet connection

➤ At least 1GB of RAM

➤ At least 3GB of available hard disk space

➤ A DVD-ROM drive

You may be able to run Visual Studio using a slower processor or with less memory, but things may be slow. I highly recommend more memory, 2GB or even more if possible. (I do fairly well with an Intel Core 2 system running Windows 7 at 1.83GHz with 2GB of memory and a 500GB hard drive.)

USING THE DVD

To access the content from the DVD, follow these steps:

1. Insert the DVD into your computer's DVD-ROM drive. The license agreement appears.

> *The interface won't launch if you have autorun disabled. In that case, click Start ➪ Run (for Windows 7, click Start ➪ All Programs ➪ Accessories ➪ Run). In the dialog box that appears, type D:\Start.exe. (Replace D with the proper letter if your DVD drive uses a different letter. If you don't know the letter, check how your DVD drive is listed under My Computer.) Click OK.*

2. Read through the license agreement, and then click the Accept button if you want to use the DVD.

   The DVD interface appears. Simply select the lesson number for the video you want to view.

WHAT'S ON THE DVD?

Most of this book's lessons contain a Try It section that enables you to practice the concepts covered by that lesson. The Try It includes a high-level overview, requirements, and step-by-step instructions explaining how to build the example program.

This DVD contains video screen casts showing how to work through key pieces of the Try Its from each lesson. The audio explains what is happening step-by-step so you can see how the techniques described in the lesson translate into actions.

I recommend using the following steps when reading a lesson:

1. Read the lesson's text.
2. Read the Try It's overview and requirements.
3. Read the step-by-step instructions.
4. Watch the video to see how I arrive at a solution to the Try It task. During the videos, I explain each step I am taking, and my reasons for choosing the methods to solve that task.

Sometimes a screencast mentions useful techniques and shortcuts that didn't fit in the book, so you may want to watch the screencast even if you feel completely confident about the material in that lesson.

You can also download all of the book's examples and solutions to the Try Its at the book's website.

Finally, if you're stuck and don't know what to do next, you can visit the P2P forums (p2p.wrox.com), locate the forum for the book, and leave a post. You can also e-mail me directly at tom@atlaspm.com, and I'll try to answer whatever questions you may have about the material in this book.

TROUBLESHOOTING

If you have difficulty installing or using any of the materials on the companion DVD, try the following solutions:

> **Reboot if necessary.** As with many troubleshooting situations, it may make sense to reboot your machine to reset any faults in your environment.

> **Turn off any anti-virus software that you may have running.** Installers sometimes mimic virus activity and can make your computer incorrectly believe that it is being infected by a virus. (Be sure to turn the anti-virus software back on later.)

> **Close all running programs.** The more programs you're running, the less memory is available to other programs. Installers also typically update files and programs; if you keep other programs running, installation may not work properly.

> **Reference the ReadMe.** Please refer to the ReadMe file located at the root of the DVD for the latest product information at the time of publication.

CUSTOMER CARE

If you have trouble with the DVD, please call the Wiley Product Technical Support phone number at (800) 762-2974. Outside the United States, call 1(317) 572-3994. You can also contact Wiley Product Technical Support at http://support.wiley.com. John Wiley & Sons will provide technical support only for installation and other general quality control items. For technical support on the applications themselves, consult the program's vendor or author.

To place additional orders or to request information about other Wiley products, please call (877) 762-2974.

INDEX

Symbols

: (colon), multiple statements, 76
' (apostrophe)
    cell values, 205
    comments, 29, 32
(number sign), variable values, 53
( ) (parentheses)
    argument list, 185
    arrays, 102
? (question mark)
    Object Browser, 24
    queries, 205

A

AbortRetryIgnore, 77
Access, 44, 353–362
    controlling, 6
    export, 356–358
    QueryTables, 299–300
    records, 353–356
    runtime error, 355
    versions, 355
Activate, 30–31
    workbooks, 46
    worksheets, 46
ActivateWord, 334, 335, 336
ActiveCell, 64
ActiveConnection
    Command, 310
    Connection, 309
ActiveWindow, 71

ActiveWorkbook, 23
    Worksheets, 67
ActiveX controls, 135–146
    chart sheets, 135
    CheckBox, 142
    CommandButton, 141–143
    Control Toolbox, 135, 140–143
    dialog sheets, 315
    embedding, OLEObject, 270–271
    events, 136
    formatting, 136
    Insert icon, 136
    procedures, 135
    versions, 140
ActiveX Data Objects (ADO), 307–313, 353
    Command, 310
    Connection, 309
    Recordset, 309–310
Add Watch dialog box, 206
add-ins, 279–293
    automation, 280
    closing, 290
    code, 280, 290
    converting files, 284–285
    creating, 280–284
    installation, 286–288
    plan, 281
    removing, 291
    security, 280
    user interface, 288–290
    UserForms, 281–284
    VBE, 290
    workbooks, 279, 280
Add-Ins dialog box, 286–288
    Ribbon Developer tab, 286
Add-Ins tab, 288

AddItem
    ComboBox, 238
    Initialize, 237
ADO. *See* ActiveX Data Objects
Advanced Properties, 284
advancetime, 367
Alignments, 249
alphanumeric strings, 186–187
American Standard Code for Information
    Interchange (ASCII), 235
Analysis ToolPak, 126–127, 288
Analysis ToolPak VBA, 288
AND, 70
API. *See* Applications Programming Interface
AppActivate ("Microsoft Excel"), 250
Application, 23, 44
    EnableEvents, 114–115
    Name, 66–67
    Workbook, 61
Application.Caller
    Forms controls, 138–139
    UDFs, 186
Applications Programming Interface (API),
    298, 356
Application.SendKeys, 322–323
Application.Volatile, 189
argument list, 185
arrays, 99–109
    boundaries, 104
    declaration statements, 102
        fixed elements, 104–105
    Double, 101
    elements, 99–100
    lists, 101
    one-dimensional, 101
    Option Base, 103
    Private, 102
    Public, 102
    purposes, 101
    Static, 102
    String, 101
    tables, 101
    two-dimensional, 101
    variables, 99
    Variant, 54
    zero-based numbering, 103
As, 49
ASCII. *See* American Standard Code for
    Information Interchange
Attachments.Add, 347
AutoCorrect list, 92
automation
    add-ins, 280
    Macro Recorder, 12
    macros, 5
    Office, 327–332
    recurring tasks, 5
    repetitive tasks, 5
    UserForm unloading, 253
    workbook events, 123–134
    worksheet events, 111–122
AVERAGE, 183

B

BackColor, 270
BASIC. *See* Beginner's All-purpose Symbolic
    Instruction Code
BeforePrint, 132
Beginner's All-purpose Symbolic Instruction Code
    (BASIC), 4
binding, 328–330
Binoculars icon, 24
Boolean, 52
boundaries, arrays, 104
Break button, Debugging toolbar, 199
Break mode
    Call Stack dialog box, 207
    VBE, 199
breakpoints, 203–204
    comments, 204

Bring To Front, 249
buttons. *See also specific buttons*
    Forms controls, 137–138
    macros, 137
    message boxes, 77
Byte, 52

C

Call, 202
Call Stack dialog box, 207
Cancel
    printing, 130, 133
    Workbook_BeforeSave, 131
Cancel button
    CommandButton, 232
    Unload Me, 226–227
    UserForms, 224
Caption, 232
Caption property
    Properties window, 221
    UserForms, 219
Case, 75
    To, 76
Cell, 44, 45
cells. *See also* ranges
    ActiveCell, 64
    Change, 114
    collections, 63–64
    colored, 185–186
    Do...Loop...While, 93
    Format Cells dialog box, 169
    Get.Cell, 315, 321
    PivotTable, 164
    Range, 63–64
    range, With, 32
    SpecialCells
        collections, 64–65
        Data Validation, 65
        Go To Special dialog box, 190
        ranges, 65

text files, 303
UDFs, 184
values, 205
variables, 51
worksheets, 43
Cells, 93
    worksheets, 64
Centering, 249
Change
    cells, 114
    Delete button, 120
    Exit, 120
Change Chart Type dialog box, 153
=CHAR(ROW()), 235
Chart
    default properties, 45
    variable declaration statements, 151
charts, 43, 151–162
    chart sheets, 152–153
    data labels, 161
    defaults, 153
    deleting, 158–159
    embedded
        loops, 157–158
        worksheets, 154–155
    index, 156
    legend, 161
    moving, 155–157
    ranges, 154–155
    rename, 159
    UserForms, 258
    variables, 160
    worksheets, 151
chart sheets
    ActiveX controls, 135
    charts, 152–153
    Forms controls, 135
    loops, 158
    PowerPoint, 365–367
    workbooks, 157
    worksheets, 155–156
    Worksheets, 63
Chart Wizard, 151

ChartObject, 151, 155, 365
Charts, 151
Charts.Add, 153
CheckBox
    ActiveX controls, 142
    Collection, 271
    UserForms, 240–241
classes, 263–264
class modules, 22, 263–277
    collections, 268–269
    embedding, 269–272
    TextBox, 266–268
    UDFs, 184
    VBE, 264
Classes pane, 23
ClearContents, 46
Click
    Caption, 232
    cmdNavigate, 261
    CommandButton, 233, 269
    Design Mode, 143
    ListBox, 237
    OptGroup, 274
Close
    Connection, 309
    dbRecordset, 310
    macros, 338
    Recordset, 310
    Workbook, 62
Close button, UserForms, 250–251
CloseOneWorkbook, 89
cmd, 232
cmdButtonGroup, 270
cmdExit
    Exit button, 261
    UserForm module, 274
cmdNavigate, 261
code. *See also* debugging
    add-ins, 280, 290
    breakpoints, 203–204
    dialog sheets, 317

macros, 21, 29–32
modules, 33
mySort, 31
Step Into button, 201
UserForms, 225–226
VBE, 36–37
workbook events, 123–126
Code window
    deleting macros, 33
    editing, 30, 50
    inserting modules, 33
    modules
        deleting, 33
        inserting, 33
        workbook, 124
        worksheet, 113
    Step Over button, 202
    VBE, 21
    workbook modules, 124
    worksheet modules, 113
CodeWindow, mySort, 21
Collection, 46
    CheckBox, 271
    PivotTables, 177–178
collections
    cells, 63–64
    Charts, 151
    class modules, 268–269
    OOP, 46–47
    ranges, 63–64
    SpecialCells, 64–65
    workbooks, 61–62
    worksheets, 62–63
colored cells, 185–186
ComboBox
    AddItem, 238
    End Sub, 238, 257
    pre-sort, 253–255
    ranges, 239
    RowSource, 238

unique items, 255–257
UserForms, 238–239
worksheets, 238
Command
    ActiveConnection, 310
    ADO, 310
    objConnection, 309
    objRecordset, 309
commands
    loops, 86
    macros, 72
CommandButton
    ActiveX controls, 141–143
    Cancel button, 232
    Click, 233, 269
    cmd, 232
    Exit button, 232
    Properties window, 141
    Sort Down, 254–255
    Sort Up, 254–255
    Unload Me, 226–227
    UserForms, 223, 232, 254–255
    View Code, 142
CommandText, 310
CommandType, 310
comments
    ' (apostrophe), 29, 32
    breakpoints, 204
    Conditional Formatting, 190
    If, 194
    macros, 30–32
    UDFs, 194
Comments, 47
CommentText, 293
Conditional Formatting
    comments, 190
    Get.Cell, 321
    ranges, 190
    UDFs, 190
conditional operators, 72–76

Connection
    ActiveConnection, 309
    ADO, 309
    Close, 309
    databases, 309
    Open, 309
ConnectionString, 309
Const, 57
constants
    lifetime, 58
    macros, 57–58
    modules, 58
    scope, 58
    values, 57
    variable declaration statements, 57
    variables, 57
Continue button, 251
Control Toolbox, ActiveX controls, 135, 140–143
controls. *See also specific controls*
    embedded, 135–150
    UserForms, 219–220, 231–248
ControlSource, TextBox, 234
copy and paste, 187
Create PivotTable dialog, Table Range field, 164
CreateObject, 331
.csv, 298
Ctl key, shortcut keys, 20
Currency, 52
CurrentRegion, 346
Customize Ribbon
    Excel Options dialog box, 10
    Main Tabs, 10

D

DAO. *See* Data Access Objects
Data Access Objects (DAO), 308
data labels, charts, 161

Data tab
    Get External Data section, 299
    Ribbon, 299
data types
    conversion, 54
    macros, 51–54
    UDFs, 185
    variable declaration statements, 53–54
    variables, 49–50, 52
Data Validation, 65
databases, 308. *See also* Access; Structured Query
    Language
    Connection, 309
database management system (DBMS), 308
DataForms, 322
Date, 52, 53
DateSerial, 96
DBMS. *See* database management system
dbRecordset, 310
Debug button, 197
debugging, 195–212
    Immediate Window, 22
Debugging toolbar
    Break button, 199
    Call Stack dialog box, 207
    Design Mode button, 199
    Immediate Window, 205
    Locals window, 205
    Reset button, 199
    Run button, 199
    Step Into button, 201–202
    Step Out button, 203
    Step Over button, 202–203
    Toggle Breakpoint button, 204
    VBE, 198–207
    Watch window, 205–206
Debugging window, 206
Decimal, 52
decision making, 69–81
    conditional operators, 72–76
    InputBox, 77–78

logical operators, 69–72
    message boxes, 76–77
declaration statements
    arrays, 102
        dynamic, 105–106
        fixed elements, 104–105
    dynamic arrays, 105–106
    variables, 50
        applications, 57
        Chart, 151
        constants, 57
        data types, 53–54
        dates, 53
        forcing, 54–56
        macros, 56
        modules, 56–57
        PowerPoint, 331
        times, 53
Default Chart button, 153
defaults
    charts, 153
    Macro Recorder, 14
        name, 34
    properties, Chart, 45
    worksheets, 44
deleting
    charts, 158–159
    hyperlinks, 205
    macros, 33
    modules, 36
DELETE, 312–313
Delete button
    Change, 120
    Macro dialog box, 33
DeleteData, 138
Description field
    Insert Function dialog, 191–193
    Macro Recorder, 15
Design Mode
    Click, 143
    Debugging toolbar, 199

Developer tab, 143
    VBE, 143
Developer tab, 10
    Design Mode, 143
    Record Macro button, 13
    Ribbon, 12, 136
dialog boxes. *See also specific dialog boxes*
    Do Not Show This Message Again, 318–321
dialog sheets, 315–321
    ActiveX controls, 315
    code, 317
    Immediate Window, 316
    UserForms, 315–316
    versions, 316
    workbooks, 315
    Worksheet_Change, 318
DialogFrame, 316
Dim, 49
Dir, 91
DisplayGridlines, 71
DLL. *See Dynamic Link Library*
Do
    For...Each...Next, 95
    While...Wend, 94
Do Not Show This Message Again, 318–321
Do...Loop, 91
Do...Loop...Until, loops, 86, 94
Do...Loop...While
    cells, 93
    loops, 86, 93
    worksheets, 93
Double, 52
    arrays, 101
    OldVal, 121
Do...Until
    AutoCorrect list, 92
    loops, 86, 91–93
Do...While, 86, 91
drawing shapes, 43
dynamic arrays, 105–106
Dynamic Link Library (DLL), 279

E

early binding, 328–329
editing. *See also* Visual Basic Editor
    Code window, 30, 50
    macros, 30–32, 50
Editor tab
    Options dialog box, 55, 66, 250
    Require Variable Declaration, 55, 250
elements
    arrays, 99–100
    fixed, 104–105
    loops, 100
    variables, 100
Else, 73
e-mail
    Outlook, 344–347
    ranges, 345–346
    worksheets, 348
embedding
    ActiveX controls
        OLE objects, 270
        OLEObject, 270–271
    charts
        loops, 157–158
        worksheets, 154–155
    class modules, 269–272
    controls, 135–150
Enabled, 245
EnableEvents, 114–115
End, 72
End Function, 184, 194
End If
    errors, 197
    Exit For, 89–90
End Sub, 33, 114, 132, 275
    ComboBox, 238, 257
    Step Out button, 203
    workbook events, 126

End With, 32
  errors, 197
Error
  Error Resume Next, 208
  If, 208
errors
  bypass, 208–209
  End If, 197
  End With, 197
  handler, 207–208
    InputBox, 207
    runtime errors, 207
  logical, 197
  Loop, 197
  macros, 329
  Next, 197
  runtime, 197, 334
    Access, 355
    error handler, 207
    Find, 208–212
    ListBox, 237
    Locals window, 205
    Watch window, 205
  syntax, 196–197
  trapping, 207–209
  UDFs, 188
Error Resume Next, 208
Euro Currency Tools, 288
events. *See also* workbook events; worksheet events
  ActiveX controls, 136
  Forms controls, 136
  ListBox, 237
  programming, 5
Excel 4.0 Macro Language (XLM), 321
Excel Options button, 10
Excel Options dialog box, 10
Exit, 120
Exit button
  cmdExit, 261
  CommandButton, 232
  UserForms, 224
Exit Do, 95
Exit For

End If, 89–90
  nesting, 95
export
  Access, 356–358
  images, 258
  Internet, 258
  modules, 36
  Word, 333
external data, 295–306
  QueryTables, 295–300
  text files, 301–303
ExtractNumbers, 192–193

F

fields, 313. *See also specific fields*
  databases, 308
Field buttons, 173
Field List, 167
File tab
  Options button, 10
  Ribbon, 10
  Save As dialog box, 284
Find, 208–212
fixed elements, 104–105
fixed-iteration loop, 86
floating-point numbers, 52
For, 94
For Next
  intCounter, 206
  loops, 276
  strValue, 206
For...Each
  Comments, 47
  loops, 47
For...Each...Next
  Do, 95
  exiting, 89–90
  loops, 86, 88–90
  nesting, 95
ForeColor, 270

Format Cells dialog box, 169
formatting
    ActiveX controls, 136
    Conditional Formatting
        comments, 190
        Get.Cell, 321
        ranges, 190
        UDFs, 190
    Forms controls, 136
    PivotTable Value area, 168–170
    TextBox, 234
Forms controls, 135–146
    Application.Caller, 138–139
    buttons, 137–138
    chart sheets, 135
    events, 136
    formatting, 136
    Forms toolbar, 136–139
    Insert icon, 136
    macros, 135
    versions, 140
Forms toolbar, 136–139
For...Next
    exiting, 89–90
    InputBox, 87
    Integer, 87, 96
    Long, 87
    loops, 86, 87–88
    nesting, 95
Frame control
    Enabled, 245
    UserForms, 222–223, 243–245
Function, 184
functions. *See also* User Defined Functions
    volatile, 188–193

G

Get External Data section, 299
Get.Cell, 315, 321
GetObject, 334
Go To dialog, 64

Go To Special dialog box, 190
GoBack, 261
GoForward, 261
GoTo, 208
Group, 249
GroupName, 243
grpCBX, 272

H

Help file, 24
Hide, 227–228
Hide Field List, 167
hierarchy, object model, 44
hyperlinks
    deleting, 205
    Immediate Window, 205
    UDFs, 187

I

icons. *See also specific icons*
    Project Explorer window, 21
    toolbars, 27
    VBE, 20
    versions, 10
iCounter, 91
If
    comments, 194
    End, 72
    Error, 208
    InputBox, 80
    multiple conditions, 73
    String, 331
    Workbooks, 88
If...Then, 72–73
If...Then...Else, 73
If...Then...ElseIf, 74
    Select, 75
images, 258

Immediate Window
    debugging, 22
    Debugging toolbar, 205
    deleting charts, 158–159
    dialog sheets, 316
    hyperlinks, 205
    queries, 205
    VBE, 22
    Word, 329
import
    Internet, 258
    Word, 338–339
Importance, 345
indefinite loop, 86
index, charts, 156
Initialize
    AddItem, 237
    charts, 258
    ListBox, 237, 246
    ReDim Preserve, 268
    TxtGroup, 267
    UserForms, 233, 268, 275
    WebBrowser, 261
InputBox, 340
    decision making, 77–78
    error handler, 207
    For...Next, 87
    If, 80
    PowerPoint, 364–365
    String, 77
    While...Wend, 94
INSERT, 311–312
Insert Function dialog, 191–193
Insert icon
    ActiveX controls, 136
    Forms controls, 136
inserting modules, 33–34, 107
instantiating, 267
IntAdd, 56–57
intCounter, 206

Integer, 50, 52
    For...Next, 87, 96
    OptionButton, 276
IntelliSense, 65–67
    message boxes, 77
Internet
    export, 258
    import, 258
    queries, QueryTables, 295–299
intSum, 56–57
iterations, 85–86

K

KeyPress, 267–268
keywords, 7

L

Label
    OptionButton, 273
    UserForms, 221, 232–234
late binding, 329–330
    Word, 340
LBound, 104
legend, charts, 161
LEN, 239
libraries, 23
lifetime constants, 58
lists. *See also specific lists*
    argument, 185
    arrays, 101
ListBox
    Click, 237
    events, 237
    Initialize, 237, 246
    loops, 248

MultiSelect, 236–237, 246
NextRow, 247
pre-sort, 253–255
RowSource, 237
runtime error, 237
unique items, 255–257
UserForms, 236–237, 246–248
LoadPicture, 252
Locals window
    Debugging toolbar, 205
    mySheet, 205
    runtime errors, 205
    values, 205
    variables, 205
Location, 154
Locked, 45
locking, 36–37
LogFile.txt, 301
logical errors, 197
logical operators
    decision making, 69–72
    If...Then...Elself, 74
Long, 52
    For...Next, 87
Loop, 197
loops, 85–97
    chart sheets, 158
    commands, 86
    Do...Loop...Until, 86, 94
    Do...Loop...While, 86, 93
    Do...Until, 86, 91–93
    Do...While, 86, 91
    elements, 100
    embedded charts, 157–158
    For...Each, 47
    For...Each...Next, 86, 88–90
    For...Next, 86, 87–88
    iterations, 85–86
    ListBox, 248
    nested, 94–95
    For Next, 276
    PivotTable, 178
    RefreshAll, 178
    Step, 90
    While...Wend, 86, 94
Loop While, 93

M

macros, 3–4
    automation, 5
    breakpoints, 203–204
    buttons, 137
    Close, 338
    code, 21, 29–32
    commands, 72
    comments, 30–32
    composing, 9–12
    constants, 57–58
    data types, 51–54
    deleting, 33
    editing, 30–32, 50
    errors, 329
    Forms controls, 135
    InputBox, 77
    message boxes, 76–77, 100, 107
    modules, 28–29
    mySort, 13
    names, 14
    plan, 12
    Quit, 338
    running, 16–17
    Step Into button, 201
    Step Over button, 202
    subroutines, 111
    text files, 301–303
    UDFs, 184, 190–191
    variables, 49–51
        declaration statements, 56
    versions, 29

Word, 329, 335–336
workbooks, 15, 62
worksheets, 62–63
Macro dialog box, 16–17
    Delete button, 33
    shortcut keys, 17
Macro Recorder, 12–16
    automation, 12
    default names, 34
    defaults, 14
    Description field, 15
    inefficiencies, 30
    modules, 28
    repetitive tasks, 12
    Stop Recording button, 15
    Stop Recording toolbar, 15
    Store Macro In field, 15
    Sub, 29
    UDFs, 184
    versions, 15
macro sheets, 20
MailItem, 344–345
Main Tabs, 10
Message Box
    OptionButton, 242
    text files, 303
message boxes
    button configuration, 77
    decision making, 76–77
    IntelliSense, 77
    macros, 100, 107
    prompt argument, 77
methods
    OOP, 43, 46
    Workbook, 62
    worksheets, 43
modules
    class modules, 22, 263–277
        collections, 268–269
        embedding, 269–272
        TextBox, 266–268
        UDFs, 184
        VBE, 264

code, 33
constants, 58
deleting, 36
export, 36
inserting, 33–34, 107
Macro Recorder, 28
macros, 28–29
Project Explorer, 33, 34
Project Explorer window, 28
rename, 34–35
standard, 22
    UDFs, 184
UserForms, 22, 225–226, 247
    cmdExit, 274
variable declaration statements, 56–57
VBE, 22
workbooks, 22, 34
    Code window, 124
    workbook events, 124
worksheets, 22
    Code window, 113
    View Code, 112–113
More Controls, 140
MouseOver, 270
MsgBox, 77
MsgBoxShowOnceOption, 318–321
MultiPage control
    Page, 245
    UserForms, 245
multiple statements, 76
MultiSelect, 236–237, 246
myChartMaker, 202
myFileName, 331
myPath, 331
mySheet
    Locals window, 205
    Nothing, 205
mySort
    code, 31
    CodeWindow, 21
    macros, 13
mySum, 186
myValue, 49, 51

N

name. *See also* rename
  defaults, Macro Recorder, 34
  macros, 14
  UDFs, 184
  UserForms, 219
  workbooks, 189
  worksheets, 189, 208
Name
  Application, 66–67
  Worksheet, 45
Name property
  Properties window, 34
  UserForms, 219
Names, ranges, 64
NameWB(), 189
nested loops, 94–95
New Formatting Rule dialog, 190
NewVal, 121
Next, 87
  errors, 197
NextRow, ListBox, 247
NOT, 71–72
Nothing, 205
Number Format button, 168

O

objConnection, 309
Object, 52
Object Browser
  Binoculars icon, 24
  Classes pane, 23
  Help file, 24
  Search, 24
  VBE, 23–24
Object field, 113, 125
Object Linking and Embedding Database
  (OLE DB), 307

object model, 44–47
  hierarchy, 44
  Office, 23
object-oriented programming (OOP), 43–47
  collections, 46–47
  methods, 43, 46
  properties, 43, 45
objRecordset, 309
ODBC. *See* Open Database Connectivity
Office
  Access, 44, 353–362
    controlling, 6
    export, 356–358
    QueryTables, 299–300
    records, 353–356
    runtime error, 355
    versions, 355
  automation, 327–332
  controlling, 6
  object model, 23
  Outlook, 44, 343–351
    email composition, 344–347
    MailItem, 344–345
    opening, 343–344
  PowerPoint, 44, 363–370
    chart sheets, 365–367
    CreateObject, 331
    creating new presentation, 363–364
    InputBox, 364–365
    Open, 331
    running presentations, 367–368
    variable declaration statements, 331
    worksheet range, 364–365
  Ribbon Interface, 9
  Val, 331
  versions, 328
  Word, 44, 333–342
    activating, 333–336
    Code window, 30
    controlling, 6
    creating documents, 336
    GetObject, 334
    Immediate Window, 329

import, 338–339
late binding, 340
macros, 329, 335–336
printing, 337–338
ranges, 337
String, 339–340
Office button, 10
Save As, 284
OKCancel, 77
OldVal, 121
OLE DB. *See* Object Linking and Embedding
Database
OLEObject, 270–271
On Error GoTo, 207
On Error Resume Next, 334
one-dimensional arrays, 101
OnKey, 153
OOP. *See* object-oriented programming
Open
Connection, 309
PowerPoint, 331
Recordset, 310
Workbook, 62
Open Database Connectivity (ODBC), 307, 308
OpenOrClosed, 190
OpenTest, 190
operating systems, 7
operators
conditional, 72–76
logical
decision making, 69–72
If...Then...Elself, 74
OptGroup, 274
Option Base, 103
Option Explicit, 54–55
OptionButton
GroupName, 243
Integer, 276
Label, 273
Message Box, 242
UserForms, 223, 241–243
Options button, 10

Options dialog box, 55, 66, 250
Options tab, 171
OR, 70–71
If...Then...Elself, 74
Outlook, 44, 343–351
email composition, 344–347
MailItem, 344–345
opening, 343–344

P

Page, 245
passwords
VBE, 37
worksheets, 78
PasswordChar, 234
photographs, 252–253
Picture, 253
PivotCache, 173–175
PivotTable, 173
Refresh button, 173
Worksheet_Change, 175
PivotChart, 171–173
Field buttons, 173
PivotTable, 171
PivotFields, 176
PivotItems, 177
PivotTable, 43
cells, 164
Field List, 167
loops, 178
PivotCache, 173
PivotChart, 171
PivotFields, 176
PivotItems, 177
Refresh menu item, 173
RefreshAll, 178
Report Filter area, 167–168
reports, 163–170
source data, 174

source table, 164
updating, 119
Values area, 168–170
Workbook_Open, 178
Worksheet_Change, 175, 177–178
PivotTable icon, 171
PivotTable Tools section
Options tab, 171
Ribbon, 171
PivotTables, 177–178
planning
add-ins, 281
macros, 12
Popular, 10
PowerPoint, 44, 363–370
chart sheets, 365–367
CreateObject, 331
creating new presentation, 363–364
InputBox, 364–365
Open, 331
running presentations, 367–368
variable declaration statements, 331
worksheet range, 364–365
Presentations.Add, 363
Preserve, 106
pre sort
ComboBox, 253–255
ListBox, 253–255
primary keys, 308
printing
Cancel, 130, 133
UserForms, 258
Word, 337–338
PrintOut, 130, 337–338
PrintPreview, 130
Private, 102
Private Sub Workbook_Open(), 132
Procedure field, 113–114, 125
procedures, 111
ActiveX controls, 135
statements, 114
Project Explorer
icons, 21

modules, 28, 33, 34
Properties window, 218
UserForms, 216, 218
VBE, 21, 124, 132
View Code, 28
Project Properties dialog box, 37
prompt argument
InputBox, 77
message boxes, 77
properties
defaults, Chart, 45
OOP, 43, 45
Properties window
Caption property, 221
CommandButton, 141
Name property, 34
Picture, 253
Project Explorer, 218
VBE, 22
Protection tab, 37
Public, 57, 58
arrays, 102
UDFs, 184
Public Declaration Function, 298

Q

queries
databases, 308
Immediate Window, 205
Internet, QueryTables, 295–299
QueryClose, 251
QueryTables
Access, 299–300
Internet queries, 295–299
Question Mark icon, 24
Quick Watch window, 206
QuickBASIC, 4
Quit, 338

R

RAND(), 188
RAND, 189
Range, 44
    cells, 63–64
    ClearContents, 46
ranges
    cells, With, 32
    charts, 154–155
    collections, 63–64
    ComboBox, 239
    Conditional Formatting, 190
    e-mail, 345–346
    Names, 64
    Selection, 64
    SpecialCells, 65
    Step Into button, 201
    Word, 337
    worksheets, PowerPoint, 364–365
real-time charts, 258
records, 313
    Access, 353–356
    databases, 308
Record Macro button
    Developer tab, 13
    Visual Basic toolbar, 13
Record Macro dialog box, 29
Recordset
    ADO, 309–310
    Close, 310
    Open, 310
recordsets, 307
    databases, 308
    Source, 310
recurring tasks automation, 5
ReDim, 106
ReDim Preserve, 106
    Initialize, 268
Refresh, 46
Refresh button, 173

Refresh menu item, 173
RefreshAll
    loops, 178
    PivotTable, 178
relational database, 308
rename
    charts, 159
    modules, 34–35
repetitive tasks
    automation, 5
    Macro Recorder, 12
reports, 163–170
Report Filter area, 167–168
Require Variable Declaration, 55, 250
Reset button, 199
Ribbon
    Add-Ins tab, 288
    Data tab, 299
    Developer tab, 12, 136
    File tab, 10
    PivotTable Tools section, 171
Ribbon Developer tab
    Add-Ins dialog box, 286
    Stop Recording button, 16
    Visual Basic button, 20
Ribbon Insert tab, 171
Ribbon Interface, 9, 10
Ribbon option, 10
RowSource
    ComboBox, 238
    ListBox, 237
Run button, 199
Run Macro button, 16
run time errors, 197, 334
    Access, 355
    error handler, 207
    Find, 208–212
    ListBox, 237
    Locals window, 205
    Watch window, 205

S

Same Size, 249
Save, 62
Save As
    File tab, 284
    Office button, 284
Saved, 45
scope
    constants, 58
    variables, 56–57
Search, 24
security, 7
    add-ins, 280
SELECT, 311
Select, 30–31
    With, 32
    If...Then...ElseIf, 75
Select a Function pane, 192
Select Case, 74–75
    worksheets, 80
Select Data Source dialog box, 299
Select Table dialog box, 300
Selection, 32
    ranges, 64
Send To Back, 249
SendKeys, 315, 322–323
SendMail, 348
SheetManager, 286, 288
=SheetName(), 189
Sheets, 63
ShellExecute, 356
shortcut keys, 14–15
    Ctl key, 20
    Macro dialog box, 17
    Record Macro dialog box, 29
Show
    AppActivate ("Microsoft Excel"),
      250
    UserForms, 225
Show Developer tab, 10

Show Field List, 167
ShowDataForm, 322
ShowModal, 250
Simple Mail Transport Protocol (SMTP), 348
Single, 52
slideshowsettings.Run, 367
SMTP. *See* Simple Mail Transport Protocol
Solver, 288
Sort, 201
Sort Down, 254–255
Sort Up, 254–255
Source, 310
source data
    cell values, 205
    PivotTable, 174
source table, 164
Special button, 64
SpecialCells
    collections, 64–65
    Data Validation, 65
    Go To Special dialog box, 190
    ranges, 65
SQL. *See* Structured Query Language
standard modules, 22
    UDFs, 184
statements. *See also* declaration statements
    multiple, 76
    procedure, 114
Static, arrays, 102
StaticRandom, 188
Step, 90
Step Into button
    code, 201
    Debugging toolbar, 201–202
    macros, 201
Step Out button
    Debugging toolbar, 203
    End Sub, 203
Step Over button
    Code window, 202
    Debugging toolbar, 202–203
    macros, 202

Stop Recording button
  Macro Recorder, 15
  Ribbon Developer tab, 16
Stop Recording toolbar
  disappearance of, 16
  Macro Recorder, 15
Store Macro In field, 15
String, 52
  arrays, 101
  If, 331
  InputBox, 77
  strVerify, 108
  UDFs, 193–194
  Word, 339–340
strText, 194
Structured Query Language (SQL), 299, 310–313
  DELETE, 312–313
  INSERT, 311–312
  SELECT, 311
  UPDATE, 312
strValue, 206
strVerify, 108
Sub, 201
  deleting macros, 33
  Macro Recorder, 29
subroutines, 111
SUM, 183
SumColor, 186
syntax errors, 196–197

T

tables. *See also* PivotTable; QueryTables
  arrays, 101
  source, 164
Table Range field, 164
text files
  cells, 303
  external data, 301–303
  macros, 301–303
  Message Box, 303

TextBox
  class modules, 266–268
  ControlSource, 234
  formatting, 234
  PasswordChar, 234
  UserForms, 234–236
ThisWorkbook, 132
Time, 233
times, 233
  variable declaration statements, 53
To, 76
Toggle Breakpoint button, 204
toolbars. *See also* Debugging toolbar; Stop
  Recording toolbar; Visual Basic toolbar
  Forms toolbar, 136–139
  icons, 27
  UserForms, 249–250
    Zoom, 252
  VBE, 27
Tools, VBA Project Properties, 37
trapping errors, 207–209
two-dimensional arrays, 101
TxtGroup, 267

U

UBound, 102, 104
UDFs. *See* User Defined Functions
Undo, 120, 121
Ungroup, 249
Unload Me, 261
  Cancel button, 226–227
  CommandButton, 226–227
  UserForms, 226–227
unloading UserForms, 253
Until, 94
UPDATE, 312
User Defined Functions (UDFs), 5, 183–194
  alphanumeric strings, 186–187
  Application.Caller, 186
  argument list, 185

cells, 184
class modules, 184
colored cells, 185–186
comments, 194
Conditional Formatting, 190
copy and paste, 187
data types, 185
End Function, 184, 194
errors, 188
Function, 184
hyperlinks, 187
Insert Function dialog, 191–193
Macro Recorder, 184
macros, 184, 190–191
name, 184
Public, 184
standard modules, 184
String, 193–194
UserForms, 184
volatile functions, 188–193
workbooks, 184
worksheets, 183, 184
UserForms, 215–229, 236–237, 246–248
add-ins, 281–284
advanced, 249–262
Cancel button, 224
Caption property, 219
CheckBox, 240–241
ActiveX controls, 142
Collection, 271
Close button, 250–251
closing, 226–228
code, 225–226
ComboBox, 238–239
AddItem, 238
End Sub, 238, 257
pre-sort, 253–255
ranges, 239
RowSource, 238
unique items, 255–257
worksheets, 238

CommandButton, 223, 232, 254–255
Continue button, 251
controls, 219–220, 231–248
creating, 216–217
designing, 218–224
dialog sheets, 315–316
Exit button, 224
Frame control, 222–223, 243–245
Enabled, 245
Hide, 227–228
Initialize, 233, 268, 275
Label, 221, 232–234
OptionButton, 273
ListBox, 236–237, 246–248
Click, 237
events, 237
Initialize, 237, 246
loops, 248
MultiSelect, 236–237, 246
NextRow, 247
pre-sort, 253–255
RowSource, 237
runtime error, 237
unique items, 255–257
maximizing size, 252
modules, 22, 225–226, 247
cmdExit, 274
MultiPage control, 245
name, 219
Name property, 219
OptionButton, 223, 241–243
photographs, 252–253
printing, 258
Project Explorer, 216, 218
QueryClose, 251
real-time charts, 258
Show, 225
ShowModal, 250
TextBox, 234–236
class modules, 266–268
ControlSource, 234

formatting, 234
PasswordChar, 234
toolbar, 249–250
Zoom, 252
UDFs, 184
Unload Me, 226–227
unloading, automation, 253
UserForm_Initialize, 275

V

Val, 331
#VALUE!, 188
values
cells, 205
constants, 57
Locals window, 205
variables, 50
(number sign), 53
Value field, 206
Value Field Settings dialog box, 168
Values area, 168–170
variables
arrays, 99
cells, 51
charts, 160
constants, 57
data types, 49–50, 52
declaration statements, 50
applications, 57
Chart, 151
constants, 57
data types, 53–54
dates, 53
forcing, 54–56
macros, 56
modules, 56–57
PowerPoint, 331
times, 53
elements, 100
Locals window, 205
macros, 49–51

need for, 50–51
scope, 56–57
values, 50
(number sign), 53
workbooks, 62
Variant, 52, 53–54
arrays, 54
VB. See Visual Basic
VBA Project Properties, 37
VBE. See Visual Basic Editor
vbModal, 250
versions, 7, 9–10
Access, 355
ActiveX controls, 140
dialog sheets, 316
Forms controls, 140
icons, 10
Macro Recorder, 15
macros, 29
Office, 328
View Code, 226
CommandButton, 142
Project Explorer, 28
UserForms, 226
VBE, 113
worksheet modules, 112–113
Visual Basic (VB), 4
Visual Basic button, 20
Visual Basic Editor (VBE), 19–25, 216
add-ins, 290
Break mode, 199
class modules, 264
code, 36–37
Code window, 21
Debug button, 197
Debugging toolbar, 198–207
Design Mode, 143
entering, 20
exiting, 24
icons, 20
Immediate Window, 22
locking, 36–37
modules, 22

Object Browser, 23–24
passwords, 37
Project Explorer, 21, 124, 132
Properties window, 22
protecting, 36–37
toolbars, 27
UserForms, 216
View Code, 113
windows, 20–22
worksheets, 20
Visual Basic toolbar
Record Macro button, 13
Run Macro button, 16
VLOOKUP, 183
volatile functions, 188–193

W

Watch window
Debugging toolbar, 205–206
Value field, 206
WebBrowser, 259–260
GoBack, 261
GoForward, 261
Initialize, 261
UserForms, 259–260
Webqueries, 295–299
WHERE, 312–313
While...Wend, 86, 94
windows. *See also specific windows*
VBE, 20–22
With, 32
advancetime, 367
cell range, 32
WithoutVariable, 51
Word, 44, 333–342
activating, 333–336
Code window, 30
controlling, 6
creating documents, 336
export, 333

GetObject, 334
Immediate Window, 329
import, 338–339
late binding, 340
macros, 329, 335–336
printing, 337–338
ranges, 337
String, 339–340
Word.Application, 334
Workbook, 23–24, 44, 45
Application, 61
Close, 62
methods, 62
Open, 62
Save, 62
workbooks, 216
Activate, 46
add-ins, 279, 280
chart sheets, 157
collections, 61–62
dialog sheets, 315
macros, 15, 62
modules, 22, 34
Code window, 124
workbook events, 124
name, 189
Saved, 45
simplification, 5–6
UDFs, 184
UserForms, 216
variables, 62
worksheets, 63
workbook events
automation, 123–134
code, 123–126
End Sub, 126
workbook modules, 124
Workbook_Activate, 127
Workbook_BeforeClose, 127
Workbook_BeforePrint, 130
Workbook_BeforeSave, 131
Workbook_Deactivate, 128
Workbook_NewSheet, 130

Workbook_Open, 126–127

Workbook_SheetActivate, 131

Workbook_SheetBeforeDoubleClick, 129

Workbook_SheetBeforeRightClick, 129

Workbook_SheetChange, 128

Workbook_SheetDeactivate, 131

Workbook_SheetPivotTableUpdate, 130

Workbook_SheetSelectionChange, 128–129

Workbook_Activate, 127

Workbook_BeforeClose, 127

Workbook_BeforePrint, 130

Workbook_BeforeSave, 131

Workbook_Deactivate, 128

Workbook_NewSheet, 130

Workbook_Open, 272

    PivotTable, 178

    workbook events, 126–127

Workbooks, 61–62

    If, 88

Workbook_SheetActivate, 131

Workbook_SheetBeforeDoubleClick, 129

Workbook_SheetBeforeRightClick, 129

Workbook_SheetChange, 128

Workbook_SheetDeactivate, 131

Workbook_SheetPivotTableUpdate, 130

Workbook_SheetSelectionChange, 128–129

Worksheet, 44, 45

    Name, 45

worksheets, 62–63

    Activate, 46

    cells, 43

    Cells, 64

    charts, 151

        embedded, 154–155

    chart sheets, 155–156

    collections, 62–63

    ComboBox, 238

    defaults, 44

    Do...Loop...While, 93

    e-mail, 348

    embedded charts, 154–155

    functions, 5

    hiding, 89

    macros, 62–63

    methods, 43

    modules, 22

        Code window, 113

        View Code, 112–113

    name, 189, 208

    passwords, 78

    ranges, PowerPoint, 364–365

    relocating, 63

    Select Case, 80

    UDFs, 183, 184

    VBE, 20

    workbooks, 63

worksheet events

    automation, 111–122

    disabling, 114–115

    enabling, 114–115

    Worksheet_Activate, 117–118

    Worksheet_BeforeDoubleClick, 116

    Worksheet_BeforeRightClick, 117

    Worksheet_Calculate, 118

    Worksheet_Change, 115–116

    Worksheet_Deactivate, 118

    Worksheet_FollowHyperlink, 117

    Worksheet_PivotTableUpdate, 119

    Worksheet_SelectionChange, 116

Worksheet_Activate, 117–118

Worksheet_BeforeDoubleClick, 116

Worksheet_BeforeRightClick, 117

Worksheet_Calculate, 118

Worksheet_Change, 114

    dialog sheets, 318

    events, 115–116

    PivotCache, 175

    PivotTable, 175, 177–178

Worksheet_Deactivate, 118
Worksheet_FollowHyperlink, 117
Worksheet_PivotTableUpdate, 119
Worksheets, 46
    ActiveWorkbook, 67
    chart sheets, 63
    Sheets, 63
Worksheet_SelectionChange, 116

X

.xla, 279
.xlam, 279
XLM. *See* Excel 4.0 Macro Language

.xls, 91, 355
.xlsm, 355
.xlsx, 355

Y

YesNoCancel, 77

Z

zero-based numbering, 103
Zoom, 249, 252

Wiley Publishing, Inc.

End-User License Agreement